# THE MEDITERRANEAN DIET COOKBOOK

# THE MEDITERRANEAN DIET COOKBOOK

*A Delicious Alternative
for Lifelong Health*

**NANCY HARMON JENKINS**

BANTAM BOOKS
NEW YORK • TORONTO • LONDON
SYDNEY • AUCKLAND

The Mediterranean Diet Cookbook

A Bantam Book / July 1994

Book design by Joyce Weston

*Library of Congress Cataloging-in-Publication Data*

Jenkins, Nancy Harmon.
    The Mediterranean diet cookbook : a delicious alternative for
lifelong health / Nancy Harmon Jenkins.
        p.      cm.
    Includes bibliographical references and index.
    ISBN 0-553-09608-7
    1. Cookery, Mediterranean.    2. Diet—Mediterranean Region.    3. Low-
fat diet—Recipes.    I. Title.
    TX725.M35J46    1994
    641.5'63—dc20                                                94-5946
                                                                    CIP

*Published simultaneously in the United States and Canada*

Bantam Books are published by Bantam Books, a division of
Bantam Doubleday Dell Publishing Group, Inc. Its trademark,
consisting of the words "Bantam Books" and the portrayal of a rooster,
is Registered in U.S. Patent and Trademark Office and in other countries.
Marca Registrada, Bantam Books, 1540 Broadway, New York, 10036.

PRINTED IN THE UNITED STATES OF AMERICA

KPH   0   9   8   7   6   5   4   3   2   1

In honor of all the women who have been my guides and companions in the kitchen over the years—my mother, Dorothy Thorndike Harmon; my sister, Jane Harmon Carr; and my daughter, Sara Carlen-Jenkins; and especially Maria Jose in Madrid; Balqiss in Beirut; Iula in Bellapais; Giulia in Rome; and last, but hardly least, Mita Antolini in Teverina di Cortona—this book is gratefully dedicated.

# CONTENTS

# ACKNOWLEDGMENTS

*W*riting about food is seldom possible without the help and generosity of some very special people. Among those who made this book possible, the most prominent is surely Fran McCullough, whose inspired idea it was and who pushed me in the gentlest possible way to finish it on time.

I'm grateful to an incredibly hardworking group of critics and testers who cooked, tasted, and kibitzed through a Maine summer when the Mediterranean sometimes seemed far away: Jane Carr, Stacey Glassman, Maureen Freeman, Frances Holdgate, Nelda McLellan, Nancy Meisle, Lolly and Jim Mitchell, and Charlotte Stancioff.

In recent journeys around the Mediterranean, I've been given warm welcomes, valuable advice, a place at the table, and occasionally a bed to sleep in by Tanya and Laura Matthews and Fatouma Mbrahim in Tunisia; Charis Leonardou, Diane Kochilas, Aglaia Kremezi, and Nicholas Stavroulakis in Greece; Nevin Halici, Tamera Neufeldt, and Nurdan Üstman in Turkey; Clara Maria Amezua, Pau and Diane Roca, and Maria Jose Sevilla in Spain; Isis Eltern, Tony May, and Faith Willinger in Italy; Sakina El-Alaoui, Luce and Jean Senouf, and Arlette Benitah in Morocco. Thanks to you all.

Thanks also to patient and long-suffering travel companions Lois Brubeck, Joanne Green, and my son-in-law Conrad Carlen; friends whose support has been incalculable, among them Ed Behr, Suzanne Hamlin, Jeffrey Steingarten, Corby Kummer, Carol Field, Fred Plotkin, and Molly O'Neill; Arlene Wanderman and Linda Russo of the International Olive Oil Council; the gang at Oldways, the two Saras, Robin, Paul, and especially Greg Drescher, whose energy and commitment were crucial to the development of the Mediterranean Diet Pyramid; last, but scarcely least, two special friends who held my hand, mostly figuratively by phone and fax, Dun Gifford in Boston and Paula Wolfert in Connecticut.

And finally, thank you to Sara and Nicholas, who have been my joy throughout our life in the Mediterranean together.

# PREFACE

The rugged stone farmhouse stands prominently on a hilltop in the midst of a valley that flows eastward from a height of land above the Val di Chiana in southern Tuscany. From the house you can look all the way down the long valley broadening gradually into the basin of the upper Tiber River, one of the roads that has always led to Rome. Our family bought the house and restored it more than two decades ago, after years of roaming around the Mediterranean, from Spain to France to Spain again, then to Lebanon and Cyprus, and finally, after a brief and unmemorable stint in East Asia, to Rome. (The father of the family was a foreign correspondent for an American news magazine; we followed where his work led him.)

The house and the community around it, which is called Teverina and is not on any map, became our home and focus in the world. It is where things happen, good and bad: Sara and Conrad were married here, and on a nearby farm Nicholas tumbled happily into a well and nearly drowned; here in this house friends gather to celebrate Thanksgiving, Christmas, Easter, Fourth of July; and here family members retreat, for solace when life becomes difficult, for peace and tranquillity when a book or a painting is due.

On the adjacent farm live Bruno and Mita Antolini, their son Arnaldo, and his wife, Maura. They are good neighbors, good friends, partners in happy times and a few sorrowful ones, constants in the changing face of the valley community as babies are born, children grow to adulthood, new people arrive with new ideas, and old people pass on. Over the course of time we have watched with them as the subsistence agriculture of this remote valley has changed from wheat, vines, and olives, grown to provide the needs of the people who live here, to tobacco, subsidized by the government and grown for distant markets.

When we first came to live in the valley, the Antolinis, like most of their neighbors, had no electricity, no plumbing, no telephone, and no tractor or other mechanized means of transportation. A profound and appealing stillness pervaded the valley, broken only by human voices and the rooster's crow. Terraces of wheat, studded with gnarled olive trees and edged with grapevines, marked the contours of the steep hillsides, and around them climbed forests of oak, chestnut, and Aleppo pine.

Today the forests are still there, but the terraces have long since been plowed into dikes and broad fields for tobacco cultivation, and the Antolinis have passed, with stunning rapidity, from a mid-19th-century way of life to a late-20th-century one without, it seems, so much as the blink of an eye. Electricity hums in their comfortable farmhouse, running everything from a *frullatora* for beating eggs to a washing machine to that icon of modern times, the television set. The telephone rings with news of family and friends. The bathroom sparkles with toilet, wash basin, and shower, and outside the little Fiat car and the big Lamborghini tractor gurgle periodically to life, ready to plow fields or carry goods and people to market.

Yet, despite all these changes, the food that Mita prepares and sets before her family twice a day has remained the same, much of it still grown and harvested on the farm—bread baked in the outdoor oven, pasta with fresh vegetables from the gardens, chickens and rabbits from the farmyard and pork from the pig that is slaughtered each year at Christmastime, mushrooms and chestnuts from the forest, and above all olive oil and wine that the Antolinis still proudly make themselves. They eat, in fact, an almost perfect Mediterranean diet, although they'd be perplexed to hear that—very low in saturated fats, very high in complex carbohydrates, lots of fresh vegetables, especially those cancer-blocking brassicas or cruciferous vegetables—cabbages, kale, turnip greens, broccoli, and so on.

This is not a book about the Antolinis or the community of Teverina, but I mention them with prominence because for me this place in the world, almost dead center in the Italian peninsula, which puts it almost dead center in the whole northern Mediterranean region, has been a place to think about food and its importance to communities and individuals, about what we grow and how we process it, how we prepare it and preserve it and share it among ourselves. Teverina, for all the changes that have taken place here, has been an example for me of what the Mediterranean diet means, in real terms and to real people.

What is this Mediterranean diet, and why should Americans, descendants of people from many different parts of the world, care?

At an international conference on the diets of the Mediterranean convened in Cambridge, Massachusetts, in early 1993 and sponsored by the Harvard School of Public Health and Oldways Preservation & Exchange Trust, the Mediterranean diet was described to an assembly of scientists, scholars, journalists, and other interested parties:

> Plentiful fruits, vegetables, legumes and grains; olive oil as the principal fat; lean red meat consumed only a few times per month or somewhat more often in very small portions; low to moderate consumption of other foods from animal sources, such as dairy products (especially cheese and yogurt), fish, and poultry; and moderate consumption of wine (primarily at meals).

It sounds simple. It sounds, in fact, quite delicious. And it is. Think of a meal that may be familiar to many Americans, especially those of Mediterranean ancestry: a light vegetable soup, made with chicken stock and chopped onions, carrots, celery, and garlic, flavored with fresh herbs and perhaps a spoonful of freshly grated cheese; a dish of pasta sauced with a little savory ground meat mixed with more chopped vegetables and herbs, the whole sautéed in olive oil; a green salad, crisply fresh and fragrant with garlic, more olive oil, and lemon juice; plenty of crusty country-style bread; a small piece of cheese; and fruit, either raw or poached in a very light sugar syrup.

Sound good? That's one example of the Mediterranean diet. There are more. Pizza is part of the Mediterranean diet, and so are rice dishes like pilaf, risotto, and paella. So are vegetable combinations with a very little meat or cheese added for flavor, hearty bean and lentil soups, fish and shellfish quickly grilled or broiled. And so too is a chunk of bread, a wedge of cheese, a few slices of onion and tomato, and a glass of good red wine to wash it all down.

The fact is that the people of the Mediterranean figured out a long time ago—back, if truth be told, in the mists of time—that good food, skillfully prepared, garnished with little more than fresh herbs, garlic, and olive oil and shared in something approaching abundance around a table with friends and relations, is not only good tasting; it's good for you too.

When the distinguished medical researcher Ancel Keys assembled a group of scientists in the early 1960s to examine diet and disease patterns around the world, the *fact* of a relationship between what people eat and the chronic diseases they

suffer—among them coronary heart disease, stroke, cancer, and diabetes—was widely accepted. What was not known, what is still being discovered, is the *nature* of that relationship.

What foods, in and of themselves, are good for us? An apple a day? A high-protein diet, such as was widely touted in the United States in the 1960s? Vegetables alone, a diet that has been embraced for religious, ethical, and health reasons by many groups throughout human history?

How are the foods that are good for us grown, prepared, and distributed? Does that have any bearing on our health?

What are the overall patterns of diets, beyond individual foods, that are most beneficial? Three meals a day? Meals rich in high-protein (and high-fat) animal products? A laboratory-produced formula of carefully balanced nutrients that accounts for all known dietary lapses and attempts to cover all bases?

The jury is still out on many of these questions, but the Harvard conference revealed a developing consensus, based on the work of Keys and his many associates then and since, that the traditional diet of people in the Mediterranean is a major factor in their *generally* good health profiles, their *generally* long lives, their *general* lack of chronic and debilitating diseases.

Central to any comparison of Mediterranean and American diets is, of course, the issue of fat. Most of the fat consumed in the United States is highly saturated fat from meat and dairy products, principally red meat and milk. In Greece, when the Mediterranean diet studies began in the early 1960s, a full 40 percent of calories in the diet came from fat, while in southern Italy the figure was 29 percent. In both cases, however, *most of the fat consumed came from olive oil.*

With the exception of some sweet desserts, the only added fat used in the recipes in this book, beyond what naturally occurs in meat, fish, and some vegetables, is from extra-virgin olive oil. Why? Not just because olive oil is traditional in the Mediterranean kitchen. High in monounsaturated fats, which lower low-density lipoproteins (LDLs or "bad cholesterol"), and with substantial amounts of valuable antioxidants such as vitamin E, olive oil can be beneficial in the diet *as long as it is not added to existing fats but replaces them.* The conclusion of the Harvard conference, based on the Mediterranean diet studies and follow-up research, was of great interest:

> . . . The possibility that a diet containing 40% of calories from fat, so long as it is very low in saturated fat and predominantly comprised of monounsaturated fat, could be healthful for most persons is something that deserves serious attention by the public health and research communities.

Medical evidence of the benefits of the Mediterranean diet are discussed more fully in the Introduction that follows. Factors other than diet, of course, also influence good health—among them heredity, exercise or the lack of it, tobacco and alcohol abuse, environmental pollutants in the air we breathe, the water we drink, the soil in which our vegetables and fruits grow, and the chemicals we add to our foods during growth and processing. It would be disingenuous to suggest that diet alone is a factor.

And it would be disingenuous to suggest that diet is nothing more than a quantifiable sum of nutrients. The Mediterranean diet, or the Mediterranean way of eating if you will, is the result of Mediterranean history and an integral part of Mediterranean culture. I like to describe it as a way of *thinking* about food. Tunisians or Turks, Cypriotes or Spaniards, rich people or poor, country folk or city dwellers, Mediterranean people are on the whole *conscious* of food in a way that most people, certainly most Americans, are not. I think it's because of this that what they eat is, on the whole, delicious—nourishing to the body because it's wholesome and to the soul because it tastes so very good.

I don't mean to suggest an obsession with food. Rather, it seems to me that in the countries of the Mediterranean there exists a deep-seated and largely unspoken consensus that eating is one of the most important things we humans do in our lives. As a great anthropologist once told me, it is our single most intimate act, far more intimate than sex because through food we literally re-create ourselves each and every day of our lives. And beyond individual needs, in Mediterranean countries there's a real sense of eating as a social act, a way of communicating, of expressing solidarity and relationship. Gathering around the table, literally breaking bread together, is both a symbol of communion and an act of communion in and of itself. And so from a very early age—probably, if it could be measured, from infancy—children absorb the cultural message that it's important to *pay attention*, to *be aware*, almost in a Zen way, of what food is, where it comes from, and how it gets to be the way it is when it comes into our lives.

This book has grown out of my own experiences over the years, living, working, cooking, and raising a family in many different countries of the Mediterranean. But it is also an outgrowth of the Harvard Mediterranean diet conference, which concluded, not surprisingly, that changing our eating habits to approach something closer to the diets of the Mediterranean could make a significant difference in American patterns of chronic disease.

No one who has picked up a newspaper in the last half dozen years needs to be

told the American diet is too high in saturated fat, salt, sugar, red meat, and processed food, and too low in fresh fruits and vegetables and complex carbohydrates (bread, pasta, legumes, and grains). The health pattern that results is one of chronic and debilitating diseases—heart disease, cancer, diabetes, and others—that affect individuals and their families while taking a tremendous toll, economically and psychologically, on the nation as a whole. Diet alone will not cure our problems, but diet is one factor in our lives that is easy to control and easy to change.

Especially with the Mediterranean diet. Why? Because the food, on the whole, is not foreign to us. This is not a diet, on the one hand, of bean sprouts and tofu-and-lentil burgers or, on the other, of artificial fats and sugars, what a friend of mine aptly calls "fake foods," created in laboratories to substitute for things we like and know we shouldn't eat. This is real food for real people, people like us.

And the food of the Mediterranean is not just familiar; it's also easy to prepare. All the recipes in this book were tested in my Maine kitchen, on a clunky old electric stove, or in the kitchens of Maine friends and neighbors, with products we bought at local supermarkets, the local health food store, and local farmers' markets. Almost everything used in the book can easily be found in such places. There are occasional ingredients—the best olives and olive oils, for instance—that may call for a special trip to a Greek, Italian, or Middle Eastern neighborhood or to a specialty foods store; and there are occasional products that may require a little effort to uncover. (The Sources list at the back of the book will help with this.)

Bringing a Mediterranean way of cooking and eating into your kitchen and dining room is not a formidable task. Because Mediterranean cooking is, by and large, home cooking and not restaurant cuisine, it is improvisational and very forgiving. You have only two cloves of garlic instead of the called-for six? Use two and don't worry. You can't find celery root, but there are loads of parsnips in the produce section? Substitute the parsnips. The chard looks good while the spinach is yellow and wilted? Use chard instead of spinach. The dish may end up a little less predominantly flavored with this or that, but somewhere in the Mediterranean, you can be certain, someone has made it like that before. Only with cakes should you be as precise as you can—and even then, only the first time out. Once you're familiar with a recipe, you can fiddle with it at will.

The most important lesson from the Mediterranean, however, is not to be found in recipes but rather in that attitude I mentioned earlier, that consciousness about food that stems from the realization that good food begins with good ingredients—truly ripe and flavorful tomatoes; fresh, crisp carrots, green beans, and peas; beets,

turnips, and potatoes that are firm and full of sweet savor; naturally raised meats, chickens, and their eggs; dairy products, yogurt and cheese, without added preservatives or stabilizers; fish, even frozen fish, with a clean and pristine scent.

This will come about only when you seek out the very best of local, regional, preferably organically and naturally raised products. Only then will you have a standard by which to measure what is not regional and natural. There are times in all our kitchens when we must use other kinds of products, but only by knowing what is best can we judge what is second-best but still a possibility. When you know the flavor of a ripe local tomato at the height of its season, when you understand what makes it taste the way it does, you will also know what doesn't measure up.

Look for the best ingredients wherever you are, whether greens or fish, wine or oil, cheese or fruit. Obviously, not all of these are going to be produced locally—wine, certain types of cheese, and olive oil almost certainly not. But look for fresh or very minimally processed food, food that has been naturally raised or grown without pesticides or chemical fertilizers.

A final note on the fat issue: We have been told of the need to cut down on fat so often and by so many authorities that it's no wonder people go to extremes in their confusion, on the one hand acting as if any and all fat were thoroughly toxic, and on the other hand shrugging their shoulders at nutritional advice because it's all so negative. Our government currently recommends that we get no more than 30 percent of our calories from fat, but a few authorities go so far as to urge a 10 percent maximum—a figure that not only is *very* difficult to achieve but also is not very palatable. And an unpalatable diet, we know from experience, is one most people won't follow for very long.

Fortunately for all of us, the Mediterranean diet is extremely palatable with great appeal to all the senses. Appetite doesn't come from knowing food is good for you—it comes from flavors and textures, from the delicious aromas that waft from a kitchen where peppers and tomatoes are simmering in olive oil with a little garlic and fresh basil, from the fragrance that rises out of a steaming soup tureen filled with chunks of seafood and leeks and a bit of orange zest, from the dazzling appearance of a bowl of crisp salad greens and ripe red tomatoes, or a platter of grilled summer vegetables, or a handsome loaf of crusty-brown country bread with a pale wedge of cheese and a sparkling glass of deep red wine to go with it. The Mediterranean diet brings to the table fragrances, colors, and textures like these along with good health and an overall sense of well-being.

A diet made up of Mediterranean dishes, like the ones in this book, will be healthful and satisfying but never austere. Keep in mind that aiming for a certain

percentage of calories from fat does not mean that every dish you eat, everything you put in your mouth, must derive *only* that percent of its calories from fat. The fat question has to be looked at in terms of the overall diet, over a period of days, even weeks. Some recipes in this book are very low in fat and some are high. Balance over time is the goal.

Remember, too, that a low fat content doesn't necessarily make a recipe healthful, nor does a high fat content indicate an unhealthful recipe. Consider for a moment a salad with a lot of fresh, nutritionally powerful but low-calorie greens and a dressing made with 2 tablespoons of olive oil; then consider a recipe for a low-fat pudding made with egg whites, lots of sugar (to compensate for the loss of taste from butter), 2 tablespoons of vegetable oil, and other ingredients. The salad, because the whole dish is extremely low in calories, shows a high percentage of calories from fat, while the sweet dessert, made of high-calorie ingredients, will seem low in fat. Yet which one belongs in a truly healthy diet?

The point is to let common sense rule. From the conclusion of the Mediterranean diet conference (see Appendix, pages 477–489), now endorsed by the World Health Organization and the Food & Agriculture Organization of the United Nations, it seems clear that any diet in which the principal fat is monounsaturated, coupled with plenty of fresh fruits and vegetables and with a strong component of complex carbohydrates in the form of bread and pasta, is a better and more healthful diet than what we have become used to in this country. This is food that is good for our bodies and, as I hope the recipes in this book will demonstrate, good for our souls as well.

## NOTE ON NUTRITIONAL DATA

Everything in this book tastes good and is good for you, in the Mediterranean context. That means that rich feast-day preparations and desserts should be consumed, as they are in the Mediterranean, for special occasions, perhaps a few times a year. Vegetarians and people with special health needs, for foods very low in fat or sodium or cholesterol for instance, will find plenty of ideas in the Mediterranean diet. The best news is that there are no hard and fast rules: if you want to make adjustments to account for special health problems, it's easy to do so.

Nutritional data accompanying the recipes are intended as guides to pursuing a healthy Mediterranean diet. If a range of servings and a choice of courses have been given for a recipe, nutritional counts reflect data for the largest number of servings of the most substantial course (such as main course versus first course). Where a range of ingredients has been given, nutritional counts have been computed on an average. Data have been supplied by Hill Nutrition.

Some nutritionists may find some of the recipes unacceptably high in fat, but it is important to remember that the fat content of an individual dish is not of much significance; it's the total fat picture over a period of several days that counts.

Fear of fat has dominated popular discussion of diet for such a long time that many otherwise normal, health-conscious people are struggling to lower the fat content of their diet from the 30 percent recommended by the USDA to 20 percent or an even more drastic 10 percent. But extremely low-fat diets are terribly hard to maintain: the food seldom really tastes good, and the effort that must go into providing even minimal flavor means that most conscientious observers would rather purchase prepared, portion-controlled, industrially manufactured food. Yet there is no real evidence that, for normally active people with no obesity, there's any good reason to pursue this course.

The fact is that the extensive public health initiatives in recent years have been based largely on research indicating the need to limit *saturated*

*continued*

fat. One of the most appealing lessons of the Mediterranean diet is that as long as *saturated* fat remains low, and the *balance* of fat is mostly *mono-unsaturated*, as is the case with the recipes in this book, the amount of total fat in the diet, even above 35 percent, is probably not an issue for active people.

The health benefits of olive oil have been discussed in other parts of this book, but it is important to remember that simply *adding* olive oil to a diet already high in saturated fat is not the order of the day. *Substituting* olive oil, however, is a major key to a better health profile.

Still, for many the overriding question is: can I lose weight on the Mediterranean diet? And the answer is simple: yes, you can, but only if you reduce the total amount of calories you consume and increase the amount of exercise you get in the normal course of everyday life. For ordinary people who do not have metabolism problems (and that includes most of us), that is the only way to lose weight.

Fortunately, the traditional dishes on which Mediterranean people have nourished themselves for generations are so delicious that no one need feel deprived in the slightest when they become mainstays of our own tables. This in itself may make it easier to lose weight. By shifting meat and other animal products away from the center of the plate, by adding lots of beautiful, fresh, seasonal produce, cooked vegetables, salads, and raw fruit for dessert, by making grains and beans in the form of bread, pasta, and delightful soups the focus of the meal, you may find that the word *diet* takes on an entirely new meaning.

# INTRODUCTION: THE MEDITERRANEAN DIET AND HEALTH

*by **Antonia Trichopoulou**, MD, Professor of Nutrition and
Biochemistry, Athens School of Public Health, and
Director, World Health Organization Collaborating Center for
Nutrition Education in Europe; and **Dimitrios Trichopoulos**,
MD, Vincent L. Gregory Professor of Cancer Prevention and
Epidemiology, Harvard School of Public Health*

*H*ow do we know that people in a particular area of the world have a healthier diet than our Western diet? Epidemiology, the study of disease patterns, provides the answer.

The frequency of most diseases varies substantially around the world. For diseases of infectious or occupational origin the importance of the environment, whether physical, chemical, or biological, is clear. But for many other common chronic diseases, including those of the circulatory system and cancer, the role played by the environment has not always been obvious. Studies of migrants have shown that whatever the disease pattern in their country of origin, they tend to acquire, sooner or later, the disease pattern of their host country, even when they remain relatively isolated within ethnic communities. For instance, the frequency of cancer of the large intestine is much lower in Japan than in the United States but rises to American levels within 20 years among Japanese immigrants to this country. We can conclude, then, that outside factors, collectively termed *environment*,

whether imposed by others or created by individuals themselves through personal choices about food, behavior, or lifestyle, are critical determinants of disease. This is not to imply that heredity is not important; it is, but genes are usually evenly distributed among nonisolated population groups and thus influence who *within* a population will develop disease. And most genes exercise their effects through interactions, whether simple or complex, with the environment.

Among the many environmental factors, qualitative or quantitative deviations from the ideal diet represent, as a group, the most important factor in the genesis of the most common killer diseases, including coronary heart disease and several forms of cancer. This should not be surprising. Only factors that vary widely among countries and population groups can account for the remarkable variability of disease patterns around the world, and few aspects of human conditions or behavior vary as much as diet. Of course, the human diet is unusually complex, involving hundreds of chemical components, and from the evolutionary point of view it is frequently challenging, since humans are the only animals who process and cook their food.

Nobody knows for sure what the ideal diet *is*, but there are good reasons to believe that the Mediterranean diet may come closer to it than any other realistic diet. What exactly is the Mediterranean diet? What evidence do we have that adopting this diet can benefit our health?

The *Mediterranean diet* is a loose term, and some doubt remains as to what precise dietary patterns apply. However, there are common elements in the diets of most Mediterranean people, and to the extent that they share lower rates of diet-related diseases, this looseness of definition represents an advantage: several variations on the Mediterranean diet may be equally beneficial. As a rule, the Mediterranean diet is low in saturated fat with added fat mostly in the form of olive oil; high in complex carbohydrates from grains and legumes; and high in fiber, mostly from vegetables and fruits. Total fat may be high—around 40 percent of total energy intake in Greece, as mentioned in the Preface—or moderate (around 30 percent of total energy intake, as in Italy). In all instances, however, the ratio of monounsaturated to saturated fats is high (usually two to one or more). This is because olive oil, which contains 60 percent or more of monounsaturated oleic acid, is the principal fat in the Mediterranean region. The large quantities of fresh vegetables and of cereals and the abundance of olive oil guarantee high intakes of beta-carotene, vitamin C, tocopherols (vitamin E), various important minerals, and several possibly beneficial nonnutrient substances such as polyphenols and anthocyanins.

Since Homeric times, the diet of the Mediterranean has been based on wheat,

olives and olive oil, legumes, green vegetables, seasonal fruits, and wine. Other components of the diet include onions and garlic, cheese and yogurt (mainly from goat's milk), and, to a certain extent, fish, fowl, and eggs. Because of limited availability, red meat has been used infrequently and, as a rule, in small quantities. Few adults in the Mediterranean region will find it difficult to recognize this pattern as the essence of their traditional diet. In comparison to the average American, the average Italian consumes 3 times as much pasta, bread, and fresh fruit; almost twice as much tomatoes and fish; 6 times more wine; and 100 times more olive oil—but 30 percent less meat from any source, 20 percent less milk, and 20 percent fewer eggs.

Any overview of the actual foods and dishes consumed in the Mediterranean region must emphasize the large quantities of whole-grain bread that accompany every meal. Pasta (not just in Italy but also in Greece and in North Africa in the form of couscous) is regularly used, frequently in addition to bread, as an added component in several soups, as a supplement to various dishes, or as a separate dish. Abundant complex carbohydrates, as well as plant proteins, are contributed by whole grains and cereals and also by legumes. In Greece bean soup, prepared with large quantities of olive oil, is considered the national food, credited with the survival of Greeks in their poverty-stricken country through the millennia.

The Mediterranean diet is frequently, and rightly, associated in the minds of many Americans with that lively salad made from fresh vegetables, olive oil, and feta cheese, known in this country as *Greek salad*. Usually prepared with tomatoes, cucumbers, onions, and olives, the original Greek salad is different from its American variant; in the Greek version, vegetables are fresher and tastier, olive oil is much more abundant, and the serving is much larger. A Greek fresh vegetable salad can also be made from just greens, herbs, olive oil, and lemon juice; again, feta cheese, made from goat's or sheep's milk, is frequently added. It is worth noting that cheese is consumed in large quantities along the northern Mediterranean shore—in fact, Greeks and French lead the world in per-capita cheese consumption.

In Greece, vegetables are usually cooked, especially in olive oil, and vegetable combinations include eggplant, zucchini, beans or okra, and almost always tomatoes, onions, and herbs. Vegetables also dominate many meat dishes, and, in the absence of meat, feta cheese is regularly added to most vegetable stews.

As might be expected, fish has been an important food for Mediterranean people since antiquity. Meat, however, has not been consumed in large quantities in the region until recently, mainly because it's been expensive and in short supply. The changing pattern has been implicated in the increasing incidence of diverticular disease and perhaps cancer of the large bowel.

INTRODUCTION

Wine consumption is high in the European Mediterranean countries, but widespread abuse of hard liquor is not. For millennia wine has been consumed in moderation, almost always during meals and as a rule in the company of friends— the ancient Greek word *symposium* means "drinking in company," but with a connotation of intellectual interchange. The philosophy that shaped the Mediterranean attitude toward wine consumption is best expressed in a passage from Plato's "Symposium" that many modern epidemiologists would approve: "I prepare but three kraters for prudent men; the one is for health, the one they drink first; the second is for love and pleasure; the third for sleep. The fourth is not ours, but belongs to licentiousness."

By the late 1950s the hypothesis linking diet in general to coronary heart disease was gaining widespread support, although reliable data linking dietary habits of individuals to their risk of developing coronary heart disease were lacking. The existing evidence was indirect: diet, in particular the composition of dietary fat, had been shown to be a critical determinant of serum cholesterol, with saturated fat increasing and polyunsaturated fat reducing serum levels; serum total cholesterol had been established as a major risk factor for coronary heart disease. At that time no distinction was made between low- and high-density lipoproteins (LDL and HDL or "bad" and "good" cholesterol).

In an effort to evaluate the hypothesis of a relationship between diet and coronary heart disease and to explore several other aspects of the etiology of this disease, Ancel Keys, M.D., and his colleagues set out to undertake what turned out to be one of the most celebrated studies in modern epidemiology, the Seven Countries Study. The study involved 12,763 men aged 40 to 59 years. The men were enrolled between 1958 and 1964 in 16 study groups or cohorts: two in Greece, three in Italy, two in Croatia and three in Serbia (both then part of Yugoslavia), two in Japan, two in Finland, one in the Netherlands, and one in the United States. The men were interviewed and examined so that information was available for virtually all characteristics that later were identified as major risk factors for coronary heart disease, including blood pressure, serum cholesterol, tobacco use, physical activity, dietary habits, and several others. After a follow-up period that lasted for at least 10 years, the study generated several important results; findings continue to be reported by investigators active in some of the original study centers. Among the most important findings were that the Mediterranean groups had lower mortality rates from *all causes together* than the northern European and American groups; that the difference in mortality and incidence was particularly striking with respect to coronary heart disease; that the mean percentages of calories from saturated and

polyunsaturated fats in the diets of the groups could account to a considerable extent for the differences in mean levels of serum cholesterol among them; and that the mean percentage of calories from saturated fats could account to a considerable extent for the differences in the incidence of coronary heart disease among the groups (an effect that could have been mediated through the detrimental effect of saturated fats on serum cholesterol).

Results subsequently reported from other investigations provided direct support for many of the findings of the Seven Countries Study and indirect support for others. Data assembled by the World Health Organization have confirmed the low rates of coronary heart disease in Mediterranean countries not only in the late 1950s but even now, when the traditional diet is not so closely followed. In 1990 the annual mortality from this disease per 100,000 persons of a "standard" age was 243 among men and 132 among women in the United States, whereas it was, respectively, 139 and 64 in Italy, 106 and 47 in Spain, 137 and 59 in Greece, and 91 and 40 in France. Mediterranean countries are also characterized by lower rates, as compared to those in the United States and northern Europe, of several non-smoking-related cancers, including those of the large bowel, breast, prostate, and ovary. The consequences of these disease patterns create surprising contrasts. According to the most recent (1992) World Health Organization data, men at the peak of their lives (45 years) have longer life expectancy in Greece than in any other European or North American country, even though Greek men are notorious for their high tobacco consumption, they rarely exercise in a systematic way, and they are served by a rather modest health care system.

For logistical reasons the dietary data in the Seven Countries Study were analyzed only as group averages and not for each individual subject in the study. Although this is not an optimal analysis, there can be no doubt that many of the differences in disease occurrence between Mediterranean groups on the one hand and northern European and North American groups on the other were due to differences in dietary patterns. For age-adjusted data, only major differences in other important disease-causing factors or conditions could explain the observed large differences in disease incidence. Such factors are genes, widespread epidemics, tobacco smoking, and low socioeconomic class. But none of these factors is likely to have played a major role: migrant studies have eliminated a genes-based explanation; no major infectious epidemic was selectively affecting northern Europe and North America; and poverty and tobacco smoking have been, if anything, more common in Mediterranean countries.

The Seven Countries Study confirmed that a diet low in saturated fat, like the

Mediterranean diet in virtually all its variations, can reduce total serum cholesterol and risk of coronary heart disease. In the process, however, the Mediterranean diet came to be perceived as just another low-saturated-fat diet. Scientists from the Mediterranean countries have tried to argue that there is much more to the Mediterranean diet than its low intake of saturated fats, but the majority of the educated public was too preoccupied with the polyunsaturated-to-saturated-fatty-acid ratio and the "reduce total fat" commandment to pay much attention. It was only in 1991 that a major editorial in the influential *New England Journal of Medicine,* by the distinguished scientists Frank Sacks and Walter Willett, revived interest in the Mediterranean diet. These authors pointed out that high levels of serum HDL cholesterol are probably as important for the prevention of coronary heart disease as low levels of serum LDL (and total) cholesterol. They argued further that a diet low in saturated fat but high in monounsaturated fat, which would reduce LDL cholesterol and increase HDL cholesterol, appears to be at least as good as a diet low in saturated fats and high in carbohydrates. Although both monounsaturated fat and carbohydrates are effective in reducing LDL, carbohydrates do not increase HDL cholesterol as much as monounsaturated fats do. Furthermore there is experimental evidence and limited human data justifying some concern about the long-term safety of a diet high in polyunsaturated fats, the diet that has been promoted by the American Heart Association, whereas the safety of a high-monounsaturated-fat diet has been demonstrated through the centuries in the people of the Mediterranean region. Willett and his colleagues and other authors also have provided evidence that partially hydrogenated vegetable fats, the basis of margarine and vegetable shortening, far from being safer than saturated animal fats, may actually increase the risk of coronary heart disease. So, it appears that among the realistic alternatives open to people accustomed to the Western diet, the Mediterranean diet stands out as apparently healthier.

Although most scientists believe that diet can in fact play a role in coronary heart disease by contributing to high cholesterol levels and subsequent atherosclerosis, an increasingly influential minority theorizes that diet may also interfere with the blood-clotting events that trigger acute coronary episodes (mainly myocardial infarction and sudden cardiac death). According to this hypothesis, long-chain polyunsaturated fatty acids, of what is chemically described as Omega-3 type, have beneficial effects, including a reduction in blood-clotting tendency and blood viscosity and an increase in the breaking up of blood clots. These fatty acids are provided mainly by fish, but also by several plants, and there is indeed evidence that eating fish may reduce the risk of coronary heart disease. Although fish is not a

defining characteristic of the Mediterranean diet, it is obviously an important part of it—certainly more important than red meat in the time-honored traditional diet of the Mediterranean.

There has been a tendency to associate the health effects of the Mediterranean diet with its fat composition, but perhaps equally important is the fact that almost all variants of this diet are high in complex carbohydrates (bread, pasta, legumes) and rich in fresh vegetables and fruits. Complex carbohydrates and fiber, derived from vegetables, fruits, cereals, or legumes, seem to play a major beneficial role in protecting against constipation, diverticular disease, and perhaps colorectal cancer and coronary heart disease. But the protective role of fresh vegetables and fruits is likely to extend to a much wider range of diseases. They have been consistently reported to be protective against, or at least inversely associated with, several common types of cancer, including those of the esophagus, stomach, large bowel, liver, pancreas, lung, bladder, cervix, and even ovarian and breast cancers. Whether the effects of vegetables and fruits are due to their high content of antioxidant vitamins like beta-carotene, vitamin C, and vitamin E, other vitamins like folate, certain minerals and trace elements, or other compounds is not clearly established. Antioxidants are strong candidates as protagonists in the disease-preventing capacity of vegetables and fruits. They are believed to prevent or neutralize the effects of oxidative processes that may be involved in the development of cancer, atherosclerosis, other chronic diseases, or aging itself. In most instances the protective effect seems to be more strongly associated with vegetables and fruits themselves than with any particular constituent nutrient or nonnutrient. Nevertheless, certain vitamins appear to protect against certain diseases in high doses that can be taken only in the form of supplements. This may be particularly true with respect to vitamin E and coronary heart disease. This field of research is rapidly developing, and it is not conclusively established that very high doses of vitamins are required. In any case it would be prudent to assume that whether vitamin supplements are taken or not, fresh vegetables and fruits should be plentiful in the diet, and the Mediterranean diet is as plentiful as any.

There are several other dimensions to the Mediterranean diet, and very few of them are linked to adverse health effects. Total fat intake, including intake of monounsaturated fat, is considered a risk factor for cancers of the large bowel and perhaps those of the prostate and the pancreas. However, the incidence of these cancers is generally lower in the Mediterranean region than in northern Europe or North America. It appears that red meat (and possibly animal protein and fat) is a more important determinant of cancer of the large bowel than monounsaturated fat, although other explanations may also apply. Consumption of red meat has been low in the traditional Mediterranean diet, although recent data suggest rapidly increasing trends. Salt intake is probably unnecessarily high in several Mediterranean countries, and this may contribute to the modestly high incidence of stroke and stomach cancer in some of these countries. Total energy intake is rather high in the European Mediterranean countries, but in the absence of excess prevalence of obesity in the region, this is actually an advantage—it implies higher energy expenditure and therefore higher levels of physical activity. Physical exercise is an important protective factor for coronary heart disease and possibly cancers of the large bowel and the prostate. Finally, the relatively low intake of milk is partly compensated by the high cheese consumption that covers, in most instances, the requirements for osteoporosis-preventing calcium.

The deleterious effects of excessive alcohol intake, both long-term and short-term, are well documented. By contrast, light to moderate drinking has been shown consistently to be associated with reduced risk of coronary heart disease by about 25 percent. Since coronary heart disease is the principal cause of death among both men and women in the developed countries, it is not surprising that light to moderate drinking has been associated with longevity and has been singled out as a likely explanation for the very low coronary mortality of the French, the so-called French paradox. Light to moderate drinking should be interpreted as two to three glasses per day for men or one to two glasses per day for women; a lower level is indicated for women because of their presumed higher sensitivity, as well as concerns that alcohol may slightly increase the risk for breast cancer.

It has been shown in several studies that alcohol increases the levels of "good" HDL cholesterol and, at least in theory, all alcoholic drinks should impart similar degrees of protection against coronary heart disease. This would be true even in lay quantitative terms, since the servings of most alcoholic beverages, including spirits, wine, and beer, contain approximately equal amounts of alcohol. Most epidemiologic studies have supported this hypothesis, but some authors have argued that wine, and in particular red wine, may be more beneficial, possibly because the latter contains compounds with antioxidant properties. Probably more important than the chemical differences between wine and other alcoholic beverages is the way wine is drunk, particularly in the Mediterranean countries—almost always during meals and in the company of family or friends, under conditions that favor moderation and discourage acute intoxication. Mature people and societies can find the balance that maximizes the beneficial health effects of wine and minimizes its adverse effects, but the balance can be a precarious one.

It is not clear whether the identified health-promoting aspects of the Mediterranean diet can fully explain the otherwise unexplained good health of Mediterranean people. Some scientists have proposed that the freshness of plant foods, various interactions among components of diet, or the pattern of eating and drinking may have elusive and difficult-to-identify synergistic effects. Others have argued that the relaxing psychosocial environment in most Mediterranean countries, the preservation of the extended family structure, the stress-releasing afternoon siesta habit, and even the mild climatic conditions may complement the beneficial effects of diet. Nevertheless few, if any, deny the central role of diet in the constellation of favorable conditions surrounding the Mediterranean people.

The Mediterranean diet and lifestyle are not the product of unusual insight or wisdom. They were shaped by climatic conditions and environmental constraints, and in many instances they represent adaptive responses to poverty and hardship. Furthermore, many of their important health-promoting components are not unique to the Mediterranean region but can be found in other areas of the world and other population groups. Still, several variations of the Mediterranean diet can be considered realistic models of a prudent diet that fits our current understanding of healthy nutrition. Indeed, it is the convergence of recent results from methodologically superior nutritional investigations with the dramatic ecological evidence represented by the Mediterranean natural experiment that has created the present momentum toward the Mediterranean diet. It would appear logical for non-Mediterraneans to adopt critical elements of this diet in their food habits and for Mediterraneans to reverse the trends that tend to draw them away from their health-promoting nutritional traditions.

Both authors of this Introduction were born and raised in Greece, but both have traveled and lived in several parts of the world. In the process, we have come to realize that individuals as well as ethnic groups can learn a lot from the experience and the cultural tradition of others. It seems to us that a healthy diet may represent one of the most important contributions of the Mediterranean people to others around the world. It is tasteful, lively, and highly variable—and it can be an integral and important component of a health-promoting lifestyle.

# MAKING THE CHANGE

*C*hanging eating habits may seem like a radical and difficult chore, but changing to the Mediterranean diet is easy because most of the foods and cooking techniques are already familiar to us. It's a shift of emphasis that's the key to cooking and eating in a healthy Mediterranean style.

Except for olive oil, there's no need for special foods in the larder—in fact, most of the foods featured in the Mediterranean kitchen are probably already in your pantry cupboard. Several different kinds of beans, both dried and canned, long-grain and short-grain rice, cornmeal for polenta and flour for bread, pasta in a variety of shapes, canned tomatoes, and condiments like dried mushrooms and herbs are common ingredients and take no special effort to acquire. If there's an Italian, Greek, or Middle Eastern neighborhood nearby, you'll have access to first-rate olives and cheese; otherwise, make a special trip some Saturday to a more distant market and spend time wandering around examining the offerings. If you're far from ethnic shopping areas like these, mail-order suppliers are a good, if sometimes rather expensive, resource.

We invent all sorts of rationales for holding back on changing diets, especially where families are involved. But there are compelling reasons for making the switch, and most of the obstacles are easily overcome. Just remember where families are concerned that change sometimes has to come slowly. Whatever you do, don't make a big deal out of it. Small, quiet, almost unnoticeable changes are more effective than noisy family food fights.

*Start off by structuring mealtimes,* if you don't do that already. It's hard for American families, with so many of us apart at lunch, but dinner at least should be a time for the family to come together and share whatever is on the table. Try to have meals on the table at the same hour each day and let people know they're expected

to be there. It's the first step in a Mediterranean direction, building a sense of food as a fundamentally communal, shared experience.

*Switch from whatever fats you now use to olive oil,* preferably extra-virgin olive oil. If you're not used to olive oil, start off with one of the light oils—light, that is, in flavor, not in calories or fat (all oils have the same number of calories; all are 100 percent fat). Since salad naturally goes with oil, begin by dressing the salad with light oil, following one of the recipes in Chapter 6. Once you've grown used to the taste, move up a notch to a more flavorful oil and start using olive oil to lightly sauté meat, chicken, or fish. More flavorful oils are wonderful for sautéing potatoes, especially with a little garlic or onion added, another way to accustom your family to the distinctive flavor. Soon you may find yourself using truly aromatic oils on steamed vegetables or baked potatoes in place of butter or sour cream. (A flowery olive oil on fresh corn in season is a magnificent treat!)

*Get out of the butter habit.* Butter is *never* on the Mediterranean table. Even at breakfast, only a little jam garnishes the bread, which is appreciated for its own good flavor. Don't add butter to vegetables either. A little olive oil serves the same function, adding richness and flavor.

In restaurants, ask how food is prepared and select items that aren't lavished with butter and cream. The best restaurants will have a cruet of fine oil to add as a garnish for unbuttered vegetables.

*Add bread in abundance to the meal.* If you don't feel like making your own, seek out a bakery with a reputation for dense, chewy, country-style loaves, preferably just plain bread without added sugar, butter, or eggs. Mediterranean tables are never without bread, which is one of the fundamental components of the Mediterranean diet.

*Begin or end each meal with a salad.* Make it from fresh crisp greens and whatever vegetables are in season—tomatoes in late summer, cucumbers, sweet peppers, scallions, broccoli flowers, spinach, and so on. Don't use iceberg lettuce—it has almost no nutritional value—but do look for dark green leaf lettuces like romaine and oak leaf, common in supermarket produce sections. Add fresh green herbs for variety, but not all at once—basil at one meal, dill at another, coriander (cilantro) if you like the flavor at a third.

*Add both more vegetables and different vegetables to the menu.* Get away from the American focus on potatoes, salad, and green peas. There's nothing wrong with any of them, but life is so much richer! Every day, try to get in at least one serving each of cruciferous vegetables (broccoli and broccoli rabe, cabbage, cauliflower, turnip and mustard greens, etc.) and beta-carotene-rich vegetables and fruits

(broccoli and broccoli rabe, carrots, sweet potatoes, spinach, and yellow squash, as well as apricots and cantaloupe). These don't have to be served separately—vegetable combinations, vegetables cooked in a sauce for pasta, vegetables served cut up in a soup are all ways to increase the quantity consumed.

*Cut down on the amount of meat consumed.* There's no reason for normal, healthy adults to eat more than 4 ounces of lean meat a day, and much less is much better. Children, of course, need even less. (If your family is used to 8-ounce portions, start cutting the portions down gradually rather than all at once.) Eat lean red meat (beef, pork, and lamb) just once or twice a week. Other meals can feature chicken, fish, pasta, rice, or vegetables.

One easy way to cut meat consumption is with stews that feature meat as an incidental to lots and lots of vegetables. You'll find recipes for such preparations throughout this book. Or make a hearty soup the main course, with plenty of bread, perhaps a little cheese, and salad to accompany it. Soup is a delicious and cheap way to get lots of vegetables on the table.

Move meat away from the center of the plate by adding complex carbohydrates like rice, beans, and pasta to fill the gap that meat once occupied. When you do serve a main course of meat or fish, get into the Mediterranean habit of offering a first course of pasta or soup to fill diners up before the meat arrives.

And if you're worried about budgetary constraints, think of this: by adding olive oil and subtracting meat, you'll probably come out even over the course of a week.

*Substitute wine in moderation for other alcoholic beverages.* If you enjoy wine with your meals, you're already well on the way to a Mediterranean lifestyle. Except among strict Moslems, wine is part of every Mediterranean meal but breakfast. The operative words here are *part of the meal.* In the Mediterranean, wine is a companion to food and almost never taken on its own. Even a glass of wine or an aperitif as a cocktail before dinner is always accompanied by something to eat—if not a full-fledged meze, then a few olives or a handful of almonds. Wine in moderation, a couple of glasses a day served with meals, seems in fact to be protective against coronary heart disease (see the Introduction for details).

If you don't care for wine, drink water instead—a bottle of still or fizzy mineral water is another standard feature on Mediterranean tables. Just don't substitute milk, which comes into the Mediterranean diet after infancy only in the form of wonderful cheeses and yogurts or a little hot milk added to morning coffee. For normal healthy adults, enough calcium should be supplied by cheese, yogurt, and vegetables.

MAKING THE CHANGE

*Don't fuss with dessert.* To me, dessert seems like useless and unprofitable time spent in the kitchen, and it's certainly not necessary on the table. (Far better to spend that time making soup.) Above all, don't buy packaged desserts, whether cakes, cookies, or ice cream—well, maybe ice cream as an occasional treat. Most packaged desserts are so loaded with saturated fat and sugar, not to mention stabilizers and other undesirable additives, that they are truly nutritional time bombs. All they really do is accustom the palate to sugary fats at the end of a meal. If you must have a sweet, the simplest of cookies is preferable to a rich cake; better yet is fresh or lightly poached fruit, which should be sweet enough in itself to satisfy any sugar addicts in the family. And with fruit you get valuable vitamins and fiber along with the sweet, something that cannot be said for other desserts.

Many restaurants will have a simple platter of fresh fruit or fruit with cheese on the dessert menu. Choose it instead of the sinfully chocolate drop-dead nightmare the pastry chef is so proud of. As more of us start asking for fruit, more fruit will be served.

*Think about the quality of the food you buy and seek out the best.* Because Mediterranean food is so simple, it's worth spending time looking for the best ingredients. How do you go about doing this? Fortunately, it gets easier with each passing season. Start with the place where you customarily shop. Many supermarkets, responding to customer demand, have established sections devoted to organically raised produce and naturally raised meats. Some supermarket chains, like Bread and Circus in the Northeast and Mrs. Gooch's in California, to name just two, are entirely devoted to healthy products like these.

If supermarkets have little to offer, look for farmers' markets and health food stores that carry local, healthy ingredients. (Call the food editor of a local newspaper or your state university's college of agriculture for information. Cooperative Extension agents can also be good information sources.)

Farmers' markets are terrific sources. When you start to frequent them, you'll also start to build up contacts with local farmers. They'll not only tell you how the food is grown or produced; they may tell you how to cook it too, and they'll start to let you know what things are coming along. The best-run health food stores and co-ops are also good outlets for local production—fruits and vegetables, whole grains and beans, free-range chickens and their eggs, all of which will be fresher and more flavorful than most supermarket offerings. Many farmers' markets and health food stores take WIC coupons and food stamps; if you're on a tightly restricted budget, keep that in mind.

In restaurants, ask questions about where food comes from and let them know that you care. The best restaurants also care and work hard to advance quality.

In the end, it's the simplicity of it all that makes the Mediterranean diet such an appealing alternative. Exotic foods, elaborate and time-consuming preparations, and special culinary techniques are not what it's all about. Good food, carefully purchased, thoughtfully if simply prepared, and lovingly served and shared: that's the secret.

## OLIVE OIL

There is a village south and east of Siena called Montisi where during the season of the olive harvest I like to drop in on a particular mill, or *frantoio* as it's called in Italy. I like this place in part because the oil produced here is the rich, green stuff of the region, oil that, when young and fresh from the *frantoio,* slides down the throat with the peppery *pizzica,* the catch at the back of the palate that is typical of oil pressed from immature, half-green Tuscan olives.

This is the oil connoisseurs seek out much as they do the fine red wines of the region. Like the wines, the oil has a unique character. It speaks of the terraced hills around Montisi with a voice that is subtly different from that of oils from nearby Lucca or Cortona. And these strong-flavored, green-tasting Tuscan oils are very different themselves from the lighter, rounder, fatter oils from Apulia in Italy's South. Which again are distinctive from the oils of Catalonia with their hints of almond and the richer, full-bodied oils from Greece and farther east in Lebanon and the bland, sweet oils from North Africa.

The olive harvest begins in Montisi, as it does throughout the Mediterranean, toward the end of autumn and the beginning of winter, as farming families who live in the village gradually strip the trees of their fruit.

The greenish violet olives, engorged with oil, are brought to the *frantoio* by the tractorload and tumbled through a hopper down into the crusher, two giant stone wheels that stand on edge and turn steadily, mashing the fruits to a thick, oily paste that is spread on round mats, once made of esparto grass, now made of plastic. The big mats are stacked high, one on top of the other, and carted by dolly to the presses. Gently but firmly the mats are compressed and the precious oil, glistening gold in the dim light of the *frantoio,* oozes out and trickles slowly down over the mats and into waiting receptacles below.

And that's it. Cloudy, greenish gold, and heady with fragrance, the new oil is ready. Most of the Montisini don't even bother filtering their oil

*continued*

because the residues precipitate, just like wine residues, with the cold winter temperature.

It is chilly in the *frantoio,* but that doesn't stop it from being a sort of community center during the brief weeks that it's operating. Besides the workers, there are farmers and farm wives dropping in to check the progress of their oil, buyers and curious onlookers, and always a group of old men of the village who do nothing much but comment on the action, comments that are sometimes received as wisdom, sometimes as the foolishness of age.

In the back room a fire burns brightly on an old hearth that just escapes antiquarian value. The men gather around the hearth, toasting thick slices of bread on long forks until they're blackened and crusty. Then they rub the slices with a cut clove of garlic and drizzle them thickly with the newly decanted oil. A sprinkle of salt from a nearby jelly jar and the bruschetta is ready, its crust softened with oil to the point that weak old teeth can masticate it with evident satisfaction. It is a scene that has been repeated every year at this time for as long as the old men can remember, for as long as they've heard tell.

Is it strange that a product as ancient as olive oil has been given new life and validity by the discoveries of modern science? Not really. Not when you understand that for thousands of years olive oil has been the foundation of the Mediterranean diet, this diet that nutritionists and medical researchers tell us approaches an ideal. Olive oil is not the only healthy factor in the Mediterranean diet by any means, but scientists suspect that it is one of the most significant. Why that is so takes a little explaining.

As nutritional science evolves, so does our knowledge about olive oil, its physical characteristics and chemical composition and its impact on human metabolism. What is clear at this point is that olive oil is unusually high in monounsaturated fats and a very good source of the elusive tocopherols (vitamin E).

Vitamin E is a powerful antioxidant; like beta-carotene and vitamin C, it fights against free radicals, damaging elements that seem to suppress the immune system and may contribute to heart disease, cancer, and lung

*continued*

disease as well as to the aging process. Free radicals are produced in the body by pollutants like tobacco smoke and fuel exhaust, but they are also a normal, constant, and inevitable by-product of human metabolism. Anything that inhibits the formation of free radicals is likely to be beneficial in disease prevention.

There are basically two kinds of fats in the diet, saturated and unsaturated. Saturated fats, like butter, cream, lard, and the fat that lies in the interstices of well-marbled steak, are recognizable because they are mostly solid at room temperature. They come mainly from animals, although tropical vegetable oils like palm oil and coconut oil are also high in undesirable saturated fat. Unsaturated fats, mostly plant-based vegetable and seed oils, are liquid at room temperature. Unsaturated fats are either polyunsaturated or monounsaturated.* All dietary fats and oils, whether of animal or plant origin, are equal in that they have about 120 calories and between 13 and 14 grams of fat to the tablespoon. All vegetable and seed oils are also equal in that they are cholesterol free.

Monounsaturated fat is the main component of olive oil, which is between 56 and 83 percent monounsaturated, depending on the olive variety. Monounsaturated fats work in the body to reduce total serum cholesterol levels by reducing low-density lipoproteins (LDLs or "bad" cholesterol) while increasing high-density lipoproteins (HDLs or "good" cholesterol). (Polyunsaturated fats, on the other hand, reduce LDLs but are less effective on HDLs.) Monounsaturated fats are highly protective against diseases associated with elevated "bad" cholesterol levels, such as heart disease. There are other oils that are also high in monounsaturated fats, but they all have drawbacks: almond and hazelnut oils, for instance, are very expensive to produce; avocado oil has an unacceptably high level of saturated fat as well; and rapeseed oil, better known as

---

* Saturation refers to the chemical structure of fat molecules. In saturated fats the molecules are completely covered, or saturated, with hydrogen atoms. In monounsaturated fats there is one unsaturated link in the chain, and in polyunsaturated fats there is more than one unsaturated link.

*continued*

*canola oil,* is highly refined and adds nothing to the foods with which it is used.

Olive oil is the only fat that is high in monounsaturated fatty acids, that is easy and relatively inexpensive to produce by simply expressing the juice of olives, and that contributes welcome flavors and textures to the foods to which it's added. Moreover, olive oil has a long tradition as the principal fat used by people with a well-documented history of long and healthy lives—the people of the Mediterranean basin.

With all the talk that goes on about reducing fat consumption, why should we bother with olive oil at all? Wouldn't it be better just to eliminate all fats from our diets? No, it wouldn't, for the very good reason that, beyond questions of taste (and fat, no matter what its structure, contributes powerfully to flavor in all our foods), our bodies need a certain amount of fat to function properly—grease for the gears, you might say, in the form of fat-soluble vitamins like A, D, E, and K and in the valuable, protective HDL cholesterol levels that, without some fat in the diet, might fall dangerously low, according to researchers.

At the Cambridge conference on the diets of the Mediterranean in 1993, Dr. Walter Willett, chairman of the Department of Nutrition at the Harvard School of Public Health, startled the assembly when he exclaimed, only half-jokingly, "As far as I'm concerned, you can take the whole food pyramid and just pour olive oil over it!" Yet there's a certain amount of logic in that assertion: The Seven Countries Study of men on the island of Crete in the early 1960s showed that they received a full 40 percent of their daily calories from fat, the fat they ate was primarily olive oil, and their mortality rates from coronary heart disease and stroke were among the lowest in the world (see Introduction).

More soberly, in an editorial article in the *New England Journal of Medicine,* Dr. Willett and Dr. Frank M. Sacks of Harvard Medical School concluded: "An alternative to a low-fat diet for lowering cholesterol levels is the traditional Mediterranean diet, . . . [in which] olive oil is a major source of energy, fat averages 35 to 40 percent of total calories, and rates of coronary disease are as low as in populations with very-low-fat diets. . . .

*continued*

[W]e believe that the majority of dietary fatty acids should be monoun-saturated rather than polyunsaturated, because diets very high in polyun-saturated fats lower HDL levels, and concern remains about the carcinogenic potential (albeit not proved) of such high amounts of polyun-saturated fats."

So the cautionary rule is: Don't *add* fat to your diet, but do *substitute* monounsaturated fats like olive oil for those you now use.

# CHAPTER ONE

# THE SMALL DISHES OF THE MEDITERRANEAN

*Meze, Antipasti, Tapas, Street Food, Bar Snacks, and*
*Other Introductions to the Meal*

T he Greek Cypriotes who used to live in the village of Bellapais had a reputation as the laziest folk on the island. And with good reason, since the infamous Tree of Idleness cast its shadow over the village square and the dusty quadrant in front of Dmitri's café. Beneath its branches mustachioed old men, clad in the black baggy trousers that were once the uniform all over the eastern Mediterranean, passed long and tranquil hours sipping thick, heavily sweetened coffee or anise-flavored ouzo, nibbling on olives or bits of the local goat's milk cheese, playing endless games of backgammon, or trictrac as they called it, and keeping an eye on village comings and goings. Unlike the women of the village, who kept up a constant chatter as they went about their work (no idleness for them), the old men were often silent, contemplative, deep into what Lawrence Durrell supposed to be a Moslem quality called *kayf*, in his words, "a fathomless repose of the will."

Bellapais was the village Durrell wrote about in *Bitter Lemons*. We lived there in the early 1970s, long after Durrell had left, in a happy lull between two periods of political struggle on the island. What kind of tree it was that cast its invidious shade over the old men I no longer even remember—walnut perhaps, since walnuts encourage indolence, or so they say. In tribute to the tree's powers, the new and sparkling café-restaurant that opened opposite Dmitri's shortly after we arrived in the village was also called the Tree of Idleness, and that was appropriate too since

it was on the terrace of the Tree of Idleness Café that we were introduced to an even more seductive form of indolence, the meze table.

The café quickly became famous island-wide for the extent and variety of its meze, or mezedakia as the Greeks say, and we became frequent and enthusiastic customers. Entire Sunday afternoons were idled away over the meze table while house guests came and went from Kyrenia, Beirut, and farther afield and the children wandered in for a bite of this or a nibble of that between the games they played—Saracens and Crusaders instead of cowboys and Indians.

The food came on white china saucers and oval platters, and the dishes piled up in the center of the table as the afternoon wore on. There would always be hummus, pureed chick-peas or garbanzos mixed with sesame paste, and baba ghanouj or melitzanosalata, charcoal-roasted eggplant pureed with garlic and olive oil, along with wedges of flat pita bread for dipping. There were always olives, both shiny plump black ones and little bitter green ones flavored with coriander, and chunks of that tangy, salty sheep's milk feta cheese that seems to have been created solely because it goes so well with black olives. These were the sine qua nons of the meze table. And then, depending on the season, there would be grape leaves, stuffed with meat and served hot or stuffed with rice and currants and served cold. And since we were only 15 minutes from the sea, there would almost always be something fishy, if only salted anchovies or canned sardines or rosy-colored taramosalata, made with salted cod's roe. But if the fishing had been good lately, there might also be a little plate of fried whitebait or a pile of sweet red mullet no more than five or six inches long or chunks of octopus braised in red wine with bay leaves and cinnamon—as well as lamb sausages flavored with grains of coriander, deep-fried and melting haloumi cheese, fresh radishes and scallions and creamy, garlic-scented yogurt to dip them in, fat fasoulia beans dressed with rich, dark green Cypriote olive oil and juice from lemons grown in the orchards below the village. And so on till the afternoon had magically melted away, till twilight began to creep along the craggy peaks above the village, till the last honey touch of sun mellowed the old Crusader-built walls around the abbey church. Then *kayf,* whether Moslem or not, really did set in, the contemplation, Durrell says, that comes of silence and ease.

What exactly is a meze? Like so many ideas about food, a meze is vastly different depending on where you are and whom you're with and what you're planning to do with the day. In its simplest form it might be like what the old men had at Dmitri's, a few black and green home-cured olives on a plate with a chunk of sheep's milk cheese and a little olive oil sprinkled over it. Add slices of cucumber and quarters of dark red sweet tomatoes, dressed with a few grains of sea salt, perhaps some pickled

green peppers or beet-dyed red turnips, and you start to have something worth talking about. Add more dishes, especially freshly cooked dishes, and you begin to approach a spread like that at the Tree of Idleness with which to while away a Sunday afternoon.

The elements of the meze table are part of a category I've called "the small dishes of the Mediterranean," a panoply of little dishes that are eaten informally and without a great deal of ceremony, whether meze in the eastern Mediterranean, tapas in Spain, antipasti in Italy, or the variety of merendas and casse-croûtes and snacks that are taken between meals all over the region.

Meze may have evolved, as Turks like to claim, to accompany their favorite alcoholic drink, raki, an anise-flavored distilled spirit that, like Greek ouzo, Arab arak, and Provençal pastis, all of which it resembles, turns cloudy when mixed with ice or water. If the Turks are right, then meze's closest cousin around the Mediterranean is surely Spanish tapas, which seem devised specifically to encourage drinkers and revive flagging spirits or at least to keep them going till a proper meal can be served.

Tapas, strictly speaking, are served only in a bar, never in a restaurant, and even more properly eaten only while actually standing up at the bar, one foot resting on the brass rail. But that custom is changing, and even in deeply traditional Andalusia, where some suspect the custom began, you'll find tapas served at restaurant tables these days. The nature of the fare is changing too. No longer will you find the things that were served free or for a couple of pesetas with a well-chilled fino or a late-night coñac in the tasca bars where the bullfighters used to hang out around the Plaza Santa Ana in Madrid, things like little cubes of coagulated lamb's blood speared with toothpicks, or *percebes,* a strange kind of goose barnacle that looks like miniature elephants' toes—tastes like them too, some would say. But there are still chunks of well-aged queso manchego or sheep's milk cheese, wedges of tortilla, the Spanish potato and onion omelet, and slices of jamon serrano, hand-cut from hams that hang over the bar with a little plastic cup beneath them to catch the dripping juices. In season you might get *gambas al ajillo,* tiny shrimps roasted in olive oil with garlic and chilies and presented in the terra-cotta dishes in which they were cooked, or in the springtime *chanquetes,* horrifyingly expensive baby eels, no more than an inch or two long and given a similar treatment. And there are always crackling fresh salted almonds, whose flavor is so complementary to the nutty taste of chilled fino sherry, and as with meze there are always olives, big fat green ones called *gordales* often stuffed with an almond or a bit of salted anchovy.

In Italy the "small dishes" are almost always served at the table, as antipasti to

THE SMALL DISHES OF THE MEDITERRANEAN

25

begin a meal. An antipasto course (the name means "before the meal," not before the pasta) is by no means invariably included in a meal; rather it indicates that the courses that follow will border on elegance or at least on showy presentation. Unlike tapas and meze, antipasti are not particularly connected with bars and drinking, although of course, like every part of an Italian meal, they are served with the appropriate wine. This is really restaurant food and almost never part of family dining except on special feast days or to impress an honored guest. In that way antipasti are more like what the French call an *amuse-gueule* or an hors d'oeuvre (literally, "outside the work"), a little something to stimulate the appetite for the real food that will follow. In a country restaurant the antipasto might be a platter of local *salumi*, all sorts of cured hams and sausages flavored with garlic or the seeds of wild fennel; there might also be a few crostini, little bread crusts topped with a mash of chicken livers and capers or with fresh ripe tomatoes minced and sprinkled with basil and salt.

Sometimes vegetables, especially fresh ones just coming into season, will star in an antipasto. They might be served raw, as in a salad like puntarelle, chicory shoots dressed with an anchovy-garlic sauce that are treasured in Rome in late winter and early spring, or they might be cooked—the first wild mushrooms of the season are often simply grilled and presented as an antipasto. Raw or cooked, a singular presentation like this carries a clear message: "This is so special it is to be savored and cherished on its own, undistracted by anything else." An admirable attitude and one we would do well to adopt.

Provençal hors d'oeuvres and crudités are similar to Italian antipasti—a platter napped with slices of rosy pink and dark red sausages, for instance, alternating with some of the spectacular early vegetables cooks in the region dote on—tiny artichokes, fennel, and broad beans to be eaten raw, or barely steamed haricots verts, the most delicious of all green beans. Or the feature might be the startling goodness of those big, deeply ridged Provençal tomatoes, thickly sliced and eaten with wedges of crusty bread and salty local jambon or with aïoli, that garlic lovers' died-and-gone-to-heaven sauce of mounted egg yolks and olive oil and cloves and cloves and cloves of garlic.

Of all these presentations, the most spectacular is surely the Italian *pinzimonio*, a cornucopia of the earliest spring vegetables, either raw or barely blanched: baby onions, tender little carrots, tiny violet artichokes, pencil-thin wild asparagus, young lettuces, cucumbers, fennel. These are served with a simple glass cruet of the finest olive oil of that year, perhaps still with the slight throat-catching edge of bitterness that denotes oil of the highest quality, along with salt and pepper—

nothing more. Each diner pours a puddle of golden-green oil in the center of the plate, adds judicious amounts of salt and pepper, scrambles them with a fork to mix, and then happily dips the vegetables, one by one, and consumes them out of hand.

Outside of restaurant kitchens, few cooks these days are both willing and able to produce a full-blown meze like the one at the Tree of Idleness or a succession of tapas like those still served in bars and cafés throughout Spain. But the idea behind these small dishes—to produce something quick and tasty out of a lively and informal attitude toward eating—is a good one, and for that reason I have also included in this chapter recipes for salads and egg dishes that seem to fit the job description well.

Many of the recipes here can be served singly or in a small group of two or at most three to keep guests happy with a bottle of wine while the cook gets on with the rest of the meal. Others can form the basis of a meal, either as a main course or as a garnish for something more substantial. Most of these small dishes are based on vegetables, beans, or grains; where meat is used, it is most often a flavor adjunct. In the midst of the bustle of modern life, this is one way to get in those five-a-day servings of fresh vegetables that we are told should be our goal. A couple of small vegetable dishes to start, a substantial green salad in the middle, and a finish of fresh fruit should keep even the most confirmed carnivore happy and healthy and perhaps even wise. And whether the small dishes come at the start or in the middle of the meal, be sure there's always plenty of good, crusty bread served with them.

Keep in mind too that the various savory pies in Chapter 3—whether pizza, Catalan *cocas*, or the spinach and cheese-stuffed tarts of the eastern Mediterranean—can make appealing small dishes or first courses, as do many of the dishes in Chapter 8. Where it's appropriate, I have made suggestions about when and how to serve. Anyone who wants to attempt a full-scale mezedakia should keep in mind that many dishes can be prepared ahead of time and indeed benefit from it.

# MARINATED OLIVES

**A**nywhere you go in the Mediterranean, at any time of day or night, you will most likely be offered olives in some form or another—large or small; green, black, or purply brown; brine-, salt-, or oil-cured; wrinkled and shriveled or plump and full of rich oil. In the eastern Mediterranean olives are eaten even for breakfast— and an excellent breakfast they make, served with the thickened yogurt called *labneh* and some fresh rounds of Arab bread. Elsewhere, olives are quintessential as tapas and on hors d'oeuvre and antipasto platters. One of the region's most ancient foods (wild olives were part of the diet of Mesolithic cave dwellers in the Grotto dell'Uzzo on Sicily some 10,000 years ago), olives, like their precious oil, define the region and its cuisine. Durrell's sonorous and much quoted line about their savor—"Older than meat, older than wine, as old as cold, clear water"—has its own antique flavor, memorable because it rings true.

Selecting olives is important. It's worth a special trip to a big-city delicatessen or an Italian, Greek, or Middle Eastern neighborhood shop for a look at what's available. We actually have a much wider variety of olives in this country than in any single market in the Mediterranean. In Italy, for instance, you can find only Italian olives, but at my favorite Italian food supplier, Al Capone in Somerville, Massachusetts, I can find Greek, Italian, French, and often North African olives, and just a few doors away is a shop selling the rather bitter green olives from the Middle East.

Most supermarket deli departments have the lusciously oily Greek black olives called Kalamata, from the region of the Peloponnisos where they originated. Even when not the best quality, they're far superior to anything that comes in a can—the texture, combined with the extraordinary burst of flavor in your mouth, makes you realize that olives really are a food and not just a garnish for cocktail canapes. Canned California olives, whether black or green, are not to be used in any of the recipes in this book.

Although many different varieties of olives are grown, many of them specifically for eating, the most significant difference for the cook is in the curing. As you know if you've ever tasted an olive right off the tree, table olives must go through a curing process to eliminate their acrid flavors. The curing, during which the olives undergo lactic fermentation just like yogurt and other fermented products, is accomplished through different mediums—a salt brine, for instance, or, when olives are very mature and black, a dry marinade directly in salt. Such home-style

curing methods are almost unchanged since Columella, the great Spanish Latin writer on things agricultural, described them back in the first century A.D. In winter months, in farmhouse cantinas and attics throughout the Mediterranean basin, olives ferment in woven willow baskets and massive earthenware amphorae, just like the 3,000-year-old ones Sir Arthur Evans found in the ruined palace storerooms of Knossos on Crete.

Once olives have been cured, they may be marinated in aromatics to add other complementary flavors such as garlic, bay leaves, fresh thyme, citrus peel, lightly cracked coriander seeds, or a little hot chili pepper. Here are my personal favorites, but use your own taste to guide you in creating olives for your table.

1   **pound small black Niçoise olives, drained**

2   **lemons**

**dash of cayenne pepper**

½   **teaspoon sweet paprika**

¼   **teaspoon ground cumin**

1   **tablespoon extra-virgin olive oil or more if necessary**

Place the olives in a bowl. Carefully pare away the zest of the lemons and slice into fine julienne (or use a zester). Peel the white rind away from the lemons and discard it. Cut the juicy yellow flesh into thin sections, discarding the seeds. Toss the zest and lemon flesh with the olives, adding the spices. Add the tablespoon of olive oil and toss again. Set aside to let the flavors blend for a couple of hours or several days before serving. To keep them longer than a few days, pack the olives in a jar; add a tablespoon of salt and enough oil to cover. The olives may be kept refrigerated for 2 or 3 weeks but should be brought to room temperature before serving. *Makes 1 pound; 16 servings*

Nutritional Data, per portion

| | | |
|---|---|---|
| Calories 27 | Carbohydrate 2g | Saturated Fat trace |
| Protein trace | Sodium 124mg | Monounsaturated |
| Fat 2g | Cholesterol 0 | Fat 2g |

THE SMALL DISHES OF THE MEDITERRANEAN

**ANOTHER METHOD:**

1   pound large black Greek olives, drained

zest of 1 orange, grated or sliced into julienne

2   bay leaves, chopped

1   garlic clove, cut into thin shavings

1   teaspoon hot red pepper flakes or to taste

1   tablespoon extra-virgin olive oil

Combine all the ingredients and mix well. Set aside to marinate for a couple of hours before serving. Or pack in a jar, as in the preceding version, to keep for 2 to 3 weeks. *Makes 1 pound; 16 servings*

Nutritional Data, per portion

| | | |
|---|---|---|
| Calories   73 | Carbohydrate   2g | Saturated Fat   1g |
| Protein   trace | Sodium   625mg | Monounsaturated |
| Fat   8g | Cholesterol   0 | Fat   6g |

---

## TREATING FRESH GREEN OLIVES

In some Italian and Greek neighborhoods, freshly harvested olives are available seasonally. If you can find them, follow the example of Niko Stavroulakis, a friend who lives in the old city of Hania on the Greek island of Crete. Niko cracks freshly harvested green olives with a hammer and leaves them for three weeks in fresh (not salted) water, changing the water each day. Then he drains them and packs them in jars, layered with lemon slices, each layer sprinkled liberally with salt. He fills the jar with olive oil, covers it, then leaves it in a cold pantry. The olives are ready to eat in another three weeks. Cracked coriander seeds are a nice addition with the lemon layers.

# TAPÉNADE

### *Black Olive Paste*

**T**he ancient Romans made a sauce called *epityrum* from black or green olives pounded in a mortar with oil, vinegar, a little cumin, and green herbs like fennel tops, rue, mint, and cilantro. Tapénade, which is similar, comes from the south of France—the word derives from the Provençal *tapéno*, meaning capers, although the principal ingredient in the sauce is black olives. The late Elizabeth David, who wrote so movingly about Mediterranean food, always added a few ounces of tuna and a little cognac to her tapénade. Mrs. David served the sauce as an hors d'oeuvre, topped with hard-boiled eggs sliced in half lengthwise. In my family it goes on the meze table with toasted flatbread and sometimes strips of raw vegetables—fennel, carrots, celery—to dip in it; it's also a first-rate topping for crostini neri.

This calls for the very best-quality brine-cured black olives you can find. Niçoise or Gaeta olives are an excellent choice. Do not use canned Spanish or California black olives; they are simply green olives processed to turn black and peculiarly lacking in either flavor or texture. If you can't find olive oil–packed tuna, use water-packed tuna and drain well.

| | |
|---|---|
| 1 | **pound black olives, pitted** |
| ½ | **cup drained capers** |
| 1 | **small garlic clove, coarsely chopped** |
| ½ | **6⅛-ounce can Italian tuna packed in olive oil, drained** |
| 2 | **tablespoons brandy** |
| ½ | **cup olive oil** |
| | **a few drops of fresh lemon juice** |

Combine all the ingredients in a blender or food processor and process very briefly. Tapénade should be a rather coarse-textured paste (the original method of pounding in a mortar, while tedious, still produces the best quality). This may be prepared up to a week ahead and stored in the refrigerator with a thin layer of olive oil poured over it, but be sure to bring it to room temperature before serving since olive oil solidifies when chilled. Stir the excess olive oil into the paste before serving. Taste and add a few drops of lemon juice if desired. *Makes 1½ to 2 cups; 6 to 8 servings (more if part of a meze)*

THE SMALL DISHES OF THE MEDITERRANEAN

# HUMMUS BI TAHINI

### *Chick-Pea Salad or Dip*

**H**ummus bi tahini and baba ghanouj (recipe follows) are essential to an eastern Mediterranean meze. Serve them with crackers or toasted triangles of Arab or pita bread (page 133) or with vegetables such as scallions and carrot, celery, and cucumber sticks for dipping. This is good finger food with a glass of wine (or arak or ouzo) before dinner, but both hummus and baba ghanouj—alone or together— can also be substantial side dishes to accompany a main-course soup or salad. Note that in this classic recipe there is just a hint of garlic so that the sweetness of the chick-peas is not masked.

In some parts of the country chick-peas are more commonly known by their Spanish name, garbanzos. Tahini, or sesame seed paste, is readily available at supermarkets and health food stores.

1   cup dried chick-peas, soaked overnight and drained

3   cups water

½   cup tahini

1   tablespoon roasted (dark) sesame oil

1   teaspoon salt or to taste

½   teaspoon ground cumin

juice of 2 lemons or more to taste

¼   garlic clove, finely minced

1   tablespoon extra-virgin olive oil

pinch of ground hot red chili (not chili powder)

GARNISH (OPTIONAL):

a little finely minced parsley

THE MEDITERRANEAN DIET COOKBOOK

Place the chick-peas in a saucepan with the water. Bring to a boil, cover, and simmer gently until the chick-peas are very tender but not falling apart. Time depends on the age and size of the chick-peas, but count on at least 30 to 40 minutes. Remove from the heat and drain, reserving about ½ cup of the cooking water. If you wish, set aside half a dozen chick-peas to use as a garnish.

Place the chick-peas in a food processor with about ¼ cup of the cooking liquid. Process in brief bursts until the chick-peas are a coarse and grainy puree, adding more liquid if necessary.

Combine the chick-pea puree in a bowl with the tahini, sesame oil, salt, and cumin. Add the lemon juice and stir to mix well, then stir in the minced garlic. Spread the puree on a deep platter, swirling the top with a spoon or fork. Then mix the olive oil with the ground chili and drizzle it over the swirls. Garnish with the reserved chick-peas and minced parsley if desired. *Makes 2½ cups; 8 to 10 servings (more if part of a meze)*

Nutritional Data, per portion

| | | |
|---|---|---|
| Calories  170 | Carbohydrate  15g | Saturated Fat  1 |
| Protein  6g | Sodium  239mg | Monounsaturated |
| Fat  10g | Cholesterol  0 | Fat  4g |

# BABA GHANOUJ

### *Roasted Eggplant Salad or Dip*

If you have a fireplace or an outdoor grill, roast the eggplant over live coals for a delectably smoky aroma.

- 1   **large eggplant, approximately ½ pound**
- 1   **large garlic clove**
- 1   **teaspoon salt or to taste**
- ½   **cup tahini**
- **juice of ½ lemon or more to taste**
- 2   **tablespoons water**
- 2   **tablespoons extra-virgin olive oil**
- 1   **teaspoon minced flat-leaf parsley**

Rinse the eggplant and prick it at least an inch deep with a fork in a dozen places. (This is important—I once had a large unpricked eggplant explode in my oven; the cleanup took days.)

Place the eggplant on a grill about 8 inches above a charcoal or wood fire that has burned down to embers. Roast the eggplant, turning frequently, for about 20 minutes or until it is soft inside and quite charred on the outside. Or roast it in a preheated 375-degree oven, turning frequently, for about 40 minutes.

Transfer the eggplant to a colander, slit the eggplant, and let the juices drain off. Discard the dark skin, mash the flesh with a fork or a potato masher, and set aside.

Peel the garlic clove and crush it with the flat blade of a knife. Place in a bowl with the salt and, using the back of a spoon, mash the garlic and salt to a paste. Stir in the tahini, then gradually beat in the lemon juice and water. Finally, fold in the mashed eggplant and beat thoroughly to combine well.

When you're ready to serve, transfer the eggplant puree to a deep platter. Mix the olive oil and parsley together and drizzle over the eggplant. ***Makes 1½ cups; about 6 servings***

Nutritional Data, per portion

| | | |
|---|---|---|
| Calories 16g | Carbohydrate 7g | Saturated Fat 2g |
| Protein 4g | Sodium 391mg | Monounsaturated |
| Fat 15g | Cholesterol 0 | Fat 8g |

# EGGPLANT DIP WITH YOGURT

**T**his is a slightly different preparation from the previous recipe, although used in much the same way. The tang of yogurt replaces the rich and nutty flavor of tahini; use nonfat yogurt if you wish.

If you cannot find poblano peppers, which are spicy without being fiery, use a mixture of green bell peppers, Italian or cubanelle peppers, and a few serranos or jalapeños to achieve a balance of spice and sweetness.

2   pounds eggplant

1   cup nonfat or low-fat plain yogurt

¼   cup extra-virgin olive oil

juice of ½ lemon

4 or 5 spicy but not fiery green peppers such as poblanos

2   large garlic cloves, peeled

1   teaspoon salt

Prepare the eggplants as in the previous recipe, grilling or roasting them until soft and black, then draining them in a colander.

Roast and peel the peppers, following the directions on page 455.

When the eggplants are cool enough to handle, strip away and discard the dark skin and mash the flesh with a fork or a potato masher, gradually mixing in the yogurt, olive oil, lemon juice, and pepper juices from the bowl.

Lightly crush the garlic cloves with the flat blade of a knife; then crush them to a paste with the salt, using a mortar and pestle. Add half the peeled peppers to the mortar and crush with the garlic paste. (Use a blender or food processor for this step if you wish, but don't put the eggplant in the blender; the texture is much better when it's done by hand.) Fold the pepper-garlic mixture into the eggplant. Cut the remaining peppers into strips and use to garnish the eggplant like the spokes of a wheel. *Makes about 2 cups; 6 to 8 servings*

Nutritional Data, per portion

| Calories   121 | Carbohydrate   13g | Saturated Fat   1g |
| --- | --- | --- |
| Protein   4g | Sodium   304mg | Monounsaturated |
| Fat   7g | Cholesterol   1mg | Fat   6g |

THE SMALL DISHES OF THE MEDITERRANEAN

# ROASTED RED PEPPER PUREE

▌like to include this scarlet puree in a white china bowl on the meze table next to a platter of dark and regal purple tapénade; it makes a dramatic contrast of both taste and color. Roasted over charcoal or wood embers, the peppers develop a lovely smoky sweetness. If the garlic seems overpowering, use just one clove.

4   large red bell peppers
3   tablespoons extra-virgin olive oil
1   tablespoon red wine vinegar
2 or 3 garlic cloves, peeled and crushed with the flat blade of a knife
½   teaspoon salt
freshly ground black pepper to taste

Rinse the peppers, roast them whole, and peel them, following the directions on page 455. Turn the peppers and their juice into a food processor and process in brief spurts until the peppers are a thick puree. Leave the processor running as you slowly pour in the oil and then the vinegar. Transfer to a serving bowl.

In a separate small bowl, crush the garlic and salt together with the back of a spoon to a smooth puree or use a mortar and pestle. Stir the garlic into the pepper puree. Taste and adjust the seasoning, adding pepper and more oil, vinegar, or salt if desired.

Serve with rounds of toast or crackers or with vegetable sticks for dipping.
*Makes about 1½ cups; 6 to 8 servings*

Nutritional Data, per portion

| | | |
|---|---|---|
| Calories  60 | Carbohydrate  4g | Saturated Fat  1g |
| Protein  trace | Sodium  138mg | Monounsaturated |
| Fat  5g | Cholesterol  0 | Fat  4g |

# ÇAÇIK

### Yogurt and Cucumber Sauce, Salad, or Dip

**A**lso called *tzatziki* in Greece, this is another healthful addition to the meze table, especially if made with nonfat yogurt. Use çaçik (jah-JEEK) as a sauce or dip or thin it with ice water to make a refreshing cucumber-yogurt soup.

When you're buying cucumbers, look for firm fresh ones that are slender for their length and free of soft spots or wilted ends. I prefer the shrink-wrapped, so-called *English cucumbers.* Cucumbers with waxed skins, which dominate so many produce markets, are on a par with California canned olives in my book. They were probably picked months ago—and they taste like it. Good-quality unwaxed Kirby or pickling cucumbers, although small, are an acceptable alternative if they're not too fat and full of seeds.

Dried mint has a sweeter, less wild taste than fresh mint and is preferred for this dish, although fresh mint is an appropriate garnish.

1    **long English cucumber or 2 slender unwaxed regular cucumbers**
**salt**
2    **garlic cloves, chopped**
1    **tablespoon white wine vinegar**
2    **tablespoons extra-virgin olive oil**
1½ **cups plain yogurt, nonfat if desired**
1    **tablespoon dried mint**
2    **tablespoons fresh mint leaves for garnish**

Peel and slice the cucumbers. (If they're very seedy, cut the cucumbers into quarters lengthwise and cut away the seeds.) Place the slices in a bowl and toss with a little salt. Set aside for 15 minutes or longer to draw some of the liquid out of the cucumbers.

In a bowl in which you will serve the çaçik, use the back of a spoon to mash the garlic to a paste with 1 teaspoon salt. Stir the vinegar into the paste and then stir in the oil. Add the yogurt and dried mint and mix well.

Rinse the salt from the cucumber slices in a colander and pat them dry with a kitchen towel. Fold them into the yogurt mixture. Garnish with fresh mint and serve with wedges of pita bread or crackers, or fresh vegetables such as carrots or

celery sticks, to dip in the sauce. *Makes about 2 cups; 6 to 8 servings; if thinned with 1 cup of water, 6 servings of yogurt soup*

Nutritional Data, per portion

| | | |
|---|---|---|
| Calories 60 | Carbohydrate 5g | Saturated Fat 1g |
| Protein 3g | Sodium 35mg | Monounsaturated |
| Fat 4g | Cholesterol 1mg | Fat 3g |

# ROASTED ALMONDS

**O**nce upon a time the Fuente del Berro district was a suburb on the eastern outskirts of Madrid, but the city has long since grown up around it. Fuente del Berro means "watercress fountain," after a spring-fed fountain on the edge of the nearby park where peacocks wandered. Entering the little barrio of single-family homes with front gardens facing cobblestoned streets, you leave the clangor of the city behind and walk into a very different, much older and more tranquil Spanish town. When we first went to live in the barrio, there were still gaslights at every street corner and a lamplighter who came around at dusk with his ladder to light the flares.

The little house in Fuente del Berro was within walking distance of Ventas, Madrid's plaza de toros, where the greatest bullfighters in the world came for the San Isidro corridas in May, and so the garden became a gathering spot before the corrida for a ritualistic glass or two of well-chilled fino sherry and a handful of these almonds. I used to fry them, but oven roasting uses much less oil—not only a healthier outcome but also less mess. The flavor of roasted almonds goes especially well with the nutty flavor of fino or palo cortado sherry—but these almonds are so delicious they can accompany any other wine just as well.

Almonds and almond oil, like olives and olive oil, are a good source of monounsaturated fat. In this country the best almonds come from natural foods stores, where a steady turnover ensures freshness. Don't buy blanched almonds, because the skin helps keep the nuts fresh. Above all, avoid nuts with any hint of rancidity. Note too that the taste of the almonds is actually better a couple of hours *after* roasting.

2 **cups unblanched shelled almonds**

2 **teaspoons almond oil or very light-flavored extra-virgin olive oil**

½ **teaspoon sea salt or more to taste**

Preheat the oven to 300 degrees. Bring a large pot of water to a boil, plunge the almonds in, and boil rapidly for 1 minute. Turn the almonds into a colander, and as soon as you can handle them but before they are really cool, slip the skins off. If any skins don't come off easily, return the offending nuts briefly to the boiling water.

Spread the skinned nuts in a baking dish large enough to hold them in a single layer. Bake for 5 minutes to dry them out. Remove from the oven and stir in the oil and salt. Return to the oven for another 10 minutes, stirring occasionally with a wooden spoon, until the almonds are a pale golden brown. During the last few minutes, check frequently to make sure they're not getting too brown. Set aside for a few hours before serving. ***Makes 2 cups; 8 servings***

Nutritional Data, per portion

| | | |
|---|---|---|
| Calories 201 | Carbohydrate 7g | Saturated Fat 2g |
| Protein 6g | Sodium 95mg | Monounsaturated |
| Fat 18g | Cholesterol 0 | Fat 12g |

THE SMALL DISHES OF THE MEDITERRANEAN

# GRILLED VEGETABLES MARINATED WITH OIL AND VINEGAR

**A**t Locanda del Gallo, a restaurant in the tiny Apulian village of Acaia (said to have been settled by Ancient Greeks, possibly Homer's Achaeans), the host prides himself on the quality and quantity of his antipasto offerings, among them seasonal vegetables simply grilled and marinated in a lightly vinegared sauce, called *a scapecce*. A selection of different vegetables makes a handsome presentation, but any one of these could be served on its own, as an antipasto or a first course.

Grilling the vegetables over charcoal or wood embers lends them an agreeably sweet and smoky flavor, but in a pinch they can be done on a stovetop grill or under a gas or electric oven broiler. Instead of being salted and drained, the eggplant is soaked in brine; the technique produces a crisp exterior and a creamy interior. The vegetables can be made a day or more ahead, but they should be brought to room temperature before being served.

2   eggplants, preferably the plum-shaped Italian ones, about 1 pound
salt
2   red bell peppers
2   yellow bell peppers
3   long, slender zucchini, about 1½ pounds
a little olive oil for brushing

THE MARINADE:

¼   cup extra-virgin olive oil
¼   cup red or white wine vinegar
2   garlic cloves, chopped
2   oil-packed anchovy fillets, minced, or salt to taste
1   tablespoon minced fresh mint, thyme, or oregano

Cut the eggplant into lengthwise slices about ½ inch thick. Place in a bowl and cover with water, measuring the amount used. Add ¼ cup salt for every 2 quarts. Set a plate in the bowl with a weight on top (a can of tomatoes is ideal) to hold the slices underwater and leave them to soak for 1 to 2 hours.

Meanwhile, rinse the peppers and cut them in half lengthwise. Remove the seeds and white membrane. Cut the zucchini on the diagonal into slices about ½ inch thick.

When you're ready to cook, prepare a medium-hot charcoal fire or preheat an electric or gas grill or oven broiler. Remove the eggplant slices from the brine and pat dry with paper towels. Brush the eggplant and zucchini slices lightly with olive oil, using a pastry brush, and grill them on each side for 10 to 18 minutes. When the slices are toasted dark brown on both sides, remove from the grill and arrange on a deep platter.

Place the pepper halves skin side down on the grill or skin side up under the broiler. Cook until the peppers are *slightly* blackened and the skin is starting to lift off and blister, about 5 to 8 minutes. (Peppers need not be cooked on both sides.) Add to the platter.

Mix the marinade ingredients together and pour the marinade over the vegetables. Cover with aluminum foil and set aside at room temperature to marinate for several hours or overnight. Serve at room temperature. *Makes 8 servings as a first course, 10 servings as part of a meze*

### Nutritional Data, per portion

| | | |
|---|---|---|
| Calories 128 | Carbohydrate 8g | Saturated Fat 1g |
| Protein 2g | Sodium 592mg | Monounsaturated |
| Fat 11g | Cholesterol 1mg | Fat 8g |

# MECHOUIA

### *Tunisian Grilled Vegetable Salsa*

In season *mechouia* (mesh-WEE-yah) appears on Tunisian tables at almost every meal, as a first course on its own, as a garnish or salad to accompany a main course, or as one of several small dishes to nibble at while waiting for more substantial food. If you add the optional garnishes of pitted black olives, hard-boiled eggs, and tuna (use the best-quality oil-packed tuna available) or refreshed salted anchovies, the dish is substantial enough to stand on its own accompanied by a good crusty bread and with fruit and cheese to follow. (Don't confuse *mechouia*, which means "roasted," with *mechoui*, which also means "roasted." The latter refers to a splendidly festive barbecued whole baby lamb.)

For the finest sweet and smoky flavor, Tunisian cooks roast the vegetables over charcoal or wood embers, but in her tiny kitchen in Sidi bou Said, on a hilltop

above the sea outside Tunis, Fatouma Mbrahim grills the peppers under a gas broiler and roasts the tomatoes and onion in a very hot oven. Either way, *mechouia* is best made at least an hour ahead of time and set aside for the flavors to meld somewhat before serving.

The ratio between sweet and hot peppers is meant only as a guide. If you want more or less heat, change the balance—but be sure to use a total of about 1½ pounds.

1   pound green and red bell peppers, about 3 medium
3 or 4 fresh chilies to taste
a little olive oil for baking
1   pound ripe but firm tomatoes, about 3 medium
2   medium onions, unpeeled
salt
4   garlic cloves
1   tablespoon ground caraway or 1 tablespoon ground or crushed
       coriander seeds
½   cup extra-virgin olive oil
juice of 2 lemons
freshly ground black pepper to taste (optional)

GARNISH (OPTIONAL):

hard-boiled eggs, coarsely chopped; pitted olives; chunks of well-
       drained tuna; or salted anchovies, boned and refreshed in
       running water

Roast and peel the peppers and chilies, following the directions on page 455. Cut the peppers and chilies into small dice, add to the bowl with their juices, and set aside.

Preheat the oven to 450 degrees. Brush a little olive oil over the bottom of a small roasting pan, then pour a little oil into your palms and rub it over the tomatoes and onions. Place the vegetables in the roasting pan and roast for about 10 minutes, turning occasionally. When the tomato skins are cracking and easy to peel, remove the tomatoes from the pan but let the onions continue roasting for another 15 to 20 minutes.

Lift the skins off the tomatoes and slice them in half, letting the juices run out.

Dice the tomatoes and toss in the bowl with the peppers. Remove the onions, discard the skins, dice the onions, and add to the other vegetables.

Pound the garlic with a little salt in a mortar or use the back of a spoon to crush the chopped garlic in a bowl with salt to a paste. Add the crushed caraway and mix the garlic paste into the vegetables. Set aside for at least an hour or until you're ready to serve.

Just before serving, mix the olive oil with the lemon juice to taste and stir into the vegetables, adding pepper if you wish. Garnish if desired and serve immediately.

*Note:* Fresh herbs or greens, such as basil or purslane, can be slivered and stirred into the salad at the last minute before serving. ***Makes about 2 to 3 cups; 6 to 8 servings***

Nutritional Data, per portion

| | | |
|---|---|---|
| Calories   200 | Carbohydrate   12g | Saturated Fat   2g |
| Protein   2g | Sodium   8mg | Monounsaturated |
| Fat   18g | Cholesterol   0 | Fat   14g |

# SLICED RADISH SALAD WITH GREEN HERBS AND TUNA

**W**e tend to use radishes only as a garnish, but this Tunisian recipe reminds us of how well the vegetable can stand on its own.

Farmers in Lebanon's fertile Beqaa Valley grow radishes as big around as tennis balls, to be eaten out of hand like apples. Use large or small radishes for this salad; just be sure that they are young and firm all the way through, not woody or hollow. Parsley is traditionally used, but try basil or cilantro for a change.

1   teaspoon sea salt or more to taste

juice of ½ lemon or more to taste

1   pound young firm radishes, trimmed

2   tablespoons minced flat-leaf parsley

¼   cup finely diced celery, about 2 ribs

¼   cup minced scallion, about 3

3   tablespoons extra-virgin olive oil

1   3¼-ounce can water-packed white tuna, drained and flaked

12   small black olives, preferably Gaeta or Niçoise, pitted

THE SMALL DISHES OF THE MEDITERRANEAN

In a small salad bowl, dissolve the salt in the lemon juice.

There are several ways to prepare the radishes. I often use all three—grate the radishes on the large holes of a grater; use a swivel peeler to peel off the red skin into the salad bowl, then quarter the white part and slice thinly. Or simply slice the cleaned radishes thinly into the salad bowl. Smaller radishes are easier simply to slice, while larger ones lend themselves better to the other treatments. Mix well with the salted lemon juice.

Add the parsley, celery, and scallions to the radishes and mix well. Set aside for at least 5 minutes. Drain away the liquid given off by the vegetables, then add the olive oil, tuna, and olives. Taste—there should be plenty of lemon flavor, but if not, add more lemon and salt to taste. Serve piled on a bed of greens. *Makes 3 cups; 6 servings*

Nutritional Data, per portion

| | | |
|---|---|---|
| Calories 102 | Carbohydrate 4g | Saturated Fat 1g |
| Protein 4g | Sodium 379mg | Monounsaturated |
| Fat 8g | Cholesterol 6mg | Fat 6g |

# RATATOUILLE, PISTO MANCHEGO, AND CAPONATA

I first encountered ratatouille, the brilliant Provençal mixture of summer vegetables stewed in olive oil, in the pages of Elizabeth David's *French Provincial Cooking*. That book, with its precise evocation of the good fresh flavors, the balance, and the attention to detail that still characterized French cooking in the early 1960s when it was published, changed my life in the kitchen as it did that of so many others. This recipe is basically Mrs. David's, with a few refinements added over the years. Make it at the height of summer, when tomatoes are at their peak.

Despite all precautions, the eggplant absorbs a lot of olive oil, making this a dish that's relatively high in fat. Use it, then, sensibly—it is a rich and delicious preparation, to be consumed in small quantities as a first course or as an accompaniment to a plain main course, perhaps an oven-roasted chicken or some exceptionally tasty grilled swordfish steaks. In Provence ratatouille often accompanies a roast leg of lamb, and it's especially good with a humble plate of meltingly soft white beans dressed with a little olive oil.

3   medium eggplants, about 1½ pounds

3   tablespoons sea salt or more to taste

1½  pounds red peppers, both sweet and hot to taste

¾   cup extra-virgin olive oil

3   medium onions, chopped

2   garlic cloves, chopped

3   medium zucchini, about 1½ pounds

4   large tomatoes, about 1½ pounds, peeled (page 454) and chopped

½   teaspoon sugar

1   teaspoon coriander seeds, lightly crushed with a rolling pin or
    coarsely ground in an electric grinder

1   tablespoon drained capers, coarsely chopped

freshly ground black pepper to taste

a handful of chopped fresh basil for garnish

a handful of pitted black olives for garnish (optional)

Rinse the eggplant and cut into 1½-inch cubes. Place the cubes in a bowl and add the salt and water to cover. Set a plate inside the bowl with a weight on it (a can of tomatoes is ideal) to hold the cubes under the brine. Set aside for 1 to 2 hours.

Roast and peel the peppers, following the directions on page 455. Cut the peppers into long strips and add to the juices in the bowl.

Heat about ¼ cup of the olive oil in a sauté pan over medium-low heat and add the onions and garlic. Cook, stirring occasionally, until the onions are very soft and melting, about 15 minutes. Do not let the onions brown. Remove the onions from the pan with a slotted spoon and add to the peppers.

Drain the eggplant cubes and pat dry with paper towels. Add another ¼ cup oil to the sauté pan and raise the heat to medium. Toss the eggplant cubes in the hot oil and fry them until they are light brown or golden on all sides, about 10 to 15 minutes. When thoroughly browned, remove with a slotted spoon and add to the other vegetables. While the eggplant is cooking, cut the zucchini into 1½-inch cubes. When the eggplant is done, brown the zucchini, adding the last ¼ cup oil as needed. (Try to add oil between frying batches, so that you're not adding cold oil to the hot vegetables in the pan.)

When the zucchini is done, add the tomatoes to the oil in the pan. Lower the

heat slightly, stir in the sugar and coriander, and simmer, stirring frequently, until the tomatoes have reduced to a thick jam, about 20 minutes. Stir in the capers.

Now combine all the vegetables with the tomato sauce, stirring carefully with a wooden spoon to avoid breaking up the vegetables. Add some salt if necessary and several grinds of freshly ground black pepper. Just before serving, stir in the basil and the black olives if desired.

Ratatouille can be refrigerated for several days, but it is best served at room temperature or even a little warmer. **Makes 8 to 10 servings**

**VARIATIONS:** Pisto manchego, from the high central plateau of Spain, is made in much the same manner except that the coriander and capers are omitted and only green peppers are used. After cooking, the whole pisto can be put into a terra-cotta baking dish and one fresh egg per serving broken over the top with a little salt and pepper and perhaps a few drops of olive oil on each egg. Placed in a hot oven, the pisto bakes until the eggs have set.

Caponata, from Sicily, is another similar preparation, but ½-inch chunks of celery are fried with the eggplant and zucchini cubes. (The celery lends a little crunch to the finished product.) Add 2 teaspoons sugar and ¼ cup red wine vinegar to the tomatoes as they cook down to give it the proper sweet-sour (*agrodolce* in Italian) flavor. Green olives, rather than black ones, will garnish caponata, which is most often served as an antipasto, although it's also very good as a side dish with meat, beans, or eggs as for pisto manchego.

Nutritional Data, per portion

| | | |
|---|---|---|
| Calories 218 | Carbohydrate 17g | Saturated Fat 2g |
| Protein 3g | Sodium 182mg | Monounsaturated |
| Fat 17g | Cholesterol 0 | Fat 13g |

# CROSTINI

Crostini are favorites on antipasto platters in country homes and restaurants throughout central Italy. Basically the preparation is simply a way of using up stale bread. Although we think of Italians as predominantly pasta eaters, bread has always been much more important in the diet throughout Italy, as is illustrated by recipes like the ones that follow—as well as panzanella (page 72) and ribollita (page 98)—which show how to extend bread beyond the obvious.

Originally crostini were thick little crusts of stale bread dipped briefly in wine or broth or salted water to refresh them, the liquid depending on what further use was to be made of the crostini. Years ago in Rome, Italian food writer Ada Boni says, crostini dipped in wine and topped with sugar were a favorite snack or merenda for young and old alike. Or you might dip them in water or broth, one side only, drizzle olive oil over the top, then lay on slices of good provola cheese and a couple of anchovy fillets set crisscross, put them in a very hot oven, and leave for just a few minutes until the cheese is melting and the bread is crisp. You can see exactly how pizza might evolve from a production like that, which must be very old indeed, perhaps as old as ovens themselves.

I must confess that I don't really like crostini dipped in liquid—the bread gets too mushy for my taste. Instead I like to grill the bread on one or both sides before piling on the topping. I suspect most people on this side of the Atlantic would agree.

The following recipes illustrate the technique, but crostini are fun to experiment with—take some leftover creamy white beans, for instance, mix with olive oil, lemon juice, and chopped garlic, and pile on crostini for Tuscan baked bean sandwiches. Or chop steamed bitter greens (arugula, broccoli rabe, collards, or turnip greens) and toss with oil, salt, and garlic; pile them on crostini and top with a few drops of balsamic vinegar. At the Taverna Giulia, a Genovese restaurant in Rome, we used to get *crostini di salmone*, topped with slices of smoked salmon and a slice of mozzarella that would melt in the oven's heat and protect the delicate salmon from drying out.

The success of crostini depends on the quality of the bread used. It should be a dense and grainy country-style loaf, either a long narrow baguette or a round boule, like the bread from the recipe on page 131.

# CROSTINI DI FEGATINI

**M**ade with chicken livers, these are among the most substantial of all crostini. My Tuscan neighbor Mita Antolini always serves them as little appetite seducers before important meals like the annual tobacco harvest dinner. In addition to a first course or antipasto, crostini are appropriate for extending a main-course salad or soup—a creamy puree of butternut squash or pumpkin goes beautifully with crostini di fegatini.

½   pound fresh chicken livers

2   tablespoons extra-virgin olive oil

½   cup minced onion

½   small garlic clove, minced

2   tablespoons minced flat-leaf parsley

2   anchovy fillets (optional)

⅓   cup vin santo or dry amontillado or oloroso sherry

2   tablespoons meat or chicken broth (pages 83 and 81) or water

1   tablespoon coarsely chopped drained capers

juice of ½ lemon

salt and freshly ground black pepper to taste

good-quality bread, slightly stale, about 12 ½-inch slices of baguette or

      6 ½-inch slices of boule cut in half, grilled on one or both sides

Pick over the chicken livers, cutting away any green spots and removing any tough bits of fiber. Rinse briefly in a colander and set aside.

In a skillet over medium-low heat, heat the oil and gently sauté the onion, garlic, and half the parsley until the onion is very soft and pale yellow, about 10 minutes. Add the anchovy fillets if desired and mash into the oil in the pan.

Pat the chicken livers dry. Raise the heat under the pan to medium, push the vegetables to the sides of the pan, and add the livers to the middle. Toss to brown them quickly. As the livers cook, chop them coarsely with a wooden spoon. After a few minutes, when their rosy color has disappeared, add the wine and broth, lower the heat to medium-low, and cook the livers for another 15 minutes or until they have changed color all the way through and most of the broth has been absorbed or

has evaporated. As they cook, continue crushing them with the wooden spoon or a fork to make a coarse paste.

If you prefer a smoother mixture, remove the livers from the pan and process briefly in a food processor. (Traditionally they are served as a coarse paste.) Stir in the capers and remaining parsley along with the lemon juice and mix very well. Taste and add salt (the capers may provide enough), lots of pepper, and more lemon juice if desired.

The chicken liver paste is best served warm or at room temperature. Serve it in a bowl, accompanied by the grilled bread. Or pile it on the bread, topping each slice with a caper or a bit of lemon zest, and arrange on a platter. *Makes 6 servings*

Nutritional Data, per portion

| | | |
|---|---|---|
| Calories 251 | Carbohydrate 30g | Saturated Fat 1g |
| Protein 11g | Sodium 373mg | Monounsaturated |
| Fat 8g | Cholesterol 166mg | Fat 5g |

# CROSTINI DI POMODORO

These are to be made only when ripe red tomatoes are in local markets.

1   **pound summer tomatoes**

¼   **garlic clove, minced**

2   **tablespoons extra-virgin olive oil**

**a little balsamic vinegar**

½   **teaspoon coarse sea salt or more to taste**

**freshly ground black pepper to taste**

**6 to 8 fresh basil leaves, finely slivered**

**good-quality bread, slightly stale, about 12 ½-inch slices of baguette or**
      **6 ½-inch slices of boule cut in half, toasted on one or both sides**

Peel and seed the tomatoes, following the directions on page 454. Dice the peeled tomatoes, then turn them into a bowl and mix with the garlic, oil, and about a teaspoon of balsamic vinegar. Add salt and pepper and a little more vinegar if you wish.

THE SMALL DISHES OF THE MEDITERRANEAN

Pile the tomato mixture on the untoasted sides of the bread. Top each with slivers of basil. Serve immediately or set aside, lightly covered with plastic wrap, for an hour or more so the bread can absorb some of the tomato juices. *Makes 6 servings*

### Nutritional Data, per portion

| | | |
|---|---|---|
| Calories  194 | Carbohydrate  30g | Saturated Fat  1g |
| Protein  5g | Sodium  433mg | Monounsaturated |
| Fat  6g | Cholesterol  0 | Fat  4g |

---

## FETTUNTA OR BRUSCHETTA

Called *fettunta* in the region around Florence, *bruschetta* (bruce-KETT-ah) in the rest of Italy, this is the simplest kind of crostini and a great favorite among workers in the olive groves and at the unheated *frantoio* where the olives are pressed. Thick slices of bread are toasted on both sides over the embers of a fire on a hearth in a side room, where the workmen gather to warm up between loads. Then they're rubbed lightly with a cut clove of garlic and drizzled richly with the fresh green oil right off the presses. This, I need hardly say, should be reserved for the very finest and freshest olive oil you can find; in fact some people, myself included, would argue that this is one of the best uses to which fine, fresh oil can be put. Fortunately more and more of the better producers are actually dating their oil, so it is easier to select for freshness.

---

# TABBOULEH

**T**he earthiness of bulgur, or burghul (cracked steamed wheat), combines beautifully with the sharp sweetness of mint and parsley and the tang of lemon in what may be the best known of all dishes from the eastern Mediterranean. Tabbouleh became a hit back in what my children call the hippy-dippy days, when the counterculture was first exploring alternatives to the conventional American diet. In one form or another (some of them pretty strange), it has remained a favorite in the deli sections of health food stores ever since. This version, more green than grain, is the way it appears on meze tables all over Lebanon.

¾ **cup medium-grain bulgur**

3 **large bunches of flat-leaf parsley, finely chopped, 2 cups**

1 **bunch of fresh mint, leaves only, finely chopped, ½ cup**

1 **bunch of scallions, thinly sliced**

2 or 3 **tomatoes, diced**

1 **lemon**

½ **cup extra-virgin olive oil**

**salt and freshly ground black pepper to taste**

**large crisp romaine lettuce leaves for serving**

Cover the bulgur in a bowl with fresh cold water to a depth of about 1 inch. Set aside to soak for 20 or 30 minutes while you chop and dice the vegetables. When the bulgur grains are nicely plump, drain them, squeezing out as much water as you can. Turn the grains into a clean kitchen towel and squeeze out the remaining water. Each grain of bulgur should be moist and plump but without a trace of liquid.

Pour the bulgur into a dry bowl, add all the chopped and diced vegetables, and mix well with your hands, squeezing slightly to release the flavors. When the bulgur is well mixed, squeeze the lemon over it. Then add the oil and toss to blend all together well.

A common mistake is to use too much bulgur in proportion to the greens. You should have a very green-looking salad in which the bulgur garnishes the parsley rather than vice versa. Taste the salad and add salt and pepper, lemon juice, and oil as desired.

To serve, arrange overlapping leaves of romaine lettuce all around an oval platter and heap the tabbouleh in the middle. Use the romaine leaves as scoops for the tabbouleh. *Makes 4 to 5 cups; serves about 8*

Nutritional Data, per portion

| | | |
|---|---|---|
| Calories 185 | Carbohydrate 14g | Saturated Fat 2g |
| Protein 3g | Sodium 14mg | Monounsaturated |
| Fat 14g | Cholesterol 0 | Fat 11g |

# THREE-GRAIN SALAD

**F**arro is an ancient type of soft wheat that has become very popular in Italy in recent years. Also called *emmer wheat,* it is available in some specialty stores, but if you can't find it, use soft-wheat berries instead. In any case, the recipe is intended as a model, and other grains and legumes might be substituted.

½ cup Italian farro or soft-wheat berries, soaked in 1½ cups water for 2
     hours

3 cups vegetable broth (page 80) or clear white chicken stock (page 81)

3 tablespoons extra-virgin olive oil or more to taste

2 tablespoons fresh lemon juice or more to taste

½ cup brown or green lentils

1 medium cucumber, peeled and diced

6 scallions, sliced on the diagonal

2 tablespoons minced yellow onion

2 tablespoons minced celery

1 tablespoon minced fresh basil, parsley, or mint

½ cup water

½ cup couscous (not instant)

salt and freshly ground black or white pepper to taste

1 teaspoon hot red pepper flakes (optional)

Drain the soaked wheat and combine with the stock in a medium saucepan. Bring to a boil, cover, lower the heat, and simmer until the grains are tender—

about 40 minutes. Use a slotted spoon to remove the tender grains from the pot, leaving the cooking liquid behind. Put the cooked grains in a bowl and immediately dress with 2 tablespoons of the oil and a tablespoon of the lemon juice, mixing well to coat the grains.

Return the cooking liquid to a boil, add the lentils, cover, lower the heat, and cook until the lentils are tender—20 minutes or longer.

Meanwhile, add the cucumber, scallions, yellow onion, celery, and herbs to the wheat grains, tossing to mix well.

While the lentils are cooking, bring the water to a boil and pour it over the couscous, tossing to mix well and soften the couscous. When the lentils are done, remove them with a slotted spoon from the cooking liquid and add to the wheat, tossing to mix well. Turn the couscous into the cooking liquid—there should be very little liquid left in the pan—and steam gently for 5 minutes or so, just until the couscous is tender. Drain the couscous well and add to the bowl with the other grains. Toss all the grains together. Adjust the seasoning, adding salt and pepper and, if you wish, the hot pepper. Set aside for 30 minutes or longer to let the grains absorb the flavoring. If necessary, add more oil and lemon juice before serving.

*Makes about 3 to 4 cups; 6 to 8 servings*

Nutritional Data, per portion

| | | |
|---|---|---|
| Calories  194 | Carbohydrate  27g | Saturated Fat  1g |
| Protein  7g | Sodium  15mg | Monounsaturated |
| Fat  7g | Cholesterol  0 | Fat  5g |

# LEBANESE CHICK-PEA AND BULGUR SALAD

1    cup dried chick-peas, soaked in water overnight, or use the quick-
      soak method (page 454)

3½ cups water

¾   cup coarse-grain bulgur

1    bunch of scallions, both green and white parts, coarsely chopped

2    tablespoons minced fresh mint leaves

⅓   cup minced flat-leaf parsley

⅓   cup fresh lemon juice

⅓   cup extra-virgin olive oil

1    teaspoon salt

freshly ground black pepper to taste

¼   teaspoon ground cinnamon

romaine lettuce leaves for serving

Drain the chick-peas and combine in a saucepan with the fresh water. Bring to a boil, cover, lower the heat, and simmer until the chick-peas are tender but not falling apart. Time will vary with the age of the beans, but count on at least 30 minutes.

Meanwhile, cover the bulgur in a bowl with warm water to a depth of 1 inch. Set aside to soak for about 20 minutes. Drain the bulgur in a fine-mesh sieve, pressing to extract as much water as possible. Then turn the bulgur into a clean kitchen towel and squeeze to extract the remaining liquid.

Add the scallions, mint, and parsley to the bulgur in a bowl and mix well with your hands, squeezing slightly to release the flavors. Then add the drained chick-peas, lemon juice, oil, and seasonings and stir to mix well. Set aside, covered, for 30 minutes or so to develop the flavors. Serve on a platter, surrounded by the romaine lettuce leaves. The leaves can be used to scoop up the salad. ***Makes 4 cups; about 8 servings***

### Nutritional Data, per portion

| | | |
|---|---|---|
| Calories  224 | Carbohydrate  27g | Saturated Fat  2g |
| Protein  7g | Sodium  287mg | Monounsaturated |
| Fat  11g | Cholesterol  0 | Fat  8g |

# LENTIL AND WALNUT SALAD

**U**nlike other beans and pulses, lentils need not be soaked before cooking. The lentils commonly used in Mediterranean kitchens are quite small and dark slate-brown or grayish green in color. Do not use Indian dal-type lentils for these dishes, because those are meant to disintegrate into a porridge when cooked.

1   cup green or brown lentils, picked over and washed

2   cups water

¾   cup chopped scallion

1   red bell pepper, diced

½   cup finely chopped flat-leaf parsley

½   cup coarsely chopped walnuts

½   teaspoon dry mustard or 1 heaped teaspoon Dijon mustard

4 to 5 tablespoons red wine vinegar to taste

⅓   cup extra-virgin olive oil

salt and freshly ground black pepper to taste

Combine the lentils with the water and bring to a boil. Turn the heat down to medium-low, cover the pan tightly, and simmer for about 20 minutes or until the lentils are cooked through but still firm enough to hold their shape.

When the lentils are done, remove from the heat, drain, and place in a bowl along with the scallions, red pepper, parsley, and walnuts.

In a separate small bowl, combine the mustard with the vinegar, beating in a little at a time until the mixture is thoroughly blended. Gradually beat in the olive oil. Pour the dressing over the lentils and toss to mix thoroughly. Add salt and black pepper and serve simply as is or on a bed of bitter greens such as arugula, chicory, or dandelion greens. *Makes about 4 cups; 4 to 6 servings*

Nutritional Data, per portion

| | | |
|---|---|---|
| Calories  289 | Carbohydrate  23g | Saturated Fat  2g |
| Protein  11g | Sodium  8mg | Monounsaturated |
| Fat  19g | Cholesterol  0 | Fat  11g |

# TURKISH BEET SALAD WITH YOGURT DRESSING

In Turkey, garlicky yogurt dressing flavored with dried mint or fresh dill is poured over raw or cooked vegetable salads. Try the same dressing with chunks of carrot or celery root or with new potatoes steamed until just tender—or serve a selection of steamed vegetables, tossed with the garlic-yogurt sauce and arranged on a deep platter. (Remember that beets will tint everything pink unless kept apart.) Whether you use mint, dill, or some other herb, use a little of the same herb, freshly minced, as a garnish.

18　small beets
1　garlic clove, chopped
1　teaspoon salt
1　tablespoon white wine vinegar
2　tablespoons extra-virgin olive oil
1　cup plain yogurt (nonfat is fine)
3　tablespoons minced fresh dill or mint

Steam the beets in water to cover, 30 to 40 minutes or until tender. Drain, peel, and cut into quarters.

Using the back of a spoon, mash the garlic to a paste with the salt in a bowl large enough to hold the yogurt. Stir in the vinegar and oil, then add the yogurt and herbs and stir to combine well.

When you're ready to serve, pile the warm beets in a serving bowl or platter and pour the yogurt sauce over them. (If you do this in advance, the beets will stain the yogurt sauce pink—which may or may not be desirable.) *Makes 6 to 8 servings*

### Nutritional Data, per portion

| | | |
|---|---|---|
| Calories  108 | Carbohydrate  16g | Saturated Fat  1g |
| Protein  4g | Sodium  396mg | Monounsaturated |
| Fat  4g | Cholesterol  1mg | Fat  3g |

# TUNISIAN BEET SALAD WITH HARISSA

**B**ig round beets are roasted in Tunisian ovens until tender, then peeled, diced, and mixed with scallions, parsley, and garlic and dressed with oil and vinegar laced with a little peppery harissa. Oven roasting produces an altogether different texture from boiling and brings out the delicate sweetness of the vegetable. In Greece, beets roasted like this are often served with a thick garlicky sauce called *skordalia* (page 291).

a little extra-virgin olive oil

6   large beets, about 4 or 5 inches in diameter

½   cup chopped scallion

¼   cup finely minced flat-leaf parsley

1   garlic clove, minced

1   teaspoon harissa (page 301) or ½ teaspoon hot red pepper flakes or
      to taste

1   teaspoon red wine vinegar

2   tablespoons extra-virgin olive oil

salt to taste

Preheat the oven to 325 degrees. Oil the bottom of a roasting pan and use a little oil to rub over the carefully rinsed and dried beets. Place the beets in the pan and roast in the oven for 2½ to 3 hours or until very tender. Remove and, when they are cool enough to handle, slip the skins off and cut the beets into cubes.

Toss the beets in a bowl with the scallion, parsley, and garlic. Dissolve the harissa in the vinegar, then beat in the olive oil. Pour the dressing over the beets. Taste for seasoning and add a little salt if necessary. ***Makes 6 to 8 servings***

Nutritional Data, per portion

| | | |
|---|---|---|
| Calories   102 | Carbohydrate   9g | Saturated Fat   1g |
| Protein   1g | Sodium   57mg | Monounsaturated |
| Fat   8g | Cholesterol   0 | Fat   6g |

# TURKISH GRATED CARROT SALAD WITH YOGURT

5 to 6 medium carrots, peeled

2　garlic cloves, crushed and chopped

1　teaspoon salt

¼　cup plain yogurt (nonfat is fine)

4　teaspoons extra-virgin olive oil

4　teaspoons fresh lemon juice

Bring a pot of water to a rapid boil and plunge the carrots in. Cook for about 5 minutes, long enough to start softening them but without really tenderizing. Remove from the heat and immediately plunge the carrots into cold water to halt the cooking and cool the carrots. When they're cool enough to handle, grate them on the large holes of the grater.

In a small bowl, crush the garlic and salt together with the back of a spoon. Mix in the yogurt, oil, and lemon juice, beating with a fork. Pour the dressing over the carrots and toss to mix thoroughly. Taste and add a little more salt if necessary. Serve piled on a lettuce leaf as a first course or in a bowl as part of a meze or as an accompaniment to a main dish. ***Makes 6 appetizer servings***

### Nutritional Data, per portion

| | | |
|---|---|---|
| Calories  63 | Carbohydrate  8g | Saturated Fat  trace |
| Protein  1g | Sodium  397mg | Monounsaturated |
| Fat  3g | Cholesterol  trace | Fat  2g |

**VARIATION:** Although Turkish cooks would consider it decidedly unorthodox, I have had great success using grated *raw* carrots in this recipe.

# TUNISIAN CARROT SALAD WITH HARISSA AND FETA CHEESE

6   medium carrots, peeled and cut into thick rounds

1   garlic clove, chopped

1   teaspoon ground caraway seeds

salt to taste

1   tablespoon harissa (page 301)

¼   cup cool water

¼   cup brine-cured black olives, pitted

¼   pound feta cheese, crumbled

¼   cup extra-virgin olive oil

2   tablespoons red or white wine vinegar

Bring a pot of water to a boil, add the carrots, and cook for 5 minutes, just until they are starting to become tender. Drain, running cold water over the carrots to halt the cooking. Chop the carrot rounds very coarsely.

In a mortar, pound the garlic to a paste with the caraway and salt. Dilute the harissa with the water. If the olives are very large, chop them coarsely. Set aside a bit of feta and a few olives for garnish.

In a bowl, combine the carrots, garlic paste, and diluted harissa. Mix together well. Add the oil and vinegar and toss once more to mix well. Sprinkle the crumbled cheese and olives over the top.

Set aside at room temperature for at least 30 minutes to develop the flavors. Garnish with the reserved olives and cheese and serve. *Makes 6 servings*

### Nutritional Data, per portion

| | | |
|---|---|---|
| Calories  190 | Carbohydrate  11g | Saturated Fat  4g |
| Protein  4g | Sodium  286mg | Monounsaturated |
| Fat  16g | Cholesterol  17mg | Fat  10g |

# MOROCCAN CARROT SALAD WITH ORANGE AND LEMON JUICE

**A**lthough called a salad in Morocco, this delightful mixture is in fact more like a soup and is served as part of the first course in small bowls with spoons. Freshly squeezed orange juice is essential here.

1½ pounds carrots, about 10 medium

1½ cups fresh orange juice

juice of 1 lemon

1   teaspoon sugar or more to taste

½   cup walnut halves

Peel the carrots and grate them on the finest holes of the grater. Mix in the orange and lemon juices and add sugar to taste—the sugar should simply accentuate the flavor of the carrots rather than give them a decidedly sweet taste. Set the carrots aside to marinate while you prepare the walnuts.

Preheat the oven to 350 degrees. Spread the walnuts on a cookie sheet and bake for 10 to 15 minutes or until they become aromatic and the papery peel can be rubbed away. Remove from the oven and rub each walnut half to rid it of as much of the skin as possible. (The skin is what gives walnuts an astringent tannin flavor.)

When you're ready to serve, spoon the carrots into small bowls and garnish each with a few toasted walnut halves. *Makes 6 to 8 servings*

Nutritional Data, per portion

| | | |
|---|---|---|
| Calories  97 | Carbohydrate  15g | Saturated Fat   trace |
| Protein  2g | Sodium  28mg | Monounsaturated |
| Fat  4g | Cholesterol  0 | Fat  1g |

# CHAKCHOUKA

### *Moroccan Salad of Cooked Tomatoes and Green Peppers*

**A**nother Moroccan starter that doesn't really seem to merit the name of salad, though that is precisely what it's called. *Chakchouka,* I was told in Morocco, is a Jewish name for this dish, indicating that the preparation comes out of the rich culinary traditions of the Moroccan Jews. This is usually served, with other small dishes, at the beginning of a meal.

8   large tomatoes, peeled and seeded (page 454) and cut into chunks
1   garlic clove, slivered
¼   cup extra-virgin olive oil
4   green bell peppers
1   small fresh green chili (optional)
1   tablespoon sweet paprika
1   tablespoon minced flat-leaf parsley
1   preserved lemon (optional; page 305)

In a skillet over medium heat, cook the tomatoes with the garlic in the olive oil, adding no water but stirring frequently, until the tomatoes have thoroughly cooked down to a thick jammy sauce—about 15 to 20 minutes. They should yield up all of their liquid, and the oil should then separate slightly away from the mass of tomatoes.

While the tomatoes are cooking, roast and peel the peppers and chili, following the directions on page 455. Cut the peppers and chili into large dice. As soon as the tomatoes have reached the desired density, stir in the peppers and chili and the paprika. Sprinkle with the parsley. If you have a preserved lemon, cut the skin into small cubes or julienne strips and stir in with the peppers.

*Chakchouka* is usually served at room temperature with pieces of bread for scooping it up. **Makes 6 to 8 servings**

Nutritional Data, per portion

| | | |
|---|---|---|
| Calories   105 | Carbohydrate   10g | Saturated Fat   1g |
| Protein   2g | Sodium   15mg | Monounsaturated |
| Fat   8g | Cholesterol   0 | Fat   6g |

THE SMALL DISHES OF THE MEDITERRANEAN

## GRAPE LEAVES

If you are lucky enough to have a backyard grapevine, select tender young leaves from the top, but be sure they're large enough to handle comfortably. Rinse them in cold running water and place in a colander in the sink. Bring a teakettle of water to a boil and pour the whole kettle over the grape leaves. This should soften them enough to make them easy to handle and roll. If they're not soft enough, repeat the procedure with more boiling water.

Canned grape leaves are of varying quality and always lack the lemony astringency of fresh ones. Most of us, however, will have to make do with them. Canned grape leaves should be rinsed in cold running water to get rid of the brine in which they're packed.

To stuff grape leaves, open a leaf carefully and spread it on the kitchen counter with the smooth topside of the leaf down, the rougher veined underside up. If the stem is attached, cut it away. Place a spoonful of stuffing at the base of the leaf, where the stem was attached, about ½ inch from the edge. Fold the bottom edge up around the stuffing, then fold in each side, right and left. Carefully roll the leaf, making a compact bundle, toward the point. Place the stuffed grape leaves in the bottom of a heavy kettle or saucepan. They should fit comfortably in the bottom of the pan without being wedged in tightly, so they can expand a little as the rice in the stuffing cooks. You can make several layers of stuffed leaves, but arrange each layer in the opposite direction from the one below. When all the little bundles are layered in place, add liquid (salted water or broth, plus lemon juice) just to cover the top layer. Set a plate a little smaller than the diameter of the pan on top of the leaves to hold them in place while cooking. Cover the kettle and follow the directions for steaming the leaves.

Turkish cooks have a theory that grape leaves stuffed with meat should be made with butter or animal fat and served hot or at room temperature, while those stuffed with flavored rice should be made with olive oil and served at room temperature or cold. I mention this only for the record—I make both meat-stuffed and rice-stuffed grape leaves with olive oil and serve them at any temperature that seems right for the rest of the meal.

# GRAPE LEAVES STUFFED
# WITH RICE

1    tablespoon dried black currants

¼    cup extra-virgin olive oil

1    medium onion, peeled and minced (½ cup)

3 or 4 scallions, both white and green parts, minced

2    tablespoons pine nuts

½    cup long-grain rice

2    medium tomatoes, peeled, seeded (page 454), and chopped or
       2 canned tomatoes, drained and chopped

salt and freshly ground pepper to taste

¼    cup hot water

¼    teaspoon ground allspice or more to taste

¼    cup fresh lemon juice

about 25 grape leaves, softened if fresh (page 62) or rinsed if canned

Put the currants in a small bowl and cover with hot water to soften while you prepare the rest of the stuffing.

Warm the olive oil in a saucepan over medium-low heat and gently sauté the onion and scallions for 15 to 20 minutes or until they are thoroughly softened but not browned. Add the pine nuts and continue cooking a few minutes longer, until golden. Add the rice and stir to coat thoroughly with the oil. Add the tomatoes, salt, and pepper and pour in the hot water. Mix well, cover, and cook over gentle heat until all the liquid has been absorbed, about 10 minutes. The rice will start to soften but will not be cooked. Remove from the heat, stir in the allspice and drained currants, and set aside, covered, for 10 minutes.

Stuff the grape leaves as described on page 62 and arrange in a heavy kettle or wide, shallow saucepan. Add lemon juice and water just to cover the grape leaves. Set a plate on top of the grape leaves, cover the kettle, and simmer gently for about 30 minutes or until the rice and grape leaves are thoroughly cooked.

Pile the cooked grape leaves on a platter. Serve garnished with lemon wedges and a drizzle of olive oil or with a sauce made from a cup of yogurt mixed with 2

chopped garlic cloves and salt to taste. *Makes 2 abundant cups stuffing, enough for about 25 grape leaves; serves 4 as a first course, 6 to 8 as part of a meze*

Nutritional Data, per first-course portion

| | | |
|---|---|---|
| Calories 277 | Carbohydrate 30g | Saturated Fat 2g |
| Protein 5g | Sodium 17mg | Monounsaturated |
| Fat 17g | Cholesterol 0 | Fat 12g |

# GRAPE LEAVES STUFFED WITH MEAT AND RICE

½  cup finely minced onion

¼  cup extra-virgin olive oil

½  pound ground lean lamb

1  cup long-grain rice

2  medium tomatoes, peeled, seeded (page 454), and chopped

2  cups water, clear white chicken stock (page 81), or rich meat stock
     (page 83)

¼  teaspoon ground allspice or more to taste

1  tablespoon minced fresh dill

1  tablespoon minced fresh mint

1  tablespoon minced flat-leaf parsley

salt and freshly ground black pepper to taste

¼  cup fresh lemon juice

about 36 grape leaves, softened if fresh (page 62) or rinsed if canned

In a skillet, gently sauté the onion in the olive oil over medium-low heat until tender but not brown. Remove the onion and cooking oil and set aside.

Add the ground lamb to the pan and cook, crumbling with a fork, until the meat has lost its pink color. Strain the meat through a sieve and discard the fat. Now return the meat to the pan together with the onion. Stir in the rice and mix to coat the rice thoroughly with the juices. Add the tomatoes and ¼ cup water. Cook for about 10 minutes or just until the rice has absorbed the juices in the pan. Then stir

in the allspice, herbs, salt, and pepper, mixing well. Set aside, covered, for 10 minutes before stuffing the grape leaves.

Stuff the grape leaves as described on page 62 and arrange in a heavy kettle or wide, shallow saucepan. Add the lemon juice and remaining water just to cover the grape leaves. (Add more water if necessary.) Set a plate over the leaves, cover the pan, and simmer for 35 minutes or until rice is thoroughly cooked.

Serve the grape leaves with a sauce made of a cup of yogurt beaten with 2 finely chopped garlic cloves and salt to taste. ***Makes 3½ cups stuffing, enough for 36 grape leaves; 6 servings as a first course, 10 to 12 servings as part of a meze***

Nutritional Data, per first-course portion

| | | |
|---|---|---|
| Calories  282 | Carbohydrate  30g | Saturated Fat  2g |
| Protein  12g | Sodium  35mg | Monounsaturated |
| Fat  12g | Cholesterol  26mg | Fat  9g |

# SPANISH TORTILLA WITH POTATOES AND ONION

I lived in Spain during the Franco years, when the country was very poor and cut off from the rest of Europe. Meat was expensive, but eggs, potatoes, and onions were always cheap and always available. For many Spaniards a tortilla española was the gastronomic highlight of the week.

Humble and poor it may well be, but there is an innate sense of balance and honesty about this omelet that has tremendous appeal. Frankly, I'd take it over a paella any day.

¼  cup extra-virgin olive oil

1  medium onion, finely chopped

2  medium potatoes, peeled and diced

salt and freshly ground black pepper to taste

6  large eggs

Use a straight-sided iron skillet for this recipe. Warm the oil in the skillet over medium-low heat and cook the onion gently for about 5 minutes or until it starts to soften. Do not let the onion brown. Add the potatoes to the middle of the pan,

pushing the onion to the sides. Continue cooking for 7 to 10 minutes, stirring and turning with a spatula, until the potatoes are also softened and thoroughly cooked. The potatoes are done when you can easily push the spatula through a little cube. Using a slotted spoon, remove the potatoes and onion from the pan, leaving the oil behind, and set aside in a bowl to cool. Add salt and pepper to taste.

In another bowl, beat the eggs with a fork until thoroughly blended. When the potato mixture has cooled enough so that it will not cook the eggs, pour the eggs over the potatoes and mix gently with a fork to make sure that all the vegetable pieces are well covered.

Turn the heat back to medium-low. When the oil in the skillet starts to sizzle, pour the egg mixture into the pan and cook, shaking the pan gently to keep the eggs from sticking to the bottom. As soon as the eggs begin to solidify around the edges, start to run a palette knife, narrow spatula, or cake icer around the edges. The tortilla will firm up gradually, beginning around the edges and across the bottom, wherever the egg mixture is in contact with the heat. The trick is to keep it from sticking to the pan, so you must keep it moving gently, both by shaking the pan and by sliding the knife around, throughout the cooking time. From time to time, lift some of the cooked egg off the bottom to let the uncooked egg run underneath. When the top is still rather liquid, invert a plate over the top of the skillet and, being careful of spilled oil, turn the plate and the skillet over. Then slide the tortilla from the plate back into the skillet to finish cooking the other side. If this seems like too much for you, you can cheat, as Spanish cooks often do. Instead of turning the tortilla over, simply run it under a preheated broiler to solidify and brown the top.

Spanish cooks consider the tortilla to be done when it is still quite moist and even a little runny in the middle. When it's done to your taste, slide it out of the pan and set aside on a plate to cool to room temperature before serving.

*Note:* Do not attempt to increase the recipe by adding more eggs. Because this is always served at room temperature, you can make several tortillas ahead of time if you have a number of people to serve. ***Makes 6 to 8 servings as finger food, 2 or 3 servings as a main course for lunch***

Nutritional Data, per portion

| | | |
|---|---|---|
| Calories 398 | Carbohydrate 21g | Saturated Fat 6g |
| Protein 15g | Sodium 133mg | Monounsaturated |
| Fat 29g | Cholesterol 425mg | Fat 18g |

# ITALIAN FRITTATA WITH ZUCCHINI

**T**his is a model recipe for *frittate*. You can use many other vegetables or even just plain onions. The vegetables need not be strictly Mediterranean either—many of the bitter greens to be found in Asian markets, such as Chinese broccoli or choy sum (flowering white cabbage), especially in the winter, are excellent in a frittata.

1 **large onion, chopped**
3 **tablespoons extra-virgin olive oil**
2 **large or 3 medium zucchini, about 1 pound, sliced ¼ inch thick**
**a handful of coarsely chopped fresh basil or parsley**
**salt and freshly ground black pepper to taste**
8 **large eggs**
½ **cup freshly grated Parmigiano cheese**

Gently sauté the onion in 2 tablespoons of the oil in a skillet over medium-low heat. Cook, stirring frequently, until the onion is soft and starting to brown—about 20 minutes. Push the onion out to the edges of the pan and add the zucchini. Cook, stirring frequently, until the zucchini is thoroughly softened and starting to brown—about 20 minutes. Remove from the heat and stir in the basil. Add salt and pepper and set aside.

Preheat the broiler and adjust a rack so that the upper surface of the omelet will be about 6 inches from the source of the heat.

In a medium bowl, beat the eggs with a fork. When the vegetables are cool enough not to cook the eggs, turn the vegetables into the egg mixture, scraping the pan well, and mix, adding a little pepper.

Return the pan to medium-high heat. Add the remaining oil and turn the pan to swirl the oil all over the bottom and up the sides. Then turn the egg mixture into the pan. Cook over medium-high heat, continually running a palette knife, narrow spatula, or cake icer around the edge of the pan to keep it loose. From time to time, lift some of the cooked egg off the bottom of the pan to let uncooked egg run underneath. When the bottom of the frittata is set, remove from the heat, scatter the Parmigiano over the top, and run the frittata under the broiler for 3 or 4 minutes, just to melt the cheese and glaze the top.

THE SMALL DISHES OF THE MEDITERRANEAN

Serve immediately or set aside and serve at room temperature. *Makes 4 servings as a main course, 8 to 10 servings as a first course*

Nutritional Data, per portion

| | | |
|---|---|---|
| Calories 335 | Carbohydrate 11g | Saturated Fat 7g |
| Protein 20g | Sodium 359mg | Monounsaturated |
| Fat 24g | Cholesterol 435mg | Fat 13g |

# OVEN-BAKED FRITTATA WITH PEPPERS AND TOMATOES

2 to 3 tablespoons extra-virgin olive oil

6    scallions, both white and green parts, coarsely chopped

2    garlic cloves, minced

1    red bell pepper, diced

1    medium zucchini, diced

1    medium yellow summer squash, diced

1    medium red ripe tomato, seeded and coarsely chopped

sea salt and freshly ground black pepper to taste

3    tablespoons minced fresh basil or basil and parsley combined

12  extra-large eggs

¼    pound fresh goat cheese, such as chèvre, crumbled

Preheat the oven to 400 degrees. In a 10- to 12-inch ovenproof skillet, heat 2 tablespoons of the oil and gently sauté the scallions and garlic, stirring frequently, for about 5 minutes or until they begin to soften. Add the red pepper, squashes, and tomato, raise the heat slightly, and continue sautéing for 5 to 10 minutes or until most of the tomato juices have evaporated and the vegetables are soft. Taste and add salt and pepper if necessary. Set aside to cool slightly.

In a large bowl, combine the herbs with the eggs and beat with a fork just to break up the yolks. Use a slotted spoon to lift the vegetables out of the skillet and add them to the eggs, stirring to combine.

Return the skillet to medium heat, adding a little more oil if necessary. When the oil is hot, add the egg and vegetable mixture and cook for just 2 minutes or so, continually lifting the bottom with a palette knife, narrow spatula, or cake icer to let uncooked egg run under the cooked part. (This procedure will heat the eggs and start the cooking process. The frittata will finish cooking in the oven.) Crumble the goat cheese over the top of the frittata and place it in the oven for about 15 to 20 minutes or until the frittata is set and the cheese is melted.

Serve hot from the oven or set aside and serve at room temperature. *Makes 6 servings as a main course, 10 to 12 servings as a first course*

Nutritional Data, per portion

| | | |
|---|---|---|
| Calories 313 | Carbohydrate 7g | Saturated Fat 8g |
| Protein 20g | Sodium 249mg | Monounsaturated |
| Fat 23g | Cholesterol 505mg | Fat 10g |

# TUNISIAN AIJJAH WITH SPICY POTATOES

The North African version of frittata is called *aijjah* or *eggah*, and is more like scrambled eggs than either frittata or tortilla. Tunisians almost always add a healthy dollop of harissa.

1   pound small new potatoes, peeled and diced

3   tablespoons extra-virgin olive oil

½   teaspoon salt or more to taste

½   teaspoon ground caraway seeds

2   garlic cloves, peeled and crushed with the flat blade of a knife

2   tablespoons tomato puree

½   cup warm water

1   tablespoon harissa (page 301)

freshly ground black pepper to taste

8   large eggs

In a large skillet over medium heat, gently sauté the potatoes in 2 tablespoons of the oil until the potatoes are softened and starting to brown—about 15 minutes.

While the potatoes are cooking, pound the salt and caraway to a powder in a mortar; then add the garlic and pound to a paste. Dilute the tomato puree with the warm water and stir in the harissa. Combine with the garlic paste.

When the potatoes are done, add the harissa-garlic mixture and cook briefly, stirring, for 5 to 10 minutes, until the liquid is reduced to a thick sauce that naps the potatoes. Remove from the heat and adjust the seasoning, adding pepper and more salt if necessary. Set aside to cool slightly.

Beat the eggs with a fork in a large bowl. Then turn the potatoes into the eggs and stir to mix very well.

Rinse and dry the skillet if necessary. Set it over medium-high heat and add the remaining oil, swirling the pan to coat the bottom and sides thoroughly. Turn the egg mixture into the pan and cook, continually lifting the cooked egg mixture from the bottom and letting the liquid eggs run underneath, in order to scramble the eggs.

When the eggs have reached the desired consistency, remove from the heat and serve immediately. ***Makes 4 servings***

Nutritional Data, per portion

| | | |
|---|---|---|
| Calories 358 | Carbohydrate 24g | Saturated Fat 5g |
| Protein 15g | Sodium 440mg | Monounsaturated |
| Fat 23g | Cholesterol 425mg | Fat 14g |

# INSALATA CAPRESE

### Fresh Mozzarella with Tomatoes and Basil

This lush combination in the red, white, and green of the Italian flag is to be made only at the height of summer's harvest, when tomatoes are dead ripe and packed with flavor and fresh basil is full of fragrance. Use imported fresh mozzarella di bufala, buffalo-milk mozzarella, if you can find it; otherwise a very-good-quality cow's milk mozzarella. Do not use the skim-milk mozzarella available in many supermarket dairy cases—it bears no resemblance to the real thing.

1½ to 2 pounds summer tomatoes, about 4 large
1    pound fresh mozzarella, preferably imported mozzarella di bufala
1    large bunch of fresh basil
salt and freshly ground black pepper to taste
3    tablespoons best-quality extra-virgin olive oil
1    tablespoon red wine vinegar or to taste

Slice the tomatoes crosswise about ½ inch thick. Cut the mozzarella into ½-inch-thick slices. Discard the basil stems (or use them to flavor a soup or sauce).

Arrange the ingredients in overlapping rows on a platter: a slice of tomato, a slice of mozzarella, a large leaf of basil, continuing until all the ingredients have been used. Sprinkle with salt and pepper. Combine the oil and vinegar, beating with a fork, and pour it over the salad. Serve immediately, with thick slices of bread to sop up the juices. *Makes 6 servings*

Nutritional Data, per portion

| | | |
|---|---|---|
| Calories   306 | Carbohydrate   10g | Saturated Fat   1g |
| Protein   15g | Sodium   66mg | Monounsaturated |
| Fat   24g | Cholesterol   53mg | Fat   6g |

# PANZANELLA

## *Italian Bread Salad*

**H**ave you ever sat around the table after the salad was finished and dipped chunks of bread in the salad dressing left in the bottom of the bowl? Then this Tuscan bread salad is for you, combining the full summer flavors of red ripe tomatoes and basil with the nutty aroma of bread.

Altopascio, a town on the heights looking over the Arno Valley west of Florence as the river courses toward Pisa, is where Tuscans say the best bread in Italy is made. "Why?" I asked the woman in the local bakery. "Because it is," she said.

Panzanella should be made with an Altopascio-style *pane integrale,* a rustic whole-grain loaf, coarse-textured and deeply flavored, preferably baked in a wood-fired oven. If you don't have access to a good hearty Tuscan loaf, make your own, using the recipe on page 131, but don't try to do this with ordinary store bread—it will make a gluey mess.

1   pound rather stale (firm but not dried out) Tuscan country-style
     bread—4 1-inch-thick slices

4   large dead-ripe tomatoes, full of flavor and fragrance

1   large red onion, about ½ pound, finely sliced

1 or 2 cucumbers, about ½ pound, peeled, quartered lengthwise, and
     finely sliced

a handful of fresh green basil leaves, 1 cup firmly packed, very coarsely
     chopped or torn

½   cup extra-virgin olive oil

¼   cup red wine vinegar

1   tablespoon balsamic vinegar

salt and freshly ground black pepper to taste

Soften the bread slices in a bowl of cool water, then squeeze each slice gently to get rid of the excess liquid. Tear the bread into chunks, discarding the thick crusts, and drop the chunks in the bottom of a salad bowl. Cut the tomatoes in half and slice thickly, about ½ inch, or cut into chunks. Add to the bread, along with the onion, cucumber, and basil leaves.

In a separate bowl, mix the oil and vinegars, adding salt and pepper. Beat with a fork to emulsify and pour over the salad. Mix well, using your hands to turn the salad, and set aside in a cool spot (do not refrigerate) for at least 30 minutes before serving to allow the flavors to develop. ***Makes 6 to 8 servings***

Nutritional Data, per portion

| | | |
|---|---|---|
| Calories 313 | Carbohydrate 38g | Saturated Fat 2g |
| Protein 7g | Sodium 358mg | Monounsaturated |
| Fat 16g | Cholesterol 0 | Fat 12g |

# FATTOUSH

### *Lebanese Toasted Bread Salad*

**T**he key ingredient in *fattoush* is sumac, a dark red, lemony astringent flavoring much used in the Middle East. It is available in this country in shops in Middle Eastern neighborhoods or by mail order from specialty food stores and spice shops. If you buy whole sumac berries, grind them coarsely or pound in a mortar.

2    small Arab flatbreads (pita)

1    small head of romaine lettuce

8    radishes, sliced or cut in half

8    scallions, both white and green parts, sliced

1 or 2 cucumbers, preferably pale-skinned Middle Eastern or Armenian
       cucumbers, peeled and sliced

1 or 2 plain brine-pickled cucumbers, not sweetened or heavily flavored
       with garlic or dill, sliced

3    medium tomatoes, cut into thick chunks

⅓    cup finely chopped flat-leaf parsley

⅓    cup finely chopped fresh mint or 2 teaspoons crumbled dried

1 or 2 garlic cloves to taste

1    teaspoon salt

¼    cup fresh lemon juice

¼    cup extra-virgin olive oil

freshly ground black pepper to taste

2    tablespoons coarsely ground sumac

THE SMALL DISHES OF THE MEDITERRANEAN

Split each of the breads in half horizontally so that you have 4 thin rounds of bread. Toast the breads lightly under the broiler, just enough to turn them pale golden and crisp. Break up the crisp toast into small pieces and put in the bottom of a large salad bowl. Pile the salad vegetables on top, in the order listed, sprinkling the parsley and mint over the top.

Crush the garlic with the flat blade of a knife and chop it coarsely. In a separate small bowl, mash the garlic with the salt, using the back of a spoon. Stir in the lemon juice and oil, beating with a fork to mix well, and pour the dressing over the salad. Grind the black pepper over the top and sprinkle the sumac on last. Take the salad bowl to the table and toss the ingredients together just before serving to keep the bread from getting soggy before it is served. *Makes 6 servings*

Nutritional Data, per portion

| | | |
|---|---|---|
| Calories  175 | Carbohydrate  20g | Saturated Fat  1g |
| Protein  4g | Sodium  598mg | Monounsaturated |
| Fat  10g | Cholesterol  0 | Fat  7g |

# PASTA SALAD FROM THE ISLE OF CAPRI

This is a specialty of Titina Vuotto at her Ristorante La Pineta on the island of Capri. I don't usually like the idea of cold pasta salads, but this one is particularly good and represents (for me at least) the intriguing way that some recipes start out as Italian, get adopted and somewhat bastardized in America, and are then readopted by Italian cooks, who add new verve and excitement to an old dish. Make sure your tomatoes are ripe and juicy.

1   **pound tomatoes**

1   **large garlic clove, minced**

1   **cup firmly packed fresh basil leaves, torn or coarsely chopped**

1   **salted anchovy or 2 small oil-packed anchovy fillets (optional)**

½   **pound fresh mozzarella di bufala or cow's milk mozzarella, diced (not skim-milk mozzarella)**

**salt to taste**

¼   **cup extra-virgin olive oil**

1   **pound tubetti, or other small pasta shapes**

Core the tomatoes and cut in half crosswise. Cut each half into 8 pieces and toss in a large salad bowl. Add the garlic and basil. If you can find salted anchovies, rinse one under fresh running water, pull away the bones, and chop the fillets coarsely; oil-packed anchovy fillets need only be chopped. Add to the salad together with the mozzarella. Toss to mix well. Taste and add a little salt if necessary. Set aside to marinate.

Bring a kettle of lightly salted water to a rolling boil and cook the tubetti until just tender. Drain thoroughly and dress immediately with the olive oil, tossing to mix well. When the pasta has cooled slightly, turn it into the tomato salad and serve immediately. ***Makes 6 to 8 servings***

### Nutritional Data, per portion

| | | |
|---|---|---|
| Calories 371 | Carbohydrate 48g | Saturated Fat 1g |
| Protein 13g | Sodium 242mg | Monounsaturated |
| Fat 14g | Cholesterol 20mg | Fat 6g |

## GREEK SALAD

### *The Classic Horiatiki Recipe*

**W**hen Antonia Trichopoulou talks about the Mediterranean diet, which she does often in her role as Director of the World Health Organization Collaborating Center for Nutrition Education in Athens, one example of good, healthy Mediterranean food that she often cites (as she did in the Introduction to this book) is Greek salad. This has evoked hoots of derision from Americans used to the kind of Greek salad we get all too often in mom-and-pop corner restaurants, the one that's made with wet iceberg lettuce, hard tomatoes, and canned California black olives, dressed with Wishbone Italian Low-Cal Dressing. The salad Antonia makes when she entertains friends and colleagues at her summer house on the sea outside Athens is altogether different. In Greece the salad is called *horiatiki,* meaning "country style." If you don't care for anchovies, try flaking a little drained white-meat tuna over the top of the salad.

This salad is robust enough to serve as a main course if accompanied by chunks of sturdy country-style bread.

THE SMALL DISHES OF THE MEDITERRANEAN

1   medium head of romaine lettuce, rinsed and torn into chunks

1   long English cucumber or 2 medium slender regular cucumbers,
     thinly sliced

4   medium tomatoes, cut into eighths

1   medium red onion, halved and thinly sliced

1   pound imported Greek or Bulgarian feta cheese, preferably sheep's
     milk feta

1   red bell pepper, thinly sliced into rings

1   green bell pepper, thinly sliced into rings

¼   cup minced flat-leaf parsley

6 or 8 anchovy fillets (optional)

about 18 Kalamata olives, pitted

⅓   cup fruity extra-virgin olive oil

juice of ½ lemon

1   teaspoon minced fresh oregano leaves or ½ teaspoon dried, crumbled

salt and freshly ground black pepper to taste

Arrange the lettuce on a deep platter. Combine the cucumbers, tomatoes, and half the onion slices in a bowl. Crumble the feta and add half of it to the vegetables in the bowl, stirring to mix well. Layer this mixture over the lettuce. Arrange the peppers over the top and sprinkle with the parsley and remaining feta. Arrange the anchovy fillets, or tuna if you'd rather, on top and scatter the pitted olives over all.

In a small bowl, combine the oil, lemon juice, oregano, and salt and pepper. Beat with a fork to mix well and pour over the salad. Toss at the table just before serving. *Makes 8 servings*

Nutritional Data, per portion

| Calories   292 | Carbohydrate   12g | Saturated Fat   10g |
| Protein   11g | Sodium   826mg | Monounsaturated |
| Fat   24g | Cholesterol   51mg | Fat   11g |

# CHAPTER TWO

# SOUPS

ené Jouveau, in *Cuisine Provençale de Tradition Populaire*, a delightful
collection of recipes, folklore, and foodways, quotes the old Provençal
saying about the region's best-known soup: "L'aïgo boulido sauvo la vido," to
which one responds with proper irony, "Au bout d'un tèms, tuio li gènt." Aïgo
boulido, Jouveau says, is nothing more or less than boiled water*, flavored with
sage and garlic and poured over a crust of toasted bread that has been drizzled
with olive oil. Boiled water saves lives, the saying goes; and the response: And after
a time, it kills people off.

Savory it may be, but aïgo boulido is not very substantial, especially on a daily
basis. Yet in its very meagerness it is typical of the make-do diets of poor country
folk all around the Mediterranean. (Poor on a seasonal schedule, that is, for the
same country folk may well become veritable gluttons at times of the year like
Christmas and Easter, when more substantial fare is available.) Italian acquacotta
(cooked water) is a similar preparation, and in Spain sopa de pan, by stressing the
bread (pan), only emphasizes the soup's niggardly, penurious, parsimonious nature. The ingredients change from one place to another, but the principle remains
the same: making do.

We made do one year in Seville. We were there for the Feria, the great post-
Easter fair, and to see the great matador Ordóñez, who had come out of retirement
once more, as he did periodically, to prove that he was still the star, if the aging star,
of the corrida. The Feria is usually the second week after Easter, a time of nearly
explosive joy like a richly earned reward for the penance of Semana Santa, Holy
Week, which the Sevillanos take very, very seriously. Decked in fragrant orange
blossoms, the city is at its loveliest, and the ladies respond, young and old alike,

---

* I had always assumed, as many people do, that *aïgo* means "garlic." It doesn't. It means "water."

dressing up in the flounce-tiered costumes of flamenco dancers with flowers tucked in their hair. Riding arrogantly behind their menfolk, they parade on handsomely groomed horses, and at night they dance the sevillana to the music of guitars.

It was romantic and prodigal, but places to stay were hard to come by. We ended up in an illegal bunk on the roof of a boardinghouse kept by a slovenly woman whose breath smelled of the candied violets she sucked between her teeth all day. We reeled about the city, drunk with the scent of orange blossoms, going from casita to casita visiting these terribly proper but warm and welcoming Sevillanos in the hospitality tents they had set up. We drank chilled fino sherry and nibbled freshly fried almonds and little pinchitos, miniature savory kebabs of pork or veal. At precisely five in the afternoon (*"a las cinco en punto de la tarde,"* we said, quoting Lorca) we went to the bullfights and then, much later, home to the woman who smelled of violets and who gave us, as part of the demi-pension for which we had paid royally, sopa de pan, crusts of bread over which garlic-flavored water was poured and to which was added, at table, by the señora herself to prevent excess, a thin drizzle of a peculiarly rancid olive oil that we suspected had been used to fry the fish at lunch.

This meager soup exists all over the Mediterranean, but I will spare you the recipe. It is instructive for cooks, however, to speculate on the enrichments that go into such skimpy fare whenever possible, because the same enrichments can turn more elaborate, but still humble, preparations into something that will not be out of place as a main course on the table, whether a vegetable minestrone or a clear chicken or veal broth with rice or little shards of pasta floating in it. The enrichments could include some (but never all) of the following:

- A thick slice of toasted country bread in the bottom of each soup plate, the bread first rubbed with a freshly cut garlic clove and drizzled with a very flavorful extra-virgin olive oil
- A handful of grated cheese, whether Parmigiano or something less costly but still full of flavor, sprinkled over the top of the soup at the moment of serving
- A swirl of olive oil spooned over the top of the soup, again at the moment of serving
- A couple of handfuls of the dried yogurt and flour mixture that Arabs call *kishik* and Turks and Greeks call *trahana,* available at shops in Greek and Middle Eastern neighborhoods
- An egg—one per serving—either poached in the soup or beaten in a

separate bowl, some of the hot broth slowly beaten into the eggs and the eggs returned to the soup—which must not, from this point, come to a boil lest the eggs scramble, but which can be stirred gently over very low heat until the eggs thicken the broth slightly

Not every one of these enrichments is appropriate for every kind of soup—you will have to use your own good judgment for that, but any one of them can help turn a humble country soup into an occasion.

The recipes that follow are for what I think of as basic Mediterranean soups, made of seafood or vegetables or beans. These soups are found, in one form or another, throughout the region. As with aïgo boulido, the ingredients change, but the principle of the thing remains the same. Think of it as theme and variation.

First, you will need four basic broths or stocks—only one, of course, if you are vegetarian. For years I have searched in vain for acceptable canned stocks or broths. I don't like them, even though I confess to using them occasionally when there is no other recourse. Along with the metallic flavor of the can, they add an unpleasant chemical taste of salt and/or sweetness to dishes in which they're used. Making stocks is really a good deal easier than pie.

Stocks freeze well, and there is added pleasure in knowing you have a freezer full of low-fat, flavorful bases for all manner of soups, stews, and sauces. When I make stock, I freeze it in ½-cup, cup, and pint containers, so I have a supply for many different purposes. But if you must thaw, say, a pint to use only ½ cup, simply bring the remaining stock to a rapid boil for about 2 minutes and refreeze.

# VEGETABLE BROTH

**Y**ou will never get the same flavor impact with vegetable broth as you do with broth made from meat, chicken, or fish, so using olive oil to unite and boost the flavors is important. Vegetable broths as such are rarely used in Mediterranean cooking—this one is for the benefit of strict vegetarians.

2   medium yellow onions, quartered

3   carrots, peeled and cut into chunks

3   dark green outer celery ribs, cut into chunks

3   garlic cloves, lightly crushed with the flat blade of a knife

2   tablespoons extra-virgin olive oil

6   plump brown mushrooms, cleaned and quartered (cremini or shiitake are more flavorful than ordinary supermarket mushrooms; wild mushrooms, if you can find them, are best of all)

1   cup dry white wine

9   cups hot water

1   fat leek, rinsed carefully

1   fennel bulb, including the leafy green tops, chopped

1   tablespoon chopped fresh thyme, or 1 teaspoon dried, crumbled

1   3-inch cinnamon stick (optional)

6   whole cloves (optional)

6   slices of dried porcini mushrooms

salt and freshly ground black pepper to taste

Preheat the oven to 425 degrees. In a flameproof glass or metal baking dish, turn the onions, carrots, celery, and garlic in the olive oil to coat them well. Roast for 15 minutes; then add the mushrooms and stir to mix well. Return to the oven for another 15 minutes, after which the vegetables should be brown and crispy on the edges and should give off a delicious aroma. Remove the dish from the oven and scrape the vegetables into a heavy stockpot or soup kettle. Add the wine to the oven dish and set over medium heat. Cook the wine, scraping up the brown bits in the pan, until it is slightly reduced, about 10 minutes, then add to the stockpot with the hot water. Add the leek, fennel, thyme, cinnamon, and

cloves. Bring the stock to a simmer over medium-low heat, cover, and cook for at least 1 hour.

Meanwhile, put the dried mushrooms in a 1-cup measure and fill with boiling water. Let soak for 15 minutes. Remove the mushrooms (do not discard the soaking liquid) and rinse under running water to get rid of grit. Chop them coarsely and add to the stockpot along with the soaking liquid, strained through a fine-mesh sieve.

When the stock has finished cooking, strain it through a double layer of cheesecloth or a fine-mesh sieve. Discard the vegetables and aromatics. Taste the broth for seasoning, adding salt and pepper if necessary—be mindful of the salt, however, because reducing the broth later may concentrate the salt too much. ***Makes about 2 quarts; 8 servings***

Nutritional Data, per portion

| Calories | 49 | Carbohydrate | 4g | Saturated Fat | 1g |
|---|---|---|---|---|---|
| Protein | 1g | Sodium | 16mg | Monounsaturated | |
| Fat | 4g | Cholesterol | 0 | Fat | 3g |

# CLEAR WHITE CHICKEN STOCK

**T**he chickens I buy in the Cortona market in Italy are plump old ladies with their heads and feet, the source of much flavor, still attached. In this country I don't even bother making chicken stock with the widely available commercial birds— you can cook them forever and still get a bland and flavorless stock because the things don't have any flavor to yield anyway. Try farmers' markets and natural foods stores for chickens raised in a certain amount of freedom and fed on nonmedicated grains (so-called free-range chickens). This is the only way to get the flavorful chickens you need for good stock, or for any other chicken dish for that matter. If you can't find a boiling fowl, use a roaster. Or use a combination of chicken necks, backs, wings, and innards.

SOUPS

1 4- to 5-pound chicken, or 4 to 5 pounds chicken parts, including
   wings and backs

2 onions, quartered

2 garlic cloves, crushed with the flat blade of a knife

1 medium to large carrot, peeled and quartered

½ cup flat-leaf parsley leaves

1 tablespoon fresh thyme or 1 teaspoon dried, crumbled

1 3-inch cinnamon stick (optional)

about 10 cups cold water

salt and freshly ground black pepper to taste

Put all the ingredients except the salt, pepper, and water in a heavy stockpot or soup kettle. Add the cold water, or more if necessary to cover the bird. Over medium-low heat, slowly bring the liquid to a simmer. For the clearest stock, carefully skim the froth as it rises to the top. When the foam has ceased rising, cover the pot and cook at a slow simmer for at least 1½ hours or longer if necessary. (A boiling fowl, depending on age, may take 2½ hours to cook thoroughly.) The bird should be so thoroughly cooked that it's starting to fall apart.

At the end of the cooking time, strain the stock through a double layer of cheesecloth or a fine-mesh sieve. Discard the vegetables and aromatics. The chicken meat will have given up most of its flavor, but if you wish to use some of it as a garnish for a soup, dice it and set aside. Taste the strained stock and add salt and pepper if desired. Be wary of too much salt—if the stock is to be reduced later, it will concentrate. Put the strained stock in the refrigerator to let the fat rise and solidify, after which it can be removed easily with a slotted spoon. *Makes 10 to 12 cups; 10 to 12 servings*

Nutritional Data, per portion

| | | |
|---|---|---|
| Calories   29 | Carbohydrate   2g | Saturated Fat   trace |
| Protein   2g | Sodium   46mg | Monounsaturated |
| Fat   1g | Cholesterol   0 | Fat   0 |

# RICH MEAT STOCK

**about 6 pounds meaty beef bones—ribs and shanks are good; a**
**knuckle bone will add richness and body**

2   **yellow onions, unpeeled but cut in half**

2   **garlic cloves, peeled and crushed with the flat blade of a knife**

2   **medium to large carrots, peeled and quartered**

1   **cup dry red wine**

**about 10 cups cold water**

¼   **cup coarsely chopped flat-leaf parsley**

1   **tablespoon chopped fresh thyme or 1 teaspoon dried, crumbled**

2   **bay leaves**

1   **whole dried red chili (optional)**

**salt and freshly ground black pepper to taste**

Preheat the oven to 425 degrees. Place the bones in a glass or metal oven dish with the onions, garlic, and carrots. Roast for about 30 minutes, stirring occasionally with a wooden spoon. The meat should be thoroughly browned and the vegetables starting to brown and crisp along the edges.

Scrape the meat and vegetables into a heavy stockpot or soup kettle. Add the wine to the oven dish and cook over medium heat, scraping up all the brown bits, until the wine has given off all its alcohol, about 10 minutes. Pour the wine into the stockpot. Add the cold water along with the parsley, thyme, bay leaves, and chili. Bring to a slow simmer over medium-low heat, skimming the froth with a slotted spoon as it rises to the surface. When the foam has ceased to rise, cover the pot and simmer for at least 2½ hours.

When the stock has finished cooking, strain through a double layer of cheese-cloth or a fine-mesh sieve. Discard the vegetables and aromatics. If you wish to use the meat, pull it away from the bones, chop coarsely, and set aside in a small bowl covered with a spoonful or two of the stock to keep it from drying out. Taste the strained stock and add salt and pepper if necessary, keeping in mind that the salt will be concentrated if the stock is reduced later. Place the stock in the refrigerator long enough for the fat to solidify, after which it can be removed easily with a slotted spoon. *Makes about 10 cups; 10 servings*

SOUPS

# FISH STOCK

**F**ish stock, ideally, is made with the heads and bones of large white-fleshed fish like cod or haddock that have been cut up for fillets. There's a good deal of flesh left on the bones and in the head, and this gives flavor to the stock. The carcasses of any white-fleshed fish can be used—monkfish, snapper, weakfish, or whatever is available at your fishmonger. Do not use oily fish such as bluefish, mackerel, or salmon, however, because the taste is too strong.

In some parts of the country it may be next to impossible to get fish trimmings for stock. In that case, use a commercially prepared fish stock or a dehydrated mix—but do add the aromatics, wine, and vegetables to give it as distinctive a taste as possible. (Bottled clam juice is usually too salty.) In the absence of anything else, use a piece of plain frozen fish fillet, add the aromatics, vegetables, and wine, and simmer for 30 minutes or so—it won't be as rich and savory as using fish heads, but it's better than plain water. (Discard the fillet and aromatics after simmering.)

> **head and bones of 1 4- to 6-pound fish, preferably haddock, cod, or**
>     **snapper**
> 2  **bay leaves**
> 1  **medium carrot, peeled and cut in half lengthwise**
> 1  **medium onion, halved**
> 12 **black peppercorns**
> 12 **flat-leaf parsley sprigs**
> 1  **cup dry white wine**
> 6  **cups cold water**
> **salt and freshly ground white pepper to taste**

Place the fish head and bones in a heavy soup kettle or stockpot along with the bay leaves, carrot, onion, peppercorns, and parsley. Add the wine and cold water.

Bring to a boil slowly, cover, turn the heat down, and simmer for 45 minutes. Strain the broth when done and discard the solids. Taste the broth and add salt and pepper if desired, keeping in mind that the salt will be concentrated if the stock is later reduced. *Makes 6 to 7 cups; 6 to 7 servings*

Nutritional Data, per portion

| | | |
|---|---|---|
| Calories 20 | Carbohydrate 1g | Saturated Fat trace |
| Protein 3g | Sodium 162mg | Monounsaturated |
| Fat trace | Cholesterol 9mg | Fat trace |

# MEDITERRANEAN FISH SOUP

### *The Basic Recipe*

**Z**arzuela, bouillabaisse, brodetto, Greek kakavia, Tuscan cacciucco, Turkish baliksi çorbasi, and so on: the flavoring of these fish and seafood soups changes from one part of the Mediterranean to another. A little chopped wild fennel and a strip of dried orange peel mark a soup as Provençal, while the bright color and slightly musty flavor of saffron may indicate Spanish or Maghrebi ancestry, and a thickening of egg yolks and lemon juice, beaten together and stirred into the hot soup so that the broth naps the pieces of seafood with a creamy velour, is a technique of Greek and Turkish cooks. But while aromas and flavors vary, the basic preparation is consistent. Aromatics—leeks, garlic, a little chopped white onion, a handful of freshly picked parsley—are gently stewed in olive oil; the fish is added, perhaps with chopped ripe tomatoes or a glass of white wine; then water or fish stock and seasonings such as salt, pepper, a branch of thyme, a bay leaf, and, on the island of Cyprus, a short length of cinnamon stick are added, and the soup is set to cook.

The procedure may look daunting at first, but it is actually very simple and logical, and the most complicated parts of the cooking can often be done well ahead and the whole thing assembled at the last minute.

These fish soups can be made with a single variety of fish, but more often they are composed of several different kinds, as well as shellfish—mussels, clams, razor clams, crabs—shrimp or rock lobster, and squid or cuttlefish or pieces of octopus. When a number of different fish are used, of course, the cook must pay careful attention to cooking times so that the result is not a mishmash of disintegrating

seafood. One caution: strong-flavored, oily fish like mackerel, salmon, and bluefish are not appropriate for these soups; save them for the grill.

It is often said that a true bouillabaisse, by all accounts the apotheosis of Mediterranean fish soup, can be made only in or near the port of Marseilles and that the preparation, to be genuine and authentic, must include the little spiny scorpion fish, called *rascasse* in French, that lend so much flavor, but very little substance, to the broth. That may well be, but a very fine, Mediterranean-style fish soup can be made anywhere in the world where there is access to a variety of first-rate fresh fish—try haddock as the main ingredient on the East Coast, fresh Alaska halibut in the Pacific Northwest, red snapper and drum in the Southeast, redfish along the gulf, or whatever looks good and fresh at the fishmonger that day. Supplies are getting better and better all over the country, and cooks in the interior, who once had to rely on a meager selection of frozen fish, now have access to excellent fresh fish. And frozen fish itself has improved enormously in quality in recent years. Even in large supermarkets the fish counter seems to be one place where the customer still has rights—don't be afraid to assert them.

Usually the fish is served together with the broth in which it has cooked as a main course. A refinement found in restaurants and bourgeois homes is to serve the broth separately, as a first course, perhaps thickened with rice or pasta or poured over slices of toasted, garlic-rubbed bread. Then the fish itself comes along as a second course, possibly with a sauce such as sauce verte (page 288) or, when tomatoes are at their peak, a fresh salsa of chopped ripe tomatoes, garlic, and basil (page 298).

½   **cup dry white wine**

½   **cup water**

18   **hard-shell mahogany or Manila clams, the smaller the better, well scrubbed**

2   **cups fish stock (page 84)**

¼   **cup extra-virgin olive oil**

2   **medium yellow onions, chopped**

1   **fat leek, white part only, rinsed well and sliced into julienne strips**

3   **garlic cloves, minced**

3   **very ripe tomatoes, peeled, seeded (page 454), and chopped, or 3 or 4 whole canned tomatoes, drained and chopped**

1   **bay leaf**

1    teaspoon minced fresh thyme or ½ teaspoon dried, crumbled

1    teaspoon sea salt or to taste

2½ pounds firm white-fleshed fish, such as wolffish, monkfish, cod,
        haddock, or halibut, boned and cut into serving pieces

1½ pounds medium (36–40 count) shrimp

4    squid, cleaned and cut into rings

freshly ground black pepper to taste

2    tablespoons minced fresh parsley


Combine the wine and water in a saucepan. Place the pan over medium heat, and as soon as the liquid starts to bubble, add the clams, cover, and steam until their shells open—about 5 to 7 minutes. Remove clams from the liquid, discarding any that haven't opened, but leave them in their shells. Strain the clam broth through a fine-mesh sieve to remove all traces of sand and add the strained liquid to the fish stock to make 3 cups.

Add the olive oil to an earthenware casserole, a Dutch oven, or a similar heavy pot that is large enough to accommodate all the ingredients and somewhat wider than it is tall. (You should have about ¼ inch of oil in the bottom of the pot.) Place over medium-low heat, and when the oil is hot, add the onions, leek, and garlic. Cook, stirring occasionally, until the vegetables have softened and turned golden, about 20 to 30 minutes. Do not let the vegetables brown.

Stir in the tomatoes, bay leaf, and thyme and continue cooking for approximately 30 minutes, until all the liquid has evaporated and the tomatoes have melted into the onions. Add the salt.

Add the fish stock, raise the heat to medium, and add the pieces of fish. Simmer for 2 minutes, then add the shrimp, and 2 minutes later distribute the squid rings over the surface of the stew. Cook for approximately 3 to 5 minutes longer or until the seafood is thoroughly cooked but not overcooked—about 10 minutes in all. Add the clams in their shells for the last 90 seconds—just long enough to heat them thoroughly. Remove from the heat and, just before serving, add generous amounts of pepper and the parsley. *Makes 8 to 10 servings*


Nutritional Data, per portion

| Calories   276 | Carbohydrate   9g | Saturated Fat   1g |
| Protein   40g | Sodium   355mg | Monounsaturated |
| Fat   8g | Cholesterol   220mg | Fat   5g |

**VARIATIONS:** A Catalan version of this, described by Colman Andrews in *Catalan Cuisine*, adds ½ cup each of dark rum and sherry plus ½ teaspoon each of ground cinnamon and ground allspice to the basic preparation—add these with the tomatoes. Provençal cooks add a teaspoon of fennel seeds and a 2-inch piece of dried orange peel, also with the tomatoes, while North Africans contribute a teaspoon of ground cumin and a little hot chili or a spoonful of harissa (page 301). For an Italian flavor, just before serving sprinkle the soup with a handful of slivered fresh basil and a big spoonful of drained capers.

# DÉLICE DE FRUITS DE MER SÈTOISE

### *Virtually Fat-Free Mediterranean Fish Soup*

**T**his is a labor-intensive recipe, but well worth the effort. Most of the work can be done a day ahead or in the morning for an evening presentation—and a handsome presentation it is, too. Because no fat is added, the small amount of fat in the dish comes from naturally occurring residual fat in the fish and shellfish—much of it in the form of beneficial Omega-3 fatty acids.

4 pounds mussels

salt

1 pound monkfish, haddock, or cod fillets

1 small bunch of flat-leaf parsley

2 medium fennel bulbs

2¼ cups water

2 cups dry white wine

1 tablespoon chopped fresh thyme or 1 teaspoon dried, crumbled

3 bay leaves

a large pinch of saffron threads

1 medium carrot, peeled and cut into chunks

1 medium yellow onion, halved

12 black peppercorns

a 2-inch piece of dried orange peel

1 pound medium-large (25 count) shrimp

4   garlic cloves, slightly crushed with the flat blade of a knife
1   pound sea scallops
3   firm but ripe tomatoes, roughly chopped, or 5 canned whole
     tomatoes, drained and chopped


Clean the mussels, discarding any that are gaping open. Soak them in a bowl of cold salted water for 30 minutes or until you're ready to cook. Cut the fish fillets into 2-inch pieces, sprinkle lightly with salt, and set aside. Finely chop the leaves only of about half the parsley—you should have 2 tablespoons—and set aside. Trim the fennel, but leave the bulbs whole.

In a saucepan large enough to hold the fennel bulbs, bring 1 cup of the water and 1 cup of the wine to a boil. Add half the thyme, a bay leaf, and the fennel bulbs and steam, covered, over medium heat until the fennel is barely tender, about 15 to 20 minutes. Remove from the heat and remove the fennel from the pan, reserving the liquid. Add the saffron to the liquid and set aside. Slice the fennel bulbs lengthwise (top to bottom) about ½ inch thick and set aside.

In another pan, bring 1¼ cups water to a boil. Add the remaining thyme and bay leaves along with the carrot, onion, the remaining parsley, the peppercorns, orange peel, and the remaining wine. Bring to a simmer, cover the pan, and cook for 10 minutes at a slow simmer. Add the shrimp and cook for 2 to 3 minutes. When the shrimp have turned pink but remain firm, remove the pan from the heat. Using a slotted spoon or tongs, remove the shrimp from the pan and set aside to cool, reserving the liquid. When the shrimp are cool enough to handle, peel and set aside.

Return the fennel-cooking liquid to the heat, and when it has reached a slow simmer, add the drained mussels. Steam, covered, in the broth until their shells open, about 5 minutes. Remove the mussels with a slotted spoon and strain the broth through a fine-mesh sieve to remove the herbs and any sandy sediment. Combine the reserved shrimp broth with the mussel broth. (The recipe can be made ahead to this point, but the cooked shrimp and mussels, the fennel, and the broth should be refrigerated if you're holding them for more than an hour or so.)

When you're ready to cook, bring the broth to a slow but steady simmer in a heavy soup kettle or a Dutch oven that is wider than it is tall. Add the garlic, scallops, and pieces of fish. Poach gently until just barely cooked, about 5 to 10 minutes. Add the tomatoes and chopped parsley, stirring to mix. Add the mussels, shrimp, and fennel and continue cooking, not more than 5 minutes, until they are thoroughly heated. Serve immediately. *Makes 8 servings*

SOUPS

# NIÇOISE MUSSEL OR CLAM SOUP

**T**his soup is traditionally made with mussels, but I have also made it with hardshell clams (cherrystones, mahoganies, or Manilas), and it's every bit as delicious.

Mussels used to be terribly hard to clean, so much so that many cooks felt it wasn't worth the effort. But with cultivated mussels widely available, it's a whole lot easier. You should still pick over mussels or clams before cooking and discard any with cracked or gaping shells. (Unlike softshell clams or steamers, the shells of hardshell clams should be firmly closed.) After cooking, on the other hand, discard any whose shells have *not* opened.

If you gather mussels or clams from the wild, be absolutely certain that the waters from which you harvest them are clean—local departments of fish and wildlife or marine fisheries (the name varies from one state to another) can advise you about where and when to harvest.

pinch of saffron threads

2 medium onions, coarsely chopped

3 garlic cloves, crushed with the flat blade of a knife

1 bay leaf

2 cups water

2 quarts hardshell clams or mussels, rinsed, the mussels cleaned of
      their beards if necessary and gaping mussels or clams discarded

3 tablespoons extra-virgin olive oil

1 leek, white part only, rinsed well and sliced

1 small fennel bulb, chopped

1 teaspoon chopped fresh thyme or ½ teaspoon dried, crumbled

**2    tomatoes, chopped, or imported canned whole tomatoes, drained and crushed with a fork**

**dry white wine as needed**

**⅓   cup vermicelli, broken into 1-inch lengths**

**salt and freshly ground black pepper to taste**

Mix the saffron in a cup with a couple of tablespoons of very hot water and set aside to steep.

Combine half the onions, 2 garlic cloves, and the bay leaf with the water and bring to a boil in a soup kettle large enough to hold all the clams or mussels. As soon as the water boils, add the shellfish and steam until they are all fully open—about 10 minutes. Discard any that have not opened after this point.

As soon as they are cool enough to handle, remove the clams or mussels from their shells and set the meat aside with a teaspoon of the olive oil drizzled over it to keep it from drying out. Strain the broth through a fine-mesh sieve to rid it of all sand. Set aside.

In another pan over medium heat, sauté the remaining onion, remaining garlic clove, and leek in the remaining olive oil until the vegetables are soft but not brown—about 10 minutes. Add the fennel, thyme, and tomato and cook together for a few minutes, until the tomato has released its juices. Add enough wine to the strained broth to make up 1 quart, then pour the liquid into the vegetables in the pan. Cook briefly to evaporate the alcohol from the wine, then add the saffron with its soaking liquid and the vermicelli and cook about 10 minutes or just until tender. Add the mussels or clams, and when they are just heated through, serve the soup over toasted bread slices. (Don't let the soup come to a boil, or the shellfish will toughen.)

Garnish with a dollop of olive oil, a little handful of minced flat-leaf parsley, or a very little grated Parmigiano cheese. *Makes 4 servings*

Nutritional Data, per portion

| | | |
|---|---|---|
| Calories 250 | Carbohydrate 23g | Saturated Fat 2g |
| Protein 14g | Sodium 85mg | Monounsaturated |
| Fat 12g | Cholesterol 29mg | Fat 8g |

# CHORBA BIL HOUT SFAXIYA

*Fish Soup in the Style of Sfax with Cumin, Chilies, and Harissa*

**T**unisia's long, undulating Mediterranean coastline forms both its northern and eastern boundaries and gives the country its reputation for fine seafood. In Sfax, midway down the east coast heading toward Libya, the twin riches of fish and olive oil come together, for this is also one of the great olive oil–producing regions of the world. The robust flavors of peppery harissa and cumin are also appreciated by Sfaxiya cooks.

Use halibut, swordfish, or salmon steaks, cut at least 1 inch thick, or thick fillets of salmon, cod, haddock, snapper, or other white-fleshed fish.

2   bell peppers, preferably both red and green

1   serrano or jalapeño chili

5   garlic cloves, chopped

1½ teaspoons ground cumin

½   teaspoon salt or more to taste

2   pounds fish steaks or fillets

freshly ground black pepper to taste

1   medium onion, minced

¼   cup extra-virgin olive oil

1   tablespoon tomato puree diluted with about ¼ cup water

½   tablespoon harissa (page 301) or more to taste

½   tablespoon hot red pepper flakes

2   bay leaves

6   cups water

a handful of minced flat-leaf parsley or cilantro for garnish

2   lemons, quartered, for garnish

Before you start to cook the fish, roast and peel the peppers and chili, following the directions on page 455. Cut the peppers and chili into strips and set aside.

Combine the garlic, cumin, and salt in a mortar and pound to a paste. Set aside.

Rinse the fish and cut, if necessary, into serving-size pieces. Sprinkle with salt and pepper on both sides and set aside.

In a heavy stockpot or soup kettle over medium-low heat, gently sauté the onion in the oil until it is thoroughly soft and golden—about 10 minutes. Add the diluted tomato puree, harissa, red pepper flakes, bay leaves, and garlic-cumin paste. Mix well and cook for 10 minutes, then add the water, bring to a boil, stirring, and add the pieces of fish. Reduce the heat and simmer until the fish is just done—10 minutes or a little less for 1-inch-thick steaks or fillets. Be careful not to overcook the fish.

When the fish pieces are done, remove from the soup and set aside. Remove and discard the bay leaves. Push the soup through a vegetable mill or puree in a blender or food processor. Return the soup to the stove and add the pepper strips and pieces of fish. Just before serving, bring back to a simmer, but do not cook.

To serve, place a slice of toasted bread in the bottom of each soup plate. Add a few pieces of fish on top. Pour the pureed broth with the pepper strips over the top. Garnish with finely minced parsley or cilantro and wedges of lemon. *Makes 6 servings*

Nutritional Data, per portion

| | | |
|---|---|---|
| Calories 253 | Carbohydrate 7g | Saturated Fat 2g |
| Protein 27g | Sodium 263mg | Monounsaturated |
| Fat 13g | Cholesterol 39mg | Fat 9g |

# CAPTAIN BAYRAM'S SOUTHERN TURKISH FISH SOUP WITH RICE

**C**aptain Bayram, skipper of the *Hasret*, a 72-foot golet or motor sailer that cruises the south Turkish coast out of the ancient port of Bodrum, makes this soup from time to time when a coastal fishing vessel ties up next to *Hasret* with a particularly good catch. The captain likes to use orfoz or lahoz, which are rather large groupers (called *mérou* in French) that inhabit the warmer Mediterranean waters. On this side of the Atlantic I have made the soup with firm white-fleshed fish like cod and haddock.

Soaking the rice overnight before cooking adds both comforting density and delicate flavor to the broth.

1   quart fish stock (page 84) plus 2 cups water, or 6 cups water

2   Turkish bay leaves

1   teaspoon dried oregano, crumbled

1   teaspoon freshly ground black pepper

1   ancho chili

1   large onion, quartered

1   large carrot, peeled and cut into chunks

2   medium ripe tomatoes, quartered, or 3 canned tomatoes, drained and quartered

1   3- to 3½-pound whole fish or about 2 pounds fish steaks or fillets: cod, haddock, halibut, sea bass, or snapper

2   tablespoons extra-virgin olive oil to taste

1   large potato, peeled and cut into bite-size cubes

⅓   cup long-grain white rice, soaked overnight in 1 cup water

2   large eggs

juice of 2 lemons

¼   teaspoon hot red pepper flakes or more to taste

salt and freshly ground black pepper to taste

finely chopped flat-leaf parsley for garnish

Combine the stock and water in a stockpot and add the bay leaves, oregano, pepper, chili, onion, carrot, and tomatoes. Bring to a boil and cook over medium-low heat until the vegetables are very soft, about 30 to 40 minutes. Strain the stock, pressing the vegetables firmly to extract all the juices.

Return the strained stock to the pan and add the fish. Cook the fish at a slow simmer until the flesh flakes easily. Boneless fillets will cook in 2 or 3 minutes, depending on their thickness; a whole fish may take 25 to 30 minutes. Remove the fish when done and, if you're using a whole fish or fish steaks, discard the skin and bones. Set the flesh aside in a bowl, drizzling 1 tablespoon of oil over the top to keep it from drying out.

Add the potato to the stock and cook, covered, over medium heat for 10 to 15 minutes or until the potato pieces are tender. Using a slotted spoon, remove and pile on top of the fish pieces. Drizzle another tablespoon of oil over the top of the potatoes.

Add the rice to the fish stock and cook, covered, very slowly and gently for another 30 to 40 minutes. The rice should disintegrate into the stock and give it a slightly gelatinous consistency. The recipe may be made ahead of time up to this point.

When you're ready to serve, add the fish and potatoes to the stock and return it slowly to a simmer. In a bowl, beat together the eggs and lemon juice until thoroughly blended. Slowly beat a ladleful of hot stock into the egg mixture and continue adding ladlefuls, one by one, beating constantly, until the egg mixture is close to the temperature of the simmering stock. Carefully stir the hot egg mixture into the stock. Continue to cook for a few minutes, stirring constantly, until the stock has thickened slightly. Do not let the stock boil, or the eggs will scramble.

When the soup is pleasantly thickened, remove from the heat and stir in the hot pepper flakes as well as salt and black pepper. Serve immediately, garnished with a little parsley. *Makes 6 to 8 servings*

Nutritional Data, per portion

| Calories | 225 | Carbohydrate | 17g | Saturated Fat | 1g |
|---|---|---|---|---|---|
| Protein | 25g | Sodium | 167mg | Monounsaturated | |
| Fat | 6g | Cholesterol | 107mg | Fat | 3g |

# MEDITERRANEAN VEGETABLE SOUP (MINESTRONE)

## The Basic Recipe

There are as many variations of Mediterranean vegetable soup, or minestrone, as there are of Mediterranean fish soup. All rely on a panoply of fresh seasonal vegetables, and for vegetarians especially they offer a rewarding study. While pancetta (unsmoked Italian bacon), bacon, or some other type of preserved pork often adds richness to the broth, the meat is just as often left out entirely, and the richness comes from a dollop of finest-quality olive oil added at the very end as the soup is served. In Italy, freshly grated Parmigiano cheese is always added at the table, and leftover minestrone forms the basis for another frugal soup, the Tuscan favorite called *ribollita* (boiled again!), the next day.

As with fish soups, the technique is similar no matter where you are: aromatics (including pancetta or prosciutto or bacon, if you wish) are sautéed in olive oil, then the vegetables and broth are added. Finally, an enrichment of oil, grated cheese, or whatever is added just before serving.

I've evolved the following basic recipe over the years from the minestrone described by Pellegrino Artusi in *La Scienza in Cucina e l'Arte di Mangiar Bene*, a great cookbook first published in Florence in 1891, still in print (my copy is the 109th edition of the original) and still used regularly in northern Italian home kitchens.

Don't be constrained by the vegetables listed, Artusi counsels—almost anything fresh and seasonal is a happy addition to this spectrum. Cabbage-family vegetables (cabbage itself, Brussels sprouts, turnips, kohlrabi, and so forth) should be added at the end or cooked separately. If cooked a long time in the soup, their strong flavors will dominate.

½  cup white beans, such as cannellini or Great Northern, or borlotti (cranberry) beans, soaked overnight, or use the quick-soak method (page 454)

6  cups rich meat stock (page 83), vegetable broth (page 80), or water

½  small green or Savoy cabbage, slivered

3 or 4 large leaves of red or white Swiss chard, slivered

1  tablespoon finely minced pancetta or prosciutto

1   garlic clove, minced

¼   cup chopped flat-leaf parsley

¼   cup finely chopped onion

2   tablespoons extra-virgin olive oil

2   celery ribs, sliced

2   medium carrots, peeled and diced

1   large potato, peeled and diced

1   large or 2 small zucchini, diced

½   pound ripe tomatoes, peeled (page 454) and chopped, or about 6
      canned whole tomatoes, drained and chopped

other vegetables, such as green beans or peas, greens (kale, turnip greens,
      broccoli), leeks, pumpkin, acorn or butternut squash, turnips,
      diced or slivered, as desired

salt and freshly ground black pepper to taste

½   cup Arborio rice

6 to 8 tablespoons freshly grated Parmigiano cheese


In a small covered saucepan, simmer the drained beans in about 2 cups of the stock until tender but not falling apart—40 minutes to 1 hour, depending on the age of the beans. When done, set aside in the cooking liquid.

Rinse the slivered cabbage and chard in running water and steam for about 15 minutes in the water clinging to the leaves, adding a few tablespoons if necessary to keep the vegetables from scorching. When the vegetables are tender but not falling apart, set aside.

Combine the pancetta, garlic, parsley, and onion and sauté gently in the oil in a heavy stockpot or soup kettle large enough to hold all the vegetables and the stock until just tender but not brown—about 10 to 15 minutes.

Add the remaining vegetables to the pot along with the remaining broth. Bring to a simmer, cover, and cook gently for 20 to 30 minutes, just until the vegetables are tender. Add the cabbage, the chard, and the beans with their cooking liquid. Taste the soup and add salt and pepper if you wish. Stir in the rice and continue cooking for 15 to 20 minutes or until the rice is done. Remove from the heat and serve immediately, with a spoonful of grated cheese on top of each serving. *Makes 6 to 8 servings*

## Nutritional Data, per portion

| | | |
|---|---|---|
| Calories 206 | Carbohydrate 31g | Saturated Fat 2g |
| Protein 9g | Sodium 183mg | Monounsaturated |
| Fat 6g | Cholesterol 5mg | Fat 3g |

**VARIATIONS:** In Majorca, roasted and peeled sweet red peppers, cut into strips, are added, along with a little hot red pepper.

In Lucca, in the lower Arno Valley, a springtime minestrone called *garmucia* includes spring onions, fresh fava beans and peas, diced hearts of small artichokes, and the tips of fresh asparagus, served up with a dollop of the fine, light olive oil for which the region is famous.

In Provence the magnificent soup called *pistou* ("Pee stew!" said Nicholas, age four, when I told him what we were having for supper) is made by stirring a healthy dollop of fragrant basil sauce, similar to Italian pesto, into the basic vegetable mixture at the end. To make pistou sauce, pound in a mortar 3 crushed garlic cloves, 1 cup firmly packed fresh basil leaves, and a pinch of salt. When the mixture is a paste, stir in 3 tablespoons freshly grated Parmigiano and 2 or 3 tablespoons extra-virgin olive oil. You may also substitute a handful of broken vermicelli for the rice in the original.

Tuscan ribollita, an old-fashioned peasant dish once scorned by the gentry and now enjoying tremendous vogue, is made with leftover minestrone, one in which rustic white or borlotti beans are dominant and bourgeois rice is absent. The leftover soup is reheated the next day with 4 or 5 slices of good country bread torn into chunks and mixed in to absorb all the soup's juices. A healthy dollop of the best-quality extra-virgin, preferably unfiltered, olive oil is poured over the top of the very thick soup before serving—robust fare!

In the eastern Mediterranean, and especially in Islamic countries, mutton or preserved mutton (qawarma) takes the place of prosciutto, pancetta, or other pork products. To give a vegetable soup an eastern flavor, sauté some lean cubed lamb with the onions and garlic and add a cinnamon stick and a small amount of allspice to the seasoning of the soup.

# TOMATO SOUP
# MEDITERRANEAN STYLE

**T**his soup has maximum impact late in August and early in September, at the height of tomato season. Take the time to seek out red, ripe, juicy tomatoes from a local farmer who grows them. There's just no point in trying to make something tasty from out-of-season and flavorless ingredients. If you find a good supply of fine tomatoes, however, make the soup in quantities and freeze it. It makes an elegant base for hearty winter vegetarian (and non) soups.

2　medium onions, coarsely chopped

1　garlic clove, crushed with the flat blade of a knife

3　tablespoons extra-virgin olive oil

about 6 pounds ripe, red tomatoes, quartered

1　teaspoon salt or more to taste

1　teaspoon sugar or more to taste

3　fresh thyme sprigs or ½ teaspoon dried, crumbled

½　bay leaf

freshly ground black pepper to taste

GARNISHES (OPTIONAL):

¼　cup slivered fresh basil leaves, 1 tablespoon ground cumin, and the
　　grated zest of 1 lemon or 1 orange; 1 tablespoon per serving finest-
　　quality extra-virgin olive oil; pinch of cayenne pepper; or a little
　　handful of small bread cubes or croutons gently browned in
　　garlic-flavored olive oil

Combine the onions and garlic with the oil and cook in a saucepan large enough to hold all the tomatoes over medium-low heat until the onions are soft and golden but not brown, about 10 to 15 minutes. Toss in the tomatoes and add the salt, sugar, thyme, and bay leaf. Stir to mix well, bring to a boil (the tomatoes will exude a good deal of juice—no more need be added), and cook, uncovered, for about 15 minutes or until the tomatoes are thoroughly cooked and disintegrating.

Puree the soup through the medium disk of a food mill. Or put the soup in a blender or food processor (in small batches if it's easier) and process until the

mixture is thoroughly pureed. Then strain through a sieve to get rid of any seeds and bits of skin. Scrape a plastic disk back and forth over the sieve to push as much of the soup through as possible. Taste and adjust the seasoning, adding salt if desired and lots of black pepper.

This pleasantly thick soup can be served in conventional soup bowls or in mugs for sipping. Garnish with one or more of the garnishes. *Makes 6 to 8 servings*

Nutritional Data, per portion

| | | |
|---|---|---|
| Calories 131 | Carbohydrate 19g | Saturated Fat 1g |
| Protein 3g | Sodium 305mg | Monounsaturated |
| Fat 6g | Cholesterol 0 | Fat 4g |

# CASTILIAN GARLIC SOUP

**S**opa de ajo, from the rather bleak high central plains of Spain, should be pleasantly flavored with warm roasted garlic. Add more than the recipe specifies if you wish. A well-flavored homemade chicken stock is important. Spanish cooks sometimes poach an egg for each serving in the rich stock. Note that you will need to serve the soup in bowls that can go into a hot oven without damage—earthenware bowls are traditionally used in Spain.

8   garlic cloves, peeled

¼   cup extra-virgin olive oil

1   tablespoon sweet paprika

½   teaspoon cayenne pepper

6   cups clear white chicken stock (page 81)

⅓   cup amontillado or oloroso sherry

¼   teaspoon ground cumin

pinch of saffron threads

salt to taste

4   ½-inch-thick slices of crusty bread

4   large eggs (optional)

freshly grated Parmigiano cheese

In a heavy soup kettle or a 2-quart saucepan, gently sauté the garlic in the oil until the cloves are golden brown, about 10 to 15 minutes. Remove the garlic and set aside.

Remove the pan from the heat and stir in the paprika and cayenne. Add the stock and sherry and stir to mix thoroughly. Return to the heat and stir in the cumin and saffron.

Crush each of the garlic cloves with a fork and stir into the soup. Taste for seasoning and add salt if desired. Let the soup simmer gently, covered, for 15 minutes.

While the soup cooks, toast the bread slices on both sides under a preheated broiler. Set aside.

If you wish to add the eggs, poach them, one at a time, in the simmering broth, just stirring the broth to make a whirlpool into which you drop the egg. Poach for 2½ minutes, just until the white firms up and encloses the egg, or longer if you prefer.

Heat the broiler again and fill each bowl with hot soup. Float a slice of toasted bread on top of each serving, sliding an egg under each slice of toasted bread if you're using eggs. (The toast will protect the egg from further exposure to heat.) Sprinkle the bread liberally with grated cheese and slide the bowls into the oven just long enough to melt the cheese on top. *Makes 4 servings*

Nutritional Data, per portion

| | | |
|---|---|---|
| Calories  278 | Carbohydrate  22g | Saturated Fat  3g |
| Protein  6g | Sodium  225mg | Monounsaturated |
| Fat  17g | Cholesterol  0 | Fat  11g |

**VARIATION:** For a more substantial vegetable soup in the same style, add 3 peeled, chopped medium potatoes and 2 cups coarsely chopped deveined spinach leaves with the roasted garlic.

# GAZPACHO SEVILLANO

**G**azpacho is one of the quintessential Mediterranean soups and, along with paella, what most people call to mind when they think of Spanish cuisine. I learned to make this soup, not surprisingly, in Spain, but it became a family favorite in Lebanon, where it was always part of our weekend picnic basket.

Make this as thin or thick as you wish by adding or withholding cold water. Sometimes I make it with no water at all, and instead of whirling the ingredients in a blender I layer them in a tall mason jar, sprinkling each layer with a little salt, sugar, cayenne pepper, and cumin. This makes gazpacho salad—very good for a change.

3½ pounds ripe, red tomatoes, peeled (page 454) and coarsely chopped
(about 6 cups)
1   garlic clove, chopped
½   small red onion, chopped
1   green bell pepper, chopped
1   English cucumber, peeled and chopped
1   cup extra-virgin olive oil
2   tablespoons sherry vinegar or more to taste
1   2-inch slice of stale white country-style bread
½   cup cold water
½   teaspoon ground cumin
pinch of cayenne pepper
salt to taste
sugar to taste

GARNISH:

finely diced cucumber, green bell pepper, onion, and/or
hard-boiled egg

Put the tomatoes, garlic, onion, pepper, and cucumber in a blender and whirl briefly (in small batches if it's easier) to puree. With the blender lid ajar, pour in the oil and vinegar while you continue to process the vegetables.

Tear the bread into small chunks and soak briefly in the cold water. When the bread is soaked thoroughly, gently squeeze out the excess water and add the soaked bread to the blender along with the cumin and cayenne. Process to incorporate thoroughly.

Taste and adjust the seasoning, adding salt and/or a small quantity of sugar if necessary (sugar brings out the flavor of the tomatoes—½ teaspoon should be adequate). More sherry vinegar also may be added to adjust the flavor. If the thoroughly pureed soup seems too thick, add ice-cold water until the desired consistency is reached.

The soup should be light and smooth, almost creamy in consistency. If it is still too coarse in texture, you may press it through a sieve. For picnic purposes it is best served thin enough to sip from a mug, but if you're serving it at table, with a soup dish and spoon, a thicker consistency is fine, and you will want to garnish each plate with the traditional gazpacho garnishes—finely diced cucumber, green pepper, onion, and hard-boiled egg. *Makes 8 servings*

### Nutritional Data, per portion

| | | |
|---|---|---|
| Calories 323 | Carbohydrate 18g | Saturated Fat 4g |
| Protein 3g | Sodium 96mg | Monounsaturated |
| Fat 28g | Cholesterol 0 | Fat 20g |

# AJO BLANCO

### *Andalusian Cold Almond-Garlic Soup*

Like gazpacho, which it resembles in technique if not in flavor, this wonderfully refreshing chilled summer soup has its origins in a simple, humble country preparation of bread, water, and garlic. Ajo blanco (the name means "white garlic"), with regional variations all over southern Spain, is enriched with pounded almonds and served cold in the searing heat of an Andalusian summer. Originally it would have been made with a darkish country bread, but modern cooks emphasize the cool whiteness of the preparation by using a more refined white-flour bread and occasionally adding cream—to my mind, an unnecessary embellishment. If you have a source of freshly harvested almonds, they will add immeasurably to the flavor of the soup; otherwise a few drops of almond extract will bring out the flavor.

¼  **pound (2 cups) shelled almonds**

½  **pound stale crusty country-style bread**

1  **cup water**

1  **cup extra-virgin olive oil**

4  **garlic cloves, minced**

1½ **teaspoons salt**

¼  **cup white wine vinegar**

1  **quart ice water**

**pure almond extract to taste**

GARNISH:

**green seedless grapes, golden raisins, peeled and cubed fresh apple, or**
       **small bread cubes fried in a little olive oil**

Blanch the almonds by dropping them into a pan of boiling water for about 1½ minutes or until the skins are loose enough to slip off. Run under cold water to cool, then skin them. Chop the almonds coarsely with a knife and place in a blender.

Cut the crusts away from the stale bread and tear the crumb into large pieces. (You should have about 3 cups of loosely packed bread.) Put into a bowl with the water, turning the bread so that it absorbs most of the water. Once the water is

absorbed, squeeze the bread gently to rid it of excess water, place it in the food processor, and process in brief spurts to a textured cream. Add the bread to the almonds in the blender. Turn on the blender and slowly pour in the olive oil, blending the contents to a thick cream.

Add the garlic, salt, and vinegar and blend to mix well. With the motor running, add about half the ice water. Transfer the soup to a glass or ceramic container, stir in the remaining water, and refrigerate the soup or put it in the freezer for an hour or so, until ready to serve. Before serving, taste and add more vinegar or salt if necessary or a few drops of almond extract to boost the flavor. The cold olive oil might thicken the soup too much, in which case you should thin it with more ice water.

Add one or two of the garnishes—more would destroy the appealing simplicity of the soup. ***Makes about 6 servings***

### Nutritional Data, per portion

| | | |
|---|---|---|
| Calories 529 | Carbohydrate 23g | Saturated Fat 6g |
| Protein 7g | Sodium 759mg | Monounsaturated |
| Fat 48g | Cholesterol 0 | Fat 36g |

## MEDITERRANEAN BEAN SOUPS

Winter in the Mediterranean is quite mercifully brief, but it can still be harsh, especially in the mountains, where snowfalls always seem to take people by surprise, as if it truly doesn't belong. Sometimes the snow catches me short too, and I have to walk a mile or so to the bottega in Teverina to get milk or coffee or eggs. "*Ha visto la neve, signora?*" Mrs. Coppini always asks—"Did you see the snow?"—as if the six inches lying on the roads, making them too precarious for driving, might have escaped my attention. And yet it snows every winter three or four times.

These hearty soups of beans, grains, and winter vegetables, cooked for days on the hearth in deep terra-cotta pots, are what keep people going in weather like that, and not just the country folk either. On via Borgognona, just off Rome's ultra-chic Piazza di Spagna, a little Tuscan restaurant called da Nino is, for all its rustic appearance, hugely popular at lunchtime with film people, journalists, and what a friend of mine calls "the in crowd." As you push through Nino's door on one of those blustery February days when the wind whips the rain along the Roman cobblestones in horizontal sheets, you will be greeted by the welcome sight of a big fiasco, the old-fashioned bulb-shaped green-glass jar in which Chianti wines used to be shipped, sitting behind the entry window, filled with white beans simmering away in a bath of water, olive oil, salt, and pepper, with just a branch of sage to flavor them. This is fagiuoli al fiasco, a famous Tuscan country dish, and a more rustic and hospitable flavor on such a wintry day you cannot imagine.

Bean soups are not just Tuscan, of course, but a staple all around the Mediterranean. Before New World beans arrived in Europe sometime after 1492, these soups were made with chick-peas (ceci in Italian, garbanzos in Spanish), lentils, and broad or fava beans. Egyptian foul or ful is another Old World bean, a small dark-skinned fava that was perhaps the very bean that fueled the bellies of the builders of the pyramids—unless that was lentils. These Old World beans still form the basis of some of the region's most loved dishes, but a vast panoply of New World beans are also used.

# MEDITERRANEAN BEAN SOUP

### The Basic Recipe

**T**his basic recipe is the soup I cook at home in Tuscany, so it should be called *zuppa di fagioli*. But the principle works, with variations, for many other bean soups. Tuscan cooks use white cannellini beans or cranberry beans (also called *borlotti*), but the soup is just as good with traditional American beans like navy beans, yellow-eyes, and pea beans, or even chick-peas. American big red kidney beans will also do in a pinch, but they are a little crude in flavor for this dish and will give it an unappetizing red color.

1    medium to large onion, coarsely chopped

2 or 3 medium carrots, peeled and coarsely chopped

1 or 2 garlic cloves, crushed with the flat blade of a knife

2    tablespoons extra-virgin olive oil, plus more to taste for garnish

2    cups dried beans, soaked overnight, or use the quick-soak method
        (page 454)

8 to 10 cups boiling water

1    tablespoon fresh thyme, or 1 teaspoon dried, crumbled

1 or 2 bay leaves to taste

about ¼ cup chopped flat-leaf parsley, plus more for garnish

salt and freshly ground black pepper to taste

In a heavy stockpot or soup kettle over medium heat, gently sauté the onion, carrots, and garlic in the oil until the vegetables are soft but not browned, 10 to 15 minutes. Add the drained beans to the stockpot along with the boiling water. Add the herbs, except the salt and pepper. (Traditional cooks hold off on the salt until the beans are thoroughly softened; the theory, which I have not been able to prove, is that salt toughens protein and hardens the beans.)

Cook the beans, covered, over low heat for 1½ to 3 hours, adding boiling water from time to time if necessary. Cooking time varies with the age of the beans, and since there is no way to tell whether dried beans are this season's crop, you have to follow your good sense. In any case, if the beans finish cooking before you're ready

to serve them, it doesn't matter—they reheat splendidly. When the beans are soft, taste and adjust the seasonings.

Before serving, you may want to remove about 1½ cups of the beans, puree them in a blender or a food mill, and return them to the pot to thicken the soup. If the soup is too thick, on the other hand, it may be thinned by adding hot water or some crushed canned tomatoes with their juices. In any case, be sure to taste the soup and adjust the salt and pepper before serving.

Serve the soup as is, with chopped parsley sprinkled over and a drizzle of the best green olive oil you can buy. Or garnish it with croutons or, to do it in true Mediterranean style, for each serving toast a thick slice of densely textured country-style bread, rub it with a cut clove of garlic, sprinkle it with olive oil and salt, and float it in the middle of the soup plate. ***Makes 8 servings***

Nutritional Data, per portion

| | | |
|---|---|---|
| Calories 220 | Carbohydrate 35g | Saturated Fat 1g |
| Protein 12g | Sodium 18mg | Monounsaturated |
| Fat 4g | Cholesterol 0 | Fat 3g |

**VARIATION:** Add a chopped tomato in season or a dollop of tomato concentrate with the herbs.

# FASSOLADA

*Greek White Bean Soup*

**T**his version of Greek bean soup reverses the usual procedure, sautéing lots of vegetables and adding them halfway through the cooking.

1½ cups large white beans or cannellini, soaked overnight, or use the
     quick-soak method (page 454)

10 cups cool water

¼ cup extra-virgin olive oil

3 medium onions, coarsely chopped

2 medium carrots, peeled and sliced

3 celery ribs, coarsely chopped

2 green bell peppers, diced

3 tablespoons tomato puree

juice of ½ lemon

salt and freshly ground black pepper to taste

Drain the beans and place in a heavy soup kettle or stockpot with the cool water. Bring to a boil, cover, and simmer for 30 minutes.

Meanwhile, heat the oil in a skillet and gently sauté the onions, carrots, and celery until the vegetables are soft but not browned—about 10 to 15 minutes. Add the peppers and continue cooking for 5 minutes or so, until the peppers are starting to soften.

After the beans have cooked for 30 minutes, pour the vegetables and their oil into the pot with them. Add the tomato puree, stirring to dissolve, and continue simmering for 30 minutes or more, until the beans are very tender. Cooking time will vary with the age of the beans. At the end of the cooking time, stir the lemon juice into the soup. Taste and add salt and pepper if necessary. ***Makes 6 to 8 servings***

Nutritional Data, per portion

| | | |
|---|---|---|
| Calories 228 | Carbohydrate 33g | Saturated Fat 1g |
| Protein 10g | Sodium 51mg | Monounsaturated |
| Fat 8g | Cholesterol 0 | Fat 6g |

# WHITE BEAN AND FARRO SOUP

**F**arro is an old-fashioned type of wheat, said to be the grain that fed the Roman armies. It has recently come back into fashion in Italy as Italians begin to appreciate and grow nostalgic for the old culinary traditions. Farro is available in this country from specialty food stores such as Dean & Deluca in New York (see address in the Resources at the back of the book), but you can substitute grains of soft white wheat (or wheat berries), available at health food stores. (Kamut is one soft-wheat grain that is often available.) Don't use hard red wheat, however, because it never becomes as tender as soft wheat.

1½ cups cannellini or borlotti (cranberry) beans, soaked overnight

1    cup farro or soft-wheat berries, soaked overnight

1    medium onion, coarsely chopped

1    garlic clove, coarsely chopped

1    celery rib, coarsely chopped

1    medium carrot, peeled and coarsely chopped

2 or 3 fresh sage leaves to taste

2 or 3 fresh rosemary sprigs to taste

2 or 3 fresh oregano or marjoram sprigs to taste or

    ½ teaspoon dried oregano, crumbled

2    tablespoons fruity extra-virgin olive oil, plus more for garnish

3    tablespoons homemade or canned tomato sauce

1    3-inch cinnamon stick

6    whole cloves

salt and freshly ground black pepper to taste

a little minced flat-leaf parsley

Drain the soaked beans and place in a saucepan. Cover with fresh water to a depth of 1 inch and cook, covered, over gentle heat until the beans are very tender—1 to 1½ hours, depending on the age of the beans. Check the beans from time to time and add boiling water as necessary—they should always be about an inch deep in boiling water.

While the beans are cooking, simmer the farro or wheat berries in water or

stock to cover until the wheat is just tender—about 15 minutes. Set aside in the cooking liquid.

When the beans are done, drain them, *reserving their cooking liquid.* Pass the beans through a food mill or puree in a blender, using a little of the cooking liquid if necessary to ease the process.

Chop the onion, garlic, celery, carrot, sage, rosemary, and oregano together. In a heavy saucepan or soup kettle over medium-low heat, gently sauté the vegetables and herbs in the oil until the vegetables are soft but not browned—about 10 minutes. Add the tomato sauce, cinnamon stick, cloves, and a little salt and pepper. Stir to mix well, cover, and cook gently together for about 15 minutes.

Add the pureed beans with about a cup of their cooking liquid and the farro or wheat berries with all their cooking liquid. Cover and let cook for about an hour or until the farro is very tender. Check the level of cooking liquid from time to time, adding bean liquid or boiling water when necessary to keep the soup from sticking. When the farro is tender, adjust the seasoning, adding salt and pepper if necessary. Remove the cinnamon stick and cloves. Serve the soup immediately, garnishing each plate with a drizzle of fruity extra-virgin oil and, if you wish, a little parsley.
*Makes 8 servings*

Nutritional Data, per portion

| | | |
|---|---|---|
| Calories 253 | Carbohydrate 42g | Saturated Fat trace |
| Protein 12g | Sodium 44mg | Monounsaturated |
| Fat 5g | Cholesterol 0 | Fat 3g |

# EGYPTIAN LENTIL SOUP

**T**he fancy version of this soup is made with a little finely ground lean lamb or beef to enrich the flavor, but a vegetarian version is just as good and more typical of the lentil soup that has nourished Egyptians since the beginning of history. I like to use a mixture of brown and peeled red lentils: the red lentils disintegrate in the soup stock and give it a lovely creaminess. (From Bharti Kirchner, an authority on Indian and Bengali food, I learned that red lentils are called *Egyptian lentils, masur dal* in Hindi—just one more on the list of culinary links between the eastern Mediterranean and the subcontinent.) All brown lentils may also be used, but they will not disintegrate.

1  large onion, coarsely chopped

1  carrot, peeled and coarsely chopped

2 to 3 ounces finely ground lean lamb or beef to taste (optional)

2  tablespoons extra-virgin olive oil

1  teaspoon ground cumin

1  teaspoon fennel seeds

1½ cups brown lentils, or 1 cup brown lentils and ½ cup red lentils

2  quarts water

1  small dried red chili (optional)

juice of ½ lemon or more to taste

salt and freshly ground black pepper to taste

GARNISH (OPTIONAL):

1  small onion, peeled and thinly sliced, the slices warmed and softened,
   but not cooked, in ¼ cup best-quality extra-virgin olive oil

lemon wedges for serving

Pick over the lentils, discarding any small stones or other debris. In a heavy stockpot or soup kettle, gently sauté the onion, carrot, and ground meat if desired in the olive oil until the vegetables are soft and the meat is very brown—about 15 minutes. Stir in the cumin and fennel and add the lentils and water. Add the chili if desired.

Cook until the lentils are tender, about 30 minutes. Remove the chili. Add the

lemon juice and taste for seasoning, adding salt and pepper if desired. Garnish each serving, if you wish, with the onion slices and their oil. Serve with lemon wedges to squeeze over the soup. **Makes 6 to 8 servings**

Nutritional Data, per portion

| | | |
|---|---|---|
| Calories 169 | Carbohydrate 24g | Saturated Fat 1g |
| Protein 11g | Sodium 8mg | Monounsaturated |
| Fat 4g | Cholesterol 0 | Fat 3g |

**VARIATION:** Add a cup of chopped green chard or spinach with the lentils.

# SEPHARDIC RED LENTIL
# AND BULGUR SOUP

**T**his is a wonderfully restorative potion to counteract the damp and chilly winds that swoop down the Bosporus in wintertime. Don't be put off by the humble ingredients. Though porridgelike in consistency, the soup has a wonderful flavor. It's adapted from a description in the collection of Sephardic recipes compiled by Viki Koronyo and Sima Ovadya, *Sefarad Yemekleri* (Istanbul, 1990).

1½ cups red lentils

3 cups water

1 cup coarse bulgur

2 cups very hot water

1 teaspoon salt or to taste

3 tablespoons extra-virgin olive oil

1 teaspoon crumbled dried red chili, hot red pepper flakes, or hot paprika

1 teaspoon ground cumin

2 medium onions, halved and finely sliced

Pick over the lentils, discarding any small stones or other debris. Bring the water to a rolling boil. Add the lentils, lower the heat, cover, and simmer for about 15 minutes. The lentils will disintegrate into a lovely pale yellow cream.

While the lentils are cooking, mix the bulgur in a bowl with the hot water. Set

aside to let the grains absorb all the water. When the lentils are done and very soft, add the bulgur to them together with any leftover soaking liquid and the salt to taste. Stir to mix well. Cover the soup and keep in a warm place.

In a skillet over medium-high heat, sauté the onions in the olive oil, stirring frequently, until the onions are soft and golden brown, about 15 minutes. Add the cumin midway through the cooking. At the end, when the onions are golden, take them off the heat and stir in the chili. Then stir the onions into the soup.

If the soup is too thick and porridgy for your taste, add ¼ to ½ cup boiling water. Heat the soup to serving temperature, but do not cook again. Serve immediately. *Makes 6 servings*

Nutritional Data, per portion

| | | |
|---|---|---|
| Calories 326 | Carbohydrate 50g | Saturated Fat 1g |
| Protein 17g | Sodium 378mg | Monounsaturated |
| Fat 8g | Cholesterol 0 | Fat 6g |

# PROVENÇAL CHICK-PEA SOUP

**O**n the island of Crete, chick-pea flour is used in bread making, while in Provence and along the Italian Riviera, chick-pea flour is used to make panisse or panissa, a sort of chick-pea polenta. Once the polenta has set, it's sliced into little cakes and deep-fried in olive oil—delicious!

Chick-pea soup is a lot easier, however, and with an impressive flavor from the addition of fennel seeds and orange peel, very typical flavors of this part of the Med. Serve the soup over toasted slices of country bread that have been rubbed lightly with garlic and drizzled with olive oil.

½  **pound dried chick-peas, soaked overnight, or use the quick-soak method (page 454)**

2  **quarts cold water**

**salt to taste**

1  **medium onion, sliced**

2  **leeks, white parts only, rinsed well and sliced**

3  **tablespoons extra-virgin olive oil, plus a little more for garnish**

1   large ripe red tomato, chopped

1   2-inch strip of orange zest, cut into julienne strips

1   teaspoon freshly ground fennel seeds

freshly ground black pepper to taste

GARNISH:

6   slices of country-style bread, lightly toasted

Drain the chick-peas, place in a heavy soup kettle or stockpot, and add the cold water. Bring to a boil, lower the heat, cover, and simmer until the chick-peas are tender and their skins are loose.

If you wish, remove the chick-peas from their cooking liquid (*don't discard the liquid*) and, when they are cool enough to handle, pull away and discard the skins, a nicety of professional chefs that need not be observed for the family table.

Puree about half the chick-peas with a little of their cooking liquid in a blender or food processor. Return to the soup (that is, the remaining chick-peas and remaining cooking liquid) and stir to blend well. The puree should be creamy but not too thick and studded with whole chick-peas. Taste and add salt if you wish. Cover and keep warm.

In a skillet over medium-low heat, gently sauté the onion and leeks in the oil until soft but not browned—about 10 to 15 minutes. Add the tomato, orange zest, and fennel and cook for 3 or 4 minutes, just long enough to thicken the sauce a little. Then turn it into the soup kettle with the chick-peas and their liquid. Taste and add more salt, if necessary, and lots of black pepper.

Bring the soup back to a gentle simmer and serve over toasted bread with a thread of olive oil drizzled on top. *Makes 6 servings*

Nutritional Data, per portion

| | | |
|---|---|---|
| Calories  225 | Carbohydrate  29g | Saturated Fat  1g |
| Protein  8g | Sodium  16mg | Monounsaturated |
| Fat  9g | Cholesterol  0 | Fat  6g |

# LEBLEBI

### *Tunisian Chick-Pea Soup*

Leblebi is a mainstay of the Tunisian diet, for rich and poor, country folk and city dwellers alike. Similar soups can be found all over North Africa, but what makes leblebi special is the elaborate selection of garnishes. You needn't use all of these by any means—a spoonful of capers and a sprinkle of chopped scallions, together with a dollop of olive oil, make a fine soup—although the more garnishes you present, the more the soup becomes worthy of special occasions.

Leblebi can also be made with chicken or beef stock, homemade of course, for an even richer presentation. If you use stock, add a little diced chicken or beef as one of the garnishes.

If you're using commercially prepared harissa (the kind that comes in a tube), be wary and add it in small quantities—it is usually much hotter than homemade.

1¼ cups dried chick-peas, soaked overnight in 2 cups water, or use the
    quick-soak method (page 454)

5    cups boiling water

1    teaspoon ground cumin or cumin seeds, or more to taste

1    teaspoon salt or more to taste

4    fat garlic cloves, coarsely chopped

1    tablespoon harissa (page 301) or to taste

1    medium onion, halved and thinly sliced, slices softened in 1
    tablespoon extra-virgin olive oil

6    ½-inch-thick slices of dense country-style bread, preferably day-old

GARNISHES:

¼    cup coarsely chopped drained capers

½    cup thinly sliced pickled turnip (page 306)

2    hard-boiled eggs, coarsely chopped, or 1 3½-ounce can best-quality
    tuna, drained and flaked

a few tablespoons ground cumin

⅓    cup harissa (page 301)

⅓    cup thinly sliced scallion, both white and green parts

a cruet of extra-virgin olive oil

2   lemons, quartered

salt and freshly ground black pepper to taste

Drain the chick-peas of their soaking liquid and place them in a 2-quart saucepan or soup kettle. Add the boiling water and place over low heat. Cover and bring the water back to a boil. Cook at a very slow simmer for about 20 minutes or until the chick-peas have started to soften but are not yet ready to eat. Time will vary, depending on the age and size of the chick-peas.

If you're using whole cumin seeds, crush them with the salt in a mortar, then add the garlic and crush to a paste. You can also grind the cumin seeds in an electric coffee grinder kept for grinding spices; place the ground cumin in a small bowl and then mix with the salt; using the back of a spoon, crush the chopped garlic into the spice mixture. Either method should produce a fine, homogenous paste of garlic, salt, and cumin.

Add the garlic-spice paste with the tablespoon of harissa to the simmering soup and stir to mix well. Continue simmering the soup for 5 minutes or so to let the flavors develop, then taste and add more salt, cumin, or harissa if desired.

Continue cooking, covered, another 15 to 20 minutes over very low heat, until the chick-peas are soft. Add the onion slices and their olive oil and cook for 15 minutes longer.

Arrange the garnishes in bowls or saucers on a tray or in a sectioned relish dish, together with the cruet of olive oil, salt, and a pepper mill.

Have ready 6 individual soup bowls. Remove the crusts from the bread slices and tear a slice into coarse, irregular chunks, each no more than ½ inch thick. Drop the bread chunks from each slice into the bottom of a soup bowl. Ladle about ½ to ¾ cup of the broth over the bread to soften it, then ladle on the chick-peas. Proceed with the rest of the soup bowls and serve immediately, passing the garnishes so that each person can add whatever is desired. *Makes 6 servings*

Nutritional Data, per portion, using eggs

| | | |
|---|---|---|
| Calories   378 | Carbohydrate   52g | Saturated Fat   2g |
| Protein   15g | Sodium   658mg | Monounsaturated |
| Fat   15g | Cholesterol   71mg | Fat   8g |

Nutritional Data, per portion, using tuna

| | | |
|---|---|---|
| Calories   381 | Carbohydrate   52g | Saturated Fat   2g |
| Protein   16g | Sodium   721mg | Monounsaturated |
| Fat   15g | Cholesterol   7mg | Fat   8g |

SOUPS

# CHICK-PEA, CHICKEN, AND RICE SOUP FROM ALEPPO

**T**his soup has been a favorite since I first had it years ago in a restaurant off Hamra Street in Ras Beirut that specialized in cuisine from Aleppo. The cinnamon marks it as from the region of the Lebanese–Syrian–South Turkish littoral, where flavors that we associate with sweet cakes and cookies, like cinnamon, clove, and allspice, are used very successfully in soups and stews. Don't let the simplicity of this deceive you—it's an astonishingly good dish for cold days and nights.

¾ cup dried chick-peas, soaked overnight, or use the quick-soak
   method (page 454)

2 quarts clear white chicken stock (page 81) with the breast meat of the
   cooked chicken diced and reserved

½ cup long-grain rice

1 medium onion, chopped

2 garlic cloves, minced

2 tablespoons extra-virgin olive oil

1 teaspoon ground cinnamon

½ teaspoon ground cumin

salt and freshly ground black pepper to taste

In a covered heavy kettle or stockpot, simmer the drained chick-peas in the chicken stock for an hour or more, until they are thoroughly cooked but not falling apart. Add the rice and continue cooking until the rice is tender but not bursting, 15 to 20 minutes. Stir in the reserved chicken and continue cooking just long enough to heat it through. Taste the stock and adjust seasoning if necessary. Cover and keep warm.

In a small skillet, gently sauté the onion and garlic in the oil until soft but not browned—about 10 to 15 minutes. Stir in the cinnamon and cumin and cook 5 minutes longer or until the aroma of the spices begins to rise. Stir the mixture into the soup, return to a simmer, taste, adding salt and pepper, and serve immediately.
***Makes 6 to 8 servings***

# CATALAN SOUP OF WHITE BEANS AND CLAMS

**I**f you can find little mahogany clams (in the East) or Manila clams (in the West), serve them in their shells. Otherwise, use the larger littlenecks and discard the shells after the clams are cooked.

**FOR THE BEANS:**

2   medium yellow onions, chopped

6   garlic cloves, chopped

2   tablespoons extra-virgin olive oil

½   pound dried white beans, soaked overnight, or use the quick-soak method (page 454)

1   quart cold water

salt to taste

**FOR THE CLAMS:**

1   pound onions, finely chopped

4   garlic cloves, finely chopped

¼   cup extra-virgin olive oil

2   pounds ripe, red tomatoes, peeled (page 454), or 1 28-ounce can whole tomatoes with liquid, coarsely chopped

1   teaspoon sugar

2   small dried red chilies, crumbled

1   cup dry white wine

salt and freshly ground black pepper to taste

2   pounds mahogany, Manila, or littleneck clams

**GARNISH:**

¼   cup finely minced flat-leaf parsley and the zest of a lemon sliced into very fine julienne shreds

SOUPS

In the bottom of a heavy stockpot or soup kettle, sauté the onions and garlic in the olive oil until vegetables are tender but not browned. Drain the beans and add them to the cooked vegetables along with the water. Bring to a boil, turn the heat down to simmer, cover, and cook the beans until tender—45 minutes to 1 hour, depending on the size and age of the beans. Add the salt. When the beans are tender but not falling apart, remove from heat and set aside.

In another kettle, gently sauté the chopped onions and garlic in the oil until the vegetables are tender but not browned—about 10 to 15 minutes. Add the tomatoes, sugar, and chilies, raise the heat slightly, and continue cooking for 5 to 10 minutes or until the tomato sauce thickens. Add the wine and raise the heat to high. Cook, stirring frequently, until the alcohol has cooked off, about 5 to 7 minutes. Taste the sauce, adding salt and pepper if necessary.

The beans and tomato sauce may be prepared ahead of time and reheated just before cooking the clams.

Scrub the clams well before cooking them and discard any that stay firmly closed. If you're using mahogany or Manila clams, simply toss the well-cleaned clams into the bubbling tomato sauce and cook until all the clams are open—about 5 to 8 minutes.

Put littlenecks, which often have more sand and grit, in a large, heavy skillet and shake the pan over medium-high heat until all the clams have opened, not more than 5 minutes. Discard the shells and any clams that have not opened and toss the clams into the tomato sauce. (Any liquid exuded by the clams can be strained through a double layer of cheesecloth or a fine-mesh sieve directly into the tomato sauce.) Do not let the clams continue cooking in the sauce, or they will toughen.

Serve the beans in shallow soup plates with the clam-tomato sauce in the center of each plate. Garnish with parsley and a few strands of lemon zest. *Makes 8 servings*

### Nutritional Data, per portion

| | | |
|---|---|---|
| Calories 286 | Carbohydrate 33g | Saturated Fat 2g |
| Protein 11g | Sodium 29mg | Monounsaturated |
| Fat 11g | Cholesterol 6mg | Fat 8g |

**VARIATION:** Substitute 2 pounds medium shrimp for the clams. Peel the shrimp, devein them if necessary, and cook in the tomato sauce 2 to 3 minutes.

# MOROCCAN HARIRA

Harira, a thick and meaty stew of beans and lentils, is found all over North Africa in one form or another. This is the version Sakina el-Alaoui makes in her Marrakesh kitchen. Sakina uses smen, Moroccan preserved butter, to fry the meat and onions. American cooks will prefer a good olive oil.

1½ cups chick-peas, soaked overnight, or use the quick-soak method
       (page 454)
1    pound very lean boneless beef
1    large onion, chopped
3    tablespoons extra-virgin olive oil
1    tablespoon freshly ground black pepper or to taste
½    cup finely chopped flat-leaf parsley
¼    cup finely chopped cilantro
1    celery rib, green tops included, chopped
1    teaspoon ground ginger
1    3-inch cinnamon stick
1    gallon water, or half water and half meat or chicken stock (page 83
       or 81)
1    cup lentils, preferably small brown lentils
1    14-ounce can whole tomatoes with their liquid
2    tablespoons canned tomato sauce
pinch of saffron threads
1½ cups water for thickener
½    cup unbleached all-purpose flour
salt to taste

Drain the chick-peas and set aside.

Cut the meat into very small pieces—about ½-inch cubes. In a large heavy soup kettle over medium heat, sauté the meat and onion in the oil, stirring occasionally, until the meat is brown and the onions are golden—about 20 minutes. Add the pepper, half the parsley, half the cilantro, the celery, ginger, and cinnamon and stir to mix well. Cook for about 5 minutes, just until the scent of the aromatics begins to

rise. Add 2 quarts of the water and bring to a boil. Turn the heat down and simmer the meat, covered, for 1½ hours.

Place the drained chick-peas in a separate saucepan with the remaining 2 quarts water and simmer, covered, for about 1½ hours or until the chick-peas are tender. Add the lentils and continue simmering, covered, until the lentils are just tender—about 20 minutes longer, depending on the age of the lentils.

Break up the canned tomatoes and add to the meat with the tomato sauce and saffron. Raise the heat to medium-high and continue cooking, uncovered, for about 10 minutes or until the sauce has reduced somewhat and the meat is very tender.

Remove the cinnamon stick from the meat stock. Add the chick-pea–lentil soup to the meat soup, stir to mix, and cook at a very bare simmer while you prepare the thickening.

Place 1½ cups water in a medium bowl. A little at a time, and beating with a fork, add the flour to make a cream. Stir the cream slowly into the soup and simmer for 15 minutes or until the broth is thick and the taste of raw flour has cooked away. Taste the soup and add salt and more pepper if desired. Garnish the soup with the reserved parsley and cilantro and serve immediately. ***Makes 10 servings***

### Nutritional Data, per portion

| | | |
|---|---|---|
| Calories 312 | Carbohydrate 39g | Saturated Fat 1g |
| Protein 23g | Sodium 122mg | Monounsaturated |
| Fat 8g | Cholesterol 26mg | Fat 4g |

# TANDIR ÇORBASI

### *Turkish Hearty Multibean Soup*

**T**his soup is supposed to be cooked in a tandir, or pit oven—the Turkish word is the same as *tandoor*, the Hindi word for the oven and for the style of cooking familiar to us from Indian restaurants. The oven and the cooking style are also typical of central Anatolia, especially the Konya region, where Nevin Halici, whose recipe this is, studies and writes about Turkish cuisine.

2    ounces finely ground lean lamb or beef

1    medium onion, finely chopped

2    tablespoons extra-virgin olive oil

¼    cup tomato puree

½    cup lentils

½    cup dried chick-peas, soaked overnight, or use the quick-soak
       method (page 454)

½    cup dried cannellini or small white beans, soaked overnight, or use
       the quick-soak method (page 454)

½    cup bulgur

6    cups rich meat stock (page 83)

1    teaspoon hot red pepper flakes

½    teaspoon freshly ground black pepper

½    teaspoon dried mint, crumbled

salt to taste

In a heavy saucepan or soup kettle, sauté the ground meat and onion in the oil, stirring frequently, until the meat is brown and the onions are golden—about 20 minutes. Stir in the tomato puree and cook for another 5 minutes, stirring constantly so that the sauce doesn't burn. Add the lentils, drained chick-peas, drained beans, and bulgur, stirring to mix well; then pour on the stock. Add the chili, pepper, mint, and salt and bring to a boil. Lower the heat, cover, and simmer slowly for 2 to 2½ hours or until the beans and chick-peas are soft and tender. Taste and adjust the seasoning, adding more salt, pepper, and mint if desired. ***Makes 8 servings***

SOUPS

Nutritional Data, per portion

| | | |
|---|---|---|
| Calories 228 | Carbohydrate 35g | Saturated Fat 1g |
| Protein 13g | Sodium 51mg | Monounsaturated |
| Fat 5g | Cholesterol 5mg | Fat 3g |

# CHAPTER THREE

# BREADS, FLATBREADS, PIZZAS, AND SAVORY PIES

*N*ear Ephesus in southern Turkey, an old woman makes *saç* bread, thin oniony layers baked on a griddle that looks like an upside-down wok perched over an open fire. In Marrakesh in Morocco, a well-to-do lady rises at dawn to set the dough for the semolina bread she herself makes each day for an extended family that includes half a dozen servants. In the crowded alleys of the medieval souk in Fez, children balance on their heads wooden trays piled with pale, dimpled loaves of dough, on their way to the neighborhood baker. In Egypt, village women bake paper-thin flatbread, as they have for at least 5,000 years, by pressing it against the hot and gritty outside of a hand-built mud oven. In Tuscany and in Greece, when the flames have died in the household oven and the walls are white with heat, housewives thrust in great round grainy loaves made weekly from wheat raised on terraces below the farmhouse and ground at the local mill. And in Naples and Nice and Marseilles, the *pizzaiuoli* work at a feverish pace, flipping flat round disks into domed ovens so hot they could fire pottery, so hot the pizza is done in two minutes flat.

You could spend a lifetime researching, cooking, and writing about all the different breads of the Mediterranean, and in the end you might feel you had only begun. In this part of the world, where the value and power of yeasted grain was probably first encountered and where bread has been such a vital element in the diet since the beginning of history, possibly even earlier, the variety of breads and yeasted products is amazing.

Ceres, in the old religion the goddess of grain and the harvest, retains her power

as a symbol of sustenance and life. Bread was one of the holiest offerings solicited for the dead god-kings of Egypt ("thousands of bread and thousands of beer," the ancient formulas intone), just as today it is raised to a sacrament in the Christian Mass. For the same reason, all over the Mediterranean the sacred loaves are baked and blessed each Friday at the beginning of the Jewish Sabbath, and bread, or cake, broken and shared between bride and groom, is the symbol of a new beginning, a new family.

The reason is simple: bread is, for the people of the Mediterranean and their cultural descendants throughout the Western world, the fundamental food. In blessing it and sharing it we recognize, if only tangentially, our connection with each other, with our past as a community, and with the earth that offers us the grain from which we grind the flour to bake our daily bread.

There is a subtler reason at work as well. For in the action of yeast we perceive in a dramatic and immediate form the very beginnings of life itself. Yeast is nothing on its own, a lump of clayey matter or, for most of us today, dry granulated dust that lies inert in the palm of the hand. But mix it with warm, salty water, stir it with ground grain—whether wheat, rye, or barley—knead it and coax it and set it to rest in a hospitable environment, and it begins to stir and grow and come alive. Then pop it into the hot womb of the oven, and it becomes something quite phenomenal, not only symbolic of life but life-giving matter, in and of itself. Food.

## INGREDIENTS

When I bake bread in this country, I use King Arthur all-purpose flour from Vermont, an unbleached, unbromated white flour ground from hard red wheat from the western prairies and untreated with chemicals. Hard red wheat is naturally high in gluten-producing protein (13 grams of protein in 4 ounces, according to the King Arthur label), which makes it best for bread making. King Arthur flour is available by mail order (see Resources at the back of the book) and in many grocery stores in the Northeast. But if you don't have access to it, look for a flour of similar strength and quality.

In the recipes that follow, I have given instructions for using active dry yeast, the granulated form that comes in little envelopes or is sold loose at health food stores.

## Working with a Sourdough Starter

But the most traditional and, in my opinion, the best leavening for bread dough is a piece of dough from an earlier baking that has been held back and kept in a cool place for at least 24 hours. You may be more familiar with the name *sourdough* for this process, although when properly maintained the dough should not really be sour at all but rather have the well-developed tang that all fermented foods, from wine to sauerkraut, derive from lactic fermentation. Sourdough is not unique to San Francisco or to Forty-Niners. Since baking began, it has been the most common way to preserve the leaven, in home kitchens as well as commercial bakeries, but since commercial yeasts became widely available, the traditional method has lapsed.

It is so very easy, however, that I urge it on anyone who intends to bake bread at least once every 10 days or so. Well do I remember, from what my children call those hippy-dippy days of yore, bakers who would proudly open a refrigerator to show you a jar of sourdough that they'd kept going for six years or more, a base of nearly solid library paste covered by a thin and yellowish liquid. Like much of what we did in those days, there was something more than a little murky and unseemly about it. There is no reason to go to such lengths, and it may help to get over that if you simply think of each baking as raising a sponge of flour, yeast, and water, then removing a cup of it and setting it aside in a covered glass jar for the next baking.

Some baking instructions will tell you to "feed" your sourdough starter, if you're not able to use it every 10 days or so, with additional flour and water. The irresistible image that springs to mind is of some earnest yuppie on an extended business trip, clutching his jar of sourdough starter so he can feed it regularly while he's away from home. Believe me, this is just too complicated. If you have to go away for a couple of weeks, for heaven's sake, leave behind the sourdough starter or reserved dough or whatever you want to call it. If it isn't any good when you get back, throw it out and start afresh. Life is too short to worry about things like that.

If you want to use the traditional method, start the following recipe. After the first rising, you will have what's called the *sponge*. Before you add the barley, rye, or whole-wheat flour, remove a cup of the sponge, transfer it to a glass container (a mason jar is perfect), cover it, and store it in the refrigerator. (The country bread recipe, having had a cup of starter removed, will make a little less than usual, but that's okay just this once.) The one important thing to remember about starter or reserved dough is that it will work best if it contains nothing but yeast, water, and unbleached all-purpose wheat flour. No eggs, butter, fats, milk, or anything of

BREADS, FLATBREADS, PIZZAS, AND SAVORY PIES

that ilk should be added to the sponge before the cup of reserved dough has been removed. The starter will keep for 10 days. (If you want to keep it longer, you should feed it with equal quantities of unbleached all-purpose flour and tepid water, ½ cup of each. Let the starter come to room temperature, stir in the flour and water, then let it sit at room temperature for an hour or so before returning it to the refrigerator.)

When you want to use starter to make bread, take a cup of reserved dough out of the refrigerator and, using a spatula, scrape it into a bowl. (In cold weather, rinse the bowl with hot water to make a warmer, more comfortable environment for the starter.) Simply substitute the cup of starter for the yeast. (I know, this increases the overall quantity of the recipe, but believe me, it will all work out in the end.) Starter works best for true bread recipes rather than quick-rising flatbreads like Arab pita and Neapolitan pizza. But in the very best *pizzerie* of Naples, the traditional leavening to this day is a piece of dough held back from the day before.

You should feel free to experiment with the starter and with other aspects of bread making. Bread is about the most forgiving thing in the entire kitchen repertoire—even when something doesn't turn out the way you wanted or expected, the smells that emanate from baking bread will convince anyone in sniffing range that wonderful things are happening.

If you work with a baking stone, which produces the best texture in breads and pizzas, note that you must put the *cold stone* in the *cold* oven, to avoid cracking the stone. Turn the oven on to the desired temperature and preheat for at least 30 minutes, even though the oven light goes off. The oven will have reached the desired temperature after 5 minutes or so, but it takes a lot longer to heat the stone thoroughly.

## BREAKFAST IN THE MEDITERRANEAN WORLD

**T**ell me what you eat for breakfast, and I will tell you who you are. Or at least I will tell you what part of the Mediterranean you come from.

In America, breakfast goes two ways. We have either big fat breakfasts (eggs and bacon, toast with butter and jam, home fries on the side) or little skinny ones (cuppa java with skim milk and artificial sweetener). And no matter which we choose, we feel guilty because we know we're not doing it right.

In Mediterranean countries many people don't even consider breakfast a meal. And it's been that way for a long time. In the late Middle Ages, Francesco di Marco Datini, an anxious, fretful, but eminently successful wool merchant from Prato, the industrial town north of Florence, took no breakfast at all. In that, says his biographer Iris Origo, Datini was like most people of his time, in Tuscany and elsewhere. Those who ate breakfast did so only for therapeutic reasons, often to combat the threat of plague. In any case, since coffee and tea were unknown, such a breakfast was but a piece of toasted bread and a glass of wine.

Farm families today have big bowls of half-milk, half-coffee, sweetened with sugar, and perhaps a wedge of stale bread to dip in it, while in cities like Madrid and Rome the bars and cafés (unlike here, they're often the same thing) are thronged in the early-morning rush hour with workers and students, standing up and hurriedly gulping cappuccino while between sips they nibble on some sort of sweet, sticky bun or, in Spain, on crisp *churros*, ropes and twists of deep-fried dough. These bar scenes are a nutritionist's worst nightmare as anxious mothers stuff their children with sugar, fat, and caffeine before putting them happily, smock fronts sprinkled with powdered sugar, on the bus for school.

There are parts of the Mediterranean, though, where breakfast would make even a home economist content: In Morocco, workers stop at street-corner holes-in-the-wall for thick purees of stewed fava beans, mixed with olive oil and redolent of garlic, with glasses of mint tea to wash it down. In Barcelona, along with the obligatory café con leche, breakfasters munch on

*continued*

*pa amb tomaquet* (pahm toh-MAH-kett), glorious small buns of baguette bread, split and lightly toasted, rubbed with garlic and halves of dead-ripe red cherry tomatoes, smashed well into the bread, and topped with olive oil.

My all-time favorite Mediterranean breakfast, however, comes from the Levant. Tewfiq Salah, a large and ebullient Palestinian who served as our occasional driver in Beirut, introduced me to this one morning many years ago at the start of a trip over the mountains to Damascus. Once the introduction was made, I was hooked for life.

The Continental Hotel, where the Beirut drivers had their headquarters, was not far from the university. In the freshness of early morning, when even in summer a breath of cool air off the sea bathes the city, I would walk up the hill to a sidewalk café to join Tewfiq for coffee and bread from a nearby bakery, fresh from the oven, its aromas rich and complex with the fragrance of yeast and roasted wheat. This was usually Arab bread, *khubz'arabee*, flat and thick, sometimes lightly sprinkled with a delicious mixture of olive oil, wild thyme called *za'atar*, sesame seeds, and crushed sumac berries with their pleasant, lemony astringency. Sometimes there was also *khubz marqouk*, mountain bread, thin as a flour tortilla and used in a similar way, like a spoon to scoop up creamy yogurt made from fresh goat's milk. With the yogurt we had olives—fat, aromatic black ones and crisp, bitter green ones—along with young scallions and radishes. And like many Middle Easterners, Tewfiq always began the day with ful medames (page 228) made with small, brown Egyptian fava beans.

This kind of breakfast is nutritional perfection—fiber-rich beans and bread, plenty of fresh vegetables, yogurt for its calcium, and an abundance of the good fat, olive oil. And for someone who grew up in New England where, even in boarding school, we had baked beans on Saturday night and warmed-over beans for Sunday breakfast, it doesn't taste all that strange either.

Try it sometime. And if you ever get to Brooklyn, you can eat a Lebanese breakfast in the little Arab restaurants along lower Atlantic Avenue, near Brooklyn Heights. The bread comes from local bakeries, too.

# ED BEHR'S MEDITERRANEAN COUNTRY-STYLE BREAD

I've learned more about the art of bread making from Ed Behr, the Vermont-based writer, editor, and general factotum of *The Art of Eating*, a quarterly newsletter, than from anyone in the Mediterranean or elsewhere. Ed seems to have a natural instinct, what my mother would have called "a good hand," for bread. Here's what he taught me:

- Use as little yeast as you can get away with.
- Let the rising be long, cool, and slow.

When you think about it, those are pretty good life principles as well.

This is a very slow-rising bread. Three days may seem excessive, but the bread develops a wonderful flavor and texture, and the bonus is that there's so little to do each day that you almost don't even notice you're making bread. I published this recipe in the *New York Times* in 1990. The editor of *Food & Wine* magazine called to say it was the best bread she'd ever baked.

2 cups very warm, almost hot, water

1 teaspoon active dry yeast

9 to 11 cups unbleached all-purpose white flour

2 tablespoons salt

2½ cups tepid water

2 cups barley, rye, or whole-wheat flour

2 or 3 tablespoons cornmeal or coarse semolina as needed

Put the very warm water in a large mixing bowl, sprinkle the yeast over it, and stir briefly with a wooden spoon to distribute the yeast through the water. Add 2 cups of the white flour, stir to mix well, cover with plastic wrap, and set aside in a cool place (50 to 70 degrees) to rise overnight. (If you're using starter, mix a cup of starter with warm water and flour, cover, and set aside to rise.)

The next day, if you wish, remove a cup of the starter sponge and store in a glass jar in the refrigerator. Add to the remaining sponge the salt, a cup of the tepid water, and the barley, rye, or whole-wheat flour. Stir or mix thoroughly with your hands. Cover the bowl again, return to a cool place, and let it rise overnight.

On the third day, add the remaining 1½ cups tepid water and about 7 cups white flour. Begin kneading in the bowl, then sprinkle a little flour over a wooden pastry board or wooden countertop and turn the dough out. Knead thoroughly for at least 10 minutes, adding flour as necessary until you have a smooth, elastic dough. Rinse the mixing bowl, dry it, dust it with flour, and put the dough back in. Cover with plastic wrap and set aside at room temperature to rise until it has increased in volume about 2½ times—about 2 to 3 hours.

Turn the dough out on the lightly floured board, punch it down, and knead briefly just to knock any air holes out. Form into 2 round (*boules*) or long (*baguettes*) loaves and place the loaves on baking sheets (if you're not using a baking stone) or on a wooden peel that has been lightly sprinkled with cornmeal or semolina. Set aside in a warm place (70 degrees or more) to rise rapidly, 30 minutes to an hour, until doubled in size.

If you're using a baking stone, set it in the cold oven and preheat to 500 degrees for at least 30 minutes. If you're using a baking sheet and no stone, simply preheat the oven to 500 degrees. When you're ready to bake, slash the tops of the loaves with a very sharp knife in 3 or 4 places. Quickly slide the loaves into the oven, directly onto the hot stone if you're using it, and bake for 15 minutes. Turn the heat down to 350 degrees and bake for 35 minutes longer.

When the bread is done and the crust is golden brown, remove the bread from the oven and let it cool on a rack. ***Makes 2 loaves, about 1¼ pounds each; 40 servings***

Nutritional Data, per portion

| Calories 134 | Carbohydrate 28g | Saturated Fat trace |
|---|---|---|
| Protein 4g | Sodium 330mg | Monounsaturated |
| Fat trace | Cholesterol 0 | Fat trace |

**VARIATION:** Tuscans prefer their bread with no salt. It's perfectly all right to leave it out if you wish.

# ARAB FLATBREAD

*Pita or Pocket Bread*

**M**iddle Eastern flatbread or pita has conquered America in the last decade or so, for reasons as inexplicable as those behind most food fads and fashions. At least part of the appeal must be the convenience of these "pocket" breads as all-purpose sandwich wrappers. You used to be able to find Arab bread only in bakeries in Middle Eastern neighborhoods, like Atlantic Avenue in Brooklyn. Then enterprising Arab-Americans began moving out of these confines and marketing Arab bread in big-city supermarkets. And now it has been taken over by commercial bread giants—with the usual loss of quality and texture that goes along with commercialization and industrialization.

If your only experience with Arab bread has been through the spongy, flabby mass-marketed products, try this recipe at least once just so you'll know the difference. Properly made Arab bread in individual flat rounds should separate fairly easily into top and bottom halves, each one with a firm, chewy, yet tender texture.

Unlike the Mediterranean country bread, homemade Arab bread doesn't keep well; in Beirut, it's bought when it's needed, and in the countryside the family's daily supply is baked each morning in the outdoor oven. For this reason, the rising or fermentation takes place over a shorter period of time. Family cooks set the sponge the night before and leave it to rise overnight. Then a quick rising at dawn means there's hot, fresh bread for breakfast.

I make Arab bread in small quantities for immediate consumption, but the recipe is easily expanded simply by doubling quantities. Leftover bread can be used in Lebanese fattoush (page 73).

1    teaspoon active dry yeast

2½   cups very warm water

6    cups unbleached all-purpose flour

1    teaspoon salt

a little olive oil for the bowl

a little cornmeal for dusting the loaves

At least 6 hours before you want the bread (or the night before if it's for breakfast), mix the yeast with half the warm water (hotter than body temperature

but not so hot that you can't hold a finger in it comfortably—about the temperature of baby's milk in a nursing bottle). As soon as the yeast is dissolved, add about 1½ cups flour and stir with a wooden spoon until you have a thick slurry. Don't worry if some of the flour remains in little undissolved globules; it will all come together in the end.

Cover with a damp kitchen towel and set aside to rise, ideally at 60 to 70 degrees. Don't worry if you can't get exactly the right temperature. (Housewives all over the Mediterranean set bread to rise in summer's heat and winter's frigid cold and all the temperatures in between, without benefit of central heat or air-conditioning.)

After 3 or 4 hours, or in the morning if the sponge has been rising overnight, stir in the remaining warm water, the salt, and 3 cups more flour. Knead with your hands in the bowl to combine the liquid and flour. Then turn the rather sticky mass out on a heavily floured bread board and knead on the board, gradually incorporating the remaining flour, until you have a compact, smooth, elastic mass. This will take a good 10 to 15 minutes.

Wipe a little olive oil around the bottom and sides of a bowl large enough to hold twice the amount of dough you now have. Place the ball of dough in the bowl and turn it to coat the dough with olive oil. Cover with a damp kitchen towel and set aside to rise. This time you will want a quicker rising, so leave the bowl in the warm kitchen or in a gas oven that has a pilot light. The bread should double in bulk within 1 to 1½ hours.

Turn the dough out onto the bread board, punch it down, and knead briefly to get rid of any air pockets. Form the dough into a long, fat sausage. Using a sharp knife or a bread spatula, slice the dough thickly into 8 or 10 slices—each slice should weigh approximately ½ pound. Form each slice into a ball and, using your hands and a rolling pin, stretch and roll each slice into a circle about 8 inches in diameter. You can stack the circles one on top of the other, but be sure to dust between them rather thickly with cornmeal to keep them from clinging to each other. Set aside while you preheat the oven.

Place a baking stone or tiles, if you're using them, in the cold oven and preheat to 425 degrees for at least 30 minutes. If you're not using a stone or tiles, simply preheat the oven to 425 degrees. Place the dough circles directly on the tiles or stone or on lightly oiled baking sheets. Bake for 8 to 10 minutes or until the bread has puffed and is a very pale gold color. Remove from the oven and set the breads on a clean kitchen towel. Cover with another clean towel. After about 5 minutes, press lightly on the towel to flatten the breads. *Makes 8 to 10 flatbreads*

THE MEDITERRANEAN DIET COOKBOOK

| Calories 278 | Carbohydrate 57g | Saturated Fat trace |
|---|---|---|
| Protein 8g | Sodium 222mg | Monounsaturated |
| Fat 1g | Cholesterol 0 | Fat trace |

# "ARMENIAN" BREAD FROM CYPRUS

**W**e used to get this bread from a bakery on a back street of Kyrenia, the delightful port town on Cyprus's north coast. At the time I accepted that it was Armenian bread, but I now realize that it was a *Turkish* bread and most likely the bakery itself was run by Turkish Cypriotes—but in the heated politics of the day, of which I was blissfully unaware, *Armenian* was more PC than *Turkish* with the Greek Cypriotes among whom we all lived.

In any case, it is utterly delicious, fragrant with fennel and thickly coated with sesame seeds like the crisp simit rings that are sold by street vendors all over the Middle East—and yet it really is bread.

As with any bread, the balance between flour and liquid depends on a number of variables, among them the humidity in the air and the age and humidity of the flour.

¾　cup warm water

1　teaspoon sugar

1　teaspoon active dry yeast

4 to 5 cups unbleached all-purpose white flour

1　teaspoon salt

1　tablespoon extra-virgin olive oil plus a little more for the bowl

¼　cup fennel seeds, lightly crushed in a mortar

1　egg white beaten with 2 tablespoons water

⅓　cup or more sesame seeds as needed

Mix together ¾ cup of the warm water (hotter than body temperature but not too hot to hold a finger in it comfortably—the temperature of a baby's nursing bottle) with the sugar and yeast in a large bowl. When the sugar and yeast have dissolved, stir in about 2½ cups flour and mix with a wooden spoon. Add another

BREADS, FLATBREADS, PIZZAS, AND SAVORY PIES

cup of flour—by now you should be able to mix the sticky flour and liquid together with your hands.

Spread ½ cup or more flour on a bread board and turn the dough out onto the board. Knead well for about 10 minutes, gradually incorporating a tablespoon of olive oil into the bread. Return the kneaded dough to the rinsed-out, lightly oiled bowl, cover with a damp kitchen towel, and set aside to rise for about 2 hours or until the dough has doubled in bulk. The ideal rising temperature is between 60 and 70 degrees, but it won't matter if the temperature is off a little in either direction.

When the dough has doubled, turn it out on the lightly floured board, punch it down, and knead slightly to get rid of any air bubbles. Spread it out and sprinkle the fennel seeds over, then roll up and knead a few more strokes to distribute the fennel seeds evenly throughout.

Cut the dough in half and form each half into a 10- to 12-inch-long sausage. Cover lightly with a damp kitchen towel and set aside for about 30 minutes to rise in the kitchen's warmth. If you're using a baking stone or tiles, set them in the oven and preheat to 425 degrees for at least 30 minutes. Otherwise, use a baking sheet with a little cornmeal scattered over it and simply preheat the oven to 425 degrees.

Just before baking, paint each loaf with the egg white mixture and pat the sesame seeds thickly all over the top and sides of each loaf. With a very sharp knife or a razor, cut slashes in the top of each loaf. Bake the loaves for about 20 to 25 minutes or until the sesame-flecked crust is russet-gold and the bread feels hollow when you knock the bottom gently. ***Makes 2 loaves; 16 servings***

<u>Nutritional Data, per portion</u>

| | | |
|---|---|---|
| Calories 163 | Carbohydrate 29g | Saturated Fat trace |
| Protein 5g | Sodium 143mg | Monounsaturated |
| Fat 3g | Cholesterol 0 | Fat 2g |

# MOROCCAN SEMOLINA BREAD

**S**emolina flour, ground from the golden heart of durum wheat, the hardest of all wheats, is a soft creamy yellow and coarser in texture than regular wheat flour. In this country it's sometimes marketed as pasta flour (it's the flour from which commercial dried pasta is made); I use Antoine's Pasta (Semolina) Flour with 14 grams of protein in 4 ounces. In North Africa, semolina flour is used to make couscous, although few home cooks make their own couscous these days since good ready-made (not precooked) couscous is widely available.

Moroccan cooks also use semolina flour to make the round bread that is served at every meal and is used to sop up the juices of stews, soups, and tagines. The first task of the day for many Moroccan women is to make the family supply of these breads, one per person for each meal. Properly made, this produces crisp-crusted bread with a beautiful yellow crumb. The kneading takes longer than with ordinary wheat flour doughs, but kneading, like shelling peas, is a good time for passive meditation—problems get solved while the dough turns to silk. The instructions in my favorite Moroccan cookbook conclude, after detailing the mixing and kneading and molding of the breads: "Send them to be baked at the neighborhood oven."

1   **tablespoon active dry yeast**

2   **cups tepid water**

4   **cups semolina flour**

1   **tablespoon salt**

1   **cup unbleached all-purpose flour plus about ⅓ cup for the bread
      board**

Rinse a small bowl in hot tap water. Add the yeast to the bowl along with about 3 tablespoons of the tepid water. Set aside while the yeast dissolves.

Put the semolina flour in a large mixing bowl. Make a well in the center and add the yeast mixture and the salt. Pull some of the semolina over the yeast mixture, then pour the rest of the tepid water over the semolina. Set aside for 5 minutes or so to let the semolina absorb the water. Sprinkle the cup of all-purpose flour over the semolina and begin to work the dough, first using a wooden spoon to mix, then, as the mixture becomes raggedy, using your hands. Knead the dough in the bowl with your hands until it is well blended, then turn the dough out on a lightly floured board and knead for at least 20 minutes, gradually incorporating

BREADS, FLATBREADS, PIZZAS, AND SAVORY PIES

some of the flour on the board. The mixture will become silky and smooth, though still a little sticky.

After 20 minutes, form the dough into a large ball and set aside. Sprinkle the rest of the ⅓ cup flour on the board. Using a knife or a dough cutter, divide the ball of dough into 6 pieces. (Don't tear the smaller pieces away with your hands, because you risk tearing the developing gluten structure.) Form each piece into a ball about the size of an orange—each one will weigh approximately ½ pound. As you form each ball, roll it lightly in the flour on the board and set aside. Let the balls rest for about 5 minutes.

Pat each ball into a round flat circle about ¾ inch thick. Set the circles on a wooden peel or bread board and prick each one with a fork in 6 or 7 places. Cover lightly with aluminum foil and set aside to rise for 30 minutes.

If you're using a baking stone, place it in the cold oven and preheat the oven to 450 degrees for 30 minutes. If you're using a baking sheet, simply preheat the oven to 425 degrees.

Place the breads on the stone or baking sheet, close the oven door, and turn the heat down to 400 degrees. Work quickly so that the oven temperature does not have a chance to drop below 400 degrees. Bake the breads for 20 to 25 minutes or until they are golden brown and cooked through. ***Makes 6 breads; 6 servings***

Nutritional Data, per portion

| | | |
|---|---|---|
| Calories 508 | Carbohydrate 103g | Saturated Fat trace |
| Protein 18g | Sodium 1,101mg | Monounsaturated |
| Fat 2g | Cholesterol 0 | Fat trace |

# BLACK OLIVE BREAD

**A**ny high-quality black olives can be used in this recipe, although wrinkly oil-cured black olives are best. Juicy black olives like Greek Kalamatas will add considerable moisture to the bread dough. If you use these olives, you may need to add a little more flour.

**FOR THE SPONGE:**

1   teaspoon active dry yeast

1½ cups warm water

1½ cups unbleached all-purpose flour

1½ cups warm water

4   cups unbleached all-purpose flour

½   teaspoon olive oil for the bowl

1   teaspoon salt

½   cup pitted black olives

1   tablespoon grated orange zest (optional)

Make a sponge at least 6 hours or the night before you plan to bake the bread. Dissolve the yeast in the warm water, stirring with a wooden spoon. When the yeast is dissolved, stir in the flour. Cover with a damp kitchen towel and set aside to rise in a room that is on the cool side—between 60 and 70 degrees is ideal.

When you're ready to bake, add 1½ cups warm water and 2 cups flour to the sponge. Stir to mix it well. If you wish to set aside starter for the next baking, transfer 1 cup of the mixture to a glass jar or bowl, cover tightly, and store in the refrigerator. Starter can be stored for a week or 10 days under refrigeration before it needs to be used or refreshed for longer storage.

Add 1½ cups more flour to the remaining yeast mixture along with the oil and salt. Stir to mix well, first with a wooden spoon and then with your hands. Spread the remaining ½ cup flour on a bread board and turn out the yeast mixture. Knead very well, incorporating the flour on the bread board, for about 15 minutes. When the dough is smooth, elastic, and satiny, return it to the rinsed bowl, the bottom and sides of which you have wiped with a little olive oil. Turn the dough in the bowl to coat it with oil, cover the bowl with a damp kitchen

BREADS, FLATBREADS, PIZZAS, AND SAVORY PIES

towel, and set aside to rise and double in bulk—about 2 hours at a temperature between 60 and 70 degrees.

Scatter a little more flour on the bread board and turn the dough out. Punch it down and knead briefly, just to get rid of any air bubbles. Spread the dough out and scatter the pitted olives over it. Now gather the dough together and knead just enough to distribute the olives throughout.

Form into 2 round loaves and set aside for the final 30 minutes of rising. If you're using a baking stone or tiles, preheat the oven to 425 degrees for at least 30 minutes. Otherwise, just preheat to 425 degrees. Place the loaves in the oven and bake for about 35 minutes, until the bread is golden brown and crusty and feels hollow when you rap on it. Turn out onto a rack and leave for at least 2 hours before cutting it. *Makes 2 loaves, 8 servings each*

Nutritional Data, per portion

| | | |
|---|---|---|
| Calories  163 | Carbohydrate  33g | Saturated Fat  trace |
| Protein  5g | Sodium  175mg | Monounsaturated |
| Fat  1g | Cholesterol  0 | Fat  trace |

# TSOUREKI

### Greek Braided Holiday Bread

**W**herever breads are made in the world, there is a clear distinction between everyday bread, made simply from flour, yeast, and water, and holiday breads, enriched with eggs, butter, sugar, and sometimes dried fruits and nuts. When *tsoureki* is made for Greek Easter, red-dyed Easter eggs are tucked into the folds of the braid. This is a more everyday-holiday version of what is essentially a brioche.

Mahleb, made by grinding the stones of a wild cherry, has a characteristic soft sweetness in which you can just detect the almondy flavor of cherries. It is available in shops in Middle Eastern neighborhoods. I buy whole kernels of mahleb and grind them in a coffee mill (kept especially for milling spices). If you can't find mahleb, substitute fennel or caraway, although the flavor will be entirely different. Or increase the amount of zest to 2 teaspoons for a stronger orange flavor.

1   ¼-ounce envelope active dry yeast

½   cup very hot water mixed with ½ cup milk

5   cups unbleached all-purpose flour plus 2 cups cake flour, plus a little more for flouring the board

½   cup (1 stick) unsalted butter, softened

¾   cup sugar

4   large eggs

1   teaspoon ground mahleb or 1 teaspoon crushed caraway or fennel seeds; or increase the orange zest to 2 teaspoons

1   tablespoon Greek brandy or ouzo

1   teaspoon grated orange zest

juice of ½ orange

¼   cup slivered or sliced blanched almonds

Warm a 6-cup bowl in hot water and dry. In the warm bowl, mix the yeast with the water-milk mixture and stir with a wooden spoon until the yeast dissolves and starts to swell. Add 1½ cups of the all-purpose flour and mix to a thick cream. Set aside, covered with a damp kitchen towel, in a warm kitchen for 2 hours or in a cool

place overnight. (This is a sponge. The dough will ferment and rise, but it will remain quite liquid—sour cream consistency.)

When the sponge is ready, beat the butter in another bowl until it is light and fluffy; then gradually beat in the sugar. Add 3 eggs, one at a time, beating well after each addition. When all the eggs have been incorporated, add the mahleb, brandy, and orange zest and juice. Stir in the sponge and mix together.

Add the remaining flour to the sponge mixture and combine gradually, stirring with a wooden spoon and then using your hands to work in the flour. Knead for about 10 minutes or until the raggedy, sticky dough becomes soft and satiny. Incorporate more flour as you knead if necessary. Do the final kneading on a lightly floured board.

Return the dough to the mixing bowl, rinsed out and lightly greased, cover with plastic wrap, and set aside to rise in a cool place for at least 3 hours or until the dough doubles in size.

Punch the dough down and knead it briefly on the lightly floured board to knock out all the air holes. Then form into three 14-inch-long sausages and braid them together. (If you wish, you can form the dough into 6 rolls and make 2 shorter braids.) Set the braid on a lightly oiled baking sheet, cover with a piece of aluminum foil, and set aside, covered loosely with foil, to rise once more for just an hour.

When you're ready to bake, preheat the oven to 350 degrees. Beat the remaining egg lightly with a tablespoon of water and paint the braid with the wash, then strew almonds all over the surface of the bread. Bake for about 45 minutes or until the crust is golden brown and shiny. ***Makes 1 large loaf or 2 small loaves; 20 servings***

Nutritional Data, per portion

| | | |
|---|---|---|
| Calories   257 | Carbohydrate   42g | Saturated Fat   3g |
| Protein   6g | Sodium   17mg | Monounsaturated |
| Fat   7g | Cholesterol   56mg |   Fat   2g |

# POMPE À L'HUILE

*Olive Oil Bread from France*

**M**adeleine Kamman, director of this country's most prestigious culinary training center at Beringer Vineyards in California's Napa Valley, introduced me many years ago to this festive bread from Provence. The round golden disk is appropriate for both Christmas and Easter, two feasts of the sun that linger in our modern calendar.

2  cups unbleached all-purpose flour

¼  cup warm milk or water

1  ¼-ounce envelope active dry yeast

5  tablespoons sugar

3  large eggs

½  teaspoon salt

½  cup extra-virgin olive oil plus a little for greasing the bowl and pan

1  tablespoon orange-flower water

2  tablespoons grated orange zest

Put the flour in a mixing bowl and make a well in the center. Pour the warm milk into the well and sprinkle the yeast on top. Set aside for about 5 minutes while the yeast gradually absorbs some of the liquid. Add a tablespoon of sugar to the yeast and, using a wooden spoon, flick some of the flour from around the sides of the well over the yeasty liquid, covering it completely. Set aside to allow the yeast to develop for at least 30 minutes.

In a separate bowl, beat 2 of the eggs with the remaining sugar and the salt until the mixture is foamy. Beat in the olive oil, orange-flower water, and grated zest. Pour this mixture into the bowl with the flour and slowly mix in all the flour from around the edges of the bowl. You can use a wooden spoon at first, but once the mixture becomes raggedy, start to use your hands. Eventually you will need to turn the dough out onto a lightly floured board and knead for at least 10 minutes to develop the gluten.

Rinse out the mixing bowl, grease it lightly with a little olive oil, and transfer the well-kneaded dough to the bowl. Cover with a damp cloth and set aside in a warm place to rise. When it is double in bulk—after about 2 hours—turn it out on

BREADS, FLATBREADS, PIZZAS, AND SAVORY PIES

the board again, punch it down, and knead very briefly just to knock out any air holes. Return to the greased bowl, cover with the damp cloth, and let rise again until doubled in bulk—about 1½ hours.

Lightly oil a 10-inch round cake pan. Punch the dough down after the second rise, knead again briefly to knock out any air holes, and roll or pat it out in a disk to fit the pan. With a very sharp knife, cut a crisscross or crosshatch pattern about ½ inch deep in the surface of the dough. Cover loosely with a sheet of aluminum foil and set aside to rise until the dough is about 1½ inches high—about 1½ hours.

When you're ready to bake, preheat the oven to 375 degrees. Beat the remaining egg with a teaspoon of cool water and use it to paint the surface of the bread (you will need only about half the egg for this). Cut the crosshatch slashes again. Bake the bread for 20 to 25 minutes. Remove from the oven and cool on a rack before turning the bread out. ***Makes one 10-inch loaf; 16 servings***

Nutritional Data, per portion

| | | |
|---|---|---|
| Calories   153 | Carbohydrate   16g | Saturated Fat   1g |
| Protein   3g | Sodium   83mg | Monounsaturated |
| Fat   9g | Cholesterol   40mg | Fat   6g |

# CRESCIA OR CIACCIA DI PASQUA

*Italian Cheese and Bacon Easter Bread*

**W**ith nuggets of cheese and bacon or prosciutto, this dense bread is made for Easter in central Italy, where the cheese used is pecorino—not hard pecorino romano but a slightly aged sheep's milk cheese. I have substituted Greek or Bulgarian sheep's milk feta with good results.

Prosciutto or pancetta will give a more authentic flavor, but slab bacon might be used instead. If it's very smoky, blanch it briefly in boiling water.

½   **cup milk**

1   **¼-ounce envelope active dry yeast**

½   **cup (1 stick) unsalted butter**

½   **cup fruity extra-virgin olive oil**

6   **cups cake flour plus more for the board**

½   **teaspoon salt or more to taste**

½   **pound sheep's milk cheese**

1   **cup freshly grated Parmigiano cheese**

2   **ounces prosciutto, pancetta, or slab bacon, diced**

1   **whole egg and 1 egg white**

**pinch of saffron threads**

**salt and freshly ground black pepper to taste**


Warm the milk to body temperature on the stove. Pour it into a small bowl and sprinkle the yeast over it. Stir with a wooden spoon to dissolve the yeast and set aside for 10 minutes.

Combine the butter and olive oil in a small saucepan and warm on the stove to melt the butter, but don't let it cook.

Add the flour and salt to a large mixing bowl, tossing the salt to distribute it evenly. Grate half the sheep's milk cheese on the large holes of a grater and cut the other half of the cheese into small cubes. Add all the cheese, the Parmigiano, and the ham to the flour and toss with your hands to coat the bits with flour.

Make a well in the center of the flour and pour in the yeast and milk. Beat the whole egg with a fork and add to the yeast along with the saffron threads,

crumbling them gently. Add a little salt and pepper. Gradually mix the flour with the liquids, drizzling the olive oil–butter mixture over the flour as you mix. Use a wooden spoon at first and then your hands. Turn the dough out on a lightly floured board for the final kneading. (Because of the added cheese and ham, the dough will not become smooth and silky like regular bread dough, but it should be soft and well mixed.)

Set the kneaded dough in the mixing bowl, rinsed out, dried, and greased lightly. Cover with a damp kitchen towel and let rise for about 1½ hours.

Butter and flour an 8-inch round springform or cake pan (3 inches deep). Knock the dough down and knead briefly, then press it into the pan, using your knuckles, and set aside, lightly covered, in a warm place to rise again for about 30 minutes.

When the dough has risen, preheat the oven to 400 degrees. Brush lightly beaten egg white over the top of the bread and bake for about 45 minutes or until the top is golden. *Makes one 8-inch round loaf; 8 to 10 servings*

Nutritional Data, per portion

| | | |
|---|---|---|
| Calories 563 | Carbohydrate 54g | Saturated Fat 14g |
| Protein 16g | Sodium 679mg | Monounsaturated |
| Fat 31g | Cholesterol 81mg | Fat 15g |

## PIZZA AND CALZONE

Making pizza at home is quick, easy, and fun—or at least it is after you've done it a couple of times. Grown-ups love it almost as much as children do. Even the most recalcitrant young eater usually can be persuaded by pizza— it's a marvelously deceptive way to introduce good-for-you food to rigidly resistant small palates.

So why does pizza evoke squawks of protest from nutritionists? Because they're talking about fast-food pizza as it's served in this country, piled high with saturated fat, sugar, and sodium. The pizza you make at home, on the other hand, is a well-balanced modern Mediterranean meal: a complex carbohydrate (the pizza dough) at the center of the plate, dressed with vegetables (tomatoes, onions, fresh peppers) and a little animal protein (anchovies, fresh mozzarella, a few slivers of ham or sausage), the whole bathed in the glow of good monounsaturated fat in the form of extra-virgin olive oil.

On its home ground, pizza is like that, a model of rectitude poised between exuberance and restraint. On its home ground, too, pizza is almost never made at home. In Italy pizza is the ultimate social food, made in public to be consumed in public, preferably in the company of friends and colleagues. But we live in America, and to the astonishment of Italians, we make pizza at home.

If you find the prospect daunting at first, don't worry. Pizza, like bread in general, is very forgiving, and since it's so fast, a mistake is easily overcome. Everyone who has ever made it, including some of the most gifted chefs in the country, has fallen victim to burned crusts, burned tops, or, the ultimate disaster, jerking the pizza onto the stone only to have the topping slide off, the dough stick to the peel, and a hell of a mess sizzling on the baking stone.

A couple of inexpensive pieces of equipment will help make the process of baking pizza or calzone easier and the results better. A baking stone, a disk or rectangle of composite stone made for use in the oven, or baking tiles (unglazed ceramic tiles from a building supply house) will

*continued*

simulate the effect of the wood-fired masonry ovens traditionally used for pizza and breads throughout the Mediterranean. And a wooden peel, a thin board with a handle and a beveled edge at the far end, makes it easier to slide the prepared dough onto the hot stone.

If you don't want to invest in these, bake your pizza or calzone on a cookie sheet or in a shallow pie plate. The crust will be softer, without the pleasing crunch and roasted flavor that comes from the stone, but it will still be a good thing.

A calzone is a pizza that has been folded over its topping to make a big tart. (The name means "big socks" or "trouser legs"—you can see how that would come about.) The dough is exactly the same, but there's usually lots of cheese inside, which becomes deliciously gooey, of course, when baked.

## BASIC DOUGH FOR PIZZA AND CALZONE

¾  teaspoon active dry yeast

1  cup very warm water

2  cups unbleached all-purpose flour

1  cup cake or soft pastry flour

1  teaspoon salt

½  teaspoon olive oil for the bowl

coarse semolina or cornmeal for the peel

Sprinkle the yeast over the warm water and set aside to let the yeast develop. Add all the flour to a large mixing bowl with the salt and toss to mix well. Make a well in the center of the flour. Pour the yeast mixture into the flour. Gradually mix the flour and liquid together, stirring with a wooden spoon at first, then with your hands. When the mixture is raggedy and pulls cleanly away from the bowl, turn it out on a lightly floured board. Knead the dough for about 6 to 8 minutes or just until it is light and elastic—the texture of a baby's bottom is what you're looking

for. Rinse out the mixing bowl, dry it, and oil it lightly. Set the dough in the oiled bowl and turn it to coat it lightly with oil. Cover with plastic wrap and set aside at a temperature between 60 and 70 degrees for 1½ to 2 hours or until the dough has doubled in volume. Turn the dough back onto the floured board, punch it down, and knead briefly just to knock the air holes out.

If you're using a baking stone, set it in the cold oven and preheat to 550 degrees for at least 30 minutes. Otherwise, just preheat the oven to 550 degrees. Divide the dough in two, using a pastry cutter or a knife. (If you try to pull it apart, you risk tearing the developing gluten.) Pat a ball of dough into a thick circle, then, using a rolling pin, roll it out on the board to about ⅛ to ¼ inch thick. Work quickly and be careful not to overwork the dough. Sprinkle a peel with coarse semolina or cornmeal and slide the circle onto the peel. If you're not using a peel, slide the circle onto a lightly oiled baking sheet or pan. Top with one of the toppings that follow or make up your own.

Open the oven door and quickly jerk the peel to slide the pizza onto the baking stone. (Or slide the baking sheet into the oven.) Close the door and set the heat at 500 degrees. Work quickly so that the oven temperature does not have a chance to drop below 500 degrees. Bake for 5 to 7 minutes or until the crust is blistered brown and the topping is bubbling. ***Makes enough dough for two 8- to 10-inch pizzas or four 6-inch long calzoni; 4 servings as a first course or accompaniment to a main-course soup or salad***

Nutritional Data, per portion

| | | |
|---|---|---|
| Calories 347 | Carbohydrate 73g | Saturated Fat trace |
| Protein 10g | Sodium 552mg | Monounsaturated |
| Fat 1g | Cholesterol 0 | Fat trace |

# PIZZA NAPOLETANA

### *Traditional Toppings for Neopolitan Pizza*

**M**argherita and marinara are the classic sauces for Neapolitan pizza and have been ever since that memorable but unrecorded moment in the 19th century when the New World tomato was firmly and finally wedded to the venerable Neapolitan flatbread called *pizza*. Marinara is a simple sauce, according to the rules established by the True Neapolitan Pizza Association, made of oil, tomatoes, oregano, garlic, and salt. Pizza Margherita is only slightly more complex: oil, tomatoes, grated

cheese, mozzarella, basil, and salt. Note the absence of garlic: Because this was the favorite of Margherita of Savoy, or so it is said, garlic was left out so that no odor might sully the breath of the queen of Italy.

Pizza can be dressed with chopped or sliced fresh tomatoes, but cooked tomato sauce is more commonly used, even in Naples, where tomatoes at their peak are among the most sensational things I have ever put in my mouth. Leftover sauce freezes well and can be used on pasta or in a soup.

The quantities for each type of topping make one 8- to 10-inch pizza. If you wish to make two *pizze alla marinara*, simply double the quantities for the remaining ingredients—but it's more fun to make two different kinds of pizza.

### *Cooked Tomato Sauce for Neopolitan Pizza*

2 or 3 garlic cloves to taste, sliced

2    tablespoons extra-virgin olive oil

3½ pounds tomatoes, cut into chunks, or 1 28-ounce can whole tomatoes
      with juice, chopped

1    teaspoon salt (omit if using canned tomatoes)

½   teaspoon sugar

In a heavy saucepan over medium-low heat, cook the garlic in the olive oil until it starts to soften, about 5 to 10 minutes. Add the tomatoes, salt if you wish, and sugar, raise the heat slightly, and cook rapidly, stirring frequently, while the tomatoes give off their juice and cook down to a thick mass—15 to 20 minutes. Watch the mixture carefully toward the end to make sure it doesn't scorch.

Put the sauce through the medium disk of a food mill. (Don't use a processor or blender, because it will grind up the tomato seeds and make the sauce bitter. The food mill will hold back a certain amount of seeds and skin, letting just the pulp go through.) If the sauce seems too thin, return it to medium-low heat and cook, stirring constantly and watching very carefully, until it is the desired consistency.
*Makes about 2 cups sauce; about 5 servings*

Nutritional Data, per portion

| Calories 119 | Carbohydrate 16g | Saturated Fat 1g |
|---|---|---|
| Protein 3g | Sodium 469mg | Monounsaturated |
| Fat 7g | Cholesterol 0 | Fat 5g |

THE MEDITERRANEAN DIET COOKBOOK

*Pizza alla Marinara*

½  recipe pizza dough (page 148)

semolina or cornmeal for the peel

1  tablespoon extra-virgin olive oil in a ¼-cup measure

¾  cup cooked tomato sauce (page 150)

6  garlic cloves, chopped or thinly sliced

½  teaspoon dried oregano, crumbled

salt and freshly ground black pepper to taste

Follow the directions on page 148 for heating the oven and preparing and shaping the pizza dough. Assemble all the ingredients for the pizza before you start to work.

Brush the dough circle with olive oil right out to the edge (you won't use all the oil). Using a wooden spoon or your fingers, spread the tomato sauce over the dough, leaving about a ¼-inch rim around the edge. Distribute the garlic and oregano over the tomato sauce and add salt (if needed) and pepper. Drizzle the remaining olive oil over the pizza—be sure to wring the oil out of the brush.

Open the oven door and quickly but smoothly jerk the dough onto the hot stone. Or slide the baking sheet into the oven. Close the door and turn the heat down to 500 degrees. Work quickly so the oven temperature does not have a chance to drop below 500 degrees. Bake for 5 to 6 minutes or until the crust is brown and the top is bubbling. ***Makes one 8- to 10-inch pizza, serving 2 as a first course***

Nutritional Data, per portion

| Calories 533 | Carbohydrate 91g | Saturated Fat 2g |
| Protein 13g | Sodium 994mg | Monounsaturated |
| Fat 14g | Cholesterol 0 | Fat 10g |

**VARIATION:** The True Neapolitan Pizza Association might not approve, but you can add ¼ cup freshly grated Parmigiano cheese to the top of the pizza just before you put it in the oven.

## Pizza Margherita

½ recipe pizza dough (page 148)

semolina or cornmeal for the peel

1 tablespoon extra-virgin olive oil in a ¼-cup measure

¾ cup cooked tomato sauce (page 150)

about 3 ounces imported mozzarella di bufala or cow's milk fior di latte,
   sliced

salt and freshly ground black pepper

1 small bunch of fresh basil leaves, rinsed well

¼ cup freshly grated Parmigiano cheese

Follow the directions on page 148 for heating the oven and preparing and shaping the pizza dough.

Brush the dough circle with olive oil right out to the edge (you won't use all the oil). Using a wooden spoon or your fingers, spread the tomato sauce over the dough, leaving about a ¼-inch rim around the edge. Distribute the mozzarella slices over the tomato sauce and add salt and pepper. Arrange the basil leaves over the mozzarella, reserving a few for garnish if you wish, then sprinkle with the Parmigiano. Drizzle the remaining olive oil over the pizza—be sure to wring the oil out of the brush.

Open the oven door and quickly but smoothly jerk the dough onto the hot stone. Or slide the baking sheet into the oven. Close the door and turn the heat down to 500 degrees. Work quickly so the oven temperature does not have a chance to drop below 500 degrees. Bake for 5 to 6 minutes or until the crust is brown and the top is bubbling. Add the reserved basil leaves just before serving. ***Makes one 8- to 10-inch pizza, serving 2 as a first course***

Nutritional Data, per portion

| | | |
|---|---|---|
| Calories 705 | Carbohydrate 92g | Saturated Fat 4g |
| Protein 25g | Sodium 1,251mg | Monounsaturated |
| Fat 27g | Cholesterol 40mg | Fat 11g |

## OTHER TOPPINGS FOR AN 8- TO 10-INCH PIZZA

- Add pitted black olives or anchovy fillets to Pizza alla Marinara (page 151) or Pizza Margherita (page 152).
- Brush the dough with oil and distribute over it ¼ pound mozzarella, sliced; ¼ cup basil leaves, slivered; ½ teaspoon salt; and lots of black pepper.
- Top the oil-brushed dough with 1 pound onions, peeled, thinly sliced, and very gently sautéed in a tablespoon of extra-virgin olive oil with a teaspoon of salt and ½ teaspoon of sugar, until the onions are very soft, golden-brown, and reduced, about 20 to 30 minutes. Top the onions with scattered walnut halves and add 2 firmly packed cups rinsed (but not drained) arugula and watercress, 2 or 3 tablespoons freshly grated Parmigiano cheese, and 2 tablespoons walnut oil.

# ARTICHOKE AND LEEK PIZZA

**T**his is a fantasy pizza, created in response to all those extravagant creations of New Age chefs who subscribe to the credo that if twice is good, four times is even better. Simplicity and restraint, more often than extravagance, are the hallmarks of good Mediterranean cooking.

½   pound imported mozzarella di bufala or cow's milk fior di latte,
      grated on the large holes of the grater

3   tablespoons extra-virgin olive oil

1   medium onion, finely chopped

about 3 ounces Italian pancetta, diced

2   medium or 4 small firm spring artichokes, trimmed as described on
      page 455 and quartered

½   cup water

freshly ground black pepper to taste

1   fat leek, rinsed well and thinly sliced

salt to taste

½   recipe pizza dough (page 148)

semolina or cornmeal for the peel

3   tablespoons freshly grated Parmigiano cheese

If you're using a baking stone, place it in the cold oven and preheat to 550 degrees for at least 30 minutes. If you're using a baking sheet, simply preheat the oven to 550 degrees. Assemble all of the ingredients for the pizza before you start to work. Mix the mozzarella with 1 tablespoon of the olive oil and set aside.

In a saucepan over medium-low heat, gently sauté the onion and pancetta in 1 tablespoon of the remaining oil until the onion is soft but not starting to brown—about 10 to 15 minutes. Add the drained artichoke pieces and stir to mix well. Add the water to keep the vegetables from scorching, along with the pepper. Cover and cook over gentle heat until the artichoke pieces are tender and most of the liquid has been absorbed—about 15 minutes. Add the sliced leek and stir to mix well. Taste for seasoning, adding salt if desired.

About 5 minutes before the oven is heated, shape the pizza as described on page 148, laying the circle of dough on a peel or on a lightly oiled baking sheet.

Brush the dough circle with a little of the remaining oil right out to the edge. Distribute the artichoke-leek mixture over the surface of the pizza. Sprinkle the grated cheese over the vegetables. Drizzle the remaining olive oil over the pizza—be sure to wring the oil out of the brush.

Open the oven door and quickly but smoothly jerk the dough onto the hot stone. Or slide the baking sheet into the oven. Close the door and turn the heat down to 500 degrees. Work quickly so that the oven temperature does not have a chance to drop below 500 degrees. Bake for 5 to 6 minutes or until the crust is blistered brown and the top is bubbling. ***Makes 1 pizza, serving 4 as a first course or an accompaniment to soup or salad***

### Nutritional Data, per portion

| Calories 574 | Carbohydrate 51g | Saturated Fat 5g |
|---|---|---|
| Protein 24g | Sodium 777mg | Monounsaturated |
| Fat 34g | Cholesterol 60mg | Fat 14g |

## CALZONE WITH THREE CHEESES

1   recipe pizza dough (page 148)

½   pound imported mozzarella di bufala or cow's milk fior di latte,
      grated on the large holes of a grater

2   tablespoons extra-virgin olive oil

2   cups peeled, seeded, and chopped fresh tomatoes or chopped well-
      drained canned whole tomatoes

1   small onion, finely chopped

¼   cup tightly packed slivered fresh basil leaves or ½ teaspoon dried
      oregano, crumbled

½   cup fresh goat's milk cheese such as chèvre

salt and freshly ground black pepper to taste

⅓   cup freshly grated Parmigiano cheese

1   large egg beaten with 1 teaspoon cold water

While the dough is rising, assemble the other ingredients and prepare the stuffing. Mix the grated mozzarella with a tablespoon of the olive oil and

set aside. Drain the chopped tomatoes, whether fresh or canned, in a fine-mesh sieve.

In a saucepan over medium-low heat, gently sauté the onion in the remaining tablespoon of oil until the onion is soft but not brown—about 10 to 15 minutes. Stir in the basil and chèvre, adding a very little warm water if necessary to cream the chèvre. Cook very briefly, just long enough to warm up the chèvre. Taste and add a little salt and pepper if desired. Set aside.

If you're using a baking stone, set it in the cold oven and preheat to 500 degrees for at least 30 minutes. If you're using a baking sheet, simply preheat the oven to 500 degrees.

About 5 minutes before the oven is heated, punch down the pizza dough and form into 4 balls. On a lightly floured board, roll a ball out into a circle about ⅛ to ¼ inch thick. Slide the circle onto a wooden peel or onto a lightly oiled baking sheet and lightly paint the edges with a little beaten egg. On one half of the circle, spoon about a quarter of the chèvre mixture, top with the drained tomatoes, and then add the mozzarella and oil. Sprinkle a little grated Parmigiano over the top. Fold the other half over and press or crimp the edges together. Proceed with the rest of the pizza dough and stuffing ingredients.

When all the calzoni are made, paint the tops lightly with the remaining oil. Slide the calzoni onto the baking stone or onto a lightly oiled baking sheet in the oven. Close the oven door, turn the heat down to 450 degrees, and bake for about 25 minutes or until the calzoni are golden brown. ***Makes 4 calzoni; 4 servings***

Nutritional Data, per portion

| | | |
|---|---|---|
| Calories 715 | Carbohydrate 83g | Saturated Fat 7g |
| Protein 29g | Sodium 854mg | Monounsaturated |
| Fat 29g | Cholesterol 113mg | Fat 8g |

# DOUBLE-CRUSTED PIZZA FROM SOUTHERN ITALY

1    recipe pizza dough (page 148)

3    pounds mixed greens such as escarole, spinach, chard, broccoli

½    pound yellow onions, halved and sliced

2    garlic cloves, crushed with the flat blade of a knife

¼    cup extra-virgin olive oil

24   black olives, pitted and coarsely chopped

¼    cup golden raisins, plumped in warm water

¼    cup pine nuts

6    oil-packed anchovy fillets, coarsely chopped

salt and freshly ground black pepper to taste

1    large egg beaten with 1 teaspoon water


While the pizza dough is rising, prepare the filling. Rinse the greens, trim away the tough stem ends, and slice the tender stems and leaves into 1-inch lengths.

In a saucepan large enough to hold all the greens, gently sauté the onions and garlic in the oil for 4 or 5 minutes, until they are light golden. Stir in the greens and mix well with the garlic and oil. Clap a lid on the pan and cook for about 5 to 7 minutes or until the greens are wilted. If necessary, add a very little water from time to time to keep the greens from scorching.

When the greens are wilted, add the olives, raisins, pine nuts, and anchovies and stir to combine with the greens. Cook over medium-low heat for just a few minutes, then taste and add salt and pepper. Set aside until ready to cook.

When the pizza dough is doubled in size, preheat the oven to 375 degrees. Divide the dough into 2 unequal portions, the larger for the bottom of the pie, the smaller for the top. Lightly grease and flour a 10-inch round straight-sided pie or quiche pan. Roll out the larger piece of dough into a very thin circle large enough to cover the bottom and sides of the pan with a little hanging over the edge. Line the pan with the dough and fill the pie with the vegetable mixture. Roll the second piece of dough into a very thin circle just large enough to fit over the top of the pie. Fold and crimp the edges to hold the crust securely in place. Paint the top with a little of the beaten egg mixture and poke a design or pattern of holes into it to let the steam

out. Bake for 40 to 45 minutes or until the pie is golden and crisp. Remove and let sit for 15 minutes before serving. ***Makes 1 double-crust pizza; 6 to 8 servings***

Nutritional Data, per portion

| Calories 338 | Carbohydrate 49g | Saturated Fat 2g |
|---|---|---|
| Protein 12g | Sodium 592mg | Monounsaturated |
| Fat 12g | Cholesterol 28mg | Fat 8g |

## SCHIACCIATA, CIABATTA, AND FOCACCIA

### *Italian Flatbreads*

*La ciaccia* is what Tuscans call these breads that have become so popular in American restaurants recently. Mita Antolini, my neighbor in Teverina, makes *ciaccia* (CHA-cha) every 10 days or so when she fires up the oven built into the outside wall of her farmhouse. The Antolinis eat freshly baked *ciaccia* for their midmorning merenda, slicing the bread in two and slipping a thick wedge of home-cured prosciutto or young pecorino cheese inside, or sometimes just a spring onion fresh from the garden, sliced and dressed with a little olive oil. With a glass of young Sangiovese wine, it's a terrific pick-me-up.

*Schiacciata* means squashed or flattened, which is what these breads are; *ciabatta* means slipper, which is one shape the bread takes; *focaccia* derives from the Latin *focus*, the hearth, which is where the breads were once baked. There is no mystery about them despite all that has been written. They are quite simply the domestic equivalent of pizza, made by women, baked in the household oven, and consumed quite casually within the family, unlike pizza, which is always made by men, baked in a public oven, and consumed with panache and a sense of display in a very public place—a nice illustration, if you will, of the difference between men's and women's roles in traditional cultures like these.

The dough for schiacciata and focaccia is just like pizza or bread dough—yeast, water, flour, perhaps a little salt. Ciabatta should have 1 or 2

*continued*

tablespoons of extra-virgin olive oil worked into the dough. To make schiacciata or focaccia, simply take a piece of pizza dough (described on page 148) or bread dough (page 131), punch it down after it doubles in bulk, and roll or pat it out on a peel or board sprinkled with a little semolina or cornmeal. The dough should form a rough circle or oval about an inch high and 8 to 10 inches or so in diameter. Dimple it all over by pressing the handle of a wooden spoon in to a depth of about ½ inch (making little wells to catch the olive oil that you will put on before baking), then cover it loosely with a sheet of aluminum foil and set it aside in a warm place to rise again. It won't rise much—perhaps another ½ inch in the next 40 or 50 minutes, while you heat the oven to 500 degrees. (If you're using a baking stone, be sure to put it in a *cold* oven, then set the temperature to 500 and leave it for at least 30 minutes.)

When the oven is hot, smear a couple of tablespoons of extra-virgin olive oil over the top of the bread. Sprinkle it with a teaspoon, or more if you wish, of crunchy sea salt and slip the bread into the oven. Close the door, turn the heat down to about 425 degrees, and bake the bread for about 25 or 30 minutes, until the top is crisp and golden. (Ciabatta is made the same way except that, since you have incorporated oil into the dough, you will not add it on top.) ***Makes 1 flatbread; about 8 servings***

**VARIATIONS:** They are legion, but among the simplest is ¼ cup or so of rosemary needles, stripped away from the stems; or a scattering of finely sliced red onion; or chopped or sliced garlic; or a wash of thin tomato sauce (thinned with water if necessary) mixed with slivers of fresh basil leaves.

# PISSALADIÈRE

### *Provençal Pizza*

This is Provençal pizza, although the name comes not, as you might expect, from pizza but from pissala, a strongly flavored anchovy paste that was once the basis of the pie. Elizabeth David's version, published more than 30 years ago in *French Provincial Cooking*, calls for a rich egg and butter dough and makes something like a savory tart or an eggless quiche. I use olive oil instead of butter but otherwise follow her recipe more or less as she wrote it. It makes, as Mrs. David noted, "a splendid first course at luncheon." In my family it is also considered a superior after-school snack. It's as good at room temperature as it is straight from the oven, something you can't say for most pizzas.

½ teaspoon active dry yeast

¼ cup warm water

1¼ to 1½ cups all-purpose flour

salt to taste

1 large egg

3 tablespoons extra-virgin olive oil

1¼ pounds yellow onions, about 2 medium, halved and thinly sliced

1 garlic clove, sliced

2 medium tomatoes, peeled (page 454) and chopped, or 3 canned whole
   tomatoes, well drained and chopped

2 tablespoons slivered fresh basil leaves or ½ teaspoon dried thyme,
   crumbled

12 oil-packed anchovy fillets or 2 salt-packed anchovies, prepared as
   directed on page 471

½ cup pitted black Niçoise or Gaeta olives

freshly ground black pepper to taste

Mix the yeast with the warm water and set aside for about 10 minutes, until it is creamy.

Put a heaped cup of flour in a mixing bowl, add a pinch of salt, and stir to mix. Make a well in the middle of the flour and add the yeast mixture and

the egg along with 2 tablespoons of the olive oil. Gradually mix the flour into the liquids and stir to combine well, adding more flour as necessary. Knead with your hands in the bowl, then briefly on a lightly floured board. When the dough is soft and smooth, put it back in the bowl, rinsed out and wiped lightly with a paper towel dipped in a little olive oil. Cover with a damp cloth and set aside to rise in a warm place for 2 hours.

Meanwhile, make the filling. In a heavy skillet over medium-low heat, gently sauté the onion and garlic in the remaining olive oil until the onion is very soft and golden but not brown—about 15 to 20 minutes. Stir in the tomatoes and continue cooking until the tomato liquid has evaporated and the sauce is thick. Add the basil, a little salt, and several grinds of pepper.

Turn the dough out on the lightly floured board, punch it down, and knead briefly to knock the air holes out. Place the dough in the center of a lightly oiled straight-sided 8-inch pie pan or quiche pan. With your knuckles, press the dough gently but rapidly outward until it is spread over the bottom of the pan and all around the sides. Spread the onion-tomato mixture over the dough. Crisscross the anchovy fillets over the top and fill in the crosses with olives. Place the pie pan on a baking sheet and put it aside to rest and rise while the oven heats.

Preheat the oven to 400 degrees. Place the baking sheet in the middle of the oven and bake for about 20 minutes. Turn the oven down to 350 degrees and bake for another 20 minutes. The crust should be golden and the filling bubbly. Remove from the oven and let sit for 10 minutes or so before serving. ***Makes 4 to 6 servings***

Nutritional Data, per portion

| | | |
|---|---|---|
| Calories 254 | Carbohydrate 33g | Saturated Fat 2g |
| Protein 8g | Sodium 67mg | Monounsaturated |
| Fat 10g | Cholesterol 40mg | Fat 7g |

# LAHM AJUN

*Armenian Pizza from Beirut*

**W**e called these "Armenian pizzas" in Beirut. The principle is the same as Neapolitan pizza, but the result is decidedly Middle Eastern, and cinnamon, allspice, and cumin give a very different flavor, especially if lamb is used instead of beef. I'm not even sure these are Armenian, strictly speaking, but they are ubiquitous throughout parts of the Levant where the Ottoman Empire once held sway. This is lovely picnic fare, and it's also a fine lunch with a hefty salad like Greek horiatiki (page 75), Lebanese fattoush (page 73), or Italian panzanella (page 72).

| | |
|---|---|
| 1 | teaspoon active dry yeast |
| ½ | cup warm water |
| 1 | cup cornmeal |
| ¾ | cup boiling water |
| 2 | cups unbleached all-purpose flour |
| 1 | teaspoon salt or to taste |
| 2 | tablespoons extra-virgin olive oil plus a little for the baking sheet |
| ½ | cup pine nuts |
| 1 | medium onion, finely chopped |
| 1 | pound ground lean lamb or beef |
| 1 | cup peeled and seeded fresh tomatoes (page 454), or canned whole tomatoes, drained, chopped |
| ⅓ | red bell pepper, finely chopped |
| 1 | cup finely chopped flat-leaf parsley |
| 2 | tablespoons minced cilantro (optional) |
| 1 | teaspoon ground cumin |
| 1 | teaspoon ground cinnamon |
| ½ | teaspoon ground allspice |
| ½ | teaspoon hot red pepper flakes or 1 small fresh red chili, seeded and finely chopped |

freshly ground black pepper to taste

Sprinkle the yeast over the warm water and set aside until the yeast dissolves. In a separate small bowl, pour the boiling water over the cornmeal and stir to combine well. Set aside.

Add the flour to a mixing bowl with a good pinch of salt. Make a well in the center of the flour. Pour in the yeast mixture and a tablespoon of the olive oil. Gradually stir the flour into the liquid, using a wooden spoon, then your hands; as you work, add the dampened cornmeal. When the mixture is raggedy, turn it out onto a lightly floured board and knead for about 10 minutes or until it is silky and smooth. Rinse the mixing bowl out, dry it, and rub it lightly with a little oil. Place the kneaded dough in the bowl, cover with a damp towel, and set aside to rise for 2 hours or until it has doubled in bulk.

Gently toast the pine nuts in the remaining tablespoon of olive oil until golden brown—just a minute or two—being very careful not to burn them. Transfer them with a slotted spoon to a paper towel to drain. In the oil remaining in the pan, gently sauté the onion over medium-low heat until very soft and light golden but not browned—about 15 minutes. Combine the pine nuts, onion, tomato, pepper, parsley, cilantro if desired, and spices with the meat and mix well with your hands, adding salt and pepper to taste. Set the meat mixture aside.

Turn the dough out on a lightly floured board, punch down, and knead briefly to knock out any air holes. Divide the dough into about 16 pieces and form each piece into a small ball. Cover the balls loosely with a piece of foil and let them rest for about 10 minutes.

Preheat the oven to 450 degrees. Roll each ball into a thin disk—not more than ⅛ inch thick—and lay it on a lightly oiled baking sheet. Spread a few spoonfuls of filling all over each disk, right out to the edges, leaving a very thin border exposed. Bake the little tarts for about 10 minutes or until the pastry is golden but still rather soft. Serve hot from the oven or lukewarm. *Makes 16 little tarts; 6 to 8 servings*

Nutritional Data, per portion

| | | |
|---|---|---|
| Calories   359 | Carbohydrate   43g | Saturated Fat   3g |
| Protein   20g | Sodium   39mg | Monounsaturated |
| Fat   13g | Cholesterol   37mg | Fat   6g |

# COCAS

### Catalan Pizza with Savory Topping

**F**ascinating how theme and variations develop in a great arc from Naples around through Liguria and Provence and on into Catalonia, then down to Valencia and out to the Balearic Islands of Majorca and Minorca. The simplicity of a little disk of bread dough spread with a savory mix of onions and garlic cooked in olive oil, eked out with a little salt fish or olives or a bit of cheese, and toasted in a hot oven must have tremendous appeal to the people who inhabit this great Western Basin of the Mediterranean. But where did it come from? How did it really originate?

This is a Majorcan version, as you can tell from the red pepper.

FOR THE DOUGH:

1  teaspoon active dry yeast

1  cup cornmeal

¾  cup boiling water

2  cups unbleached all-purpose flour

salt to taste

2  tablespoons extra-virgin olive oil

FOR THE TOPPING:

2  red bell peppers, finely chopped

2  medium very ripe tomatoes, peeled, seeded (page 454), and chopped

1  medium yellow onion, finely chopped

1  tablespoon minced flat-leaf parsley

1  tablespoon sweet paprika

1  tablespoon extra-virgin olive oil

freshly ground black pepper to taste

Prepare the dough as in the preceding recipe for lahm ajun. While the dough rises, prepare the vegetables. Mix them all together with the paprika and a little salt.

Preheat the oven to 400 degrees. Turn the dough out on the lightly floured board. Punch it down and knead lightly to knock out any air holes. Cut the dough into 4 equal parts and form each part into a ball. Roll each ball out to not more than

¼-inch thickness. Place the dough circles on a lightly oiled baking sheet and turn the edges up very slightly to hold the topping. Drain any excess liquid from the vegetable mixture and spread some of the mixture over each circle. Sprinkle with olive oil and add a little more salt and freshly ground pepper if you wish. Slide the baking sheet into the oven and bake for 5 minutes, then turn the heat down to 300 degrees and bake 20 to 30 minutes longer or until the vegetables are cooked through and the crust is golden. *Makes 4 servings*

Nutritional Data, per portion

| | | |
|---|---|---|
| Calories  491 | Carbohydrate  85g | Saturated Fat  2g |
| Protein  11g | Sodium  11mg | Monounsaturated |
| Fat  12g | Cholesterol  0 | Fat  9g |

**VARIATION:** Any of the pizza toppings may be used on cocas, which are, after all, but one variation of the basic theme. I recommend the chopped greens with olives, raisins, and pine nuts in the Double-Crusted Pizza from Southern Italy (page 157).

# GREEK SAVORY PIES

**T**he list of ingredients for these savory pies often begins with a pound of unsalted butter to be melted and brushed over the transparent layers of filo pastry. This is certainly an indigestible dish and not, I think, one we would like to have set before us more than once or twice a year. In Greek home kitchens, olive oil is much more likely to be used, making a pastry that is not only lighter and more digestible but crisp, crackly, and very attractive. For layering the filo, a plastic spritzer bottle filled with oil is very useful.

The production of homemade filo (or phyllo) pastry is labor-intensive and requires skills I've never acquired. I use frozen commercial filo for these pies.

Prepare a filling according to one of the following recipes. This can be done a day ahead or in the morning if you want to serve the pie at dinner.

1   **package frozen commercial filo pastry**

½   **cup extra-virgin olive oil, preferably in a spritzer bottle**

1   **recipe for filling**

Preheat the oven to 375 degrees. For individual pies, you will need 8 sheets of filo, or one for each pie, plus a couple more for mistakes. Remove the sheets from the package and cover them with a very lightly dampened cloth. Cover the rest of the filo tightly with plastic wrap and return it to its package in the freezer.

Spray a baking sheet lightly with oil, or paint it lightly with a pastry brush. Working quickly because filo dries out very fast upon exposure to air, remove a sheet of filo and spread it on your work surface, keeping the remaining filo sheets covered with the damp cloth. Open the sheet to its full extent, imagine it divided in half, and spray or brush the left half very lightly with olive oil. Then fold the right half over the left to make a long rectangle. Leaving a 1-inch margin around the edge, drop an abundant ¼ cup of filling in the lower right-hand corner of the rectangle. Fold up the lower edge and fold in the right-hand edge of the rectangle, then flip the corner over the filling in a northwesterly direction to make a triangle. Continue flipping the triangle, as if you were folding a flag, until you come to the end of the rectangle. Spray or brush the surface very lightly with olive oil, trim off any ragged edges with kitchen shears, and set the plump triangle of filo-encased filling on the baking sheet.

When all the filo has been filled, slide the baking sheet into the oven and bake for about 20 minutes or until the tops are golden and crisp.

To make a 10-inch round pie, you will need 12 sheets of filo, 6 for the bottom of the pie and another 6 for the top, plus a few extra for mistakes.

Paint or spray lightly the bottom and sides of a 10-inch straight-sided round springform pan with olive oil. Working quickly, remove a sheet of filo, smooth it on the work counter, and brush or spray quickly and lightly with olive oil. Set the filo in the bottom of the pan with the excess dough draping up and over the sides. Continue with 5 more sheets of filo, spraying or painting each lightly with oil and stacking them one on top of the other, each sheet crosswise to the one below. Use a light hand with the oil—overdoing it will make the pie greasy.

When all 6 layers are in place, turn the filling into the pie casing, smoothing it out on all sides. Repeat the process of oiling and layering 6 more sheets of filo to make a top for the filling, again setting the sheets crosswise to each other. When the top layers are in place, use scissors to trim away the excess pastry, leaving about 1½ inches extending beyond the rim of the pan. Spray or brush this extension lightly with water, then roll it in, folding the top and bottom layers together to form a rim around the edge of the pie. Use the remaining oil to spray or brush over the top of the pie. Slide the pie into the preheated oven and bake for about 40 minutes or until the top is golden and crisp. ***Makes 8 servings***

### Nutritional Data, per portion, with cheese filling

| | | |
|---|---|---|
| Calories 443 | Carbohydrate 36g | Saturated Fat 8g |
| Protein 14g | Sodium 711mg | Monounsaturated |
| Fat 28g | Cholesterol 81mg | Fat 14g |

### Nutritional Data, per portion, with greens and cheese filling

| | | |
|---|---|---|
| Calories 461 | Carbohydrate 40g | Saturated Fat 6g |
| Protein 14g | Sodium 620mg | Monounsaturated |
| Fat 29g | Cholesterol 69mg | Fat 16g |

# CHEESE FILLING FOR TIROPITTA

**C**ottage cheese or ricotta is a pale substitute for flavorful Greek cheeses like anthotiro, manourgi and mizithra, which can sometimes be found here in shops specializing in Greek foods. Some Greek cheeses, like the feta in the recipe, are very salty, so taste and add salt judiciously.

1½ cups crumbled feta cheese

1   cup small-curd cottage cheese, ricotta, or similar Greek cheese

2   tablespoons freshly grated Parmigiano cheese

¼   cup unbleached all-purpose flour

2   large eggs

salt and freshly ground black pepper to taste

½   cup finely minced flat-leaf parsley

1   teaspoon minced fresh thyme or ½ teaspoon dried, crumbled

½   cup finely minced fresh dill

2   teaspoons dried mint, crumbled

½   cup finely minced scallion, both white and green parts, about 1 bunch

Using a wooden spoon, mix the cheeses together in a medium bowl. Sprinkle the flour over and stir it in. Beat the eggs with a fork in a small bowl and stir them into the cheeses to make a well-blended but not smooth and creamy mass. Taste the mixture and add salt, if necessary, and lots of pepper. Add the green herbs and stir to mix well.

# GREENS AND CHEESE FILLING FOR HORTOPITTA OR SPANAKOPITTA

**O**ne of the healthiest parts of the diet of Greek countryfolk, everyone agrees, is the enormous consumption of greens—sweet, bitter, and sour, both wild and cultivated—called generically, *horta*. The range is enormous, so there's almost always something in season, whether lemon balm or purslane, wild fennel or dandelion greens, garden kale or wild chicory. Gathered year-round, greens like these are eaten on their own, tossed into farmhouse cooking pots, or brought to market for city dwellers. The open-air farmers' market in Haniá in western Crete lines both sides of the long street leading down to the port, and most of the vendors are selling masses of *horta*, some of it, like beet greens and *rathikia* or wild chicory, identifiable, some of it utterly mysterious.

To mimic the flavor somewhat (but only somewhat) of a Greek hortópitta, combine spinach with any other bitter greens you can find in the market—kale, mustard greens, dandelions, and so forth. The pie may also be made with spinach alone, in which case it's called *spanakopitta*; it will be somewhat milder in flavor.

2    10-ounce bags of fresh spinach, very carefully washed

1    pound curly endive or escarole or other bitter greens, well washed

1    medium onion, minced

12 to 18 scallions, both white and green parts, finely sliced

2    tablespoons extra-virgin olive oil

½    cup finely minced fresh dill

½    cup finely minced flat-leaf parsley

salt and freshly ground black pepper to taste

2    large eggs

¾    cup crumbled feta cheese

1    cup small-curd cottage cheese, ricotta, or similar Greek cheese

1    tablespoon freshly grated Parmigiano cheese

1    tablespoon plain dry bread crumbs

Rinse the greens very carefully and discard tough stems or wilted leaves. Place them in a large pot over medium heat, cover, and steam in the water clinging to their leaves until they are very tender—about 15 minutes. Uncover and stir the

greens down periodically. Drain in a colander and squeeze dry. (If you squeeze the greens over a small bowl, you can add the liquid to a vegetable stock or sauce.) Chop the greens rather coarsely on a board—you should have about 2 cups of chopped greens—and turn into a mixing bowl.

Gently sauté the onion and scallions in the olive oil over medium-low heat until the vegetables are very soft but not brown—about 10 to 15 minutes. Add to the greens along with all the other ingredients, one at a time, stirring after each addition.

**VARIATION:** To make a Lenten spinach pie, leave out the cheeses and eggs altogether.

# CHAPTER FOUR

# PASTA, RICE, BEANS, AND OTHER GRAINS AND LEGUMES

## PASTA

*I* was living in Rome in the mid-1970s when an editor at the *International Herald-Tribune* in Paris rang looking for story ideas. Did I ever make pasta at home? he asked. Of course, I said. Well, then, why not write about it for the newspaper? I loved to cook, but I'd never written about it.

Gradually as we talked, I realized with a frisson of anxiety that the editor meant making pasta *from scratch* at home, something no one does in Rome, where there's a *pastificio* making fresh pasta in every piazza as well as shops full of first-rate dried pasta from all the best commercial pasta makers throughout Italy. By then, however, vanity and ambition had won an easy victory over veracity, and I vowed that, if anyone could learn to make pasta, surely I could—and write about it to boot.

So I got out Marcella Hazan's first book, *The Classic Italian Cookbook*, truly a bible for me in those days and still a source of great comfort when the going gets tough, and I read—and weighed and measured and kneaded and rolled and cut and then hung the frangible strips of pasta to dry. Not content with ordinary egg pasta, I made green-colored pasta with spinach as well. We had a very large dining room at the Palazzo Taverna with 12 chairs around the massive table. By the time the children came home from school, all the chairs were draped, backs and seats alike, with ribbons of pasta, and so was the table. Enchantment! "Is it a birthday party?" Nicholas asked.

Fortunately I had a stalwart assistant at the time, Giulia d'Amurri, who kept my fantasies focused and even showed me how to use my thumb to push out orecchiette, or little ears, of pasta—they come, like Giulia's husband, Premio, from Apulia.

For lunch, of course, we had pasta. But how long to cook it fresca-fresca like this, so fresh you could almost eat it out of hand? Giulia knew. She brought an enormous quantity of water to a boil, dumped in a handful of salt and a huge quantity of pasta, gave it a stir with a long wooden ladle, and said: "*Basta dire un Ave Maria.*" It took a little longer than a Hail Mary, but not much.

That was the only time I ever made pasta from scratch by hand, and I see no reason ever to do it again. Imported Italian pasta, like De Cecco and Delverde, to name just two of the many good imported brands available, is much better than most commercially available "fresh" pasta, which is simply machine-made, machine-extruded pasta that is sold before it is dried. Making pasta truly by hand is an effort that only the dedicated and gifted can really enjoy as something more than an occasional counter to rainy-day boredom. It is a wonderful product, however, and for those who would like to try, I heartily recommend Marcella Hazan's brilliant first book, now incorporated with her second and published as *Essentials of Classic Italian Cooking* (Knopf, 1992). For the rest of us I offer a bit more than a baker's dozen of quick, easy pasta recipes, ones that require little or no forethought and that prove, if proof be necessary, that pasta—macaroni, spaghetti, vermicelli, tagliolini, whatever—is the original fast food.

For American appetites, especially when pasta is the main course offered (that's not a bad idea, either), I count on a pound of pasta for six people. Each pound of pasta, no matter what shape it takes, needs about 5 quarts of very rapidly boiling salted water (a couple of tablespoons of salt for this quantity). When the water is boiling furiously, plunge the pasta in and immediately stir with a long wooden spoon. Cover the pan until the water is once again boiling furiously. Then remove the lid and let it cook very briskly, giving it a stir from time to time, until it is done to your pleasure—more or less al dente, which is a very relative term. Of course different shapes and sizes of pasta cook at different rates—only by testing, biting into a strand or a piece, will you know for sure when it is done.

Have a colander ready and a warm bowl in which to put the drained pasta (warm the bowl by adding a couple of ladles of boiling pasta water as it finishes cooking). A moment before the pasta reaches perfection, drain it into the colander

and then turn it into the warm bowl (first emptying the bowl of pasta water) to be sauced.

Another method that can be useful for certain recipes is to drain the pasta two or three minutes *before* perfection and then turn it into the sauce on the stove. Let the pasta heat in the sauce that extra two or three minutes: the pasta will absorb the flavor of the sauce, and the whole will be more homogeneous. In either case, unless the recipe specifically states otherwise, dress the pasta as soon as it is done. Never run water over the pasta after it has been drained—that myth about rinsing starch away doesn't hold up. Then serve the pasta immediately.

One other caution: We Americans tend to serve too much sauce for the pasta, almost as if the pasta were there only to eke out the sauce, sort of a Mediterranean-style Hamburger Helper. The reverse, in fact, is true: the sauce is there simply to garnish the pasta. In the recipes that follow, proportions have been calculated Italian style, and it would be a mistake to change them. One of the great cornerstones of the Mediterranean diet is the importance of carbohydrates (pasta, bread, grains, beans) and the role played by savory sauces in lending pleasure and excitement to these essentially rather bland parts of the meal. To reverse that would be to increase the amount of fat, and often the amount of meat, at the expense of those valuable carbohydrates. Besides, it wouldn't taste good.

Pay attention to ingredients. The best-quality canned whole tomatoes are better than fresh tomatoes in many parts of the country and at many times of the year. Garlic should be plump and firm, each individual clove properly swollen to fill its papery husk. Herbs *for the most part* are better fresh than dried—and staples like parsley are always available fresh—although dried oregano, fennel seeds, and bay leaves are exceptions. Don't bother using dried basil, however.

# SPAGHETTI AJO-OJO-PEPERONCINO

### *Spaghetti with Garlic, Oil, and Hot Red Peppers*

**R**ome and Naples dispute the origin of this dish, which is so simple it can hardly be said to have been invented at all. For all its simplicity, it's remarkably satisfying: Romans turn to ajo-ojo-peperoncino for sustenance in the wee hours when the night is beginning to flag. I keep the ingredients on hand for similar occasions, returning from a long trip, for instance, or when hungry guests show up unexpectedly. The quality of the dish depends on the quality of the olive oil—this is where you should use that extraexpensive, extralush oil your cousin brought you from her last trip to Spoleto.

If you serve spaghetti ajo-ojo-peperoncino as a first course, follow it with a vegetable combination like oven-braised winter vegetables (page 418) or plain roast or grilled chicken or fish.

If you wish to add freshly grated Parmigiano cheese, do so by all means. Italians think the addition of cheese to sauces that have an abundance of garlic is odd.

6   quarts water

salt to taste

1   pound spaghetti, linguine, vermicelli, or other long thin pasta

½   cup extra-virgin olive oil

4   plump garlic cloves, minced

1   small dried hot red chili, broken into 2 or 3 pieces, or ¼ teaspoon hot
      red pepper flakes or more to taste

¾   cup minced flat-leaf parsley

freshly ground black pepper to taste

In a large pasta kettle, bring the water to a rolling boil. Add a couple tablespoons of salt and plunge the pasta in. Give the pasta a stir with a long-handled spoon and cover the pan. As soon as the water boils again, remove the lid and cook—linguine will probably take about 10 minutes, thinner pasta a little less.

While the pasta is cooking, heat the oil in a pan that will hold all the drained pasta over medium-low heat. Add the garlic and cook very gently until the garlic softens and just begins to turn golden—about 10 minutes. Then add the red pepper and parsley together with a ladleful of the pasta cooking water, turn the heat up a little, and let the sauce simmer for about 5 minutes. When the pasta is almost done, drain it in a colander and turn it immediately into the pan, mixing the pasta and sauce together well. Let it simmer together for about a minute or so—nothing need be too exact here—and then serve it immediately with salt and pepper. *Makes 6 servings*

### Nutritional Data, per portion

| | | |
|---|---|---|
| Calories  448 | Carbohydrate  58g | Saturated Fat  3g |
| Protein  10g | Sodium  267mg | Monounsaturated |
| Fat  20g | Cholesterol  0 | Fat  15g |

**VARIATION:** Linguine with Tuna (alla Sabatiello)

This recipe comes from a splendidly detailed and informative book, *La Cucina Napoletana*, by Jeanne Caròli Francesconi, first published in 1965. Anyone curious about the magnificent culinary heritage of Naples, a city that retains its exuberant character despite generations of crime, poverty, and neglect, should learn Italian to read this book. Francesconi says *alla sabatiello* comes from Saturday, *sabato*, when you could throw this together after coming home from work—a reminder that as late as 1965, many Italians still worked a six-day week.

The ingredients and procedure are exactly the same as for the spaghetti except that a 6-ounce can of the finest olive-oil-packed tuna, drained and flaked with a fork, is added to the pan with the parsley.

# LINGUINE WITH CAPERS, BLACK OLIVES, AND ANCHOVIES

**T**his Neapolitan recipe includes anchovies, once widely used in pasta and pizza as a substitute for the more expensive salt. Anchovies, omnipresent in Mediterranean cuisine, are a lingering heritage from Roman liquamen (or garum), the sauce of fermented fish, very like Vietnamese or Thai fish sauce, that was enormously appreciated as a flavoring in ancient times. Those who don't like the flavor can simply leave the anchovies out, but do try it at least once with them—I think you'll be surprised by how the flavors blend.

The best anchovies are those packed in salt that you buy by the piece in Greek and Italian shops. Otherwise, canned oil-packed anchovies are a reasonable substitute.

Use the very best richly flavored olive oil you can find.

1   **whole salted anchovy or 6 oil-packed anchovy fillets**

2   **tablespoons drained capers, preferably large ones**

1   **cup pitted black olives, preferably Gaeta**

6   **quarts water**

**salt to taste**

¼   **cup extra-virgin olive oil**

2   **garlic cloves, peeled**

½   **cup minced flat-leaf parsley**

**freshly ground black pepper to taste**

1   **pound linguine, vermicelli, spaghetti, or other long thin pasta**

If you're using salted anchovies, prepare as directed on page 471; or drain oil-packed anchovies. Cut the fillets into small pieces. If you're using salted capers, put the capers in a sieve and run water over them until most of the salt has been rinsed away. Chop the capers coarsely. Chop the pitted olives very coarsely.

Bring the water to a boil in a large kettle and add salt. Meanwhile, place the oil in a pan over low to moderate heat, add the garlic, and sauté gently until the garlic softens and starts to turn golden—about 10 minutes. Then add the capers and olives with a ladleful of the boiling pasta water. Add the parsley and a little more water if you wish, together with several grinds of pepper. Let it cook slowly together for about 5 minutes.

Meanwhile, cook the pasta, following the directions on page 172.

While the pasta boils, draw the saucepan away from the heat and add the chopped anchovies to the sauce ingredients. Mix well, pressing with the back of a spoon to dissolve the anchovies in the sauce.

As soon as the pasta is done, drain it, turn it into the warmed pasta bowl, immediately add the sauce, and turn to mix together well. Serve at once. **Makes 6 servings**

### Nutritional Data, per portion

| | | |
|---|---|---|
| Calories  398 | Carbohydrate  59g | Saturated Fat  2g |
| Protein  11g | Sodium  682mg | Monounsaturated |
| Fat  13g | Cholesterol  2mg | Fat  9g |

# PASTA ALLA CHECCA

### with a Raw Tomato Sauce

**T**his style of pasta can be found all over Italy in the summer, when tomatoes and basil are at their peak. In Rome it's called pasta alla checca. What does *alla checca* mean? No one has ever given me a satisfactory explanation. The sauce should be made in advance, but if you're going to hold it for more than a couple of hours, add the basil only an hour before serving. The raw salsa clings best to curly fusilli or small pasta shells.

Look for the very best, ripest, fullest-flavored tomatoes in local farmers' markets. There's just no point in making this dish unless tomatoes are at their peak. But when they're at their peak, if you're like me, you'll want to make it two or three times a week.

Some cooks sharpen the pasta sauce with a teaspoon of balsamic vinegar, added with the oil.

6   **large ripe, red tomatoes**

1   **garlic clove, minced**

2   **medium red onions, halved and thinly sliced**

1   **cup loosely packed fresh basil leaves**

1   **teaspoon salt or more to taste**

**freshly ground black pepper to taste**

½   **cup extra-virgin olive oil**

1   **pound fusilli or conchiglie**

6   **quarts water**

PASTA, RICE, BEANS, AND OTHER GRAINS AND LEGUMES

Over a bowl large enough to hold all the ingredients except the pasta, cut the tomatoes into small pieces and mix them and their juices with the garlic and onions. Tear the basil leaves into shreds and add to the bowl. Add the salt, pepper, and oil and toss to mix well. Cover the bowl with plastic wrap and set in the refrigerator until ready to use.

Cook the pasta in boiling salted water according to the directions on page 172. While the pasta cooks, rinse a pasta serving bowl in hot water to warm it. Remove the bowl of sauce from the refrigerator and uncover it. As soon as the pasta is done, drain it and turn it into the warmed bowl. Immediately pour the cold sauce over and mix well. Serve at once. ***Makes 6 servings***

Nutritional Data, per portion

| | | |
|---|---|---|
| Calories  504 | Carbohydrate  71g | Saturated Fat  3g |
| Protein  12g | Sodium  651mg | Monounsaturated |
| Fat  21g | Cholesterol  0 | Fat  15g |

# SPAGHETTI OR VERMICELLI ALLA POMAROLA

### *with a Sauce of Preserved Tomatoes*

In the winter, when fresh tomatoes are not available, Italian cooks don't hesitate to use canned ones. In fact many Italians, like my Tuscan neighbor Mita Antolini, put up jars and jars of *pomarola* in the early fall, when tomatoes are at their peak, to have good sauce through the winter. Use good-quality whole peeled canned tomatoes for this sauce (to preserve your own *pomarola*, see page 302). In summer, when fresh tomatoes are in season, you can use dead-ripe ones.

1   small onion, chopped

1   garlic clove, chopped

1   medium carrot, peeled and chopped

¼   cup minced flat-leaf parsley

¼   cup extra-virgin olive oil

1   28-ounce can whole tomatoes with their juice, chopped

¼   cup slivered fresh basil leaves, or ½ teaspoon dried oregano, crumbled

1½ pounds spaghetti, vermicelli, tagliatelle, or other long thin pasta

6   quarts water

salt to taste

freshly ground black pepper to taste

½   cup freshly grated Parmigiano cheese (optional)

In a heavy saucepan over medium-low heat, gently sauté the onion, garlic, carrot, and parsley in the oil until the vegetables are soft but not brown—about 10 to 15 minutes. Add the tomatoes, raise the heat to medium-high, and cook rapidly, stirring frequently, until the tomato liquid has evaporated and the tomatoes have reached a thick jammy consistency—about 20 minutes. (If you're using dried herbs, add them with the tomatoes.)

Cook the pasta in boiling salted water according to the directions on page 172.

Taste the sauce and add salt and pepper if necessary. Stir in the fresh basil. When the pasta is done, drain it and immediately turn it into a warmed bowl (use a little of the pasta water to warm the bowl). Top with half the cheese. Turn the pasta in the sauce at the table just before serving. Pass the remaining cheese with the pasta. *Makes 8 to 9 servings*

### Nutritional Data, per portion

| | | |
|---|---|---|
| Calories   361 | Carbohydrate   62g | Saturated Fat   1g |
| Protein   11g | Sodium   411mg | Monounsaturated |
| Fat   8g | Cholesterol   0 | Fat   5g |

# SPAGHETTI OR LINGUINE ALLA PUTTANESCA

### with Tomatoes, Olives, and Capers

**M**ost Italians claim this is a famous Roman dish, usually prepared by ladies of the night to revive themselves after their tiresome labors. Neapolitan food historian Jeanne Caròli Francesconi contradicts that. In Naples, she says, it was called *alla marinara* until sometime in the late 1940s, when a local celebrity, Eduardo Colucci, playfully rebaptized it *alla puttanesca*. Colucci was known as much for the table he set at his little terrace house on the island of Ischia as he was for the personalities, Italian and foreign, who graced it.

1 medium onion, chopped

2 garlic cloves, chopped

1 medium carrot, peeled and chopped

⅓ cup extra-virgin olive oil

1 whole salted anchovy, prepared as directed on page 471,
    or 4 oil-packed anchovy fillets

½ cup minced flat-leaf parsley

2 to 3 pounds very ripe fresh tomatoes, seeded and chopped,
    or 1 28-ounce can whole tomatoes with their juice, chopped

½ teaspoon dried oregano, crumbled

2 tablespoons drained capers, preferably large ones

1 cup pitted black olives, preferably Gaeta

salt and freshly ground black pepper to taste

1½ pounds linguine, vermicelli, spaghetti, or other long thin pasta

6 quarts water

In a heavy saucepan or skillet over medium-low heat, gently sauté the onion, garlic, and carrot in the oil until the vegetables are wilted but not starting to brown—about 10 to 15 minutes. Chop the anchovy fillets and add them to the vegetables together with half the minced parsley. Cook, stirring and pressing the anchovies with a wooden spoon, until they have melted into the sauce—about 5 minutes.

Now raise the heat slightly to medium or medium-high and add the tomatoes and oregano. Cook rapidly, stirring frequently, until the tomato juice has evaporated and the tomatoes are reduced to a jam—about 20 minutes. Off the heat, stir in the capers and black olives. Taste for seasoning, adding salt and pepper if desired.

While the sauce is cooking, boil the pasta in lightly salted water, following the directions on page 172. Drain the pasta, turn it into a warm bowl, and pour the sauce over. Sprinkle the remaining parsley over the top. Turn the pasta in the sauce at the table immediately before serving. **Makes 8 to 9 servings**

Nutritional Data, per portion

| Calories 409 | Carbohydrate 66g | Saturated Fat 2g |
|---|---|---|
| Protein 12g | Sodium 524mg | Monounsaturated |
| Fat 12g | Cholesterol 1mg | Fat 8g |

# ORECCHIETTE ALLA BARESE

### *Little Ears with Broccoli Rabe*

**T**he name in Italian gives no hint of it, but *orecchiette alla barese* are always cooked with a sauce made of broccoli rabe or rapini, a type of strongly flavored broccoli that is increasingly available in supermarket produce sections. (Like its cousins in the cruciferous vegetable family, broccoli rabe has important health benefits.) If you can't find broccoli rabe, substitute regular broccoli, but the flavor will not be as sharp and interesting.

This quick and easy preparation is a great favorite in the Italian South, especially in the olive oil–producing district around Bari, where the orecchiette are homemade. Orecchiette are a fairly standard variety of dried pasta and available in many supermarkets, but if you can't find them, use farfalle (butterflies), small shells, or fusilli (corkscrews) instead. The preparation is not appropriate for long stringy pasta like spaghetti or linguine.

2   bunches of broccoli rabe or 2 large heads of broccoli
salt to taste
2   garlic cloves, minced
3   tablespoons extra-virgin olive oil
6   oil-packed anchovy fillets or to taste
1   teaspoon hot red pepper flakes or 1 small dried red chili, chopped,
      seeds and all
1   pound orecchiette or other pasta
4   quarts water
freshly ground black pepper to taste

Clean and coarsely chop the broccoli rabe. Bring about 1 inch of lightly salted water to a boil in a heavy saucepan. Add the broccoli rabe and cook until it is tender and only a few tablespoons of liquid are left in the bottom of the pan—about 5 to 10 minutes, depending on how finely the vegetable is chopped. Set the pan of broccoli rabe aside, but keep it warm.

In a separate skillet or sauté pan, gently sauté the garlic in the olive oil until it is soft, then melt in the anchovy fillets by crushing them in the garlicky oil with a fork.

Add the red pepper and stir to mix well. Turn the garlic-pepper oil into the broccoli rabe and mix.

Cook the pasta in lightly salted boiling water until done, as directed on page 172. Drain the pasta and immediately combine with the seasoned broccoli rabe. Turn it into a warm serving bowl, add pepper, and serve immediately. (Don't add or pass grated cheese.) *Makes 6 servings*

### Nutritional Data, per portion

| | | |
|---|---|---|
| Calories 403 | Carbohydrate 67g | Saturated Fat 1g |
| Protein 16g | Sodium 460mg | Monounsaturated |
| Fat 9g | Cholesterol 2mg | Fat 6g |

# MITA'S TUSCAN SUGO

Mita Antolini, my Tuscan neighbor, uses this sauce to dress pasta or gnocchi di patate, little potato dumplings, that she makes for Sunday lunch.

1   medium onion, finely chopped

2   garlic cloves, finely chopped

¼   cup minced flat-leaf parsley

1   celery rib, finely chopped, leaves and all

1   small carrot, peeled and finely chopped

3   tablespoons extra-virgin olive oil

¼   pound ground very lean beef, veal, or pork

1   chicken liver, cleaned and finely chopped (optional)

⅓   cup dry white wine

1   28-ounce can imported Italian plum tomatoes or 4 or 5 large ripe
      tomatoes, chopped

salt and freshly ground black pepper to taste

1   small bunch of basil, leaves and tender tips, slivered, about ⅓ cup

1½  pounds tagliatelle or other long flat pasta

6   quarts water

½   cup freshly grated Parmigiano cheese or more to taste

PASTA, RICE, BEANS, AND OTHER GRAINS AND LEGUMES

Sauté the onion, garlic, parsley, celery, and carrot in the olive oil in a skillet over medium heat, stirring frequently, until the vegetables are soft but not brown—about 10 to 15 minutes. Add the ground meat and chopped chicken liver, raise the heat slightly, and cook the meats, stirring constantly, until they have lost all trace of rosiness—about 10 minutes.

Pour in the wine and bring to a boil. Turn down the heat and let the wine cook off until just a few tablespoons are left in the pan—about 5 to 10 minutes. Then turn the can of tomatoes, juice and all, into the pan, raise the heat again, and cook, chopping the tomatoes with a wooden spoon, until the sauce is dense and thick, the tomatoes are reduced almost to a puree, and the juice has cooked down to a few tablespoons—about 20 minutes. Taste for seasoning, adding salt and pepper if desired. Stir in the slivered basil. Set the sauce aside and keep it warm while you prepare the pasta.

Cook the pasta in salted boiling water according to the directions on page 172. Drain the cooked pasta in a colander, turn it into a heated bowl, and immediately dress with the hot sauce. Sprinkle a little of the cheese over the top and pass the remaining cheese at the table. *Makes 8 to 9 servings*

Nutritional Data, per portion

| | | |
|---|---|---|
| Calories  404 | Carbohydrate  64g | Saturated Fat  2g |
| Protein  16g | Sodium  525mg | Monounsaturated |
| Fat  9g | Cholesterol  12mg | Fat  5g |

# BUCATINI ALL'AMATRICIANA AND PENNE ALL'ARRABBIATA

**T**hese two pastas and their variations are favorites in Roman trattorias. All'amatriciana, with little pieces of cured pork in the sauce, comes from the Abruzzese town of Amatrice. So do many of the hosts of the old Roman trattorias, osterias, and tavole calde, where the common people take their meals, and so all'amatriciana has become a Roman style of pasta. *Penne all'arrabbiata*, without the cured pork, simply means "enraged pasta," referring to the heat of the peppers, which are also valuable for restoring flagging energies (see the puttanesca recipe, page 180). The popularity of all these pastas has benefited considerably from the *nostalgie de la boue* that from time to time afflicts upper-class Romans, intellectuals, film people, and aristocrats, who frequent working-class eating places at times of the night when the working classes are soundly asleep—a bit like Parisian partygoers slumming for bowls of soupe à l'oignon at five o'clock in the morning.

### Bucatini all'Amatriciana

**Y**ou don't have to make this with bucatini—other suitable pasta shapes include rigatoni, penne, and ziti.

- 1 large garlic clove, minced
- 1 medium onion, finely chopped
- 2 ounces pancetta or slab bacon, finely diced
- 3 tablespoons extra-virgin olive oil
- 1½ pounds tomatoes, preferably plum tomatoes, peeled and seeded (page 454) and chopped, or 1 16-ounce can Italian plum tomatoes with their juice, chopped
- salt and freshly ground black pepper to taste
- 1 pound bucatini or other short thick pasta
- 6 quarts water
- freshly grated cheese, preferably pecorino romano

In a saucepan over medium heat, gently sauté the garlic, onion, and pancetta in the oil, stirring occasionally, until the meat renders a little fat and the vegetables just

begin to brown—about 15 to 20 minutes. Add the tomatoes and stir to mix. Cook the tomatoes for about 5 minutes, and when they start to give off their juice, lower the heat and simmer, stirring occasionally, until the sauce is dense, about 20 minutes. Add salt and pepper.

Meanwhile, cook the pasta in lightly salted water according to the directions on page 172. Drain it, turn it into a warmed serving bowl, and pour the sauce over it. Serve immediately, passing the grated cheese. **Makes 6 servings**

Nutritional Data, per portion

| | | |
|---|---|---|
| Calories 444 | Carbohydrate 64g | Saturated Fat 3g |
| Protein 13g | Sodium 391mg | Monounsaturated |
| Fat 15g | Cholesterol 11mg | Fat 8g |

## Penne all'Arrabbiata

**C**ontrol the heat of the dish by using more or less hot red pepper.

¼ cup extra-virgin olive oil

3 large garlic cloves, minced

1½ pounds tomatoes, preferably plum tomatoes, peeled and seeded (page 454) and coarsely chopped, or 1 16-ounce can imported Italian tomatoes with their juice, chopped

1 or 2 dried hot red chilies, broken into pieces, or 1 teaspoon hot red pepper flakes or to taste

salt to taste

1 pound penne or other short thick round pasta

6 quarts water

Heat the oil in a heavy saucepan over medium-high heat and sauté the garlic, stirring constantly, until it is just beginning to turn golden—about 10 minutes. Add the tomatoes and chilies, reduce the heat to medium-low, and continue cooking until the tomatoes are soft and the sauce is dense but not pureed—about 20 minutes. Remove from the heat and taste for seasoning, adding more salt if necessary.

THE MEDITERRANEAN DIET COOKBOOK

Cook the pasta in lightly salted water as directed on page 172. Drain thoroughly, turn into a warm serving bowl, and pour the sauce over it. Serve immediately. *Makes 6 servings*

### Nutritional Data, per portion

| | | |
|---|---|---|
| Calories 386 | Carbohydrate 62g | Saturated Fat 2g |
| Protein 11g | Sodium 273mg | Monounsaturated |
| Fat 11g | Cholesterol 0 | Fat 8g |

# PASTA WITH CLAMS AND HERBS, LUCCARESE STYLE

Cesare Casella at Ristorante Vipore near Lucca makes this pasta sauce from the rich mixture of garden herbs growing around his hillside restaurant. Use whatever is available to you: parsley, sage, rosemary, and thyme, of course, plus a little sorrel if you can find it, and any other herbs growing in your garden or in the produce section of your supermarket. Good choices include borage, lovage, basil, chives, chervil, savory, lemon balm, oregano. I would not use dill, cilantro, or mint because they tend to dominate, and what you're looking for in this sauce is an intriguing mixture and balance.

Note that this is not a clam sauce—the clams are there to enhance the herbs rather than vice versa.

3    dozen mahogany, Manila, or other small hardshell clams
½    cup dry white wine
1    medium onion, finely chopped
2    tablespoons extra-virgin olive oil
¾    cup finely chopped fresh herbs
salt and freshly ground black pepper to taste
1    pound linguine, spaghetti, or other long thin pasta
6    quarts water
1    medium tomato, diced (optional)

Scrub the clams very well, discarding any that are gaping open. Place in a large heavy kettle with the wine and ½ cup water. Bring to a boil and cook over high heat,

stirring occasionally, until all the clams have opened fully—about 5 to 7 minutes. Off the heat, use a slotted spoon to remove the clams from the kettle and set them aside to cool. Discard any that don't open.

Strain the broth in the kettle through a very-fine-mesh sieve to get rid of any sand. Reduce the broth over medium heat to about ½ cup. Set aside, but keep it warm.

When the clams are cool enough to handle, pull them out of their shells and discard the shells. If the clams are large, chop them coarsely.

Rinse the pan the clams were cooked in and return it to medium-low heat. Gently sauté the onion in the olive oil until very soft and golden but not brown— about 20 minutes. Add the herbs and reduced clam broth. Stir and simmer for about 5 minutes, just long enough for the herb aromas to penetrate. Taste, adding salt and pepper if necessary. Set aside and keep warm.

Cook the pasta in the lightly salted water until not quite done, as directed on page 172. Drain the pasta and immediately turn it into the pan with the sauce. Set the pan over medium heat and turn the pasta in the sauce. Let cook for a few minutes longer, just until the pasta is done to taste and has absorbed some of the flavors of the sauce. Add the clams, along with the tomato if you're using it, to the sauce and continue stirring over medium heat just long enough for the clams to warm up. Serve immediately. *Makes 6 servings*

### Nutritional Data, per portion

| | | |
|---|---|---|
| Calories 387 | Carbohydrate 61g | Saturated Fat 1g |
| Protein 17g | Sodium 299mg | Monounsaturated |
| Fat 6g | Cholesterol 18mg | Fat 4g |

# PASTA WITH SHRIMP IN AN ORANGE SAUCE

1   red bell pepper

1   pound medium-large (25-count) shrimp

½   dried red New Mexico or Anaheim chili

2   tablespoons extra-virgin olive oil

½   medium onion, finely chopped

1   garlic clove, finely chopped

⅓   cup dry white wine

3   tablespoons fresh orange juice

grated zest of 1 medium orange

12  Kalamata olives, pitted and coarsely chopped, or 18 Gaeta or Niçoise
       olives, pitted

salt, if necessary, and freshly ground black pepper

1   pound tagliatelle or fusilli

6   quarts water

Roast and peel the red pepper, following the directions on page 455, and cut it into long thin strips. Set aside. Peel the shrimp, deveining if necessary. Cut each one into 3 pieces and set aside. Chop the chili, seeds and all, and set aside.

Over medium-low heat in a pan large enough to hold all the ingredients except the pasta, sauté the onion in the olive oil, stirring frequently, until it is very soft but not brown—about 15 minutes. Add the garlic and shrimp, raising the heat slightly, and toss them in the oil until the shrimp turns pink—about 2 to 3 minutes. Add the wine and cook, stirring frequently, until the sauce is slightly reduced—about 5 minutes—then stir in the orange juice, zest, and chili.

Bring the sauce back to a boil and stir in the roasted pepper strips and the olives. The sauce should be thick enough to coat the pasta. If it seems too thin, remove the shrimp and reduce the sauce by boiling rapidly; then return the shrimp to the thickened sauce. Taste and add salt if necessary and pepper. Keep the sauce warm while you cook the pasta.

Cook the pasta in lightly salted water according to the directions on page 172. Drain in a colander, turn into a heated bowl, and toss with the shrimp sauce. Serve immediately. *Makes 6 servings*

Nutritional Data, per portion

| | | |
|---|---|---|
| Calories 425 | Carbohydrate 62g | Saturated Fat 1g |
| Protein 23g | Sodium 443mg | Monounsaturated |
| Fat 8g | Cholesterol 93mg | Fat 5g |

# SPAGHETTI CON ZUCCHINI, PATATE, E RICOTTA

**T**his is a meager dish, one that comes out of the poor peasant culture of Apulia, down in the heel of Italy—meager but rich and delicious in combination, a reflection of how simplicity and poverty and imagination can come together to create something good. As with all simple dishes, the quality of the ingredients is what makes the difference. Use the smallest (no more than 4 inches long) and freshest zucchini you can find and waxy potatoes with good flavor. If you can't find Yellow Finns, Red Bliss potatoes will do.

At Ristorante Bacco in Barletta, near Bari, they use the local ricotta salata, a hard grating cheese, for this. An aged pecorino, if you can find it, will be good, but don't use pecorino romano, which is too strong for this dish.

**salt to taste**

6    **quarts water**

3    **medium Yellow Finn potatoes, peeled, halved, and sliced ½ inch thick**

1    **pound spaghetti or spaghettini, broken into pieces about 2 inches long**

**6 to 8 very small zucchini, thinly sliced**

⅓    **cup fruity extra-virgin olive oil**

**lots of freshly ground black pepper**

½    **cup grated ricotta salata, pecorino, or Parmigiano cheese, or more to taste**

Have all the ingredients prepared before you start to cook, because the cooking goes very quickly once begun. Fill a serving bowl with very hot water to warm it for the pasta.

In a large pot, bring the lightly salted water to a boil. Add the potato slices and boil for 8 minutes. Add the spaghetti and stir with a long-handled spoon. Cover the

pot and bring the water back to a boil. Set the lid ajar and continue boiling for 8 minutes. Add the zucchini slices and boil, uncovered, for 4 minutes or until the potato slices are cooked through and the spaghetti is just tender but not soft and mushy.

Drain, reserving ¼ cup of the cooking liquid. Immediately turn the pasta and vegetables into the warm serving bowl and pour the reserved cooking liquid and olive oil over the pasta. Add salt and pepper and sprinkle 2 or 3 tablespoons of grated cheese over the top. Serve immediately, passing the remaining cheese at the table. **Makes 6 servings**

Nutritional Data, per portion

| | | |
|---|---|---|
| Calories   488 | Carbohydrate   73g | Saturated Fat   2g |
| Protein   14g | Sodium   482mg | Monounsaturated |
| Fat   16g | Cholesterol   7mg | Fat   10g |

# TRENETTE AL PESTO

In Italy, pesto is freshly made at the height of the season when local basil is at its flavor peak. It is a rare treat, one that Italian cooks handle with joy and respect. Italians are discreet with pesto, reckoning that a little of this rich and highly flavored sauce goes a very long way. A big spoonful of pesto may be stirred into a hearty minestrone of summer vegetables (just as it is in the very similar Niçoise pistou on page 98), and I'm also fond of a small (1 teaspoon, no more) dollop of freshly made pesto to top a grilled or poached fish. In all cases, the accent is on fresh. Otherwise pesto is almost always used only in this classic Genovese dish of slender trenette noodles mixed with a few slices of small new potatoes. The sweetness of the potatoes accents the robust flavor of the sauce, and the contrasting textures of pasta and potatoes add further interest.

Traditionally, as the name implies, pesto is made with mortar and pestle, and many cooks believe that is still the best way to extract the fullest flavor from basil and garlic. It takes time, however, so the following recipe uses a blender or food processor. But someday when you have a little extra time, try making pesto the old-fashioned way, focusing on the materials at hand and the aromas that rise from the mortar. You'll be amazed at where your thoughts might lead.

PASTA, RICE, BEANS, AND OTHER GRAINS AND LEGUMES

3   cups packed tender young basil leaves

3   heaped tablespoons pine nuts

1½  teaspoons coarse salt

½   cup extra-virgin olive oil or more to taste

3.  fat garlic cloves, crushed with the flat blade of a knife and very finely
    minced

½   cup freshly grated cheese, preferably a mixture of Parmigiano and
    an aged Tuscan pecorino or pecorino sardo; otherwise, use all
    Parmigiano

salt to taste

6   quarts water

3   medium potatoes, peeled and sliced not more than ¼ inch thick

1   pound trenette, linguine, tagliatelle, or other long flat thin pasta


Put the basil, pine nuts, and salt in a food processor or blender and process
steadily while you add the oil in a thin but constant stream. The sauce should
achieve the consistency of a slightly grainy paste but not a fine puree. Add the garlic
and process very briefly, just to mix. When the sauce is the right consistency,
transfer it to a bowl and, using a spatula, fold in the grated cheese. (If you're using a
mortar, just continue to work in the cheese with the pestle.) If the sauce is too thick,
work in more olive oil. Taste and adjust the seasoning.

Pesto can be made ahead and stored in the refrigerator for a few days or in the
freezer for a few weeks. If you plan to store it, leave the cheese out. Transfer the
pesto to a refrigerator container, pour a thin film of oil over the top, cover, and
store. When you're ready to use it, let the pesto thaw if necessary, then stir in the oil
on top and the grated cheese.

Bring the lightly salted water to a rolling boil. Drop in the potato slices and boil
for 5 minutes, then drop in the pasta. Stir with a wooden spoon, cover the pot, and
bring back to a boil. Uncover and boil the pasta and potatoes together for 10 to 12
minutes or until the potatoes are thoroughly cooked and the pasta is done to taste.

While the pasta is cooking, stir a couple of tablespoons of hot pasta water into
the pesto and rinse a big pasta bowl with boiling water to warm it.

As soon as the pasta is done, drain it, turn it into the warmed bowl, and pour
the pesto over it. Toss gently to mix the pesto and serve immediately, passing more
cheese if desired. *Makes 6 servings*

Nutritional Data, per portion

Calories  595  Carbohydrate  78g  Saturated Fat  5g
Protein  17g  Sodium  791mg  Monounsaturated
Fat  26g  Cholesterol  6mg  Fat  17g

# SPAGHETTINI CON SALSA DI NOCE

### Spaghettini with Walnut Sauce

1  pound walnuts in the shell

2  garlic cloves, minced

2 to 3 tablespoons extra-virgin olive oil as needed

¼  cup minced flat-leaf parsley

salt to taste

1  pound spaghettini, spaghetti, linguine, or other long pasta

6  quarts water

¼  cup ricotta cheese

freshly ground black pepper to taste

½  cup freshly grated Parmigiano cheese

Shell the walnuts and pound to a paste in a mortar or in a food processor. If you're using a food processor, add a tablespoon of water; otherwise the walnuts might become overprocessed and exude their oil.

In a saucepan over medium-low heat, gently sauté the garlic in a tablespoon of olive oil until the garlic is soft but not brown—about 10 minutes. Add the walnuts and parsley with a pinch of salt. Stir to combine the ingredients well and cook for about 5 minutes, adding another tablespoon or more of oil if it seems necessary to keep the walnuts from burning.

Cook the pasta in lightly salted water according to the directions on page 172. While the pasta is boiling, add 2 tablespoons of the pasta water to the walnut sauce and continue cooking the sauce over very low heat. Blend the ricotta into the sauce, using a fork to mix it well. Taste and add salt if necessary and lots of freshly ground pepper.

As soon as the pasta is done, drain it, turn it into a heated bowl, and immediately turn the sauce over the pasta and mix well, adding about half the grated Parmigiano. Serve immediately, passing the rest of the cheese at the table. *Makes 6 servings*

Nutritional Data, per portion

| | | |
|---|---|---|
| Calories 607 | Carbohydrate 64g | Saturated Fat 5g |
| Protein 19g | Sodium 428mg | Monounsaturated |
| Fat 32g | Cholesterol 12mg | Fat 11g |

# FETTUCCINE WITH RICOTTA OR CHÈVRE AND ASPARAGUS

You can vary the vegetable in this springtime pasta—fresh young peas are delicious, as are small artichoke hearts or very tender young fava beans if you can find or grow them. Just be sure that the raw, prepared vegetable weighs about ¾ pound—that is, shelled peas or fava beans, artichoke hearts trimmed down to their cooking size.

Most cooks will not be able to find wild fennel, but those in northern California and other parts of the country where this delightfully fragrant herb grows on the edge of highways and in abandoned lots should take the opportunity to use the green tops. Don't substitute fennel seeds or cultivated fennel—the flavor is too crude.

¾    **pound tender young asparagus**

1    **garlic clove, crushed with the flat blade of a knife**

3    **tablespoons extra-virgin olive oil**

2    **tablespoons minced fresh mint**

2    **tablespoons minced fresh green wild fennel if available**

1    **pound fettuccine**

**salt to taste**

6    **quarts water**

½    **pound fresh creamy ricotta or mild goat cheese (chèvre)**

**a little freshly grated nutmeg if desired**

**freshly ground black pepper to taste**

½    **cup freshly grated young pecorino or Parmigiano cheese**

Trim off the tough ends of the asparagus stalks and cut the tender parts into 2-inch lengths. In a sauté pan, gently stew the garlic clove and asparagus in the oil until the vegetables are tender but not brown—about 15 minutes. Stir in the mint and, if you can find it, the wild fennel. Set aside.

Meanwhile, cook the pasta in lightly salted water as directed on page 172. While the pasta cooks, extract about ½ cup of the cooking liquid and mix it in a small saucepan with the ricotta. Set the saucepan over low heat and gently cream the ricotta with the cooking liquid. When the ricotta is warm, taste and add salt and a little pepper. If you don't have wild fennel, add grated nutmeg if you wish to the cheese sauce.

Drain the pasta and combine immediately with the cheese sauce, tossing to mix well. Arrange on a warm platter and pour the asparagus, garlic, and oil over the top. Sprinkle a few tablespoons of grated cheese over and serve immediately, passing the rest of the grated cheese at the table. *Makes 6 servings*

### Nutritional Data, per portion

| | | |
|---|---|---|
| Calories 453 | Carbohydrate 57g | Saturated Fat 5g |
| Protein 19g | Sodium 389mg | Monounsaturated |
| Fat 17g | Cholesterol 98mg | Fat 8g |

## COUSCOUS DE POISSON

### *North African Fish Couscous*

Couscous is the North African pasta, made from semolina wheat flour and water, the basic carbohydrate, along with bread, on Moroccan and Tunisian tables. Like pasta, it's often served on its own, with a thin but spicy sauce. For special occasions a grander couscous is produced, with a variety of vegetables and meats or fish.

Traditionally cooks made the couscous grains at home, a laborious process. Nowadays, even in North Africa, most couscous is bought ready-made (but not instant). You can find a good quality at many health food stores, but the best is fine-grain Diafra couscous from Morocco. (As far as I know, Diafra couscous is not imported to this country; if you're traveling to France, however, you are sure to find it in neighborhood shops that cater to the large North African population.)

PASTA, RICE, BEANS, AND OTHER GRAINS AND LEGUMES

Fatouma Mbrahim made this couscous for me one afternoon in Sidi Bou Said, a compact hilltop village outside Tunis.

In a tiny kitchen equipped with an ancient refrigerator that sat up on table legs, a four-burner stove that ran on bottled gas, a toaster oven, a sink the size of my bathroom sink at home, and a marble countertop that served as cutting board, storage area, and work table all together, Fatouma turned out a magnificent feast for 26 people. It included the couscous with all its accompanying sauces, as well as a delightful mixture of salads to garnish the main course—*mechouia*, the Tunisian favorite of finely minced grilled tomatoes, peppers, onions, and garlic (page 41); *salade d'aubergine*, made from roasted eggplant mixed with garlic pounded to a paste; *salade des concombres*, simply sliced cucumbers (the ridged, narrow sweet kind that are sometimes called Armenian or Lebanese cucumbers in this country), dressed with a light soured cream; and *salade des betteraves*, beets roasted in the oven, peeled, sliced, and mixed with oil, lemon juice, and pounded garlic.

Fatouma was born in Algeria—her family moved to Tunis after the French war—and she says her couscous, because it uses fruit as well as vegetables, is more Algerian than Tunisian. Others tell me that the fish couscous of Tunis typically includes quinces and is less spicy than couscous from other parts of the country.

A couscousière is a special two-part pot for preparing couscous, available at kitchen supply stores (or see Resources at the back of the book). The savory stew goes in the bottom half, and the couscous grain goes in the top, so that the steam rising from the stew cooks the grain. You can fabricate a couscousière with a stockpot for the bottom and a colander that will just fit into the top. Line the colander with a double layer of cheesecloth to keep the grains from falling through the holes. (A tight seal between the bottom and top is important to force the steam through the holes of the top and into the couscous. Tunisian recipe books say to dip a strip of muslin in a flour and water paste, but Fatouma seals hers with wet strips of newspaper.)

Fatouma's recipe, as you will see, is basically a vegetable couscous with the fish cooked apart in a little of the vegetable sauce. If you wish, you can omit the fish from the meal and serve a vegetarian couscous. The pumpkin featured in many Mediterranean recipes is drier in texture and flavor than our pie pumpkins. A good hard dark orange winter squash (Hubbard, acorn, buttercup, etc.) makes a fine substitute.

An elaborate couscous like this should not be made for fewer than eight people. The following recipe will easily serve 10.

4   onions, coarsely chopped

10  tablespoons extra-virgin olive oil

4   medium tomatoes, peeled (page 454) and coarsely chopped, or 1 28-
    ounce can whole tomatoes, drained and chopped

2   tablespoons harissa (page 301) diluted with ½ cup hot water

¼   cup canned tomato puree or liquid from the canned tomatoes

4   white turnips, peeled and cut in half

4   medium russet potatoes, peeled and cut in half

4   medium carrots, peeled and cut in half

about 6½ cups water

salt and freshly ground black pepper to taste

½   cup dried chick-peas, soaked overnight, or use the quick-soak
    method (page 454)

4   cups couscous, preferably fine-grain

2   cups very hot water

about 2 pounds orange squash or pumpkin, peeled and cut into serving
    pieces

1   fat or 2 slender leeks, rinsed well and cut into chunks

4   medium zucchini, cut in half lengthwise

2   green bell peppers, quartered

2   quinces, quartered and cored, or 2 very firm cooking apples,
    quartered and cored

½   teaspoon saffron threads crumbled into ½ cup warm water

1   teaspoon ground cumin

2   pounds fresh fish steaks, fillets, or cleaned whole fish: halibut,
    haddock, snapper, monkfish, or the like

1   small green cabbage, cut into 8 wedges

¼   cup harissa (page 301) diluted with ¼ cup hot water for serving

Place the onions with 2 tablespoons of the olive oil in the bottom of a couscousière and set it over medium-low heat. Cook gently, stirring occasionally, until the onions start to soften, about 15 minutes. Then add the tomatoes, stir, raise the heat to medium, and continue cooking, uncovered, for about 10 minutes or

until the fragrance starts to rise. Stir in the 2 tablespoons harissa diluted in ½ cup water and the tomato puree and cook for another 5 minutes.

Add the turnips, potatoes, and carrots to the tomatoes with a quart of the water, salt, and lots of freshly ground pepper. Bring to a simmer and cook, uncovered, for 15 minutes.

Drain the chick-peas and place them in a separate small pan with water to cover to a depth of 1 inch. Bring to a boil and cook, covered, for about 20 minutes. Set aside, but do not drain.

The recipe can be done ahead up to this point. The couscous must be prepared about 1 hour before you start to cook it, and the cooking process itself, while not laborious, will take a good hour and 20 minutes. Give yourself plenty of time, much of which can be spent doing other things while the couscous steams.

About 1 hour before you're ready to cook the couscous, prepare it by tossing the couscous grains in a large, shallow bowl with about a tablespoon of salt to mix well. Then take the remaining ½ cup oil in a measuring cup or jug in your left hand (if you're right-handed) and pour it slowly, a little at a time, over the grains while you stir them with the fingers of your right hand, coating each grain with oil. Add a cup of very hot tap water to the jug and repeat the procedure, mixing the water in a small amount at a time until the couscous has absorbed it. Smooth over the top of the couscous and set it aside for about 45 minutes to soften.

Layer the squash, leeks, and zucchini on top of the vegetable stew, then layer the green peppers and quince sections on top. Pour the chick-peas with their cooking liquid over the stew. Add the saffron with its soaking liquid, the cumin, and another cup of water.

When the couscous grains are ready, bring the vegetable stew to a simmer. Extract about ½ cup of the sauce liquid and set it aside for cooking the fish and cabbage sections.

Set the top of the couscousière onto the bottom half, sealing the gap between them as described. Rub the palms of your hands lightly with a little olive oil and rub the couscous grains between your palms to get rid of any lumps. Go over it carefully—in a good couscous each grain is separate and soft, which will never happen without this gentle rubbing. Add the couscous to the top of the couscousière, rubbing the grains between your palms as you do so. When all the couscous has been added, gently smooth over the top of the couscous with a wooden spoon and leave, uncovered and without stirring (this is very important), until the steam begins to rise between the grains. This can take up to 30 minutes. Once the steam starts to rise, time the couscous to cook, undisturbed, for 20 minutes.

THE MEDITERRANEAN DIET COOKBOOK

Meanwhile, in a saucepan that will hold the whole fish or the fish pieces in one layer, cook the fish over medium heat in the reserved sauce liquid, adding ½ cup water or more if necessary. Cover the fish and steam until it is done and the flesh flakes easily. Steaks or fillets will take about 8 to 10 minutes; a whole fish about 12 to 15 minutes, depending on thickness. Transfer the fish to a platter, reserving the cooking liquid. Cover the fish lightly with a sheet of foil and set it in a barely warm oven while you continue with the couscous.

Put the cabbage sections in a saucepan with the reserved fish liquid, cover, set over medium heat, and cook until done to taste, about 15 minutes. (Slightly underdone cabbage adds a nice texture contrast to the very soft vegetables. The cabbage is cooked apart so that its strong flavor doesn't overcome the more delicate flavors of the stew.) Add the cabbage sections to the fish to keep warm.

When the couscous has steamed for 20 minutes, remove the top of the couscousière and spread the couscous grains out, handling them gently, on a shallow platter or tray. Have ready a cup of very hot tap water with a teaspoon or more to taste of salt dissolved in it. Using a wooden spoon or wooden spatula, repeat the same action as before, pouring the salted water from your left hand, stirring very gently with your right hand, using the wooden spoon until the grains have cooled enough so you can use your fingers. Let the couscous sit for about 10 minutes, resting and absorbing the salted water.

(If you wish, add the juices in which the fish and cabbage cooked to the vegetable stew at this point.)

Return the couscous grains to the top half of the couscousière and set it once more over the simmering stew, sealing the gap as described above. Again let it steam, uncovered and undisturbed, for 20 minutes.

When the couscous is done, serve it immediately, mounding it on a warm serving platter and garnishing it with all the vegetables, including the cabbage. Drizzle a ladleful of the sauce over the couscous and vegetables and over the platter of fish and cabbage. Serve, passing the rest of the sauce in a bowl along with the harissa garnish. ***Makes 10 abundant servings***

Nutritional Data, per portion

| | | |
|---|---|---|
| Calories 780 | Carbohydrate 115g | Saturated Fat 3g |
| Protein 34g | Sodium 150mg | Monounsaturated |
| Fat 24g | Cholesterol 24mg | Fat 15g |

PASTA, RICE, BEANS, AND OTHER GRAINS AND LEGUMES

## RICE AND OTHER GRAINS

Second only to fine wheat flour in its importance in the Mediterranean diet, in some parts of the region rice is considered superior, a grain to be reserved for Sunday dinner and similar special occasions.

Short-grain rice is grown in Italy's Po Valley and Piedmont, in the great wetlands of the Camargue at the mouth of the Rhône in Provence, and in the vast and beautiful Albufera lagoon south of Valencia on the east coast of Spain. In these regions of the western Mediterranean, dishes like risotto and paella have evolved to take advantage of the plump grains that swell as they absorb the liquid and develop a creamy consistency. Risotto should be very creamy but not at all soupy. Paella and similar Spanish preparations aim for something a little drier than risotto but still with the grains enveloped in their aromatic sauce.

Farther east, in Greece, Turkey, and the Levant, long-grain rice, originally from India and Persia, is preferred for pilafs, cooked by first sautéing the rice in cooking fat (butter, oil, sheep's tail fat, or clarified butter) with aromatics and then adding boiling stock or broth. Unlike risotto, the aim with pilaf is a slightly drier, but still moist, rice in which each grain is separate.

Beyond long-grain and short-grain, a number of different types of rice are available in American markets. One of the most attractive is basmati, originally from India, now grown in Texas. Pecan rice and popcorn rice are not (as I thought for years!) rice grains mixed with pecans or popcorn but rather rice with a peculiarly nutty and delicious flavor. Basmati, pecan, and popcorn rice can be used for pilafs, but they are not suitable for risotto or paella.

What about brown rice? It is unquestionably a healthful product, but it is not used in the Mediterranean except by macrobiotics. Brown rice is better for pilaf than risotto, although you will have to increase cooking times considerably. I have never had any success with brown rice in a risotto or paella—the grains simply don't absorb the liquid properly. Try it, by all means, but be prepared for a dish that is different from what you expected. It will still be full of flavor.

# BASIC RICE PILAF

Long before I ever lived in a Mediterranean country, a Greek friend in New York taught me how to make rice like this. I have never forgotten it, though I use olive oil now instead of the butter Elias used.

This is the most basic rice of all and should be served as an accompaniment to other dishes, whether roasted or grilled meat or fish, vegetables, or beans. The almonds, pine nuts, and raisins are a garnish and may be left out if you wish.

2½ cups light chicken stock (page 81)

¼ cup coarsely chopped blanched almonds

¼ cup pine nuts

2 tablespoons extra-virgin olive oil

1 medium onion, finely chopped

1½ cups long-grain rice

1 3-inch cinnamon stick

salt and freshly ground pepper to taste

¼ cup golden raisins, plumped in warm water

Heat the stock to a slow simmer while you prepare the rest of the pilaf.

In a saucepan over medium heat, gently sauté the almonds and pine nuts in the olive oil, stirring constantly, until they are brown, about 5 minutes, being careful not to burn them. Remove them with a slotted spoon and set aside.

Add the onion to the oil in the pan and cook, stirring frequently, until the onion starts to soften but not to brown—about 10 minutes. Stir in the rice and continue cooking and stirring until the rice begins to turn a very pale brown—about 5 minutes. Immediately pour in the hot stock, add the cinnamon, and season to taste with salt and lots of pepper. Stir the rice briefly to mix well, then lower the heat and cook, covered, until the liquid has been absorbed, about 15 to 20 minutes. Remove from the heat and, still covered, set aside for 5 minutes without disturbing. Then remove the lid, discard the cinnamon stick, stir in the reserved nuts and drained raisins, and serve the rice. *Makes 6 servings*

# TOMATO AND OTHER VEGETABLE PILAFS

**U**se fresh very ripe and flavorful tomatoes when in season. Otherwise a good brand of canned tomatoes should be used.

1½ cups clear white chicken stock (page 81) or vegetable broth (page 80)

1 pound tomatoes, peeled (page 454), or 2 cups canned whole
    tomatoes, drained

1 medium onion, chopped

½ garlic clove, crushed with the flat blade of a knife

2 tablespoons extra-virgin olive oil

¼ teaspoon ground cinnamon

½ teaspoon sugar

1½ cups long-grain rice

salt and freshly ground black pepper to taste

about ¼ cup chopped fresh green herbs such as parsley, basil, or cilantro
    (optional)

Heat the stock to a slow simmer while you prepare the rest of the pilaf.

Chop the peeled tomatoes coarsely and drain off their excess juice in a sieve. If you're using canned tomatoes, crush them coarsely with a fork.

Gently sauté the onion and garlic in the oil in a saucepan over medium-low heat until the vegetables are soft but not browning—about 15 minutes. Add the tomatoes, cinnamon, and sugar and cook over gentle heat for about 5 minutes or until they are soft. Add the rice and stir to mix well. Cook for another 5 minutes, then pour in the simmering stock. Stir once to mix, then cover and cook for about

15 minutes or until the rice is tender and the liquid has been absorbed. Remove from the heat and set aside, covered, for 5 minutes.

Stir in the herbs and serve immediately. ***Makes 6 servings***

Nutritional Data, per portion

| | | |
|---|---|---|
| Calories  243 | Carbohydrate  44g | Saturated Fat  1g |
| Protein  5g | Sodium  21mg | Monounsaturated |
| Fat  6g | Cholesterol  0 | Fat  4g |

**VARIATIONS:** If you wish, stir in a couple of tablespoons of freshly grated Parmigiano cheese with the herbs. Other vegetables can be used instead of the tomatoes. A pound of fresh leeks, the white part and just a little of the green, can be cut into 1-inch slices and stirred in with the onions and garlic until the leeks start to soften. Similarly, a pound of well-washed spinach, torn into pieces, can be added with the onions and garlic and cooked until it starts to wilt. If you're using leeks or spinach, however, increase the stock to 2½ cups and do not add cinnamon or sugar. A teaspoon of lemon juice can be stirred into a spinach pilaf.

### Risotto

Plump, short-grain Italian rice, specially grown for risotto and similar techniques, is the only rice to use. Arborio is most widely available in American markets, but you might also run into Vialone Nano or even Carnaroli, the best rice of all but difficult to find even in Italy.

Rice for risotto is characterized by a soft, starchy exterior coating that absorbs the cooking liquid a little at a time and swells to the requisite thick, creamy consistency, each grain thoroughly napped with sauce. For this reason risotto rice must never be soaked or rinsed before cooking—all you will do is loosen and dissolve the starchy exterior.

Venetians, who are the best cooks of risotto, say a proper risotto is *all'onda,* that is, like a wave, just rippling with the sauce that is created simply by cooking the rice in an aromatic liquid that may also include a vegetable (or two or three) or seafood. Risotto requires more attention on the part of the cook than pilaf, but the results are well worth it. It is an elegant dish.

Risotto is usually made with quantities of butter, but I find that a good light extra-virgin olive oil is even better.

PASTA, RICE, BEANS, AND OTHER GRAINS AND LEGUMES

# RISOTTO ALLA ZUCCA

### Risotto with Pumpkin or Squash

**A**lessandra Martini, who was the chef at the now-defunct Ristorante Il Cigno in the main square of Mantua, made this risotto with the local zucca, a type of pumpkin that is drier and less sweet than our pie pumpkins. I visited the restaurant on a blustery day in late fall, exactly the right weather for this kind of food. The rice shimmered on the plate like a golden harvest moon. I have substituted butternut squash, but other dark-yellow- or orange-fleshed winter squashes are just as good.

Use the recipe as a model. Other vegetables can be used, alone or in combination, depending on the season: in spring, asparagus, trimmed and cut into 1-inch chunks, or freshly shelled green peas; in summer, tomatoes, zucchini, or sweet peppers, roasted and peeled; in autumn, fresh fennel or celery, coarsely chopped (include some of the chopped leaves and green tops of these plants); and in winter, artichoke hearts, trimmed and cut into chunks, or small beets, peeled and chunked, for a fantastic pink risotto. You could even try fruit for an interesting challenge: My favorite Roman trattoria specializes in *risotto con fragole* (strawberries), an absolute knockout.

6 cups clear white chicken stock (page 81) or vegetable broth (page 80)

¼ cup extra-virgin olive oil

2 medium yellow onions, halved and thinly sliced

1 small butternut squash, peeled and coarsely chopped, 2 to 3 cups

2 cups Arborio rice

¾ cup freshly grated Parmigiano cheese

freshly ground black pepper to taste

1 teaspoon salt or more to taste

Heat the stock to a bare simmer and keep simmering *very* gently while you prepare the risotto.

In a heavy kettle or saucepan large enough to hold all the rice when cooked, gently sauté the onions in the oil over medium-low heat until the onions are thoroughly softened but not browned—about 15 minutes. Add the squash and stir well to coat the pieces with the oil. Cover and cook for about 5 to 10 minutes or until the squash is soft enough to be broken up with a spoon. (Other vegetables, like

celery or artichoke hearts, will remain firm after 5 minutes of cooking—it doesn't matter.) If the squash starts to scorch, add a little water or stock. The squash should be very soft, almost a puree.

When the squash is soft, add the rice and stir to mix well. Add a ladle or two of simmering stock and stir. As soon as the rice has absorbed the liquid, add more, and continue adding simmering liquid, ladle by ladle, stirring constantly. There should always be liquid visible in the pan. Do not add all the liquid at once; this will produce boiled rice or pilaf instead of risotto. The rice is done when it is al dente, with a bit of a bite in the center. Each grain should be well coated with brilliant yellow sauce, which should be dense and rather syrupy looking. When it is done, the risotto should be thick enough to eat with a fork. (You might not need to use all the liquid.) Total cooking time varies from 20 to 30 minutes, depending on the degree of doneness desired.

When the rice is cooked, remove the pan from the heat and immediately stir in about ¼ cup of the cheese and the pepper. Let it sit for 5 minutes or so, to settle the flavors, then taste and adjust the seasoning, adding salt as needed. Serve immediately and pass more cheese at the table. *Makes 6 to 8 servings*

Nutritional Data, per portion

| | | |
|---|---|---|
| Calories 338 | Carbohydrate 50g | Saturated Fat 3g |
| Protein 9g | Sodium 483mg | Monounsaturated |
| Fat 11g | Cholesterol 7mg | Fat 6g |

# RISOTTO CON FUNGHI PORCINI

*Risotto with Dried Wild Mushrooms*

**T**his wonderful dish is made from the humblest of ingredients, wild mushrooms scavenged in the forest after late-summer rains and dried on racks in the farmyard while the sun is still strong. The best dried mushrooms are funghi porcini, or cèpes, imported from Italy or France, although I have also made *risotto con funghi* with Chinese and Polish dried mushrooms.

Wild porcini can be found in bosky meadows and woodlots all over the northern United States, but they don't have the same intensity of flavor that porcini have in Italy. (On the other hand, our wild chanterelles are streets ahead of Italian chanterelles in flavor.) If you like to go mushrooming and you're confident of what you find, by all means dry your own (see instructions, page 396) to concentrate the flavor.

3   **ounces dried porcini**

5   **cups light chicken, beef, or vegetable stock (pages 80–83)**

1   **small yellow onion, minced**

¼   **cup extra-virgin olive oil**

2   **cups Arborio rice**

**about ¾ cup freshly grated Parmigiano cheese**

**salt and freshly ground black pepper to taste**

Prepare the dried mushrooms at least 45 minutes before you're ready to start cooking. Place the mushrooms in a bowl and cover them with hot (not boiling) tap water. Set aside to let the mushrooms absorb the water for at least 30 minutes. Remove the mushroom pieces, *reserving the water in which they soaked.* Put the pieces in a colander or sieve and rinse in running tap water to rid them of any grit. Chop the mushrooms coarsely and set aside.

Now filter the mushroom-soaking liquid through a fine sieve or several layers of cheesecloth to get rid of any grit. Add the mushroom-soaking liquid to the stock for the risotto. When you're ready to start the risotto, bring the stock to a bare simmer and keep it simmering *very* gently while you cook.

In a heavy kettle or saucepan large enough to hold all the rice when cooked, gently sauté the onion in the oil over medium-low heat, stirring continuously until

the onion is thoroughly softened but not browned—about 15 minutes. Stir in the rice and turn it for a couple of minutes until it is thoroughly coated with the oniony fat. Now stir in the chopped dried mushrooms and a ladleful (about ½ to ¾ cup— no need to be exact) of simmering stock.

As soon as the rice has absorbed the liquid, add more, and continue adding simmering stock, ladle by ladle, stirring constantly. There should always be liquid visible in the pan. Do not add all the liquid at once; this will produce boiled rice or pilaf instead of risotto. The rice is done when it is al dente, with a bit of a bite in the center. Each grain should be well coated with the sauce, which should be dense and rather syrupy looking. When it is done, the risotto should be thick enough to eat with a fork. (You might not need to use all the liquid.) Total cooking time will be 20 to 30 minutes, depending on how soft you want the rice to be.

Remove from the heat and stir in about ¼ cup of the grated cheese. Set aside for 5 minutes or so to let the flavors settle, then taste for seasoning, adding salt and pepper as desired. Serve immediately, passing more cheese at the table. ***Makes 6 to 8 servings***

### Nutritional Data, per portion

| | | |
|---|---|---|
| Calories 334 | Carbohydrate 50g | Saturated Fat 3g |
| Protein 10g | Sodium 204mg | Monounsaturated |
| Fat 11g | Cholesterol 7mg | Fat 6g |

PASTA, RICE, BEANS, AND OTHER GRAINS AND LEGUMES

# RISOTTO AI FRUTTI DI MARE

### Seafood Risotto

**A** rather firm-textured seafood is required here. Lobster and shrimp are obvious choices, but you can also use cubed monkfish or any combination of these. Be careful of cooking times in preparing seafood—putting a lot of money into fish only to ruin it by overcooking is one of those things that can seriously depress a cook.

This is a little more complicated than other risotti, but the seafood can be prepared ahead of time with no detriment to the final preparation.

1   pound medium-large (25 count) shrimp, heads removed but shells
        left on, or 1 live 1½-pound lobster, or ¾ pound cooked lobster
        meat, or ¾ pound monkfish fillet, cut into small cubes

5   cups fish stock (page 84)

¼   cup extra-virgin olive oil

pinch of cayenne pepper

2   garlic cloves, minced

1   small yellow onion, minced

1   carrot, peeled and finely chopped

1   celery rib, finely chopped

2   cups Arborio rice

½   cup dry white wine

¼   cup minced flat-leaf parsley

¼   cup freshly grated Parmigiano cheese (optional)

salt and freshly ground black pepper to taste

First prepare the seafood if necessary. Live lobster should be steamed in a very little water until just barely cooked, about 10 minutes, then shelled and the meat cut into bite-size pieces and set aside. Shrimp should be peeled and, if large, cut into smaller pieces and set aside. The shells and other residue can be added to the cooking stock for the risotto, simmered gently for 30 minutes, and strained. (The seafood and the stock can be prepared ahead of time and refrigerated.)

When you're ready to cook, bring the strained stock to a slow simmer and keep it simmering *very* gently while you prepare the risotto.

In a heavy kettle or saucepan large enough to hold all the cooked rice, warm the oil over medium heat and, when it is shimmering, add the seafood. Stir the seafood in the hot oil just until the aroma of the fish begins to rise, about 7 to 10 minutes. The monkfish or shrimp should lose its raw translucence but not be thoroughly cooked. Stir in the cayenne pepper, remove the seafood with a slotted spoon, leaving the aromatic oil behind in the pan, and set aside. (This procedure gives an important flavor boost to the risotto.)

Now lower the heat, stir the garlic, onion, carrot, and celery into the pan, and cook, stirring, until the vegetables are soft but not brown—about 10 to 15 minutes. Stir in the rice and mix until the rice is thoroughly coated with the aromatic oil. Add the wine and cook, stirring, until the rice has absorbed most of it, about 5 minutes.

As soon as the wine is absorbed, start adding the simmering stock. Add a little at a time, ladle by ladle, stirring constantly and not adding more until the previous addition has been mostly absorbed. There should always be liquid visible in the pan. Do not add all the liquid at once; this will produce boiled rice or pilaf instead of risotto. After the first 20 minutes of cooking, stir in the reserved seafood. The rice is done when it is al dente, with a bit of a bite in the center. Each grain should be well coated with the sauce, which should be dense and rather syrupy looking. When it is done, the risotto should be thick enough to eat with a fork. (You may not need to use all the liquid.) Total cooking time should be about 25 to 30 minutes.

Remove from the heat and stir in the minced parsley and, if desired, the grated cheese. Taste and adjust the seasoning with salt and pepper. Serve immediately.

**Makes 6 to 8 servings**

Nutritional Data, per portion

| | | |
|---|---|---|
| Calories 313 | Carbohydrate 43g | Saturated Fat 1g |
| Protein 15g | Sodium 179mg | Monounsaturated |
| Fat 8g | Cholesterol 76mg | Fat 6g |

# RISOTTO NERO

### *Black Rice with Squid and Their Ink*

**T**his is a very special dish and not for fainthearted cooks who may quail at the prospect of cleaning their own squid. Cooking and eating in the Mediterranean style is not simply a question of a certain balance of nutrients. It is also an attitude toward food, a sense of understanding and respect for the origins of foods and how they come to us. What better way to develop that than by cleaning your own squid? In any case, if you leave the cleaning to a fishmonger, he or she will most likely throw away the most important feature, the little silvery iridescent sac that holds the drops of precious ink that give this risotto its name and its flavor.

This is a very rich dish—although not particularly high in fat or calories. Serve it as a main course, perhaps with a vegetable like the Gratin of Eggplant with an Orange-Tomato Sauce (page 385) to start with and a simple seasonal salad after, with bread and a little cheese.

about 1½ **pounds squid**

1 **medium onion, minced**

1 **garlic clove, minced**

2 to 3 **tablespoons extra-virgin olive oil**

½ **cup minced flat-leaf parsley**

1 **small dried hot red chili (optional)**

¼ **cup dry white wine or dry vermouth**

4 to 5 **cups fish stock (page 84) or mixed fish stock and water**

2 **cups Italian short-grain rice (preferably Vialone Nano, though
Arborio will do nicely)**

**salt and freshly ground black pepper to taste**

½ **cup freshly grated Parmigiano cheese**

Prepare the squid: Pull the hood gently away from the body and tentacles. Rinse the hood under running water and remove the beak or bone that runs up the side of the hood and looks like a piece of transparent cellulose—make sure you get all of it out of the hood. Discard the beak and set the hood aside. Cut the tentacles away from the body just below the eyes. Rinse the tentacles and set aside.

Now seek out the ink sac, a shiny iridescent pouch in the upper part of the body. Hold the sac over a saucer or small bowl and poke it with a knife so that you can scrape out the small quantity of dark ink that will gush forth. Once the ink has been removed, discard the rest of the body and add a tablespoon or two of water to the saucer to keep the ink from coagulating or drying up.

Slice the hoods into ¼-inch-thick rings and cut the tentacles in half. Pat the squid dry on a paper towel. (The squid can be cleaned ahead of time and refrigerated until ready to cook. Be sure to cover the ink with plastic wrap or foil to keep it from drying out.)

When you're ready to cook, gently sauté the onion and garlic in 2 tablespoons of the olive oil over medium-low heat until the vegetables are soft but not brown—about 10 to 15 minutes. Set aside a heaped tablespoon of minced parsley for garnish and stir the remaining parsley in with the onions, along with a little more olive oil if necessary. Add the chili, broken into pieces, if desired.

Stir just to soften the parsley, then add the pieces of squid. Raise the heat to medium and cook until the squid pieces have become thoroughly opaque and given off a good deal of liquid—about 7 to 10 minutes. Add the wine. Scrape the squid ink into the pot with the squid pieces and bring to a simmer, stirring frequently. (The risotto can be prepared up to an hour ahead to this point so that you have only the rice to prepare at the end.)

When you're ready to cook the rice, bring the fish stock to a steady simmer in a separate pan. In the rice pan, bring the squid and its inky liquid to a steady rolling simmer and add the rice. Stir well to coat the rice thoroughly and bring it quickly back to simmering temperature. Add the stock a ladle at a time, stirring almost constantly, adding the next ladle as soon as the previous one has been almost, but not quite, absorbed. By the time the rice is cooked, each grain should be tender, just a little resistant in the center, and thoroughly napped with the dark and creamy sauce. Total cooking time varies from 20 to 30 minutes depending on the desired degree of doneness. Remove from the heat and stir in the salt and pepper, a few tablespoons of the grated cheese, and the reserved parsley. Serve immediately, passing the extra cheese. *Makes 6 servings*

Nutritional Data, per portion

| | | |
|---|---|---|
| Calories 436 | Carbohydrate 60g | Saturated Fat 3g |
| Protein 25g | Sodium 316mg | Monounsaturated |
| Fat 10g | Cholesterol 220mg | Fat 5g |

PASTA, RICE, BEANS, AND OTHER GRAINS AND LEGUMES

# ARROZ AL HORNO

### Rice Baked in the Oven

**V**alencia is the heartland of Spanish rice growing, and most of it is cultivated in flooded paddy fields around the broad, silvery lagoon of the Albufera, just south of the city of Valencia. On Sundays, Valencians troop out to little beachside and village restaurants to eat rice in one form or another. In an encyclopedic Valencian cookbook I counted two dozen different rice preparations, all of them, justifiably, considered native to the region.

Naturally the best rice cooks come from the great rice-growing regions. Lourdes March, who showed me how to cook this dish—and who has written a book about rice cookery, *El Libro de la paella y de los arroces*—is from Valencia. Spanish cooks like Lourdes use large, round, rather shallow terra-cotta dishes, called *cazuelas* or *cassolas*, for baking *arroz al horno*. A round or rectangular glass ovenproof dish is a good substitute.

Note that the first step produces a rich broth called *cocido*. You can do this well in advance—up to a month, in fact, if you freeze the stock. But if you already have a good, deep-flavored stock on hand in the freezer, you can use it instead. If you do make the cocido from scratch, serve the broth as a first course before the rice. Garnish the broth with toasted garlic croutons and chopped chives or scallion tops.

FOR THE COCIDO:

- 1   6-pound stewing hen
- ½   pound pork ribs or meaty pork bones
- 2   medium carrots, halved lengthwise
- 1   large leek, quartered lengthwise and rinsed well
- 1   white turnip, quartered
- 3   quarts cold water
- 1½ teaspoons saffron threads
- 2   teaspoons salt

Place the hen, pork, carrots, leek, and turnip in a large stockpot. Add the cold water and bring to a simmer over moderate heat. Simmer, covered, for 1 hour, then uncover, skim if necessary, and stir in the saffron and salt. Cover again and simmer for 3 hours. Remove from the heat and let cool for 30 minutes. Strain into a large bowl and let cool completely. Cover and refrigerate overnight. Skim the fat from the surface before using.

(This makes far more cocido than is necessary. What can I say? Freeze what you don't use right away. The stock is a delicious base for many soups, stews, and risotti. It can be refrigerated for up to 3 days or frozen for up to 1 month.)

**FOR THE RICE:**

½   **cup dried chick-peas, soaked overnight**

4½  **cups cocido or rich meat stock (page 83)**

½   **cup extra-virgin olive oil**

1   **large or 2 medium potatoes, peeled and sliced**

4   **medium ripe tomatoes, 3 cut in half horizontally, 1 peeled and**
    **chopped (page 454)**

1   **small head of garlic**

1   **pound lean boneless pork loin, cut into ½- to 1-inch cubes**

**salt and freshly ground black pepper to taste**

1   **tablespoon sweet paprika**

1½ **cups Spanish round-grain rice (arroz bomba) or Arborio rice**

Drain the chick-peas and put them in a small saucepan with about 1½ cups of the cocido. Set over medium heat and cook, covered, until the chick-peas are soft and most of the liquid has been absorbed, at least 40 minutes. When the chick-peas are done, set them aside with their cooking liquid.

Heat the olive oil in a skillet over medium heat until it starts to shimmer. Then add the potatoes and sauté, turning once or twice, until they're browned—about 10 minutes. Remove from the cooking oil and set aside. Add the tomato halves to the oil, cut side down, and sauté until the cut sides begin to brown (don't turn them over). Remove and set aside. Rub the head of garlic firmly to brush away loose skin, but leave the head itself intact. Add to the oil in the pan and cook, turning frequently, until the outside of the garlic is thoroughly browned—about 10 minutes. Remove and set aside.

Now remove and discard all but 2 tablespoons of the oil in the skillet. Add the pork cubes to the remaining oil and cook, turning frequently, until the pork cubes are thoroughly browned—about 15 minutes. Stir in salt and an abundance of black

pepper. Add the chopped tomato and cook for about 2 minutes or until the tomato has softened.

Remove the skillet from the heat and stir in the paprika and rice, mixing well. Set aside.

Before assembling the finished dish, preheat the oven to 400 degrees. Bring the remaining stock or cocido to a simmer on the top of the stove.

Place the reserved garlic in the center of the baking dish. Arrange the pork-rice mixture all around and distribute the chick-peas and their liquid over the top of the rice, pressing them down into the rice a little with the back of a spoon. Nestle the tomato halves in the rice mixture and spread the potato slices over the top.

Pour the simmering broth over the top and bake, uncovered, for 20 to 25 minutes or until the rice is just tender and the broth has been mostly absorbed. Remove the dish from the oven, cover loosely with foil, and let sit for another 5 minutes before serving. ***Makes 6 servings; 15 servings of cocido only***

### Nutritional Data, per portion, cocido

| | | |
|---|---|---|
| Calories 30 | Carbohydrate 2g | Saturated Fat trace |
| Protein 2g | Sodium 339mg | Monounsaturated |
| Fat 1g | Cholesterol 1mg | Fat trace |

### Nutritional Data, per portion, rice

| | | |
|---|---|---|
| Calories 590 | Carbohydrate 65g | Saturated Fat 4g |
| Protein 27g | Sodium 322mg | Monounsaturated |
| Fat 25g | Cholesterol 48mg | Fat 17g |

# SPANISH RICE WITH SPRING VEGETABLES

This celebration of the spring garden calls for fava beans, also called *broad beans*. Look for small, tender, early favas, and if you can't find them, simply increase the quantities of the other green vegetables to compensate.

¼   cup extra-virgin olive oil

1   medium onion, minced

4   garlic cloves, crushed with the flat blade of a knife

1   red bell pepper, sliced lengthwise into thin strips

½   pound small waxy potatoes, such as Red Bliss, cut into halves or quarters if more than 1 inch in diameter

½   cup drained canned tomatoes, lightly crushed

5   cups vegetable broth (page 80) or vegetable broth and water combined

salt and freshly ground black pepper to taste

pinch of saffron threads

½   pound fresh green beans, the smaller the better, cut into 2-inch lengths if large

4   small, firm artichokes, prepared as directed on page 455 and quartered

about 1 pound fresh fava beans, shelled

½   pound fresh green peas, shelled

½   pound tender fresh asparagus, trimmed and cut into 2-inch lengths

2   cups short- or medium-grain rice, preferably imported Spanish rice for paella

In a saucepan or casserole large enough to hold all the ingredients, warm the oil over medium heat. Add the onion, garlic, and red pepper strips and cook, stirring occasionally, until the vegetables are soft but not brown—about 15 minutes. Add the potatoes and tomatoes and continue cooking for 5 to 10 minutes, until the

potatoes just begin to soften and the tomato juice is somewhat reduced. Add the broth and stir in a little salt and pepper together with the saffron.

When the broth begins to boil, add the green beans and artichokes. Cover and cook for 10 minutes. Add the favas, peas, and asparagus. Pour in the rice, stir to mix well, cover, and cook until the rice is tender but not soft and falling apart—about 15 to 20 minutes. Remove from the heat and let stand, covered, for about 5 minutes. Just before serving, taste and adjust the seasoning, adding salt and pepper if desired.
**Makes 8 servings**

Nutritional Data, per portion

| | | |
|---|---|---|
| Calories   409 | Carbohydrate   70g | Saturated Fat   1g |
| Protein   12g | Sodium   115mg | Monounsaturated |
| Fat   10g | Cholesterol   0 | Fat   7g |

# PAELLA VALENCIANA

**T**he most famous dish in the entire repertoire of *la cocina española*, paella is also the most misunderstood and maligned. And that, alas, is true on its home ground as much as abroad.

A true *paella valenciana*, say those who know, can be made *only* with the round, short-grain rice grown in the region from Valencia south and called *arroz bomba* or *calasparra*; it includes *only* chicken, rabbit, and snails; it is seasoned *only* with saffron and paprika; and it should be made *only* over an open fire, preferably of orange wood and vine cuttings. Moreover, it must be made *only* in a wide, round, flat-bottomed pan, itself called a *paella*, a word that comes, so it is said, from the Latin *patella*, for a similar pan. So a paella, it would seem, is a dish cooked in the pan, not necessarily a dish made with rice.

Well, not necessarily. A paella, it turns out, is many things.

"We call all sorts of dishes paella, but real paella is made in the *huerta* [the market gardens], of chicken, rabbit, and garden vegetables—the green things you have in season," says Tinuka Lassala, who comes from Valencia and learned to cook rice from her father. Originally, she explains, paella was cooked *only* by men and *only* for the midday meal. All other rice dishes, those cooked by women and those served in the evening, no matter what their content, were not paella.

I am beginning to get the sense of this, after years of trying to understand.

Paella, I think, is a little like barbecue, which once meant an event at which large pieces of meat (whole hogs, whole sides of beef) were cooked outdoors in or over a pit fire by men, usually black, for other men, usually white, to eat. And now it means any kind of grilling over any kind of fire, as long as it takes place outdoors.

Paella, in the same way, once meant a specific dish, also—curiously here in Spain, where men are so protective of their machismo—cooked by men, also cooked outdoors, usually in or close by the fields, *la huerta*, where the vegetables for the paella grow. And just as with barbecue sauce, each cook has his own recipe, often with a secret or two tucked inside, for a paella that is, really, the only true and authentic way to make it "the way our grandfathers did." And, again as with barbecue, the recipes and techniques have been widely dispersed and adopted by all kinds of indifferent and doubtless, truth be told, unskilled cooks, all kinds of equivocal garbage has been thrown into the pot, and the dish has gone forth into the world, minus its reputation and pedigree with but two things intact—the rice and the pan in which to cook it.

The best paella I ever had was in a restaurant on the beach just outside El Grao, the bustling port of Valencia, a restaurant so humble it just escaped shabbiness, a quality that was emphasized by the sand that drifted in on the wind across the dunes outside. The cook was a woman, unusually, but the rest was deeply traditional—there were the open fires of orange wood and vine cuttings on the long kitchen hearth, there were the broad flat pans, there was the rice, the product of the vastly beautiful paddies of the Albufera lagoon south of the city.

Amparo, the cook, red-haired, serene, and stout, made two paellas, one with fish (shrimps, langoustines, squid sliced into rings), one with chicken, rabbit, and snails. She explained the difference between them: for the fish paella, the rice is sautéed in hot oil with the squid and then the liquid is added; for the more traditional one, chicken and rabbit, browned in fat, simmer in a broth to which the rice is added later. "My grandfather made a wonderful paella," she said. "Around here it's the men who make it, y'know."

The following recipe is my adaptation of paella, based on what I've observed over the years from cooks like Amparo, Tinuka, and Lourdes March, another top-notch Valencian rice cook. This paella is not authentic, at least in part because there are so many ingredients, beginning with the rice, that are hard to find in this country. But it is very good. If at all possible, try to cook it over an open fire (a wood fire, that is, not a charcoal grill), because you can control the heat so much more easily. Failing that, a gas ring (a large gas ring) is second best. If your only heat

PASTA, RICE, BEANS, AND OTHER GRAINS AND LEGUMES

source is electricity, you'll need to use several burners set at different levels to control the heat.

If you cannot find a paella pan (see Resources), use a large, heavy, flat-bottomed sauté pan or skillet. The skillet must be large enough to hold all the meats and shrimp spread out in one layer, with enough space in between for the rice.

As for ingredients: You must use a round, short-grain rice. Italian Arborio rice is an acceptable substitute for Spanish short-grain rice like calasparra. Rabbit is authentic, but pork can be substituted. The dry beans used in Spain are big white ones called *garrafones*; use large lima beans instead. The green beans used are flat ones like our romano beans, but any large string beans can be substituted, as long as they are fresh (no frozen food is ever used). I also add shrimp to the mixture simply because so many people expect it. If you want to be superauthentic, leave the shrimp out. Another unauthentic touch: I take the skin and excess body fat off the chicken to cut down on undesirable fat. The recipe calls for 6 cups of chicken stock, but you might need less—the rule is 2 cups of liquid for each cup of rice, but there is a good deal of liquid in the tomatoes and other vegetables.

This large paella is an abundant dish that needs nothing but a crisp green salad to follow.

1   cup large white lima or cannellini beans, soaked overnight, or use the quick-soak method (page 454)

1   quart water

6   chicken legs, skin and excess fat removed

6   chicken thighs, skin and excess fat removed

½   cup extra-virgin olive oil or more if needed

2   pounds rabbit, cut into small pieces, or country-style pork spareribs, each cut into 3 pieces

1   pound medium-large (25 count) shrimp, unshelled if desired

3   cups finely chopped white or yellow onion

6 to 8 artichokes, prepared as on page 455, quartered

2   cups fresh tomato sauce, chopped fresh tomatoes, or canned whole tomatoes, drained and chopped

1   teaspoon saffron threads soaked in ¼ cup water

1   pound green beans, cut into 2-inch lengths

2　tablespoons sweet paprika

salt to taste

2　fresh rosemary sprigs

6　cups clear white chicken stock (page 81), simmering

4　cups round short-grain rice

Drain the beans and place in a saucepan with the water. Bring to a simmer and cook, covered, until the beans are soft but not falling apart, at least 30 to 40 minutes, depending on the age and size of the beans. When the beans are done, set them aside in their cooking liquid.

In a large, heavy, round flat-bottomed skillet or paella pan, brown the chicken pieces in the olive oil over medium heat, turning frequently to brown on all sides. This will take about 20 minutes. As the chicken browns, remove the pieces and set aside.

Add the rabbit or pork to the pan and brown, turning frequently. When the meat is brown on all sides, after about 20 minutes, remove and set aside.

Add the shrimp to the pan, raise the heat slightly, and cook quickly, tossing the shrimp. When the shrimp has changed color and become opaque, in about 5 minutes, remove and set aside.

Lower the heat to medium-low and, in the oil remaining in the pan, gently sauté the onion until soft and starting to brown, about 15 minutes, adding a little more oil to the pan if necessary.

Meanwhile, bring 2 cups water to a boil in a saucepan and add the drained artichokes. Boil for about 10 to 15 minutes or until the artichokes are just tender. Do not drain.

Add the tomatoes to the onions, raise the heat to medium, and cook, stirring frequently, until the tomatoes thicken and their liquid starts to evaporate—about 20 minutes. Pour in the saffron with its soaking water and stir to mix well. Add the green beans, the artichokes with their cooking water, and the beans with their cooking water. Stir in the paprika. Cook the vegetables over medium heat, stirring frequently, for about 20 minutes or until the sauce is once again rather thick.

Arrange the pieces of chicken and rabbit or pork around the edges of the pan and sprinkle about 2 teaspoons salt, more or less, over the sauce. Put the rosemary sprigs in the center. Add simmering stock to the pan, a cup at a time, until the liquid comes to the tops of the rivets in a paella pan or about 1 inch from the top of a skillet. Add

the rice, sprinkling it around the pieces of meat so that it is completely immersed in the liquid. Don't stir the rice, but use a thin spatula to move it gently down into the liquid. Bring to a boil and cook for about 30 minutes, gradually decreasing the heat as the rice absorbs the liquid. (If you must add more stock to cook the rice thoroughly, it should be simmering.)

When the rice is thoroughly cooked, dry, and tender but not falling apart, add the reserved shrimp, distributing them over the surface. Remove the pan from the heat and let rest for 5 to 10 minutes, then serve immediately. ***Makes 8 to 10 servings***

Nutritional Data, per portion

| | | |
|---|---|---|
| Calories   731 | Carbohydrate   87g | Saturated Fat   4g |
| Protein   49g | Sodium   273mg | Monounsaturated |
| Fat   20g | Cholesterol   158mg | Fat   11g |

# POLENTA WITH TEVERINA DRIED WILD MUSHROOM SAUCE

**P**olenta is simply the Italian name for the American staple cornmeal. There is no need to buy imported Italian polenta since cornmeal is the same thing and what is available in local markets will often be fresher and a good deal cheaper than imported polenta. Most Italian polenta is made from yellow corn, but up in Friuli, in the northeasternmost corner of the country, white corn is often used instead. White or yellow, the important thing is that the meal be stone-ground for the finest flavor. Coarsely ground cornmeal produces a more characteristic polenta than finely ground.

The wild mushrooms prized in Teverina are porcini, harvested every year in late summer and early autumn by countryfolk who scour the hillsides for the elusive treasure. Part of the harvest is eaten fresh or sold in the market in Cortona, but in good years a large part of the yield will be cleaned, sliced, dried in the sun, and stored for wintertime sauces like this one. For more wild mushroom information, see page 396.

Packets of dried porcini, or cèpes as they're called in France, are widely available in specialty food stores. Or see Resources at the back of the book.

1½ ounces dried porcini

1 pound sweet Italian sausages, cut into pieces not more than ½ inch
thick

2 tablespoons extra-virgin olive oil

1 medium onion, minced

1 medium carrot, peeled and minced

1 celery rib, minced

¼ cup minced flat-leaf parsley

1 28-ounce can plum tomatoes with their liquid, coarsely chopped

½ teaspoon chopped fresh thyme or ¼ teaspoon dried, crumbled

3 or 4 fresh rosemary sprigs to taste, coarsely chopped

salt and freshly ground black pepper to taste

6½ cups water

1½ cups yellow cornmeal

¾ cup freshly grated Parmigiano cheese

Put the dried porcini in a small bowl, cover with very hot water, and set aside
for 30 minutes to soften.

Meanwhile, sauté the sausage in its own fat in a heavy skillet or saucepan over
medium-high heat, stirring and turning frequently, until it loses its pink color,
about 10 minutes. Drain the sausage slices on a rack spread with paper towels.
Drain the fat from the skillet and wipe clean with a paper towel.

When the porcini are soft, drain them in a sieve lined with a double layer of
damp cheesecloth set over a small bowl to catch the liquid. Rinse the porcini in
running water to rid them of any grit, then chop coarsely. Reserve the chopped
porcini and their soaking water.

Heat the olive oil in the skillet over medium-low heat and gently sauté the
onion, carrot, celery, and parsley until the vegetables are soft but not brown—
about 15 minutes. Stir in the tomatoes, thyme, and rosemary. Simmer the sauce
gently, uncovered, until it is thickened, about 20 to 25 minutes. Stir in the reserved
mushroom liquid, the porcini, and the sausage. Continue cooking, uncovered, for
15 to 20 minutes. The sauce should be very thick. Taste and add salt and pepper if
you wish. Set aside, but keep it warm while you make the polenta. Or make a day in
advance and store, covered, in the refrigerator until you're ready to cook. Warm the
sauce up to simmering before serving.

To make the polenta, bring the water, lightly salted, to a rolling boil in a heavy medium saucepan. Slowly and steadily pour in the polenta, stirring constantly as you pour. When all the cornmeal has been added, reduce the heat to a gentle simmer; cook, uncovered, stirring frequently, until the polenta is thick and creamy, about 20 to 30 minutes.

Pour the polenta into a warm platter—one with a high rim to keep the sauce from spilling over. Make a well or depression in the middle of the polenta and pour the sauce over it. Sprinkle about ¼ cup of the grated cheese over the top and serve immediately, passing the remaining grated cheese at the table. ***Makes 6 to 8 servings***

Nutritional Data, per portion

| Calories 350 | Carbohydrate 32g | Saturated Fat 6g |
|---|---|---|
| Protein 16g | Sodium 726mg | Monounsaturated |
| Fat 18g | Cholesterol 40mg | Fat 4g |

## BULGUR PILAF

**B**ulgur or burghul, from the eastern Mediterranean, is wheat that has been steamed, dried, and cracked. It is widely available at health food stores and some supermarkets. Be sure you don't buy precooked bulgur. Bulgur pilaf is a delightful, nutty change from rice.

3   cups meat, chicken, or vegetable stock (pages 80–83)
1   medium onion, chopped
2   tablespoons extra-virgin olive oil
1¼ cups medium-grain bulgur
1   large ripe tomato, coarsely chopped, or 3 canned tomatoes, drained
        and coarsely chopped
salt and freshly ground black pepper to taste
¼   cup minced flat-leaf parsley

Bring the stock to a gentle simmer over medium-low heat.

In another heavy saucepan over medium-low heat, gently sauté the onion in the oil until it is soft but not brown—about 10 to 15 minutes. Add the bulgur and stir to

coat well with the oil. Stir in the tomatoes, raise the heat to medium, and cook briefly, 4 or 5 minutes, to soften the tomato. Add the simmering stock and a little salt if desired. Cover and cook over medium heat for 5 minutes, then lower the heat and simmer for 10 to 15 minutes or until the bulgur is tender and little steam holes form on the surface. Remove from the heat and set aside, covered, for 10 minutes. Uncover the pot, taste the bulgur, and add more salt if desired and plenty of pepper. Just before serving, stir in the parsley and fluff the grains. **Makes 6 servings**

Nutritional Data, per portion

| | | |
|---|---|---|
| Calories   171 | Carbohydrate   27g | Saturated Fat   1g |
| Protein   5g | Sodium   32mg | Monounsaturated |
| Fat   6g | Cholesterol   0 | Fat   4g |

**VARIATION:** Turkish cooks sometimes add a little finely chopped fresh mint with the parsley.

## BEANS AND PULSES

Dried beans and pulses—lentils, kidney beans, lima beans, chick-peas (or garbanzos), broad beans (or fava beans), and so on—come in such variety, and the varieties change so often from place to place, that they deserve an encyclopedia of their own. Lentils, chick-peas, and fava beans are Old World beans, with a history that goes back almost to the very beginnings of Mediterranean agriculture. Esau's Biblical mess of pottage was probably a well-cooked stew of lentils made savory with garlic and leeks and quite possibly with a little olive oil on top.

New World beans, which also go back to the beginnings of agriculture, only on *this* side of the globe, include the whole panoply that botanists call kidney beans or Phaseolus (the name of the genus) and were unknown in the Mediterranean until sometime after 1492. Unlike the potato and the tomato, which were slow to gain acceptance, New World beans were quickly adopted all over Europe, presumably because they could be cooked and eaten in ways that were already very familiar. And they quickly became very important in the everyday fare of people, especially in the Mediterranean, with its almost vegetarian diet. Long before our ancestors under-stood protein and its critical role in human development, they knew that beans, properly prepared, can give the same sense of nourishment and ample satisfaction that meat does and that beans cooked with a small amount of meat—a little chopped bacon or ham, a wing of preserved goose, or a few sausages—are even

more satisfying, extending that small amount of meat to serve many more people than the meat might do on its own.

The world of beans is vast. I look for new varieties every time I travel and bring them home both to eat and to plant. In the market in San Sebastian in the Atlantic north of Spain, I found black beans that were as shiny as agates (and very precious too, I could tell by the price), while in Roman markets there are tiny lentils like delicate green and brown shells, almost too pretty to eat. In this country too there are dozens of varieties, many quite regional—I think of Sivvy beans in the Carolina Lowcountry, Jacob's cattle beans and yellow eyes in Maine, and Anasazi beans in New Mexico and Arizona.

Everywhere in the Mediterranean, simple, humble bean dishes are served as main courses, first courses, or part of an hors d'oeuvre. Chick-peas or garbanzos in Provence, pale cannellini beans or speckled borlotti in Tuscany, small green flageolets or haricots secs, dark lentils, white or brown favas, dried beans or fresh—whatever the local beans of choice, they are handled in a similar fashion from Beirut to Barcelona and back again. The beans are soaked overnight (unless they are fresh), the soaking water is discarded, fresh water is added to the pot, often with aromatics (but no salt), and the beans are cooked until very tender. Then they are drained and mixed with good olive oil, a little vinegar or lemon juice, and more flavorings—garlic, onion, chopped green herbs, spices like cumin or red pepper flakes. Served at room temperature, they make a substantial addition to meze tables, and they can also be gussied up with seafood and made to star as a main course at dinner. Fashionable Florentine restaurants serve white Tuscan beans topped by a healthy dollop of best Beluga caviar—garlic and sapphires in the mud, perhaps, but it works.

Dried beans store well and should always be in your pantry cupboard, but beware of beans that have been kept too long—the older they are, the longer it will take to cook them. Buy beans from a store with a quick turnaround or, better yet, directly from a farmer who can tell you exactly when they were harvested. Despite my predilection for fresh food freshly prepared, I keep a few emergency cans of high-quality cooked beans, especially chick-peas and white cannellini, in the pantry. American Prairie brand canned beans are organically raised and preserved with nothing but water and salt. Rinsed quickly under running water and added to a soup, dressed with a little oil and lemon and tossed with chips of onion, or combined with pasta, those cans of beans have often meant the difference between success and failure in providing for unexpected guests.

The great problem with beans, of course, is flatulence, which can produce both

snickers and a goodly amount of discomfort for those who are sensitive to the digestive gases produced by beans. The problem can be dealt with, if not eliminated entirely, by discarding the water in which the beans have soaked. (I think it was Elizabeth David who told how French country women save the bean water to use in the laundry for getting rid of stubborn stains. I've never tried it, though I think of it every time I pour the soaking water down the drain.)

Most dried beans must be soaked before they are cooked—lentils are an exception. For soaking methods, see page 454.

# TUSCAN BEANS WITH OLIVE OIL AND AROMATICS

Like bread, beans are a wonderful foil for great olive oil, which may be why the Tuscans, who produce some of the world's finest oils, are also among the world's champion bean eaters. Use a fine, estate-bottled, green, fragrant olive oil (it need not be Tuscan) with these.

The following is a model recipe and can be adapted to many different kinds of beans, including non-Mediterranean beans like Mexican black beans or Asian adzukis. Remember that cooking time can vary greatly with the size and age of the beans.

1½ **cups dried white beans, such as cannellini**

7 **cups cold water**

**any or all of the following aromatics: 1 small onion, quartered; 1 garlic**
**clove, lightly crushed; 4 or 5 fresh sage leaves; 2 bay leaves;**
**12 black peppercorns; 1 small dried hot red chili**

¼ **cup best-quality extra-virgin olive oil**

**salt and freshly ground black or white pepper to taste**

1 **tablespoon minced flat-leaf parsley**

Pick over the beans, discarding any small stones or discolored beans. Place the beans in a bowl and cover with 3½ cups of the cold water. Set aside to soak overnight or for at least 6 hours. Or use the quick-soak method (page 454).

When you're ready to cook, drain the beans, discarding the soaking water. Place

the beans in a pot and add 3½ cups fresh water and any or all of the aromatics. Do not add salt. Bring the water to a boil, turn the heat down, cover the beans, and simmer gently for 30 minutes to 1½ hours, adding *boiling* water from time to time if necessary to keep the beans from scorching. Be attentive: if the water gets low, the beans will scorch very quickly. Cooking time depends on the size and age of the beans, which is hard to assess. At the end of 30 minutes, start testing the beans to judge how tender they are and continue testing periodically until the beans are done. They should be very tender but not falling apart.

Remove the beans from the heat and drain them, *reserving the cooking liquid.* Discard the aromatics used in cooking the beans. At this point, if you wish, remove about ½ to ¾ cup cooked beans and crush them gently, using a fork, in about ½ cup of the reserved cooking liquid. Then stir in the crushed beans with the whole cooked beans. Add more cooking liquid if you wish to reach the desired consistency. Or leave all the beans whole and add ½ cup or more of the reserved cooking liquid.

While the beans are still hot, add olive oil and stir to coat the beans well. Dress them with one of the following combinations or devise your own:

- 1 garlic clove, minced, and 6 scallions, both white and green parts, sliced on the diagonal
- a little chopped raw onion and finely slivered fresh green chilies
- the juice of ½ lemon along with ½ teaspoon ground cumin and chopped fresh hot red chilies or a pinch of hot red pepper flakes
- finely minced fresh green herbs—basil, dill, fennel tops, chervil, sage, lovage, borage, or others

After dressing the beans, taste and add salt and freshly ground black or white pepper if desired.

Plain beans, dressed with oil and lemon juice or vinegar, can also be served as a first-course or antipasto salad, garnished with a little handful of pitted black olives, coarsely chopped if large; or a small can of best-quality tuna, flaked over the top along with a little handful of capers; or 3 or 4 medium shrimp per serving, peeled, quickly sautéed in olive oil, and tossed with salt, pepper, and a green herb; or—if you're feeling extravagant—a big spoonful (as much as you can afford) of best-quality Beluga caviar.

Whatever the flavors or garnishes, however, the beans should be sprinkled with minced parsley before serving. Serve hot or at room temperature. **Makes 6 to 8 servings**

Nutritional Data, per portion

| | | |
|---|---|---|
| Calories 189 | Carbohydrate 23g | Saturated Fat 1g |
| Protein 9g | Sodium 6mg | Monounsaturated |
| Fat 7g | Cholesterol 0 | Fat 6g |

# PASTA AND BEANS

Pasta fazool, pasta cooked with beans, is a humble Italian peasant and working-class dish, made famous in the great Dean Martin song "That's Amore" ("When the stars make you drool . . ."). As any vegetarian will tell you, it's an ideal way to boost protein through the combination of grains (pasta) and legumes (beans). This is soupy enough to be served in bowls rather than on plates.

1    pound dried white beans, such as cannellini or Great Northern,
         soaked overnight, or use the quick-soak method (page 454)

¼   cup fruity extra-virgin olive oil, plus more for serving

1    medium onion, coarsely chopped

2    medium carrots, peeled and coarsely chopped

1    celery rib, coarsely chopped

2 or 3 garlic cloves to taste, minced

1    cup finely chopped ripe plum tomatoes or canned whole plum
         tomatoes, drained

1    fresh rosemary sprig, finely chopped

about 7 cups boiling water

½   pound fusilli, small pasta shells, small ziti, or fettuccine or tagliatelle
         broken into roughly 2-inch lengths

salt and freshly ground black pepper to taste

¼   cup minced flat-leaf parsley

freshly grated Parmigiano cheese for garnish

Drain the beans and set aside.

Heat the oil in a large heavy saucepan over medium heat and gently sauté the onion, carrots, celery, and garlic until the vegetables are soft but not brown, about

10 minutes. Add the beans to the vegetables along with the tomatoes, rosemary, and about 6 cups boiling water. Bring back to a boil, reduce the heat, and simmer, covered, until the beans are tender—1 to 1½ hours, depending on the age and size of the beans. Add more boiling water from time to time as necessary: the beans should always be covered with simmering liquid.

When the beans are very tender, transfer about 2 cups beans and their liquid to a food processor and process to a thick puree. Or put them through the medium disk of a food mill. Stir the puree back into the beans.

Add the pasta and another cup of boiling water to the beans in the pot. Cook, stirring constantly, until the pasta is tender, about 10 minutes. Remove from the heat. Taste and add salt and lots of black pepper.

Serve in a warm soup tureen or in individual warm bowls, garnished with a drizzle of olive oil, a sprinkle of parsley, and some Parmigiano. Pass more cheese and olive oil with the beans. **Makes 6 to 8 servings**

Nutritional Data, per portion

| | | |
|---|---|---|
| Calories 378 | Carbohydrate 61g | Saturated Fat 1g |
| Protein 18g | Sodium 25mg | Monounsaturated |
| Fat 8g | Cholesterol 0 | Fat 6g |

# EGYPTIAN BEANS WITH OLIVE OIL AND LEMON

### Ful Medames

These are the beans that Lebanese taxi drivers and others eat for breakfast with yogurt and bread. Ful medames are a delicious staple all over the Middle East, not just for breakfast but throughout the day. My son Nicholas quotes a saying he picked up on his travels: ful, he says, are the rich man's breakfast, the shopkeeper's lunch, the poor man's supper. The aroma of these beans on the stove can send displaced Middle Easterners into paroxysms of desire.

The beans used are very fragrant, small brown favas, called *Egyptian fava beans* or *ful* (FOOL). They are available in Middle Eastern shops (see Resources at the back of the book for suppliers).

2     cups dried Egyptian ful or other beans, soaked overnight, or use the
      quick-soak method (page 454)

2     garlic cloves, peeled

1     teaspoon salt

½     cup fresh lemon juice

¼     cup extra-virgin olive oil

½     cup finely chopped flat-leaf parsley

6 or 8 scallions

1     lemon, cut into wedges

Drain the beans, place them in a saucepan, and cover with fresh water. Place over medium heat and bring to a boil. When the beans are boiling, turn the heat down to a steady simmer, cover the pan, and cook, just simmering, until the beans are thoroughly tender. Count on 1 hour, more or less, depending on the freshness of the beans. Add a little boiling water from time to time to make up for the water that is absorbed by the beans—the beans should always be covered with water. When the beans are done, remove from the heat and drain, *reserving the cooking liquid*.

Crush the garlic with the flat blade of a knife and chop it slightly. Put the chopped garlic in a bowl with the salt and, using the back of a spoon, mash the garlic to a paste with the salt. Add the lemon juice and mix well.

Remove about 1 cup beans and mash them with about ½ cup of bean liquid to a coarse, runny texture with a fork. Mix with the garlic, then, using a slotted spoon, add the unmashed beans and stir to combine it all well. If the mixture is too dry, add a little more of the bean-cooking liquid. Stir in the olive oil and pour onto a deep serving platter. Garnish the platter with parsley, scallions, and lemon wedges and serve, hot or at room temperature, with Arab flatbread (pita; page 133) to use as scoops. *Makes 4 to 6 servings*

Nutritional Data, per portion

| | | |
|---|---|---|
| Calories 268 | Carbohydrate 35g | Saturated Fat 1g |
| Protein 14g | Sodium 379mg | Monounsaturated |
| Fat 10g | Cholesterol 0 | Fat 7g |

# TURKISH BEANS WITH POTATOES, CELERY ROOT, AND CARROTS

2    cups dried large white beans, soaked overnight, or use the quick-soak method (page 454)

2    bay leaves

1    medium onion, coarsely chopped

2    garlic cloves, crushed with the flat blade of a knife

¼    cup extra-virgin olive oil plus more for serving if desired

1    large potato, peeled and cut into chunks

1    medium celeriac (celery root), peeled and cut into chunks

2    medium carrots, peeled and cut into chunks

salt and freshly ground black pepper to taste

¼    cup finely minced flat-leaf parsley

Drain the beans and put in a large heavy saucepan with the bay leaves and fresh water to cover to a depth of 1 inch. Bring to a boil, turn the heat down, and simmer, covered, for 30 minutes. Check the water from time to time and add more boiling water if necessary. The beans should always be covered with water.

While the beans are cooking, gently sauté the onion and garlic in the oil in a large heavy saucepan until they are soft but not brown—about 10 to 15 minutes. Add the potato, celery root, and carrots and stir to coat well with the oil. Cook over medium heat for about 10 minutes or until the vegetables start to soften. The vegetables should not brown.

When the beans have cooked for 30 minutes, add the vegetables with more boiling water if necessary to cover. Add ½ teaspoon salt and continue cooking until the beans are very tender—another 30 minutes or longer, depending on the size and age of the beans.

When the beans are very tender, remove from the heat and taste, adding more salt if necessary and lots of pepper. Just before serving, stir in the parsley. Add more olive oil at the table if desired. ***Makes 6 to 8 servings***

## Nutritional Data, per portion

| | | |
|---|---|---|
| Calories  274 | Carbohydrate  41g | Saturated Fat  1g |
| Protein  13g | Sodium  46mg | Monounsaturated |
| Fat  8g | Cholesterol  0 | Fat  6g |

**VARIATION:** Greek cooks add 2 or 3 fresh or canned tomatoes, coarsely chopped, instead of the celery root.

# TUNISIAN CHICK-PEAS WITH SPICY VEGETABLES

**T**unisians usually serve a combination of beans in this peppery sauce, though chick-peas on their own are fine too. Don't be limited by the vegetable selection listed—add, subtract, or substitute at will, keeping in mind cooking times and balance of flavors.

1    cup dried chick-peas, soaked overnight, or use the quick-soak
        method (page 454)

2    medium onions, coarsely chopped

⅓    cup extra-virgin olive oil

2    tablespoons tomato puree

1    tablespoon harissa (page 301) or 1 dried red New Mexico or Anaheim chili

1    cup cold water

1    cup very hot water

3    medium carrots, peeled, cut in half lengthwise, and sliced about
        1 inch thick

2    small white turnips, peeled and cut into rough chunks

salt to taste

1    pound Swiss chard, preferably green, but red will do

4    fresh red or green bell peppers

about 1 cup yellow winter squash in chunks: butternut, acorn, Hubbard,
        or any other firm-textured squash

freshly ground black pepper to taste

¼    cup minced flat-leaf parsley

minced cilantro and lemon wedges for garnish

Drain the chick-peas and set aside. In a large heavy saucepan over medium-low heat, sauté the onion in the oil until it is soft and just beginning to brown—about 10 minutes. Stir the tomato puree and harissa into the cold water, add to the onions, and bring to a slow simmer.

If you're using a dried red chili instead of the harissa, rinse any dust off the outside, break the chili into pieces, discarding the stem (for less heat, discard the seeds and inner white membranes), and soak in the hot water for about 30 minutes. Add the chili pieces and soaking water to the onions with the tomato puree.

Have a teakettle of boiling water ready. Stir the onion-chili mixture and simmer for 5 minutes to develop the flavors. Then stir in the drained chick-peas and add boiling water to cover to a depth of 1 inch. Reduce the heat and simmer the beans, covered, for about 40 minutes, stirring from time to time and adding a very little boiling water if necessary.

Add the carrots and turnips to the stew along with water to cover, adding a teaspoon of salt if you wish. Continue cooking, covered, for 10 minutes.

While the carrots and turnips are cooking, trim the chard of any coarse or fibrous stem ends, then slice across the leaves to make thin chiffonades. Slice the bell peppers lengthwise into strips no more than 1 inch wide. Add the chard, pepper strips, and squash chunks to the beans along with more water if necessary. Cook for 10 to 15 minutes, by which time all the vegetables should be soft and the beans should be very tender. If there's too much soupy liquid in the pan, raise the heat and cook, uncovered, to reduce the pan juices.

Taste and adjust the seasoning, adding more salt if desired and a lot of black pepper. If the bean stew isn't hot enough, stir in a little more harissa or ground red chili (not commercial chili powder). Stir in the parsley and serve, garnished with minced cilantro and lemon wedges if you wish. *Makes 8 servings*

Nutritional Data, per portion

| | | |
|---|---|---|
| Calories 250 | Carbohydrate 31g | Saturated Fat 2g |
| Protein 8g | Sodium 170mg | Monounsaturated |
| Fat 12g | Cholesterol 0 | Fat 8g |

# BAKED CHICK-PEAS IN TOMATO SAUCE

*A Lenten Dish from Greece*

1   pound dried chick-peas, soaked overnight, or use the quick-soak
    method (page 454)

3   medium onions, halved and thinly sliced

2   green bell peppers, sliced lengthwise

1   fresh green jalapeño chili, seeded and finely chopped

3   tablespoons extra-virgin olive oil

3   garlic cloves, crushed with the flat blade of a knife

2   cups canned crushed tomatoes

½   cup finely chopped flat-leaf parsley

1   teaspoon dried oregano, crumbled

2   bay leaves, crumbled

salt and freshly ground black pepper to taste

Drain the soaked chick-peas. Place in a pot, cover with fresh cold water, and bring to a boil. Simmer for 30 to 45 minutes or until the chick-peas are starting to soften.

While the chick-peas are cooking, prepare the sauce: Gently sauté the onions, peppers, and chili in the oil over medium-low heat until the vegetables are soft but not brown—about 15 minutes. Add the garlic and stir to mix well, then stir in the tomatoes, parsley, oregano, and bay leaves and simmer, uncovered, for about 10 minutes or until the sauce is thickened.

Preheat the oven to 300 degrees. When the chick-peas have started to soften, remove them from their cooking liquid with a slotted spoon and stir into the vegetable sauce. Transfer the mixture to a casserole—preferably a round earthenware casserole. Add ½ cup or more of the liquid in which the chick-peas cooked, just enough to cover them. Taste for seasoning and add salt and pepper if desired. Cover and bake for 1 to 1½ hours, until very tender. Keep the chick-pea-cooking liquid warm and add a little to the beans from time to time if needed. The chick-peas and vegetables should always be just covered with liquid. *Makes 6 servings*

## Nutritional Data, per portion

| | | |
|---|---|---|
| Calories 397 | Carbohydrate 60g | Saturated Fat 2g |
| Protein 17g | Sodium 154mg | Monounsaturated |
| Fat 12g | Cholesterol 0 | Fat 7g |

**VARIATION:** On the island of Crete, cooks might substitute the juice of one or more bitter or sour oranges, sometimes called *Seville oranges*, in place of ½ cup of the tomatoes.

---

### ABOUT LENTILS

The finest lentils are the smallest—little brown *lenticchie* from Rome and southern Italy or slate-colored *lentilles du Puy* from central France—but they are very hard to find in this country and very expensive if you do find them. Ordinary grayish brown lentils will have to do instead, but don't use Indian lentils in Mediterranean recipes unless instructed specifically to do so. In Indian cuisine, lentils are meant to disintegrate somewhat and form a delicious, thick sauce for rice and other staples. In Mediterranean cuisine, the opposite end is desired: lentils are intended, for the most part, to remain intact, especially when served as an accompaniment or a salad.

Lentils are often cooked with some sort of preserved pork or bacon, and delicious they are. In Italy, good luck in the new year comes from eating as many lentils as possible for Capo d'Anno, the first of the year. New Year's lentils are served with cotechino, a large pork sausage delicately flavored with nutmeg that is poached and sliced and accompanied by a piquant salsa verde.

---

# PELLEGRINO ARTUSI'S LENTILS WITH AROMATICS

**A**rtusi, the great 19th-century Tuscan cook and recipe compiler, recommends these lentils to go with cotechino or zampone, another similar poached sausage. They also make an excellent accompaniment to roast pork or roast lamb.

½ pound brown or green lentils

3 cups cool water

2 small onions, peeled

1½ garlic cloves, peeled

1 bay leaf

salt and freshly ground black pepper to taste

1 small carrot, peeled and finely chopped

2 tablespoons minced flat-leaf parsley

½ celery rib, finely chopped

2 tablespoons extra-virgin olive oil

½ cup rich meat stock (page 83) or clear white chicken stock (page 81)

Pick the lentils over carefully to get rid of any small stones or pieces of grit. Rinse them under running water. Place in a saucepan over medium heat with the cool water. Add one of the onions, a garlic clove, the bay leaf, and salt and pepper and bring to a boil. When the water is boiling, turn it down, cover the lentils, and simmer for about 30 minutes—or until the lentils are thoroughly cooked and tender. (Time varies even more than with other legumes, depending on the age of the lentils.)

While the lentils are cooking, prepare the rest of the vegetables. Finely chop together the remaining onion and the ½ garlic clove. Combine in a heavy saucepan with the carrot, parsley, and celery and sauté gently in the olive oil until the vegetables are soft but not brown—about 15 minutes. Stir in the stock or, if you're planning to serve with a cotechino or zampone sausage, the same quantity of degreased liquid in which the sausage was cooked. Simmer gently. When the lentils are tender, drain them and stir into the vegetable mixture. Simmer for 5 minutes to concentrate the flavors. Serve the lentils with the sliced sausage or with slices of roast pork (see recipe for àrista, page 349). *Makes 6 servings*

Nutritional Data, per portion

| | | |
|---|---|---|
| Calories 190 | Carbohydrate 27g | Saturated Fat 1g |
| Protein 11g | Sodium 12mg | Monounsaturated |
| Fat 5g | Cholesterol 0 | Fat 4g |

# LENTIL AND GREEN OLIVE SALAD

Lentils make a delightful salad, especially in late winter or early spring, when the first bitter greens and young onions are sprouting. Dressed with the finest dark green olive oil and a spritz of lemon juice, lentils have an earthy sweetness that offsets the assertive flavors of early greens and turns them into a protein-rich first course or a main course when accompanied by good crusty bread and a wedge of cheese.

½   **pound brown or green lentils**
1   **small onion, peeled**
1   **garlic clove, peeled**
1   **bay leaf**
**salt and freshly ground black pepper to taste**
1   **cup pitted imported green olives, coarsely chopped**
1   **red bell pepper, cut into long thin strips**
⅓   **cup extra-virgin olive oil**
3   **tablespoons fresh lemon juice**
**bitter greens such as arugula, chicory, frisée, radicchio, or tender**
      **dandelions**
**zest of ½ lemon, cut into fine julienne strips**
1   **tablespoon minced flat-leaf parsley**

Pick the lentils over carefully to get rid of any small stones or pieces of grit. Rinse them under running water. Cook with the onion, garlic, bay leaf, salt, and pepper as described in the preceding recipe.

When the lentils are done, drain them, discarding the cooking vegetables, and mix while still warm with the olives, red peppers, olive oil, and lemon juice. Taste and adjust the seasoning if necessary. Serve piled on a bed of bitter greens. Garnish with the julienne strips of lemon and minced parsley. ***Makes 6 servings***

Nutritional Data, per portion

| | | |
|---|---|---|
| Calories 274 | Carbohydrate 25g | Saturated Fat 2g |
| Protein 11g | Sodium 549mg | Monounsaturated |
| Fat 16g | Cholesterol 0 | Fat 10g |

# CHAPTER FIVE

# FISH AND SEAFOOD

Spurred by questions about the healthfulness of high-fat animal products, Americans are eating more fish than ever before. Still, the high point for annual fish consumption recently was just under 15 pounds per person, compared to 46 pounds of chicken and 63 pounds of beef. Moreover, what the increase reflects is that people who have always eaten fish are simply eating more, while those who didn't eat fish still don't.

Pity them! Not only is fish good for you—low in fat and cholesterol for those who are concerned about heart disease (and who isn't?) and full of high-quality proteins, vitamins, and valuable trace minerals like selenium, copper, and zinc that are hard to get from other sources—it's also just plain good. And fish is quick and easy to prepare. As Mediterranean cooks know well, fish and seafood generally benefit from the simplest preparations—poaching, steaming, roasting, or grilling, whether whole fish, boneless fillets, or steaks. The sauce for the fish is most often prepared apart, whether a plain and delicious mix of good olive oil, lemon juice, and a sprinkling of fresh herbs or a slightly more complex combination like Lebanese samki harra (page 258), made with chopped garlic and cilantro and flavored with hot chilies and cumin.

The supply of fresh seafood in American fish markets and supermarket fish counters has improved enormously in recent years, especially with the development of farm-raised fish like catfish, tilapia, and salmon. Don't be put off by fish labeled "fresh-frozen." That may seem an anomaly, but if the fish is handled correctly and flash-frozen at sea or on shore soon after it is caught, fresh-frozen can be even better than many so-called fresh varieties, which may have been carried at sea, iced down in the hold of the fishing vessel, for as long as 10 days before reaching port. (Be sure to ask if the fish has been frozen, especially if you're not planning to use it

right away. If it has been thawed at the fish market, which often happens, you will not want to refreeze it without cooking it first.)

Much traditional advice to the buyer of seafood is old-fashioned—look for rosy gills, we are told, or clear eyes or shiny skin. Professional chefs in fancy restaurants may have that luxury, but the rest of us seldom get to look at gills, eyes, or skin these days because fish usually comes to us already cut into fillets or steaks, rarely as whole fish. I rely on my nose to tell me when fish is fresh and when it is not. It's pretty infallible. If you do make a mistake, don't be afraid to take the offending beast right back to the person you bought it from and ask for a refund. You may not get it, but you will have made your point.

A word about shellfish and cholesterol: Despite the bad rap they used to get, most mollusks and crustaceans are low in cholesterol. (Errors in measurement by food scientists led to the mistake.) Clams, mussels, and scallops have fewer than 35 milligrams of cholesterol in 100 grams (about 3½ ounces) of raw fish (the yolks of large eggs have 225 milligrams each); lobster has 95 milligrams, shrimp (America's favorite seafood after canned tuna) 150, and squid 230. But even with squid's relatively high count, many nutritionists recommend it except for people on rigidly low-cholesterol diets. The reason? Squid, like most other seafood, is very low in fat. Only 13 of the 92 calories in a 3½-ounce serving of squid come from fat, and the small amount of fat is made up partly of Omega-3 fatty acids, which may be valuable in combating heart disease.

Although some of the health benefits attributed to fish may simply be the result of eating less meat (every time you eat a portion of fish, you eat one less of meat), there is considerable evidence that fish may be more healthful in and of itself. One reason, scientists believe, is the presence of polyunsaturated Omega-3 fatty acids, which interfere with the formation of blood clots and help to prevent the buildup of plaque in blood vessels. Blood clots and plaque are initial steps in the progression of atherosclerosis, which, if uncorrected, can lead to heart disease. Oils present in fish may also act against inflammatory and immune reactions, which characterize diseases like arthritis and psoriasis.

The fish richest in Omega-3 fatty acids are those denizens of deep, cold waters that carry fat in their muscles, especially Atlantic salmon, mackerel, herring, bluefish, albacore, and bluefin tuna. Swordfish is also a good source of Omega-3 fatty acids. White-fleshed fish like cod, haddock, halibut, and snapper, because they don't carry fat in their muscle tissue, are not great sources of Omega-3 fats, but they should not be avoided for that reason. On the contrary: as *very*-low-fat sources of protein, they should be a significant part of the diet.

Many of the species traditionally used in the Mediterranean are rarely available here—or there, for that matter—but fortunately fish recipes and preparations are highly adaptable. In the recipes that follow I have suggested a number of different varieties where it is appropriate. I often substitute haddock, cod, halibut, or snapper, even farm-raised catfish or salmon, in Mediterranean recipes, and they work just fine. Salmon, especially, although not a traditional Mediterranean fish, is appearing in Mediterranean markets at a rapidly increasing rate, primarily because of the marketing skill of Norwegian aquaculturists. Monkfish, widely available in American fish markets, is always an appropriate choice for Mediterranean preparations, and bluefish and mackerel, if they are small, can be substituted for sardines— though if you have access to fresh sardines, snap them up and rush them home as quickly as you can. To my mind, there's no better fish in the world than a sparkling-fresh sardine, wrapped in a grape leaf blanket with its little head poking out and grilled over charcoal embers.

About lemon: In Spain I was told that lemon wedges are used only on fish that is not fresh. This seems overly fastidious; I always include lemon wedges in the garnish for fish.

FISH AND SEAFOOD

# POACHED WHOLE FISH

*The Basic Recipe*

**P**oaching, or very gently boiling, fish in water to cover is traditionally reserved for whole fish, usually a rather large fish, such as a whole salmon or sea bass. It makes an elegant presentation for a dinner party or wedding feast.

The technique requires not only a large fish but a large kettle in which to cook it. A fish-poaching kettle is a long, oval, deep pan. Old-fashioned French poaching pans come with a rack inside, very convenient for lifting the whole fish out once it is cooked. If your fish kettle lacks a rack, use a double layer of cheesecloth instead. Set in the middle of the cheesecloth, the fish can be lowered into the simmering liquid and retrieved when it has finished cooking.

FOR A 6-POUND WHOLE SALMON OR SEA BASS:

**4 to 6 cups fish stock (page 84) or water and wine simmered for**
      **20 minutes with a few bay leaves, a sliced onion, and a few**
      **parsley sprigs**
**1 or 2 cups good-quality dry white wine as needed**
**a little handful of whatever green herbs you will use for garnish—**
      **parsley, basil, dill, tarragon, fresh thyme**

Place the fish in the kettle and cover it with cool water. Then remove the fish and measure the quantity of water. This will tell you how much liquid you need to cover the fish. If the stock and wine available do not measure up, don't worry—just add water to bring the liquid up to the right level.

Place the liquid and herbs in the fish kettle and bring to a very slow simmer— the liquid should be just shuddering. Put the fish on the rack or the double layer of cheesecloth and gently lower it into the liquid. Cover and let it continue cooking at a shuddering simmer. The so-called Canadian rule dictates that fish should cook for 10 minutes for each inch of thickness, measured at the thickest part of the fish, but this often leads to overcooking. For a whole fish, I use the Canadian rule minus 10 minutes—thus a 4-inch-thick salmon cooks for 30 minutes and no more. Fish this large continues to cook from interior heat once it is removed from the pan.

Grasping the rack or the cheesecloth (use rubber gloves and old kitchen towels to protect your hands from the heat), lift the fish out of the pan and set it on a platter to cool slightly. *Do not discard the fish stock*; it has now become even richer in flavor, and if you have no other immediate use for it, set it aside to cool slightly, remove and discard the herbs, and then freeze the stock for future use.

To serve the fish immediately, place it on a warm platter and pour over it about half of the following mixture, beaten together with a fork before it is poured.

¼  garlic clove, mashed to a paste with ½ teaspoon salt

½  cup best-quality extra-virgin olive oil

3  tablespoons fresh lemon juice

salt and freshly ground white pepper to taste

1  tablespoon finely minced fresh flat-leaf parsley, basil, dill, tarragon, thyme, or other herbs

Garnish the platter with sprigs of the herb used in the sauce. Pass the remaining sauce for guests to serve themselves.

For a banquet or buffet presentation, the top layer of skin between the head and the tail (the part that will be eaten) is carefully removed while the fish is still warm. Spoon a few tablespoons of fish stock over the flesh to keep it from drying out. Serve the fish at room temperature, garnished, just before serving, as described.

A homemade mayonnaise, incorporating some of the minced fresh herbs, or an aïoli (page 293) can also be served with the room-temperature fish. *Makes 16 to 20 servings*

Nutritional Data, per portion

| | | |
|---|---|---|
| Calories  178 | Carbohydrate  trace | Saturated Fat  2g |
| Protein  18g | Sodium  43mg | Monounsaturated |
| Fat  11g | Cholesterol  49mg | Fat  6g |

# STEAM-POACHED FISH FILLETS OR STEAKS

### *The Basic Recipe*

**T**he technique called *steam-poaching* (or *poach-steaming*) is similar to poaching but requires less liquid. Fillets or steaks can be poached in an ordinary large skillet or saucepan—preferably one with a lid that fits securely on top, though a large sheet of heavy aluminum foil, in a pinch, makes a perfectly good lid. This is a good, quick, easy preparation for people who want to eat a very-low-fat diet or just a single light dish to recover from a feast. In addition to the fish listed here, salmon is a good choice; though somewhat higher in fat than the others, it is an excellent source of beneficial Omega-3 fatty acids.

2　pounds boneless fish fillets or steaks: haddock, cod, snapper, monkfish, bass, sole, or similar fish

1　cup fish stock (page 84), fish stock and dry white wine, or half wine and half water plus 1 bay leaf, ¼ teaspoon dried thyme, crumbled, a few parsley sprigs, and a pinch of salt if desired

GARNISH:

olive oil–and–lemon sauce from preceding recipe, mayonnaise, aïoli (page 293), or, for a very-low-fat garnish, yogurt sauce for fish (page 290) made with nonfat yogurt

To determine the cooking time, measure the fish fillets or steaks at the thickest part (an *approximate* measure will do). Place the liquid in a shallow skillet large enough to hold all the fish in one layer. Slowly bring the liquid to a bare simmer. Lower the fish pieces into the simmering liquid and immediately clap a lid on the pan. Or cover the pan with aluminum foil, pressing it down around the edges. Cook at a very slow simmer for about 7 minutes for each inch of thickness. The fish is done when it is opaque all the way through (check steaks next to the bone to be sure they are done). Using a spatula, remove the fish pieces and place on a warm platter.

Raise the heat to high and boil the liquid down to about one-third the original quantity. Stir in the olive oil–and–lemon sauce and pour half of it over the warm

fish pieces. Serve immediately, passing the rest of the sauce for guests to help themselves. (If you're using mayonnaise or aïoli, set aside half of it in a little china bowl to be passed at table. Off the heat, carefully mix the reduced poaching liquid, a spoonful at a time, into the remaining mayonnaise or aïoli, then spoon the mixture over the pieces of fish and garnish the platter with a sprinkling of minced fresh herbs.) *Makes 6 to 8 servings*

Nutritional Data, per portion

| | | |
|---|---|---|
| Calories 223 | Carbohydrate 1g | Saturated Fat 2g |
| Protein 22g | Sodium 98mg | Monounsaturated |
| Fat 15g | Cholesterol 66mg | Fat 11g |

# BAKED OR ROASTED FISH

### *The Basic Recipe*

**F**ish suitable for baking include whole fish; chunks or center cuts, with the bone, of large fish such as haddock, sea bass, salmon, or similar fish; and fish steaks cut 1½ to 2 inches thick. For whole fish or center-cut chunks you'll need about ½ pound per person; for boneless steaks or thick fillets, ¼ pound per serving.

¼   cup extra-virgin olive oil

at least 3 pounds whole fish or center-cut fish chunk, or 1½ to 2 pounds
        boneless steaks or thick fillets

¼   cup dry white wine or fresh lemon juice

1   garlic clove, minced

salt and freshly ground black pepper to taste

1   tablespoon fresh or dried herbs: fresh parsley, rosemary, dill, or
        cilantro, fresh or dried thyme or oregano

½   teaspoon hot red pepper flakes (optional)

lemon wedges and best-quality extra-virgin olive oil for serving

Preheat the oven to 425 degrees. Rub a small amount of olive oil over the bottom of a roasting pan large enough to hold all the fish in one layer. Rub the fish or steaks with a little more oil and place in the pan. Combine the remaining olive oil

FISH AND SEAFOOD

with the wine, garlic, salt, pepper, herbs, and hot pepper. Pour the mixture over the fish, making sure all the pieces are well coated.

Roast the fish for 15 to 20 minutes—steaks will take less time than whole fish or chunks. Baste the fish frequently with the pan juices. Remove the fish from the oven and test for doneness—the flesh should be opaque all the way through to the bone. If the fish is not done, return it to the oven for another 5 to 10 minutes.

When the fish is cooked, transfer it to a warm serving platter or warm plates and spoon the juices over the top. Serve immediately with lemon wedges and a little pitcher of best-quality extra-virgin olive oil. *Makes 6 to 8 servings*

### Nutritional Data, per portion

| | | |
|---|---|---|
| Calories 152 | Carbohydrate trace | Saturated Fat 1g |
| Protein 19g | Sodium 68mg | Monounsaturated |
| Fat 8g | Cholesterol 57mg | Fat 6g |

# GRILLED FISH

### The Basic Recipe

Fish steaks, cut 1½ to 2 inches thick—halibut, swordfish, and tuna are all good choices—are really best for grilling. Fillets are usually too delicate, and large whole fish are tricky—too often the outside is charred before the inside is cooked. If you're lucky enough, however, to find *small* whole fish, such as sardines, imported red mullet, small mackerel, or bluefish, they will be exquisite cooked over charcoal or the embers of a wood fire for a real Mediterranean-style treat.

Count on ¼ pound boneless fish steaks per serving, a little more with the bone in, and add a little extra for enthusiastic appetites.

1   teaspoon finely minced garlic, about 3 cloves

½   cup extra-virgin olive oil

¼   cup fresh lemon juice, orange juice, or dry white wine

1   tablespoon balsamic vinegar or sherry vinegar

pinch of cayenne pepper or hot red pepper flakes (optional)

½ teaspoon ground cumin; or 1 teaspoon or more chopped fresh herbs
such as rosemary, dill, parsley, thyme, cilantro, basil, or mint; or
½ teaspoon dried thyme or oregano, crumbled

freshly ground black pepper to taste

2 pounds fish steaks

lemon wedges for garnish

Combine all the ingredients except fish and lemon wedges and mix well. Using a clean paintbrush or pastry brush, paint the fish steaks liberally on both sides and set them aside, lightly covered with a piece of aluminum foil, to marinate for at least 30 minutes.

Build up a fire, using good hardwoods if you're cooking in a fireplace or the best hardwood charcoal (not fake-wood briquettes) if you're using a grill. Let the fire burn brightly and die down until you have a nice bed of hot coals or embers. Large pieces of fish can be set directly on the grill, but to prevent smaller ones from falling through and burning up, you may want to use a special grid made for fish.

When you're ready to cook, brush a little plain olive oil on the cooking surface and set it 4 to 6 inches from the source of heat. Arrange the fish steaks so that they have equal access to the heat source. Cook for about 4 or 5 minutes on each side, turning once. Test for doneness—fish should be opaque all the way through—by inserting the tip of a sharp knife near the bone or in the center of a boneless piece of fish. Remove immediately to a hot platter.

The remaining marinade should be heated just to the boiling point and either poured over the cooked fish or passed at the table along with lemon wedges. ***Makes 6 to 8 servings***

Nutritional Data, per portion

| | | |
|---|---|---|
| Calories 224 | Carbohydrate 1g | Saturated Fat 2g |
| Protein 19g | Sodium 50mg | Monounsaturated |
| Fat 16g | Cholesterol 29mg | Fat 12g |

### Saucing Plainly Cooked Fish

Check Chapter 6 for other ideas about dressing plainly cooked fish. Many of the small dishes in Chapter 1 are also appropriate. Try any of the following: Turkish çaçik (page 37), roasted red pepper puree (page 36), tapénade (page 31), Tunisian mechouia (page 41), or eggplant dip with yogurt (page 35).

FISH AND SEAFOOD

## ABOUT TUNA AND SWORDFISH

Tuna and swordfish are springtime treats in Rome, served with tiny sweet peas, *piselli romaneschi*, from the market gardens of the Roman *campagna*. For me this particular combination is always associated with the season's first opportunity to dine al fresco at Passetto, a lovely restaurant just outside Piazza Navona. The cook uses thin tuna or swordfish steaks, just ½ inch thick, quickly sautéing them on both sides in a mixture of butter and fragrant oil, and serves them with a *contorno* (accompaniment) of delicate peas cooked until they become a creamy not-quite puree of intense flavor and sweetness.

The finest tuna of all is bluefin, but you will probably not find it in your market because the resource has been seriously threatened by overfishing. In any case, most of the catch goes to Japan for sashimi—as it does also in the Mediterranean. But there are many equally delicious members of this family, such as yellowfin and albacore, and all are suitable for Mediterranean treatments.

In buying tuna and swordfish, look for moist fish with good clear color and no off tints or aromas. Yellow flesh in swordfish means it's old, as does a dark brown color in tuna. Usually both fish exhibit distinctive dry edges or gaping layers of flesh when they've been kept around too long. But as with other fish, your nose will tell you—tuna, especially, gets a strong ammonia odor when it's over the hill. Both tuna and swordfish are better fresh than frozen—or "previously frozen," in the current marketing parlance.

Fresh tuna and swordfish are usually available as steaks. Very thick ones—up to 4 inches—are best cooked with the oven roasting technique described on page 243. For other purposes I prefer steaks that are not more than 2 inches thick. Although the flavor of tuna and swordfish is very different—tuna is usually more assertive, more unmistakably fish yet with a meaty quality that is very appealing—they can be used interchangeably in the following recipes.

Because their flavor and texture are somewhat reminiscent of meat, tuna and swordfish are good introductory fish for nonlovers of seafood. While tuna and swordfish aren't especially lean, they're not high in fat either, except for albacore tuna; much of their fat, moreover, is in the form of beneficial Omega-3 fatty acids (see page 238).

# BRAISED TUNA OR SWORDFISH IN WHITE WINE

*A Pan-Mediterranean Recipe*

1   medium onion, thinly sliced

1   crushed garlic clove, chopped

1   red bell pepper, cut into julienne strips

1   tablespoon extra-virgin olive oil or more if needed

1   fresh tuna or swordfish steak, approximately 1½ inches thick,
      weighing 1 to 1¼ pounds

salt to taste

1   cup dry white wine

½   cup pitted black olives, preferably Kalamata, coarsely chopped

1   tablespoon drained capers, coarsely chopped

1   tablespoon finely shredded lemon zest


In a heavy sauté pan large enough to hold the tuna and vegetables comfortably, gently sauté the onion, garlic, and pepper strips in the oil over medium-low heat until the vegetables are soft—about 10 to 15 minutes.

Pat the fish steak dry with paper towels. Push the vegetables to the edge of the pan and turn the heat up to medium-high. Quickly sear the fish on both sides, adding more oil if necessary. The vegetables shouldn't brown, however—remove them with a slotted spoon if they start to brown and put them back when you've finished the fish. When the fish is nicely seared on both sides, sprinkle it with a little salt. Add the wine to the pan and let it come to a boil. Then turn the heat down to low, cover the pan, and braise the fish and vegetables in the wine for 8 to 12 minutes, depending on how well done you'd like the fish.

Add the olives, capers, and lemon zest and stir to mix well with the vegetables. Continue cooking just until the olives are heated through—about 3 to 5 minutes. Then transfer the fish to a heated platter and distribute the vegetables over and around it. Turn the heat to high and rapidly boil down any juices remaining in the pan until reduced to 2 or 3 tablespoons of syrupy glaze. Add to the fish and serve immediately. *Makes 4 servings*

FISH AND SEAFOOD

# PROVENÇAL BRAISED TUNA OR SWORDFISH

This is an adaptation of a method mentioned in René Jouveau's lovely *Cuisine Provençale de Tradition Populaire*. Note that the only fat comes from the olives and the fish itself, the amount depending on the type of fish used.

2   large onions, roughly chopped

2   large ripe tomatoes, roughly chopped, or canned whole tomatoes, drained and chopped

1   large lemon, very thinly sliced

salt and freshly ground black pepper to taste

2   tablespoons coarsely chopped fresh rosemary needles

2   pounds tuna or swordfish steak, 1½ to 2 inches thick, skinned if necessary

⅓   cup chopped black olives, preferably oil-cured

2   bay leaves

3 or 4 fresh thyme sprigs

1   cup dry white wine

Preheat the oven to 375 degrees. Strew half the chopped onion in a heavy kettle or casserole, preferably one with a tight-fitting lid. Cover the onion with half the chopped tomatoes and top them with a layer of half the sliced lemons. Sprinkle with salt, pepper, and about a third of the rosemary. Set the fish on top—it can be in several pieces, but they should fit together to make a compact layer. Add a little more salt and pepper and half the remaining rosemary. Spread the remaining lemons over the fish, followed by the remaining tomatoes and remaining onions. Top the final onion layer with a little more salt and pepper and the remaining rosemary and strew the black olives over all. Tuck the bay leaves and sprigs of thyme into the pot and pour the white wine over all.

Seal the kettle with heavy-duty aluminum foil, then add the lid. Bake for 1½ hours. *Makes 6 to 8 servings*

### Nutritional Data, per portion

| | | |
|---|---|---|
| Calories   203 | Carbohydrate   10g | Saturated Fat   2g |
| Protein   25g | Sodium   242mg | Monounsaturated |
| Fat   7g | Cholesterol   38mg | Fat   3g |

# SALADE NIÇOISE ROYALE

**T**raditional salade Niçoise was always served as an hors d'oeuvre or first course, and purists refused to admit tuna, or even potatoes, to the composition of this Provençal favorite. Gradually, however, over the years, canned tuna—but always the very best oil-packed white tuna—began to creep in more and more. And then someone had the brilliant idea of using a piece of fresh tuna, grilled like a steak over live coals, and voilà, salade Niçoise had become a main-course dish. You will still find traditionalists who turn up their noses at this modern version, but it makes a wonderful summertime treat and splendid fare for a special celebration, especially since so much of the dish can be prepared in advance. For an elegant presentation, roast the peppers over the grill until the skins are black and blistered, following the directions on page 455. Slice the peeled peppers into long thin fingers and use as described.

FISH AND SEAFOOD

1   pound fresh green beans, the smaller the better, trimmed

1   pound small waxy potatoes such as Red Bliss, Yellow Finn, or Russian
    fingerling

9   tablespoons extra-virgin olive oil

3   tablespoons red wine vinegar

salt and freshly ground black pepper to taste

3 or 4 hard-boiled eggs to taste (optional)

1   head of romaine lettuce, green leafy tops only

1   pound fresh ripe red tomatoes

1   large red onion, very thinly sliced

1   green bell pepper, very thinly sliced

1   red bell pepper, very thinly sliced

½   cup black Niçoise or Gaeta olives, pitted

8   oil-packed anchovy fillets (optional)

½ to ¾ cup tightly packed fresh basil leaves

2   pounds fresh tuna steak, about 2 inches thick

1   garlic clove, finely chopped

1   teaspoon salt

2   tablespoons finely minced fresh chives or scallion greens

1   tablespoon drained capers, rinsed and chopped

The green beans, potatoes, and eggs can be prepared well ahead of time—in the morning, say, for an evening meal. Simply rinse the beans and place in an inch of rapidly boiling salted water. Cook until the beans are tender—about 7 to 10 minutes—or to taste. Remove from the heat, drain, and immediately refresh in cold running water to preserve the color. Set aside as soon as the temperature has reduced and cover lightly with a piece of foil.

Scrub the potatoes and cook them in rapidly boiling salted water to cover until they are done, about 20 to 30 minutes, depending on the size and variety; be careful not to overcook. When done, remove from the heat, drain immediately, and run a little cold water over them to halt the cooking process. Peel them if you wish. Small potatoes can be served whole, but larger ones can be sliced rather thickly—not less than ¼ inch thick. Potatoes should be dressed immediately while still warm. Mix together 3 tablespoons of the olive oil and 1 tablespoon of the wine vinegar, adding

salt and pepper to taste; pour over the potatoes and toss gently. The potatoes will absorb most of the dressing. Set aside until ready to assemble the salad.

Boil the eggs in the usual manner, drain, and cover with cold water. Set aside.

If you're planning to use live coals to cook the fish, prepare the fire about an hour before you plan to serve so as to have plenty of time for a good bed of coals to build up. (If you're using an electric or gas grill or broiling the fish in the oven, just preheat for about 5 or 10 minutes.)

While the fire is readying itself, arrange the elements of the salad on a large oval platter, leaving room in the center of the plate for the fish. Arrange the lettuce as a bed for the other ingredients. Slice the tomatoes and sprinkle with salt. Pile the tomatoes at one end of the platter. Pile the dressed potatoes at the other end and arrange the green beans along both sides. Scatter the onion and pepper rings over the other vegetables and arrange the black olives and anchovies on top. Slice the hard-boiled eggs and add the slices. Finally, strew the fresh basil leaves over everything.

Set the grill or broiling pan about 5 or 6 inches away from the heat. Paint the grill or pan with a little of the olive oil—the oil will smoke a little when it's hot enough. Place the tuna steak on the grill or in the broiling pan and cook for about 8 minutes on each side, turning once. Like red meat, high-quality tuna is best if it's not thoroughly cooked—a little pink or even red in the middle is tasty. Remove the fish from the grill when it's done and drop it in the center of the salad platter.

While the tuna is cooking, prepare the dressing: Crush the garlic and salt together in a small bowl, using the back of a spoon, until it is a paste. Then, using a fork, beat in the remaining oil and vinegar along with the chives, capers, and salt and pepper.

As soon as the tuna is in place, pour the dressing over the vegetables and serve immediately. ***Makes 8 servings***

### Nutritional Data, per portion

| | | |
|---|---|---|
| Calories 396 | Carbohydrate 24g | Saturated Fat 4g |
| Protein 28g | Sodium 438mg | Monounsaturated |
| Fat 22g | Cholesterol 38mg | Fat 14g |

# SICILIAN SWORDFISH IN
# FOIL PACKETS

**T**his is a fine recipe for entertaining because there's no last-minute mess to contend with. You can prepare the packets ahead of time and pop them in the oven for 15 minutes before serving. Use any good-quality imported green olives—the small, firm, rather bitter green ones are fine—but in the absence of good-quality green olives, imported black olives will do. Though usually made with swordfish, the recipe works just as well with tuna.

Note that the recipe is for only two servings, but it can be expanded indefinitely.

1   ½-pound swordfish or tuna steak, about 1½ inches thick

a little flour for dusting the steak

1 to 2 tablespoons extra-virgin olive oil as needed

1   small onion, thinly sliced

½   garlic clove, minced

¼   cup chopped pitted green olives

1   2-inch strip of lemon zest, finely slivered

1 or 2 teaspoons tomato puree, diluted with 1 cup dry white wine

salt and freshly ground black pepper to taste

Dust each side of the fish steak lightly with flour, shaking off the excess. Heat 1 tablespoon oil in a sauté pan over medium-high heat and sauté the fish quickly in it just until it is golden on each side. (It will continue cooking later.) Remove the fish and set aside.

Lower the heat and in the oil remaining in the pan gently sauté the onion and garlic until they are soft, about 10 to 15 minutes, adding the second tablespoon of olive oil if necessary. Then add the olives and lemon zest and cook for 2 to 3 minutes. Add the tomato puree diluted with wine, raise the heat slightly, and cook over medium heat for another 2 to 3 minutes, until the wine is reduced and the sauce is thick.

Place the fish on a large square of aluminum foil or parchment paper. Pile the sauce on top and fold up the ends of the foil to form a loose but tightly sealed packet. The fish can be prepared well ahead of time and refrigerated, but allow time to bring it back to room temperature before cooking.

When you're ready to cook, preheat the oven to 425 degrees. Put the room-temperature packet on a cookie sheet or in a shallow baking pan and roast for 15 minutes. Remove. Divide the steak into 2 serving pieces and serve with the sauce spooned over them. *Makes 2 servings*

Nutritional Data, per portion

| | | |
|---|---|---|
| Calories   348 | Carbohydrate   9g | Saturated Fat   3g |
| Protein   22g | Sodium   523mg | Monounsaturated |
| Fat   17g | Cholesterol   40mg | Fat   10g |

**VARIATIONS:** For a more traditional Sicilian *agghiotta*, substitute a tablespoon each of golden raisins, pine nuts, and capers for the green olives and lemon zest. The raisins should be plumped in a little hot water, the pine nuts lightly toasted over low heat, and the capers desalted by rinsing (page 471) if they require it.

You can also prepare this in a single baking dish or gratin dish, piling the sauce on top of the fish pieces and baking in a hot oven for 15 to 20 minutes, until the fish is thoroughly cooked and the sauce is bubbly on top.

# ISTANBUL'S PANDELI RESTAURANT FISH PACKETS

Up a flight of stairs from the entrance to Istanbul's historic old Egyptian Market is Pandeli Restaurant, a beautifully antiquated place with watery blue and green Iznik tiles that make me think I'm in an aquarium. The house specialty is sea bass fillets wrapped in parchment paper and steamed over charcoal on the kitchen grill. Why doesn't the parchment burn? Because, the chef explained, it's soaked in water first. Maybe . . . but I prefer to use the infallible aluminum foil. Put these paper- or foil-wrapped bundles on the grill about 4 or 5 inches from the heat or simply let them steam-roast in a hot oven.

The great virtue of this presentation is—no cooking pots to clean up afterward! You can expand this recipe indefinitely.

FISH AND SEAFOOD

1½ teaspoons extra-virgin olive oil

1   ¼-pound piece of swordfish or boneless fillet of sea bass, snapper, or
     haddock

2 or 3 very small potatoes, peeled, or 1 medium potato, peeled and cut
     into 3 or 4 pieces

2 or 3 pearl onions, peeled, or 2 2-inch lengths of scallion, trimmed

1   thick slice of tomato, diced

3 or 4 long thin strips of green bell pepper

salt and freshly ground white pepper to taste

pinch of sweet paprika mixed with a pinch of cayenne pepper

1   teaspoon fresh lemon juice

Pull out a square of heavy-duty aluminum foil or parchment paper large
enough to make a loose packet around the fish and the vegetables. Smear ½
teaspoon of the oil on the foil and set the fish in the middle.

Bring a small pot of water to a boil and throw in the potatoes. Bring back to a
boil and cook for 4 or 5 minutes, then drain immediately.

Pile the parboiled potatoes, onions, tomato, and pepper strips on top of the
fish. Sprinkle with salt, pepper, and the paprika/cayenne mixture. Drizzle the
remaining oil and the lemon juice over the top.

Pull up the sides of foil and seal to make a loose but tightly sealed packet. The
packets can be prepared well ahead of time and refrigerated, but allow time to bring
them back to room temperature before cooking.

When you're ready to cook, preheat the oven to 425 degrees. Place the packets
on a cookie sheet in the preheated oven and cook for 20 to 25 minutes or until the
fish and vegetables are cooked all the way through.

To cook on the grill, prepare the fire ahead of time to build up a good, thick bed
of coals. Set the packet on a grid about 8 inches from the source of heat and leave for
about 20 minutes. Shift the packet around from time to time to ensure even cooking.

Serve the fish in the packet and break the packet open at the table—the
fragrance released is remarkable. *Makes 1 serving*

Nutritional Data, per portion

| | | |
|---|---|---|
| Calories  296 | Carbohydrate  26g | Saturated Fat  2g |
| Protein  23g | Sodium  101mg | Monounsaturated |
| Fat  11g | Cholesterol  39mg | Fat  7g |

# OVEN-BRAISED SALMON OR HALIBUT STEAKS

2   pounds salmon, halibut, swordfish, or other fish steaks, about 1 inch
     thick

a little flour for dredging the fish

3   tablespoons extra-virgin olive oil

3   medium yellow onions, thinly sliced

1   garlic clove, minced

1 or 2 bay leaves

1   teaspoon salt or more to taste

½   teaspoon sweet paprika

juice of ½ lemon

Lightly dredge the fish steaks in a little flour, shaking them to remove excess. In a pan over medium-high heat, fry the steaks in 2 tablespoons of the oil just long enough to brown them, 2 or 3 minutes on each side. They will not be cooked through. Transfer the steaks to an oven dish that will hold them in one layer. Preheat the oven to 375 degrees.

Add the onions, garlic, bay leaves, and salt to the pan in which the fish cooked, together with the remaining tablespoon of olive oil. Stir to mix with the oil and cook, covered, over medium-low heat, stirring occasionally, until the onions are very soft and golden brown—about 10 to 15 minutes. At the end of the cooking time, remove the bay leaves and stir in the paprika and lemon juice. Mix well and return to the heat just long enough to warm up the lemon juice.

Distribute the onion mixture over the top of the fish steaks, covering them as much as possible. Bake for 20 to 25 minutes or until the top is golden brown and the steaks are thoroughly cooked. *Makes 8 servings*

### Nutritional Data, per portion

| | | |
|---|---|---|
| Calories  209 | Carbohydrate  7g | Saturated Fat  2g |
| Protein  19g | Sodium  318mg | Monounsaturated |
| Fat  11g | Cholesterol  51mg |   Fat  6g |

# SOUTHERN ITALIAN BAKED FISH
# WITH CAPERS AND OLIVES

**M**any kinds of fish are appropriate for this treatment, including tuna and swordfish. Or try thick salmon, sea bass, haddock, cod, snapper, or grouper fillets or halibut steaks or thick slices of monkfish. This dish could as easily be Greek as Italian—if you want to make it more so, add a tablespoon of fresh (or a teaspoon of dried) chopped oregano with the bread crumbs.

4   teaspoons extra-virgin olive oil

2   pounds boneless fish

1   cup very ripe tomatoes, peeled and seeded (page 454), or 1 cup
      drained imported canned tomatoes

½   teaspoon sugar

1   teaspoon fresh lemon juice

1   tablespoon drained capers, rinsed

¼   cup chopped pitted green olives, preferably large imported Italian
      olives

salt and freshly ground black pepper to taste

½   cup unseasoned dried bread crumbs

Preheat the oven to 400 degrees. Use a teaspoon of oil to coat the inside of a baking dish large enough to hold all the fish in one layer. Place the fish in it.

Chop the tomatoes and mix with the sugar and lemon juice in a small bowl. Add the capers and olives and mix again. Taste for seasoning and add salt and pepper as desired. Pile the tomato sauce on top of the fish pieces. Distribute the bread crumbs over the top and drizzle on the remaining oil. Place in the oven and bake for 35 to 40 minutes or until the fish is thoroughly cooked, the sauce very bubbly and browned. *Makes 6 to 8 servings*

Nutritional Data, per portion

| | | |
|---|---|---|
| Calories  221 | Carbohydrate  6g | Saturated Fat  2g |
| Protein  28g | Sodium  234mg | Monounsaturated |
| Fat  9g | Cholesterol  43mg |   Fat  4g |

## THREE LEBANESE WAYS WITH FISH

We lived in Beirut in the early 1970s, right before Lebanon lurched into a 15-year war of unparalleled brutality. Most of the people I knew in Beirut have long since fled, gone to the earth's far corners. Most of them still harbor a heart-stabbing desire for the city that once was—sparkling, vivacious, beautiful, and temperamental, perched on its peninsula over the dazzling sea and backed by the stormy, snow-capped range of Mount Lebanon.

Not the least of Beirut's charms was the city's incredibly evolved cuisine that drew from a cross-cultural mix of all the people who had stopped there or passed through—Arabs and Persians, Egyptians, Turks and Armenians, Greeks, French, Italians, and of course the Lebanese themselves, fierce defenders of a heritage that went back to the ancient Phoenicians. The people of the coastal cities, Tyre and Sidon, Beirut and Byblos, had been seafarers and traders since the days of old Phoenicia, and seafood thus was a rich part of their diet, whether prepared in the French manner on the terrace of the glamorous seaside St.-Georges Hotel or in a more rustic fashion in the little outdoor restaurants that surrounded the Crusader port of Byblos, one of the oldest cities in the world. The following recipes are among treasured mementos of that time.

# SAMKI HARRA

### Lebanese Fish in a Cilantro-Chili Sauce

Use the hot chili judiciously in this recipe. Mediterranean food is not intended to be as piquant as, say, Mexican. The goal is a sense of heat but not overwhelming hotness.

1   cup chopped walnuts
2   pounds boneless firm-textured white fish fillets such as cod, scrod,
        haddock, or snapper
a little flour for dusting the fish
4 to 5 tablespoons extra-virgin olive oil as needed
2   cups finely chopped onion
4   garlic cloves, coarsely chopped
1   cup chopped cilantro
3   cups fish stock (page 84)
1   teaspoon hot red pepper flakes or to taste
½   teaspoon ground cumin
¼   cup fresh lemon juice or more to taste
salt and freshly ground black pepper to taste

Pound the walnuts, using a mortar and pestle, almost to a paste. Or process them in a food processor. Set aside.

Dust the fish pieces lightly with flour. Heat 2 tablespoons of the olive oil in a skillet over medium to high heat and, when the oil is almost smoking, sauté the fish, a few pieces at a time, for 2 or 3 minutes on each side. Don't worry about thoroughly cooking the fish since it will continue to cook in the sauce. As each piece is done, remove and set aside. (You may need to add a little more oil from time to time.)

When all the fish has been sautéed, discard any remaining oil and wipe the pan out with paper towels. Add 2 tablespoons fresh oil and over medium-low heat gently cook the onion and garlic until thoroughly softened and starting to brown—about 15 to 20 minutes. Add the cilantro and stir to incorporate thoroughly. Then add the stock, reserved walnut paste, hot pepper, and cumin. Cook the sauce over gentle heat for about 15 minutes, stirring occasionally, to develop the flavors. Then add the reserved fish pieces and continue cooking for 8 to 10 minutes or until the fish flakes apart easily.

Transfer the fish pieces to a warm platter. Add the lemon juice to the sauce, mixing thoroughly. Taste and adjust the seasoning, adding more lemon juice, salt, black pepper, or red pepper if desired. Pour the sauce over the fish.

Serve immediately, accompanied by plain boiled rice or rice pilaf (page 201).
**Makes 8 servings**

Nutritional Data, per portion

| | | |
|---|---|---|
| Calories 277 | Carbohydrate 9g | Saturated Fat 2g |
| Protein 24g | Sodium 126mg | Monounsaturated |
| Fat 16g | Cholesterol 52mg | Fat 7g |

# KOUSBARIYA

### Lebanese Fish Baked in a Tomato-Cilantro Sauce

2    pounds firm-textured white fish fillets such as cod, scrod, haddock, or snapper

a little flour for dusting the fish

¼    cup extra-virgin olive oil

1    medium onion, halved and thinly sliced

1    garlic clove, chopped

3    very ripe tomatoes, seeded and chopped, or 4 canned whole tomatoes, drained and chopped

1    tablespoon ground cumin

1    cup minced cilantro

salt and freshly ground pepper to taste

Cut the fish into serving-size pieces about 1 inch thick. Lightly dust the fish pieces with flour. Heat 2 tablespoons of the olive oil in a heavy sauté pan over medium to high heat and, when it is almost smoking, add the pieces of fish. Sauté the fish, a few pieces at a time, for 2 or 3 minutes to a side. (The fish will continue cooking later.) Remove each piece as it is cooked and set aside.

FISH AND SEAFOOD

When all the fish is done, discard the frying fat and wipe the pan out with paper towels. Add the remaining 2 tablespoons of oil to the pan and over medium-low heat gently sauté the onion and garlic until soft but not brown—about 10 to 15 minutes. Add the tomatoes and cook, stirring occasionally, until the tomatoes have given off their juices and started to thicken—about 10 minutes more. Stir in the cumin and cilantro. Taste for seasoning and add salt and pepper if necessary.

Preheat the oven to 350 degrees. Arrange the fish pieces in a shallow baking or gratin dish and cover them with the sauce. Bake for about 20 minutes or until the fish is thoroughly cooked and the sauce is bubbling. *Makes 8 servings*

Nutritional Data, per portion

| | | |
|---|---|---|
| Calories  167 | Carbohydrate  6g | Saturated Fat  1g |
| Protein  21g | Sodium  68mg | Monounsaturated |
| Fat  6g | Cholesterol  49mg |   Fat  4g |

# SAYYADIEH

### *Lebanese Fish with a Fragrant Onion Sauce*

2   pounds thick white fish fillets such as haddock, cod, or snapper

a little flour for dusting the fish

salt to taste

¼   cup extra-virgin olive oil

⅓   cup pine nuts

2½ cups finely chopped onion

3   cups water

juice of 1 lemon or more to taste

1   cup long-grain rice

finely minced flat-leaf parsley for garnish

Cut the fish into serving-size pieces and lightly dust each piece with flour mixed with a little salt. Set the pieces of fish on a cake rack and put them aside to dry.

In 2 tablespoons of the olive oil in a skillet over medium-low heat, gently sauté the pine nuts until uniformly brown, about 5 to 10 minutes, being careful not to

burn them. Remove from the heat as soon as they are done, scooping them out with a slotted spoon, and set them aside.

In the oil in the pan, sauté the fish until lightly browned on each side. Remove from the pan and set aside, covered, in a warm oven.

Add the remaining 2 tablespoons olive oil to the pan along with the onion and cook gently over medium-low heat, stirring frequently, until golden in color but not crisply fried. The onion should be melting in the oil rather than sizzling. (This can take up to 40 minutes over gentle heat.) When the onion is golden brown, add the water, cover the pan, and continue cooking for about 20 minutes, until the onion is thoroughly softened into a sauce. Be careful not to cook the liquid away—you can add a little boiling water if the sauce becomes too dry.

Remove the onion sauce from the heat. Spoon a cup of the sauce into a smaller saucepan. Add the lemon juice and continue cooking over medium-low heat until the sauce is reduced and thickened—about 10 to 15 minutes. Remove from the heat and stir in the reserved pine nuts. Set aside. This is the lemon sauce to go on top of the fish and rice.

Add enough water to the remaining onion sauce to make 2½ cups. Bring this to a boil in another saucepan and add the rice. Cover and cook, stirring occasionally, until the rice is done and all the liquid has been absorbed—about 20 minutes. Be careful not to burn the rice. When the rice is done, set aside, covered, for 5 minutes to absorb all the liquid before serving.

To serve, pile the rice on a warm platter with the fish pieces distributed on top or around the rice. Bring the lemon sauce back to a simmer and pour it over the top of the fish. Sprinkle with a little parsley and serve immediately. *Makes 8 servings*

Nutritional Data, per portion

| Calories 301 | Carbohydrate 25g | Saturated Fat 2g |
|---|---|---|
| Protein 25g | Sodium 80mg | Monounsaturated |
| Fat 11g | Cholesterol 65mg | Fat 7g |

FISH AND SEAFOOD

# LA BOURRIDE SÈTOISE

*Provençal Seafood with Aïoli*

**T**he little Mediterranean port of Sète was a frequent overnight stop for us in the late 1960s when we were traveling, for reasons I can't remember, between Madrid and the French Alps above Grenoble. I do remember why we stopped in Sète, which was at the time a rather unseemly fishing port, not at all *touristique*, especially in winter, when a chill mist often wrapped the harbor. The French poet Paul Valéry is buried in the cemetery there, and we once went to visit his grave. But the real reason for stopping was an extraordinary dish served in the restaurants of the *vieux port*, a Sètoise version of the aïoli-rich seafood stew called *bourride*. It is usually served with small new potatoes, steamed until tender, and toasted crusty bread spread with a little of the aïoli.

1   quart fish stock (page 84), preferably made from the heads and bones
      of the fish used in the bourride

2   pounds monkfish or other firm-fleshed white fish fillets such as
      haddock, snapper, even swordfish

1   large leek, rinsed well and sliced, including a little of the green

1   garlic clove, sliced

2   tablespoons extra-virgin olive oil

1   medium orange

1   teaspoon minced fresh thyme or ½ teaspoon dried, crumbled

1   tablespoon fennel seeds

2   bay leaves

18  medium shrimp, shelled and deveined if necessary

¼   cup good-quality cognac

1   tablespoon tomato puree diluted with 2 tablespoons water

1½ cups aïoli (page 293)

⅓   cup minced flat-leaf parsley

slices of crusty country bread, toasted (optional)

In a small saucepan, heat the stock to a bare simmer. Cut the fish into serving pieces and set aside.

In a heavy soup kettle over medium-low heat, cook the leek and garlic in the olive oil, stirring occasionally, until the vegetables are soft but not brown, about 10 to 15 minutes. Meanwhile, carefully pare away the zest of the orange using a swivel peeler. Cut the zest into several pieces, then add it along with the thyme, fennel, and bay leaves.

Raise the heat to medium-high and add the shrimp. Sauté briefly, tossing the shrimp with the vegetables. Add the cognac, and as soon as it begins to boil, light it with a match, averting your face. Stir rapidly with a wooden spoon until the flames die down. Using tongs, remove the shrimp and set aside.

Stir the diluted tomato puree and the simmering fish stock into the kettle. (The recipe can be prepared ahead to this point.)

Bring the stock to a slow simmer and add the fish pieces. Cook for 7 to 15 minutes, depending on how thick the fish pieces are. Add the reserved shrimp for the last 4 minutes of cooking time.

When the fish and shrimp are cooked through, remove them and set the shrimp aside in a warm place. Arrange the fish pieces on a warm serving platter. Spoon a little of the hot stock over the fish and set in a slow oven to keep warm while you finish the sauce.

Divide the aïoli approximately in half. Mound half of it in a small bowl to be passed at the table; put the other half in the top of a double boiler.

Use tongs to remove and discard the bay leaves and orange zest. Reduce the stock by boiling rapidly until it is thickened and concentrated—about 15 to 20 minutes. You should have about one-third the original quantity, about 1½ cups. Remove the stock from the heat and incorporate it, a spoonful at a time and stirring constantly, into the aïoli in the double boiler. When all the stock has been incorporated, it should be as thick as heavy cream—thick enough to coat a spoon. If the sauce is not thick enough, set it over boiling water, stirring constantly, until it has thickened. Pour the sauce over the fish on the platter, garnish with the reserved shrimp, sprinkle with the parsley, and serve immediately, passing the small bowl of aïoli for guests to add at their pleasure.

You can also serve the bourride on toast slices in individual serving bowls, pouring the thickened aïoli cream over and dropping a dollop of aïoli on each serving. *Makes 8 servings*

Nutritional Data, per portion

| Calories 552 | Carbohydrate 5g | Saturated Fat 7g |
|---|---|---|
| Protein 27g | Sodium 180mg | Monounsaturated |
| Fat 49g | Cholesterol 115mg | Fat 36g |

FISH AND SEAFOOD

# TUNISIAN FISH WITH PRESERVED LEMONS AND OLIVES

**A**t the elegant restaurant Dar El Jeld at the top of the old medina in Tunis, they make *kabkabous*, a traditional fish preparation from the southern quadrant of the Mediterranean, with fillets of sea bass, or loup de mer. Sea bass, raised on aquaculture farms in California, is often available in American markets, but other fish are also suitable: monkfish, haddock, cod, snapper, or any other firm-textured white fish with rather plump fillets (not sole or flounder). Madame Jait, one of the restaurant's proprietors, told me the dish is "not Tunisienne but Tunisoise," meaning from Tunis the city, with its cuisine of the Mediterranean littoral, not Tunisia the country, which draws more deeply from Africa and the desert for inspiration. At Dar El Jeld they do not add harissa or hot pepper to the sauce, as they would farther south, just a little cumin stirred in at the end—"because to add it sooner," says Madame Jait, "would make the sauce bitter."

1½ pounds fish fillets

salt and freshly ground pepper to taste

about ½ teaspoon saffron threads

½ garlic clove, minced

1 medium onion, minced

2 tablespoons extra-virgin olive oil

1 medium green bell pepper, cut into long strips

1 medium very ripe tomato, finely chopped, or 1 tablespoon tomato
   puree diluted with 1 cup hot water

1 tablespoon harissa (page 301) or ½ teaspoon ground medium-hot
   dried red chili (not chili powder) (optional)

¼ cup drained capers, rinsed and coarsely chopped

1 preserved lemon (page 305), rinsed and cut into small pieces

½ cup pitted olives, preferably mixed green and black

2 tablespoons white wine vinegar

½ teaspoon ground cumin

Rinse the fish fillets in running water and pat dry with paper towels. Sprinkle on both sides with salt, pepper, and the crumbled saffron. Set the fillets aside on a rack until you're ready to cook them.

In a skillet over medium-low heat, gently cook the garlic and onion in the oil until the onion is soft but not brown—about 10 to 15 minutes. Add the green pepper strips and cook just until wilted, then add the tomato and, if you wish, the harissa. Continue cooking over low heat until the sauce is reduced and thickened—about 5 to 10 minutes.

Add the fish pieces to the sauce and cook for about 7 to 10 minutes or until done. Transfer the fish pieces to a heated platter. Stir the capers, preserved lemon, and olives into the fish sauce along with the vinegar. Simmer for 5 minutes, adding the cumin at the very end. Taste and adjust the seasoning, adding salt if necessary.

Pour the sauce over the fish on the platter, arranging the lemons and olives around the edge. Serve immediately, accompanied by rice pilaf (page 201) or plain steamed potatoes to sop up the sauce. At Dar El Jeld the plate is garnished with cherry tomatoes and little onions about the same size, both cooked in the fragrant sauce of the fish. *Makes 6 servings*

Nutritional Data, per portion

| | | |
|---|---|---|
| Calories 207 | Carbohydrate 9g | Saturated Fat 2g |
| Protein 22g | Sodium 1,395mg | Monounsaturated |
| Fat 10g | Cholesterol 47mg | Fat 6g |

# GRATIN OF COD AND SPINACH

**T**his dish is traditionally made with salt cod, but I find it difficult to persuade Americans, outside of some more adventurous restaurant chefs, that there is virtue in that old-fashioned treat. Make this with fresh cod or any other firm-textured white fish, such as haddock or snapper; salmon fillets are also a good choice, setting up a nice contrast between the pink fish and the deep green spinach.

2   pounds fresh spinach, rinsed well
1   medium onion, chopped
1   garlic clove, chopped
2   tablespoons extra-virgin olive oil
1   tablespoon Dijon mustard
salt and freshly ground black pepper to taste
1½ pounds fish fillets, the thicker the better
juice of ½ lemon or more to taste
¾   cup fine dry unseasoned bread crumbs

Cook the spinach in a large kettle over medium heat, using only the water clinging to its leaves, for about 10 to 15 minutes. When spinach is tender, remove from the heat, drain, and chop rather coarsely.

In a small saucepan or skillet over medium-low heat, gently sauté the onion and garlic in 1 tablespoon of the oil until the onion is softened but not browned—about 10 to 15 minutes. Stir in the mustard and combine this mixture with the chopped spinach, stirring to mix it all together. Taste and add salt and pepper if desired. (The recipe can be prepared ahead up to this point.)

When you're ready to cook, preheat the oven to 450 degrees. Lightly oil the bottom and sides of an oval gratin dish large enough to hold the fish in one layer. Spread half the spinach mixture in the bottom of the dish, then set the fish pieces on top. Sprinkle with salt, pepper, and the lemon juice. Then top with the remaining spinach. Strew the bread crumbs over the top and drizzle the remaining tablespoon of oil over the crumbs.

Bake for about 20 to 30 minutes, depending on the thickness of the fillets, or until the fish is thoroughly cooked and the spinach is bubbling. Serve immediately.
*Makes 6 servings*

Nutritional Data, per portion

Calories 235  Carbohydrate 18g  Saturated Fat 1g
Protein 27g  Sodium 373mg  Monounsaturated
Fat 7g  Cholesterol 49mg  Fat 4g

# OVEN-ROASTED FISH WITH VEGETABLES

**S**urrounded as it is by three seas—the Atlantic, the Mediterranean, and the Mare Cantabrico arm of the Atlantic—Spain is famous for the quality of seafood in markets, restaurants, and homes. All the more curious, then, that the Spanish are champion meat eaters and have been ever since the entire nation received a papal dispensation from Friday fish to lend strength for the crusade against Islam. Today we know the Christian forces would have been even stronger, and possibly brainier, had they eaten seafood. (True, they won in the end—but it took them 700 years, all told, to do so.) Despite their predilection for meat, modern Spanish home cooks favor oven-roasting fish for its quick, easy preparation and lack of fuss.

Besugo, or sea bream, is the fish of choice in Spain, but any large fish with firm-textured white flesh will do. Red snapper is ideal. The fish should be cooked whole for the best flavor.

1 whole 4-pound red snapper, cleaned and scaled

salt

1 lemon, thinly sliced

⅓ cup extra-virgin olive oil

2 medium onions, halved and thinly sliced

2 pounds small new potatoes, peeled and sliced ¼ inch thick

2 large bell peppers, preferably 1 red and 1 green, sliced ¼ inch thick

1 medium tomato, sliced ¼ inch thick

1 teaspoon saffron threads, crumbled and dissolved in ¾ cup dry white wine

2 tablespoons dry unseasoned bread crumbs

FISH AND SEAFOOD

Rinse the fish inside and out and pat dry. With a sharp knife, make 3 deep vertical slashes, almost to the bone, on each side of the fish. Sprinkle a little salt over each lemon slice and press a slice into each of the slashes. Tuck the remaining lemon slices into the belly cavity.

In a large skillet, heat 2 tablespoons of the oil over medium-low heat. Add the onions and sauté gently, stirring occasionally, until they are soft but not brown, about 10 to 12 minutes. Using a slotted spoon, remove the onions from the oil and spread them in a roasting pan large enough to hold the fish.

Preheat the oven to 400 degrees. Add another tablespoon of oil to the pan and over medium-high heat fry the potato slices, turning occasionally, until they are golden brown, about 15 minutes. Using the slotted spoon, remove the potatoes from the oil and distribute over the onions in the baking dish. Now add the pepper strips to the pan and cook, stirring occasionally, until softened, about 5 minutes.

Set the fish on the bed of potatoes and onions and distribute the pepper strips and tomato slices over it.

In a small bowl, whisk the remaining oil with the saffron-infused wine until blended. Pour over the fish and sprinkle the bread crumbs, with a little salt if you wish, on top.

Bake for 35 to 40 minutes or until the fish is firm and cooked through. Remove from the oven, cover lightly with aluminum foil, and set aside for 10 minutes or so before serving. ***Makes 8 servings***

Nutritional Data, per portion

| | | |
|---|---|---|
| Calories  239 | Carbohydrate  10g | Saturated Fat  2g |
| Protein  26g | Sodium  95mg | Monounsaturated |
| Fat  11g | Cholesterol  44mg | Fat  8g |

## ABOUT SHRIMP

Shrimp is one seafood that takes particularly well to freezing—a good thing since most of the shrimp available in our fish markets has been previously frozen, even when it looks fresh. If you should find fresh shrimp in season, cook them as simply and briefly as possible—on the grill or steamed, following the recipe on page 271—and serve them with a little olive oil, a squeeze of lemon juice, and some crunchy sea salt.

Don't turn your nose up at frozen shrimp, however: it's fine in the recipes that follow. I have used both frozen shrimp and "previously frozen" shrimp (meaning the vendor has thawed the frozen shrimp before putting them on display). If at all possible, buy solidly frozen shrimp and thaw them in your refrigerator—the quality and texture will be superior. Unless otherwise specified, I use medium-large (about 25 to the pound) shrimp, headless but with their shells on to protect flavor and freshness, then peel the shrimp at some point during the cooking process. Mediterranean recipes often call for shrimp served with their shells on, but this is messier eating than most Americans are comfortable with.

# SKEWERED SHRIMP WITH GARLIC, LEMON, AND OLIVE OIL

This is one of those recipes whose simplicity belies its dramatic effect on the taste buds. The shrimp can be cooked under a gas or electric grill but achieve their most noble flavor when grilled over charcoal or wood embers. Use the largest shrimp you can find for this dish, although the marinade is also good with smaller specimens. The shrimp are delicious served with a *contorno*, or accompaniment, of white cannellini beans. This is one recipe where you'll want to leave the shells on and peel the shrimp at the table.

4    pounds fresh shrimp, preferably very large, with their shells on

½    cup extra-virgin olive oil

1    teaspoon sea salt

freshly ground black pepper to taste

3 or 4 garlic cloves to taste, finely minced

3    tablespoons fresh lemon juice

½    bay leaf for each shrimp

¼    cup minced fresh green herbs such as parsley, basil, or tarragon

lemon wedges for garnish

Spread the shrimp out in a shallow glass or ceramic baking dish. Combine the oil, salt, pepper, garlic, and lemon juice, beating to mix well. Pour over the shrimp and set aside to marinate for at least 30 minutes, turning the shrimp occasionally in the marinade. (Refrigerate the shrimp if you're holding them longer than 30 minutes.)

Build up a charcoal or wood fire in plenty of time to have a good bed of hot coals when you're ready to cook. Or preheat an oven broiler and adjust the rack.

Thread the shrimp on skewers, alternating with halves of bay leaf. Lightly oil a grill and set the skewers on the grill over the fire, about 4 inches from the source of heat. Grill for about 3 minutes on each side. As soon as the shrimp are done, transfer to a heated platter. Sprinkle with the herbs and serve immediately with the lemon wedges. *Makes 8 servings*

Nutritional Data, per portion

| | | |
|---|---|---|
| Calories 331 | Carbohydrate 6g | Saturated Fat 3g |
| Protein 38g | Sodium 458mg | Monounsaturated |
| Fat 18g | Cholesterol 279mg | Fat 12g |

**VARIATION:** Scallops, threaded horizontally, are equally good marinated and grilled on skewers. Or alternate scallops and shrimp for a handsome presentation.

# STEAMED SCAMPI OR SHRIMP FROM LUCCA

Late one summer afternoon after a long walk in the green foothills of the Apuane Alps, a friend and I staggered into the garden of Ristorante Vipore in the hills overlooking Lucca and the Arno River coursing slowly to the sea. We had had nothing but oranges and chocolate since breakfast, but it was that awkward hour of the day, far too late for lunch and way too early for dinner. That didn't stop Cesare Casella, who had bought live scampi that morning in the fish market in Viareggio. These were the real thing, not giant shrimp but miniature rock lobsters, and Cesare quickly steamed them in a broth that was fragrant with the wild thyme that grows on the hillsides along with chips of tomatoes, a little hot pepper, white wine, and sea salt. He served them with a simple dollop of olive oil on each plate. We ate in the garden, peeling the shellfish and dipping them in oil, and washed them down with a good Franciacorta white from Ca' del Bosco while the late sun flushed the rosy walls of Lucca across the Valdarno.

Scampi don't exist in this country. Freshwater crawfish are a poor cousin, and lobsters are too strongly flavored for such a delicate treatment. Use the freshest large shrimp you can find and plan on four or five to a serving. Any leftovers can be used in a salad or to garnish a fish stew.

1   cup fish stock (page 84)

1   cup good-quality dry white wine

a handful of fresh thyme leaves

1   4-inch strip of lemon zest

1   medium onion, chopped

1   medium very ripe tomato, peeled and seeded (page 454) and diced

1   small dried hot red chili

1   tablespoon sea salt

freshly ground black or white pepper to taste

4   pounds jumbo shrimp, as fresh as possible

½ to 1 cup best-quality extra-virgin olive oil

In a saucepan large enough to hold all the shrimp, combine all the ingredients except the shrimp and olive oil and bring to a boil over medium heat. Turn the heat down to low, cover the pan tightly, and simmer for 15 minutes to develop the flavors.

Add the shrimp, stirring to mix well, cover the pan again, and cook, boiling rapidly, for 5 to 7 minutes, depending on the size of the shrimp. All the shrimp should have turned bright pink; be careful not to overcook. Remove the shrimp from the liquid and pile on a heated platter.

Boil the cooking liquid rapidly until it is reduced to about 1 cup. It should be rather thick and a little syrupy. Pour the liquid over the shrimp. Serve with a clear glass pitcher or cruet (so you can see the color of it) of best-quality olive oil along with a little bowl of sea salt, a pepper mill, and some lemon wedges. Add slices of a crusty, country-style loaf for sopping up juices. *Makes 8 to 10 servings*

Nutritional Data, per portion

| | | |
|---|---|---|
| Calories  315 | Carbohydrate  5g | Saturated Fat  3g |
| Protein  30g | Sodium  678mg | Monounsaturated |
| Fat  19g | Cholesterol  225mg | Fat  14g |

# GRATIN OF SHRIMP AND POTATOES

**T**his is a boon-to-the-busy-cook dish that can be prepared ahead of time and assembled for last-minute cooking. Precede it with a simple vegetable soup (not one in which tomatoes dominate, however), follow it with a salad of bitter greens and sliced fennel, add a loaf of good crusty bread to the menu and some fruit for dessert, and you have a meal that's as good for company as it is for family.

2    medium onions, peeled

salt to taste

3    very ripe tomatoes, peeled and seeded (page 454) and chopped, or
        1 cup chopped well-drained imported canned whole tomatoes

1    green bell pepper, chopped

1    small jalapeño chili, seeded and sliced (optional)

2    garlic cloves, chopped

1    tablespoon minced flat-leaf parsley

1    bay leaf

3    tablespoons extra-virgin olive oil

juice of ½ lemon

freshly ground black pepper to taste

6    medium red-skin or other waxy potatoes, peeled and sliced about
        ½ inch thick

2    pounds medium-large (25 count) shrimp

Cut one of the onions in half and slice each half as thinly as possible. Put the slices in a bowl and toss them with a tablespoon of salt. Set aside for 20 to 30 minutes.

Finely chop the second onion and mix it with the tomatoes, pepper, chili, garlic, and parsley. Crumble the bay leaf and mix into the vegetables along with 2 tablespoons of the olive oil and the lemon juice. Taste the sauce and add salt and pepper if desired. Set aside.

Bring a saucepan of water to a boil over high heat, add the potatoes, and boil for 10 to 15 minutes or until the potatoes are tender but not falling apart. Drain the potatoes and set aside. (The recipe can be prepared ahead up to this point.)

FISH AND SEAFOOD

When you're ready to cook, preheat the oven to 400 degrees. Meanwhile, peel the shrimp and devein if necessary. Rinse the salted onions in a colander to remove the salt and toss to dry.

Smear the remaining tablespoon of olive oil over the bottom and sides of an oval gratin dish or a glass baking dish. Distribute the sliced onions and potatoes over the bottom of the dish, arrange the peeled shrimp on top, and pile the tomato mixture on top of the shrimp, covering the shrimp completely. Cover the dish with foil and bake for 20 to 30 minutes, until the sauce is bubbling, the shrimp are thoroughly cooked, and the potato slices are tender. Remove the foil for the last 5 minutes of cooking to let the top brown. Serve immediately. ***Makes 6 servings***

Nutritional Data, per portion

| | | |
|---|---|---|
| Calories 341 | Carbohydrate 35g | Saturated Fat 1g |
| Protein 29g | Sodium 290mg | Monounsaturated |
| Fat 10g | Cholesterol 186mg | Fat 6g |

## CATALAN SHRIMP IN A SWEET RED PEPPER SAUCE

**T**his recipe and the next are often made with Mediterranean rock lobster (the kind that have no claws), but they are just as good, possibly even better, with shrimp. This dish is delicious with a rice or bulgur pilaf (pages 201, 222); or try it with steamed wheat berries.

2   red bell peppers

2   pounds medium-large (25 count) shrimp

3   tablespoons extra-virgin olive oil

½   medium onion, minced

¼   cup minced flat-leaf parsley

4   medium very ripe tomatoes, peeled and seeded (page 454) and chopped,
       or 1½ cups chopped well-drained canned imported tomatoes

½   cup dry white wine

1   tablespoon cognac

½   teaspoon saffron threads

½   teaspoon cayenne pepper

Roast and peel the red peppers, following the directions on page 455. Cut the prepared peppers into strips and set aside.

Peel the shrimp and devein if necessary. Heat 2 tablespoons of the oil in a sauté pan over medium heat and sauté the shrimp, stirring frequently, for a couple of minutes on each side. Remove the shrimp from the oil and set aside.

Lower the heat to medium-low, add the remaining tablespoon of oil to the pan, and gently sauté the onion and parsley until the onion is soft but not browned— about 10 to 15 minutes. Add the peppers and tomatoes and cook until most of the tomato juice has boiled away and the sauce is thick and jammy—about 20 minutes.

Add the wine and cognac and raise the heat to boil away the alcohol, then stir the reserved shrimp back in together with the saffron and cayenne. Stir to combine well and cook for an additional 2 or 3 minutes, until the shrimp are thoroughly warmed and the flavors have melded. Serve immediately. *Makes 6 servings*

Nutritional Data, per portion

| | | |
|---|---|---|
| Calories   240 | Carbohydrate   8g | Saturated Fat   1g |
| Protein   26g | Sodium   192mg | Monounsaturated |
| Fat   9g | Cholesterol   186mg | Fat   6g |

# GRILLED SHRIMP WITH A CATALAN ALMOND SAUCE

**T**his is one time when the shrimp should be served with their shells on— messy, yes, but utterly delicious.

2   tomatoes, peeled and seeded (page 454) and chopped

½   cup blanched almonds

6   tablespoons extra-virgin olive oil

2   garlic cloves, peeled

1   teaspoon minced flat-leaf parsley

½   teaspoon freshly ground black pepper

1   teaspoon hot red pepper flakes

juice of ½ lemon

2   tablespoons sherry vinegar

2   pounds medium-large (25 count) shrimp

Prepare a charcoal fire or preheat a gas or electric grill. Set the chopped tomatoes to drain in a fine-mesh colander or sieve.

In a small sauté pan over medium-low heat, toast the almonds in a tablespoon of the oil, stirring frequently, until the almonds are golden brown—about 5 to 7 minutes—being careful not to burn them. Transfer the almonds to a mortar, food processor, or blender. In the oil remaining in the pan, gently sauté the garlic cloves, stirring frequently, until they are golden—about 15 minutes. Add the garlic to the almonds along with the parsley, black pepper, and hot pepper. Pound in the mortar or process or blend, gradually adding in the drained tomatoes to make a thick sauce. (If you're using a food processor or blender, be careful not to overprocess; the mixture should be a little granular from the almonds.)

Transfer the sauce to a bowl and beat in the lemon juice and vinegar. Reserve 2 tablespoons of the remaining oil and beat the rest into the sauce. Set the sauce aside.

Toss the shrimp with the reserved 2 tablespoons oil. Cook the shrimp on the hot grill, about a minute to a side, until the shells are papery and the flesh is thoroughly cooked. Pile the shrimp on a platter and serve the sauce in a separate bowl (less messy); or pour the sauce over the hot shrimp and serve (very messy but delicious). *Makes 6 servings*

### Nutritional Data, per portion

| | | |
|---|---|---|
| Calories 333 | Carbohydrate 6g | Saturated Fat 3g |
| Protein 28g | Sodium 188mg | Monounsaturated |
| Fat 23g | Cholesterol 186mg | Fat 15g |

# CALAMARI AND POTATO STEW FROM THE ISLE OF CAPRI

**A** short walk from Capri's main piazza you come to a sign for Titina Vuotto's Ristorante La Pineta. Down a flight of steps, and then another and another, the smell of something delicious growing ever more pronounced, you finally come to the restaurant itself, built into the cliffs of that amazing island. Here on a terrace looking out at the blueness of the distance, you can feast on her clean, pure cooking, which is deeply rooted in the traditions of Capri and the sea around it.

Titina uses totani, a type of squid native to the Mediterranean; calamari are a fine substitute. To keep squid from toughening, they must be cooked on high heat very briefly or on gentle heat for a long time, the method used here.

2   pounds squid, cleaned

2   garlic cloves, chopped

1   small dried hot red chili, crumbled or broken into pieces

2   tablespoons extra-virgin olive oil

1   cup dry white wine

1   teaspoon salt or to taste

2   pounds waxy potatoes, peeled and cut into chunks (small new
        potatoes can be left whole)

1   pound tomatoes, peeled (page 454) and chopped

¼   cup minced flat-leaf parsley

juice of ½ lemon

freshly ground black pepper to taste


Most squid available from American fishmongers are ready to cook, and you should not need to clean them unless you have caught them yourself, an unlikely scenario. (If you know how to catch squid, surely you must know how to clean them. If not, see the instructions for risotto nero, page 210.) Cut the squid hoods or bodies into rings about ½ inch thick. Cut the tentacle sections in half lengthwise.

In a heavy saucepan large enough to hold all the ingredients, gently sauté the garlic and chili in the oil until the garlic starts to soften, about 2 minutes. Add the

squid and continue cooking, stirring occasionally, until the squid give off liquid—about 10 minutes. Add the wine and salt and let come to a gentle simmer.

Cook the squid in the wine for 2 or 3 minutes, then add the potatoes and tomatoes. Stir to combine everything, then cover and leave to cook very, very slowly for 40 minutes. When the potatoes are cooked through, stir in the parsley and lemon juice. Taste and adjust seasoning, adding salt if necessary and pepper. Serve immediately. *Makes 6 to 8 servings*

Nutritional Data, per portion

| Calories | 251 | Carbohydrate | 25g | Saturated Fat | 1g |
| Protein | 20g | Sodium | 340mg | Monounsaturated | |
| Fat | 5g | Cholesterol | 264mg | Fat | 3g |

# MIDYE PILAKI

### *Turkish Potato and Mussel Stew*

**S**erve this in soup plates with lots of crusty country bread, toasted if you wish, to sop up the delicious juices.

6   **dozen mussels, about 6 pounds**

2   **medium onions, halved and thinly sliced**

6   **garlic cloves, peeled**

¼   **cup extra-virgin olive oil**

2   **large ripe tomatoes, peeled and seeded (page 454) and diced, or**
         **4 canned whole tomatoes, drained and diced**

2   **large potatoes, peeled, halved, and sliced about ¼ inch thick**

2   **medium carrots, peeled and cut into chunks**

**salt and freshly ground black pepper to taste**

⅓   **cup finely chopped flat-leaf parsley**

Pick over the mussels, discarding any that are gaping. Clean them under running water, removing any beards that cling to the shells. In a heavy wide shallow pan, bring about 2 inches of water to a boil. Add the mussels, cover the pan, and steam until all the mussels have opened, stirring occasionally to make sure all the

mussels are cooked—about 7 to 10 minutes. Remove the mussels from the pan (do not discard the water). Discard any that have not opened. Remove the mussels from the shells and discard the shells. Put the mussels aside in a dish, covered with a spoonful of their cooking liquid to keep them from drying out.

Strain the mussel liquid through a double layer of cheesecloth or a fine-mesh sieve. You should have about 2 cups of cooking liquid. Set aside.

In the rinsed and dried pan, gently sauté the onions and garlic in the olive oil until the vegetables are soft but not browned—about 10 to 15 minutes. Add the tomatoes and cook for just a few minutes to release their juices. Add the potatoes and carrots together with the mussel liquid, cover the pan, and cook the vegetables over medium-low heat until the potatoes and carrots are tender and have absorbed most of the liquid—about 20 to 30 minutes. Stir the mussels back in and continue cooking very gently, just long enough to heat the mussels thoroughly. Taste the sauce and add salt and pepper—additional salt might not be necessary if the mussels are salty. Off the heat, stir in the parsley. Serve immediately. ***Makes 8 servings***

Nutritional Data, per portion

| | | |
|---|---|---|
| Calories 214 | Carbohydrate 19g | Saturated Fat 1g |
| Protein 14g | Sodium 297mg | Monounsaturated |
| Fat 9g | Cholesterol 28mg | Fat 6g |

# TURKISH UNSTUFFED MUSSELS
# WITH RICE

**O**ne of the enticing offerings of a Greek or Turkish meze are sweet plump mussels, their shells stuffed with a savory mixture of rice, pine nuts, currants, and other good things. The dish is addictive, but the preparation is tedious to say the least. Each mussel shell must be opened, stuffed by hand, and tied up again, a process that's best achieved in a restaurant or taverna kitchen with plenty of hands for the work, as I learned to my despair the one time I tried it. Converting the preparation into an unorthodox but delicious pilaf is my solution. It's a richly flavored dish and is best followed by a large but simple green salad made with arugula, watercress, and fennel and a cooked fruit dessert, like the pears or the apricots and figs described on pages 428 and 429.

2   tablespoons dried black currants

6   pounds fresh mussels, about 6 dozen

salt

2½ cups fish stock (page 84) or clear white chicken stock (page 81)

2   tablespoons extra-virgin olive oil

2   tablespoons pine nuts

1   large onion, finely chopped

2   medium ripe tomatoes, peeled (page 454) and chopped, or ¾ cup
        canned whole tomatoes, drained and chopped

1   teaspoon ground allspice

¼   cup finely chopped flat-leaf parsley

¼   cup minced fresh dill

2   cups long-grain rice

freshly ground black pepper to taste

Put the currants in a cup or small bowl and fill it up with very hot water. Set aside to plump the currants.

Pick over the mussels, discarding any that are gaping. Trim them of any beards and rinse in fresh running water. Place the mussels in a heavy soup kettle or a large saucepan with an inch of lightly salted water and bring to a boil. Cover and steam

the mussels until they are all open, stirring them occasionally with a wooden spoon—about 7 to 10 minutes. Remove from the heat, discarding any that have not opened. Discard the mussel shells and set the meats aside. Strain the cooking liquid through a double layer of cheesecloth or a fine-mesh sieve and add to the stock. Rinse and dry the pan and return it to the stove.

Place a tablespoon of the olive oil in the pan and gently toast the pine nuts over medium-low heat until they are brown—about 5 to 7 minutes—being careful not to overcook. Using a slotted spoon, remove the pine nuts from the pan and set aside. Add the remaining tablespoon of oil to the pan and gently stew the onion in the oil until softened but not browned—about 5 to 10 minutes. Add the tomatoes, allspice, half the parsley, and all the dill to the pan. Cook, stirring occasionally, until the tomatoes give up their liquid and thicken slightly, about 15 minutes. Add the rice and turn it gently in the sauce until all the grains of rice are coated.

Add enough hot water to the combined stocks to make 3 cups and pour it into the pan with the rice. Add the drained currants, stir the rice to mix everything together, bring to a boil, and turn the heat down to simmer. Cover the rice and simmer gently for about 15 minutes, until the rice is thoroughly cooked but still a little resistant to the bite. Stir in the reserved pine nuts and mussels, cover again, and remove the pan from the heat. Set aside, still covered, for about 5 minutes to let the rice absorb every bit of liquid. Taste and add salt and pepper if desired. Serve immediately, sprinkled with the remaining parsley. *Makes 8 servings*

Nutritional Data, per portion

| | | |
|---|---|---|
| Calories  327 | Carbohydrate  47g | Saturated Fat  1g |
| Protein  17g | Sodium  341mg | Monounsaturated |
| Fat  7g | Cholesterol  31mg | Fat  4g |

# CHAPTER SIX

# DRESSINGS, SAUCES, CONDIMENTS, AND PRESERVES

*I*n the Mediterranean kitchen salads are dressed simply, with a rich and flavorful olive oil, the very best extra-virgin oil the cook can afford, often the product of the family's own groves of stately olive trees. To this good oil will be added a little (often a very little to American taste) vinegar or lemon juice, salt, and pepper. This is the quickest and easiest dressing in the world to prepare, and when you have the best oil you can find and the quality of your other ingredients matches it, there is no need for a cupboard full of bottled dressings.

Mediterranean cooks are puzzled by the American rage to change the flavor of good oil by steeping intense aromatics in it. Add the aromatics to the dressing, not the oil, and use it right away. Additions of chili or garlic, rosemary or basil will disguise the character of an indifferent oil, such as canola or corn oil, but steeping chili peppers or garlic in the best extra-virgin olive oil only masks its lush, fresh, and elegant flavor.

Whether vinegar or lemon juice, acid should be added with a judicious hand. American salad dressing is both overly sweetened and overly acid by Mediterranean standards. This would be simply a matter of taste were it not for the wine issue—an acid dressing makes salad inappropriate to serve with wine, and there's always wine to finish at the end of the meal and perhaps a bit of cheese to go with the salad. Ergo . . . a good olive oil–to–acid proportion is about three to one; four to one is better if you expect to have wine with the salad. A few drops of balsamic vinegar are not inappropriate in a dressing for a very simple green salad, but balsamic vinegar should not be treated as an expensive cure-all for salad dressing woes—rather, it's a precious ingredient to be treated with respect and understanding.

# A SALAD DRESSING MADE WITH WINE AND WINE VINEGAR

**A**t a dinner party north of Venice I watched the hostess, Marina Danieli, one of Italy's growing number of women wine makers, prepare salad dressing at the table. The spectacle was clearly intended for effect, and the effect was profound. The room stilled, the handful of guests spellbound by the captivating performance, as Marina thoughtfully measured quantities in a massive archaic chased-silver spoon. It was a ritual: vinegar and salt in just proportions mixed in the monumental bowl, like a chalice, of the great spoon and poured over the salad; then aceto balsamico, the true, traditional, artisanally made stuff that is so hard to find and so much appreciated when it is found, mixed again in the great spoon with some of the good red wine from her vineyards. And then, of course, a lavish abundance of olive oil, poured over the greens just before tossing.

You do not have to make your own wine to achieve this perfect match, but it helps to use a very good, full-bodied red—you are, after all, using only a spoonful. These are the proportions I worked out later, but the magic, of course, is in the silver spoon.

1 tablespoon very-good-quality aged red wine vinegar

1 teaspoon sea salt

1 tablespoon very-good-quality red wine

1 teaspoon balsamic vinegar, preferably artisanally made aceto balsamico tradizionale

½ cup fruity extra-virgin olive oil

Mix the ingredients together in the order given and pour over clean dry salad greens. ***Makes a scant ¾ cup, enough for 8 to 10 servings of salad***

Nutritional Data, per portion

| | | |
|---|---|---|
| Calories 97 | Carbohydrate trace | Saturated Fat 2g |
| Protein 0 | Sodium 148mg | Monounsaturated |
| Fat 11g | Cholesterol 0 | Fat 9g |

# LEMON AND GARLIC DRESSING
# FOR SALADS OR VEGETABLES

This dressing is common throughout the eastern Mediterranean for plain green salads, for composed salads, and as an all-purpose dressing for steamed fresh vegetables (artichokes, asparagus, green beans) or crudités—raw or parboiled fresh seasonal vegetables served as a first course. It's delicious poured over hot steamed new potatoes, sprinkled with a little chopped tarragon or chives.

½  **garlic clove, crushed with the flat blade of a knife**

1  **teaspoon fine sea salt**

1  **tablespoon fresh lemon juice**

3  **tablespoons fruity extra-virgin olive oil**

**freshly ground black pepper to taste**

Chop the garlic coarsely and put it in the bottom of a clean, dry salad bowl with the salt. Using the back of a spoon, crush the salt and garlic together to make a smooth, homogeneous paste. Add the lemon juice and stir to dissolve the salt, then add the olive oil. Mix all together well in the bottom of the bowl. Pile on the salad, but don't mix it until you're ready to serve. When you serve it, toss the salad in the dressing and add some pepper. *Makes ¼ cup, enough for 4 to 6 servings of salad*

Nutritional Data, per portion

| | | |
|---|---|---|
| Calories  61 | Carbohydrate  trace | Saturated Fat  1g |
| Protein   trace | Sodium  246mg | Monounsaturated |
| Fat  7g | Cholesterol  0 | Fat  6g |

# VINAIGRETTE

### French Salad Dressing with Mustard and Vinegar

**G**o easy on the mustard—this isn't *sauce à la moutarde*. For plain green salads or for sliced fresh tomatoes at the height of the season, these are the proportions to use, the mustard counterpointing the sauce as garlic does in the preceding recipe. For steamed artichokes or leeks, increase the quantity of mustard to 1 teaspoon. On the other hand, a very thick and mustardy vinaigrette, with perhaps a tablespoon of mustard, makes a pungent sauce for grilled squid and octopus—an astute choice of the chef at Restaurant Avlì in Réthimnon, Crete.

½   teaspoon Dijon mustard

2   tablespoons aged red wine vinegar or sherry vinegar

½   cup fruity extra-virgin olive oil

½   teaspoon salt or more to taste

freshly ground black pepper to taste

In a salad bowl or a small bowl, mix the mustard with the vinegar until it is thoroughly dissolved. Add the oil and salt and beat vigorously with a fork or wire whisk to blend. Taste the dressing and adjust the seasoning, adding more salt if necessary—but mustard is often very salty. Just before pouring it over the salad, grind in black pepper to taste. *Makes ½ cup, enough for 8 servings of salad*

Nutritional Data, per portion

| | | |
|---|---|---|
| Calories 121 | Carbohydrate trace | Saturated Fat 2g |
| Protein 0 | Sodium 146mg | Monounsaturated |
| Fat 14g | Cholesterol 0 | Fat 11g |

**VARIATION:** Substitute 3 tablespoons bitter (Seville) orange juice for the vinegar and use on a plain green salad or bean salad garnished with a handful of roasted walnuts.

# AN ANCHOVY SAUCE
# FOR BITTER GREENS

**T**his is made expressly for puntarelle, or chicory shoots, a delight of the early-spring table in Rome. They're sold already cleaned, a tedious task, in the Campo dei Fiori market. I haven't seen puntarelle in other parts of Italy, and the few times I've found imported ones on the menu of a New York restaurant, they have been deeply disappointing. But the pungent sauce can be used for other greens as well, especially bitter greens like endive and chicory. It's even good with plain romaine lettuce.

2   garlic cloves, crushed with the flat blade of a knife

4 to 6 oil-packed anchovy fillets to taste; or 2 whole salt-packed
     anchovies, prepared as directed on page 471

1   tablespoon red wine vinegar or sherry vinegar or more to taste

¼   cup extra-virgin olive oil

freshly ground black pepper to taste

Pound the garlic cloves in a mortar with the coarsely chopped anchovy fillets. When the paste is very smooth, stir in the wine vinegar. Slowly beat in the olive oil, using a fork to mix well. Taste and adjust the seasoning, adding pepper if desired. (There should be sufficient salt from the anchovies.) *Makes a scant ½ cup, enough for about 8 servings of salad*

Nutritional Data, per portion

| | | |
|---|---|---|
| Calories   67 | Carbohydrate   trace | Saturated Fat   1g |
| Protein   1g | Sodium   92mg | Monounsaturated |
| Fat   7g | Cholesterol   1mg | Fat   6g |

# SAUCE VERTE

### *A French Green Sauce for Fish*

**T**his sauce is often served as an accompaniment to a plain poached salmon (page 240) or other large whole fish. It's delightful on plain steamed vegetables—perhaps a selection of green broccoli, white cauliflower, and small orange carrots. If you serve it with vegetables, cut down the number of anchovy fillets—or leave them out entirely if you don't care for the flavor. For the finest texture, use a mortar and pestle; for speed, use the food processor as directed for salsa verde (following recipe).

| | |
|---|---|
| 1 | quart water |
| 1 | small bunch of fresh watercress, leaves and tender stems only, about 2 loosely packed cups |
| 10 | fresh spinach leaves, stems discarded, about 2 loosely packed cups |
| 1 | 1-inch-thick slice of stale country-style bread, crusts removed |
| 1 | tablespoon drained capers or more to taste |
| 4 | oil-packed anchovy fillets, chopped, or 1 salt-packed anchovy, prepared as directed on page 471 and chopped (optional) |
| 2 | tablespoons minced shallot |
| 1 | tablespoon minced fresh tarragon leaves |
| ¼ | cup minced flat-leaf parsley |
| ⅓ to ½ | cup fruity extra-virgin olive oil to taste |
| 2 | tablespoons white wine vinegar or sherry vinegar or lemon juice or to taste |
| | salt and freshly ground black pepper to taste |

Bring the water to a rolling boil and drop in the watercress and spinach. Boil for 60 to 90 seconds or until the leaves are soft. Drain well in a colander. Finely chop the greens on a cutting board.

Tear the bread into chunks—you should have about 1 cup—and put in a small bowl. Cover with water and let the bread absorb the water for about a minute, then drain and squeeze as dry as you can. Set aside.

In a mortar, pound the capers and anchovies, if desired, to a paste. Add the shallot, tarragon, and parsley and pound to mix well, then add the blanched

chopped greens and continue pounding. Pound in the soaked bread and, when the mixture is smooth and homogeneous in texture, start to add the olive oil, as if for a mayonnaise, a little at a time and turning constantly with a small wooden spoon. Once about half the oil has been incorporated you can add the rest in a thin, steady stream, stirring continually. Add oil until the sauce is the desired consistency. Stir in a tablespoon of the vinegar or lemon juice. Taste the sauce for seasoning, adding salt, pepper, and more vinegar or lemon juice as desired. ***Makes about 1 cup, enough for 8 to 10 servings***

Nutritional Data, per portion

| | | |
|---|---|---|
| Calories   105 | Carbohydrate   4g | Saturated Fat   1g |
| Protein   2g | Sodium   128mg | Monounsaturated |
| Fat   10g | Cholesterol   1mg | Fat   8g |

# SALSA VERDE

### *Italian Green Sauce for Fish or Meat*

**A**n Italian edition of sauce verte, salsa verde goes with bollito misto, a northern Italian extravaganza of simmered veal, chicken, sausage, tongue, and more; but it's even better with plain poached, steam-poached, grilled, or oven-baked fish. Make it in a processor, following these directions; or, for a finer texture, make it with a mortar and pestle, as directed in the preceding sauce verte recipe. In essence, this is another version of pesto.

6    ounces shelled walnuts, about 1½ cups

½    cup coarsely chopped flat-leaf parsley

1    tablespoon coarsely chopped fresh basil

2    garlic cloves, coarsely chopped

2    small cornichons

yolk of 1 hard-boiled egg

½    cup extra-virgin olive oil

1    tablespoon red wine vinegar or sherry vinegar or fresh lemon juice

salt and freshly ground black pepper to taste

DRESSINGS, SAUCES, CONDIMENTS, AND PRESERVES

Bring a pan of water to a rolling boil. Drop in the walnuts and boil for 45 seconds. Drain immediately. Using a small, sharp knife, peel away the bitter outer skin. Add to the bowl of a food processor. (You can skip this tedious procedure if you wish, but the sauce has a fresher, sweeter flavor with peeled walnuts.)

Add the parsley, basil, garlic, and cornichons. Turn the machine on and add the egg yolk. Continue processing, adding the olive oil in a slow stream, until the sauce is very smooth. Add the vinegar and process to mix well. Taste for seasoning, adding salt, pepper, and more vinegar if necessary. ***Makes about 2 cups; 32 servings***

Nutritional Data, per portion

| | | |
|---|---|---|
| Calories 67 | Carbohydrate 1g | Saturated Fat 1g |
| Protein 1g | Sodium 7mg | Monounsaturated |
| Fat 7g | Cholesterol 7mg | Fat 3g |

# A YOGURT SAUCE FOR FISH OR VEGETABLES

For a fat-free sauce, use nonfat yogurt, but be sure no gelatin or other thickening agents have been added to the yogurt.

2   cups plain yogurt

1   long English cucumber

salt to taste

½   cup coarsely chopped fresh mint leaves or finely chopped fresh dill

1   garlic clove, finely chopped

freshly ground white or black pepper to taste

Drain the yogurt in a sieve lined with a double layer of cheesecloth or use a conical yogurt drainer (page 300) for 30 minutes to throw off some of the whey and thicken the yogurt slightly.

Peel the cucumber (in stripes if you wish) and slice thinly. Put the cucumber slices in a colander and sprinkle about a tablespoon of salt over them. Toss to coat the slices well and set aside to drain for about 30 minutes.

Turn the drained yogurt into a bowl. Rinse the cucumber slices under running water to rid them of salt, toss, and pat lightly with paper towels to rid them of excess water. Chop the cucumber slices rather coarsely and stir into the yogurt with the mint and garlic. Taste and add more salt if desired and pepper. *Makes 2 cups; 32 servings*

Nutritional Data, per portion

| | | |
|---|---|---|
| Calories 10 | Carbohydrate 1g | Saturated Fat trace |
| Protein 1g | Sodium 11mg | Monounsaturated |
| Fat trace | Cholesterol trace | Fat 0 |

# SKORDALIA

### *Greek Garlic Sauce for Fish or Vegetables*

Skordalia can be made with either firm-textured country bread or a baked potato or, as in this recipe, both. If you use potato, however, you *must* make the sauce with a mortar and pestle, because a blender or food processor will do strange and unpleasant things to the texture of potatoes.

This sauce often accompanies salt cod for the Friday meal in Greece, but it's also traditional to serve it with little boiled beets—the beets will color the sauce pink where it touches them. In Macedonia, according to Greek cooking authority Diane Kochilas, the bread might be replaced with a cup of finely chopped walnuts.

1    large russet potato, about ½ pound

1    inch-thick slice of firm country bread, crusts trimmed, cubed, about
     ⅔ cup

3    large garlic cloves, chopped

salt to taste

½    cup extra-virgin olive oil

¼    cup drained yogurt (page 299)

juice of ½ lemon or more to taste

Preheat the oven to 500 degrees and bake the potato for at least an hour or until it is very soft. Discard the potato skin and mash the flesh with a fork. You should have about ⅔ cup.

DRESSINGS, SAUCES, CONDIMENTS, AND PRESERVES

Tear the bread into chunks, place in a bowl, and cover with cool water. Leave for just a minute or so, for the bread to absorb the water, then drain and squeeze the bread as dry as you can.

With a mortar and pestle, pound the garlic with about a teaspoon of salt until it is very smooth. Add the bread and continue pounding until the mixture is creamy, then pound in the potato flesh. Add the olive oil as if for a mayonnaise, a little at a time and stirring constantly. When about half the oil has been added, stir in the drained yogurt (an unorthodox touch to lighten the sauce). When all the oil has been added, you should have a thick, homogeneous, rather creamy mass. Stir in the lemon juice. Taste the sauce and adjust the seasoning, adding more salt, pepper, and lemon juice if desired. *Makes 1 cup; 16 servings*

Nutritional Data, per portion

| | | |
|---|---|---|
| Calories 83 | Carbohydrate 5g | Saturated Fat 1g |
| Protein 1g | Sodium 23mg | Monounsaturated |
| Fat 7g | Cholesterol 0 | Fat 6g |

# AÏOLI

### *Garlic Mayonnaise*

**A**ïoli, sometimes called the "butter of Provence" because it is so integral to the cuisine, is simply a mayonnaise incorporating quantities of fresh garlic—usually two cloves per person in Provence. That is a lot, and you might wish to use less (I do—three or four cloves for this recipe), but since the whole point of aïoli is garlic, by all means don't stint. The quality of the garlic is most important—it should be fresh and plump with swollen cloves. Reject any shriveled cloves or any in which the core is developing a green sprout.

Traditionally aïoli is made with egg yolks and garlic pounded in a mortar. A lighter sauce can be made in the blender with a whole egg and an egg white, but the blender does odd things to the taste of garlic, so I prefer to make the lighter mayonnaise in the blender, then fold the garlic paste in separately by hand. I always use organic eggs, but if you're not sure of your egg source and worried about salmonella, don't try this recipe.

1   **whole egg**

1   **egg white**

**salt to taste**

**1 to 1½ cups fruity extra-virgin olive oil as needed**

**juice of ½ lemon or more to taste**

4   **garlic cloves, coarsely chopped**

Make the mayonnaise by whirling the egg and egg white in a blender with a little pinch of salt. Remove the center knob from the blender lid and, with the blender churning, start to pour in the olive oil, a very thin thread at first, until the mixture starts to thicken. Stop the blender and pour in a few tablespoons of lemon juice, then start the blender again and continue adding oil, a little more thickly as the mixture emulsifies and mounts. When all the oil has been added, turn the blender off and set aside.

Combine the garlic in a small bowl or a mortar with a teaspoon of salt and pound the garlic or crush it with the back of a spoon until you have a thick and homogeneous paste. Now use a spatula to scrape the mayonnaise into the garlic paste and turn gently to incorporate everything. Taste and add more salt and lemon juice if desired.

DRESSINGS, SAUCES, CONDIMENTS, AND PRESERVES

If the mayonnaise breaks down and separates while you're blending it, remove it all from the blender and start over again with a fresh egg. Whirl the egg until it is light and add, bit by bit, the broken-down mayonnaise and more oil and lemon juice. It should be easy to reconstitute the mayonnaise. Then proceed as directed. *Makes about 1¼ cups; 20 servings*

Nutritional Data, per portion

| | | |
|---|---|---|
| Calories 126 | Carbohydrate trace | Saturated Fat 2g |
| Protein 1g | Sodium 6mg | Monounsaturated |
| Fat 14g | Cholesterol 11mg | Fat 11g |

# LEBANESE GARLIC SAUCE

This garlic sauce, *toum bi zeit* or garlic with oil, is a Lebanese version of aïoli minus the eggs. Zahle, a town on the Damascus Road at the edge of the great central Beqaa Valley of Lebanon, was once famous for the quality of its grilled chicken. Travelers en route to Damascus or to the impressive Roman ruins at Baalbek always scheduled a stop at a roadside restaurant in Zahle for grilled or roasted chicken served with *toum bi zeit*. This is also a critical ingredient in my favorite Beirut street food, a humble chicken sandwich made on small loaves of French bread and glorified with a thick smear of *toum bi zeit*. It is as delicious with grilled, poached, or roasted fish as it is with chicken.

This is for people who truly adore garlic.

6   garlic cloves, coarsely chopped
½   teaspoon sea salt
1   1-inch slice of country-style bread, crusts removed
3   tablespoons extra-virgin olive oil
3   tablespoons boiling water
1   tablespoon fresh lemon juice

Using a mortar and pestle, crush the garlic with the salt until you have a very smooth paste. Tear the bread into chunks and place them in a bowl. Cover with warm water, then squeeze the bread as dry as you can. Add the bread to the garlic, a

little at a time, and continue pounding to get a smooth paste. Now, using the pestle, stir in the olive oil, 1 tablespoon after another, and then the boiling water, 1 tablespoon after another. Stir in the lemon juice. You should have a smooth, thick paste. Serve in a bowl to accompany chicken, fish, or steamed vegetables. *Makes ½ cup, enough for 8 servings*

Nutritional Data, per portion

| | | |
|---|---|---|
| Calories 66 | Carbohydrate 4g | Saturated Fat 1g |
| Protein 1g | Sodium 130mg | Monounsaturated |
| Fat 5g | Cholesterol 0 | Fat 4g |

# SALSA ROMESCO

**A** Catalan sauce for fish and seafood, this is characteristic of a number of Spanish sauces in which almonds, bread, and garlic are fried and then pounded in a mortar or whirled in a blender. The process gives a pleasantly rough texture and a complex and rather nutty flavor. This is a variation of the sauce with grilled shrimp on page 275. Almonds, bread, and garlic fried in olive oil sounds Arab to me—did this come to Spain with the Moors?

Try salsa romesco with grilled or steam-poached fish or stir a healthy dollop into a bowl of fish stew. Spaniards often refer to this sauce as *muy piquante*, very hot, but I don't think most Americans, accustomed to Mexican and Southeast Asian food, will find it so. If you want to make it hotter, add more chilies.

2  **dried New Mexico (Anaheim) chilies**

1  **small dried hot red chili or more to taste**

½  **cup extra-virgin olive oil**

6  **whole garlic cloves**

½  **cup blanched almonds**

1  **2-inch-thick slice of stale country-style bread, crusts removed**

1  **medium very ripe tomato**

1  **tablespoon sherry vinegar or more to taste**

**salt (optional)**

DRESSINGS, SAUCES, CONDIMENTS, AND PRESERVES

Break up the dried chilies, discarding some or all of the seeds (which is where the heat is concentrated). In a small skillet over medium-low heat, fry the chilies in ¼ cup of the olive oil until the color starts to change, about 3 to 5 minutes. Transfer the chilies with a slotted spoon to a blender or food processor. In the oil remaining in the pan, fry the whole garlic cloves, stirring frequently, until golden brown, about 5 to 7 minutes. Remove them and add to the chilies. Add the almonds to the pan and fry (adding a little more olive oil if necessary), stirring, until golden brown, about 5 minutes. Add to the chilies. Finally, add 2 tablespoons oil to the pan and fry the bread on both sides until golden, about 5 to 7 minutes. Add to the chilies, breaking the bread into smaller pieces, together with any oil remaining in the pan.

Process or blend the fried ingredients in brief spurts, stirring down occasionally, to get a coarse bread-crumb texture.

Slice the tomato in half; squeeze out and discard the seeds. Chop the tomato coarsely and add to the blender with the vinegar. Process to a coarse paste. Now, with the blender running, add the remaining oil in a thin stream until it is thoroughly blended in and you have a thick, mayonnaiselike mass but with texture from the bread and almonds. Remove and scrape into a bowl. Taste and adjust the seasoning, adding salt if you wish or a little more vinegar. ***Makes about 1¼ cups; 20 servings***

Nutritional Data, per portion

| | | |
|---|---|---|
| Calories 90 | Carbohydrate 5g | Saturated Fat 1g |
| Protein 1g | Sodium 32mg | Monounsaturated |
| Fat 8g | Cholesterol 0 | Fat 6g |

# SAUCE ROUILLE

**T**his simple, colorful sauce adds body and interest to Provençal fish stews and soups. A spoonful is dropped in the center of each bowl of soup for serving, and the rest is passed at the table, heaped in a small china bowl. It is also a fine garnish for any plain grilled or poached fish. To French tastes it's a fiery sauce; to Mexicans and many Americans it's on the mild side. Like the preceding romesco sauce, it can be made more or less hot by adjusting the amount of chilies.

The variation with egg is wonderful with steamed new potatoes or with big russets, baked in the oven for an hour at 500 degrees and then cracked open and a dollop of the sauce dropped inside.

2  **red bell peppers**

2  **fresh New Mexico (Anaheim) chilies or dried chilies soaked in hot**
   **water for 20 to 30 minutes**

2  **garlic cloves, crushed and chopped**

**salt to taste**

3  **tablespoons dry unseasoned bread crumbs**

⅓  **cup extra-virgin olive oil**

**cayenne pepper or Tabasco sauce if desired**

Roast and peel the fresh peppers and chilies, following the directions on page 455.

If you're using dried chilies, remove them from the soaking water, discard the seeds and membranes, and scrape the red pulp away from the skins with a spoon. Discard the skins.

In a mortar, crush the garlic to a paste with a little salt. Add the peppers and chilies with the roasting juices and pound with the pestle to a homogeneous mass. Stir in the bread crumbs, then the olive oil. Taste and add a little cayenne if desired to make a hotter sauce. ***Makes about ¾ cup sauce, enough for 6 servings***

Nutritional Data, per portion

| Calories 131 | Carbohydrate 5g | Saturated Fat 2g |
|---|---|---|
| Protein 1g | Sodium 30mg | Monounsaturated |
| Fat 13g | Cholesterol 0 | Fat 10g |

DRESSINGS, SAUCES, CONDIMENTS, AND PRESERVES

**VARIATION:** In Provence the sauce is sometimes made like a mayonnaise or an aïoli, an egg yolk stirred with olive oil to a compact mass, then the pounded red peppers and garlic stirred in. This is rich. Another alternative uses a whole egg and an egg white, as in the aïoli on page 293.

# FRESH TOMATO AND BASIL SALSA

Like a Mexican salsa, this is a good all-purpose garnish for all manner of grilled meat or fish. And like a Mexican salsa, it's also very good on its own, scooped up with toasted triangles of Arab flatbread (pita, page 133). Make this only at the height of the season with fresh local tomatoes.

4 or 5 medium very ripe tomatoes

1   small red onion, peeled

1   garlic clove, peeled

⅓  cup tightly packed fresh basil leaves

2   tablespoons fruity extra-virgin olive oil

2   teaspoons red wine vinegar or sherry vinegar or more to taste

salt and freshly ground black pepper to taste

½  teaspoon sugar if needed

Cut the tomatoes in half and squeeze out and discard the seeds. Dice the tomatoes evenly and toss them in a bowl. Dice the onion and garlic and add to the tomatoes. Sliver the basil leaves as finely as you can and add to the tomatoes. Add the oil and vinegar and toss to combine well. Taste and add salt and pepper. If the mixture is too sharp, add the sugar; if it's not sharp enough, add a little more vinegar. *Makes about 2½ cups; 40 servings*

Nutritional Data, per portion

| | | |
|---|---|---|
| Calories   11 | Carbohydrate   1g | Saturated Fat   trace |
| Protein   trace | Sodium   2mg | Monounsaturated |
| Fat   1g | Cholesterol   0 |   Fat   1g |

## PERSILLADE AND GREMOLATA

*Two Pick-Me-Ups for Tired Food*

A Provençale persillade or an Italian gremolata is not really a recipe so much as a technique. Here's how it works: Suppose a piece of fish is cooked a little too simply, or a sauce, no matter how carefully directions were followed, comes out tasting a little faded, lacking in verve and interest. Then a French or Italian cook will turn to a persillade or a gremolata to perk up the dish, adding it at the very end, either stirring it into the sauce or sprinkling it over the top of meat or fish—or braised beans or vegetables.

To make a persillade, simply mince together a little handful of flat-leaf parsley and a couple of garlic cloves, more or less to taste. For a gremolata, add the finely chopped or grated zest of half a lemon. Gremolata is traditionally served over the top of Milanese osso buco, but it adds vigor and sparkle to other dishes as well.

# LABNEH

### *Lebanese Yogurt Cheese*

**T**hough often called *yogurt cheese*, this isn't, of course, cheese at all since no rennet or other coagulant is used. It's simply thickened yogurt in which the whey has been drained away.

Labneh is a marvelous substitute for fresh cheeses, however, especially if made with low-fat or nonfat yogurt. In Lebanon it's used as a spread for warm pieces of Arab bread (pita), especially at breakfast, and it's always among the dishes on the table for a meze. Beat the labneh with a little sugar or honey and vanilla and substitute it for whipped cream, crème fraîche, or clotted cream; serve it with fresh fruits or with any of the fruit desserts or sweet cakes in Chapter 9.

For a different taste, add a mixture of chopped green herbs (basil, tarragon, sorrel, lovage) and a little finely minced garlic to make a low-fat substitute for those high-fat French garlic cheeses. Just don't try to substitute labneh or yogurt for cream in cooking—it breaks down when heated to the boiling point.

Experiment with different brands of yogurt until you find one that pleases you. Small producers, like Stonyfield Farm in the Northeast, often make the best. Just be sure it's a pure yogurt made with acidophilus and other living cultures and with no added gelatin or other thickeners.

Use a colander lined with a triple layer of cheesecloth. Pour a quart of pure yogurt into the cheesecloth and set the colander in the sink or in a bowl to catch the whey. Set a plate or a piece of plastic wrap or aluminum foil lightly over the top to keep the dust off and leave for up to 24 hours. The yogurt just gets thicker as it keeps on dripping. When it's the thickness you desire, scrape it into a refrigerator container, cover it, and refrigerate it. It will keep for 10 days or more. Any whey that drifts to the top can be poured off before using.

An especially useful device is a plastic draining cone made for draining yogurt (see Resources). I set the cone over a tall, straight-sided measuring jug—the mouth of the jug must be wide enough for the cone to sit down in the jug without falling through. ***Makes 1½ to 2 cups, depending on how long you let it drip; 32 servings***

Nutritional Data, per portion

| | | |
|---|---|---|
| Calories 10 | Carbohydrate 1g | Saturated Fat 0 |
| Protein 1g | Sodium 10mg | Monounsaturated |
| Fat 0 | Cholesterol 0 | Fat 0 |

# HARISSA

### North African Hot Sauce

This hot pepper sauce adds piquancy to all manner of North African stews and couscous and is often eaten on its own, smeared on a piece of bread. Commercial harissa is available in tubes, but this version, similar to what's sold in the great Central Market in Tunis, is far superior. As with any hot sauce, you can vary the heat by balancing medium-hot and very hot chilies. Some cooks add a very little cumin to the blend. The chilies used in Tunisia are different from the ones I have suggested. The goal is to achieve a complex and pleasing balance of piquant flavors.

12  medium-hot dried chilies such as New Mexico (Anaheim)

2   hot dried chilies such as pasilla or ancho

1   very hot dried chili such as arbol

2   tablespoons coriander seeds

1   tablespoon caraway seeds

sea salt to taste

5   garlic cloves, coarsely chopped

extra-virgin olive oil as needed

½   teaspoon ground cumin (optional)

Cover the dried chilies with hot water and set aside for 20 to 30 minutes to soften.

Meanwhile, pound the coriander and caraway in a mortar with about ¼ teaspoon salt to a soft but grainy powder. Add the garlic and pound to a paste.

Drain the chilies and discard most of the seeds and membranes. Using a spoon, scrape the softened pulp into the mortar. Pound with a pestle to a coarse paste. Pound in about ¼ cup oil, a tablespoon at a time. Taste and add salt and cumin if desired. The sauce should be very thick but easy to spread. If you're not going to use it right away, put it in a jar, smoothing the top with the bowl of a spoon, and pour a little more oil over the top to seal it. It will keep, refrigerated, for 2 or 3 weeks. *Makes about ½ cup; 8 servings*

DRESSINGS, SAUCES, CONDIMENTS, AND PRESERVES

## Nutritional Data, per portion

| | | |
|---|---|---|
| Calories  120 | Carbohydrate  11g | Saturated Fat  2g |
| Protein  2g | Sodium  6mg | Monounsaturated |
| Fat  10g | Cholesterol  0 | Fat  6g |

Except for people who live on farms and naturally go about the business of preserving the harvest, most American cooks these days seem daunted by the idea of preserving just about anything and consuming it weeks later. The next three recipes, however, are incredibly easy. The products, all of them delicious in very different ways, have been made for generations in their countries of origin, and they add much to the table in terms of taste and texture. I include them both to illustrate the ease of the process and because of the delectable nature of the results.

# POMAROLA

### *Easy Canned or Frozen Tomato Sauce*

**W**hy, you may well ask, should I go through the labor of preserving tomatoes when such good-quality canned tomatoes are available in every supermarket?

Well, maybe you have a garden with a great quantity of tomatoes that are just reaching their peak of ripeness. Or maybe you frequent a farmer's market with outstanding tomatoes. Or maybe you simply want to be certain that the ingredients you use throughout the year are the finest quality, raised without pesticides and preserved without any added shelf-stabilizing junk.

Mita Antolini, my Tuscan friend and neighbor, puts up about 300 jars of these tomatoes every year in late August and early September, when her own tomato crop is intense with flavor and goodness. This forms the foundation of her pantry and the basis of all the soups, stews, and sauces that she makes through the winter.

When she makes pomarola, Mita sets herself up under the shade tree in her front yard, where she has her outdoor work table. She grinds the tomatoes through a hand-cranked machine that holds back the skin and seeds and passes the juicy pulp through. When all the tomatoes have gone through the *passa-pomodori*, she heats up the *cucina economica*, a little wood-fired cook stove in the summer kitchen, and cooks the sauce briefly with some aromatic vegetables and a little olive oil.

Years ago Mita, like all the other women in this valley, used to fill clean beer and soda-pop jars with the pulp. Nowadays even in Italy beer and soda come in cans, and Mita uses the Italian equivalent of modern mason jars with self-sealing lids. She sets the jars in a boiling water bath and cooks them for about 30 minutes. Retrieved from the boiling water, the jars sit on a rack to cool while their lids pop, snap, and click as they seal—there's no more satisfying sound for the tired Tuscan housewife who rests from her labors blissfully aware that there's enough in the larder to last through the long months until tomatoes come around in the garden again.

It's not necessary to put up 300 jars of tomatoes at once. I often find myself at the end of the summer with an embarrassment of riches as far as tomatoes go, perhaps just six or seven pounds of irresistibly delicious fruit from a trip to the farmer's market. This is an easy way to debarrass oneself of the glory of ripe tomatoes. The quantities are not inflexible—if you have 10 pounds, or even 18 pounds, you can do the same thing, though I find it's scarcely worth bothering for quantities less than about 5 pounds.

Any ripe tomatoes can be used, but the best are the ones grown for this purpose—plum tomatoes, or their equivalent, with a good ratio of meaty paste to juice. (I recently found an heirloom American variety called *hog's heart*, bizarre looking, but they made wonderful preserves.) If you haven't grown the tomatoes yourself, I urge you to buy and use only tomatoes that have been grown organically, without pesticides or chemical fertilizers.

5    **pounds tomatoes at their peak of flavor**
2    **garlic cloves, peeled**
1 or 2 **medium yellow onions to taste, peeled**
1    **celery rib**
1    **medium carrot, peeled**
**salt and freshly ground black pepper to taste**
⅓    **cup extra-virgin olive oil**
**sugar (optional)**

Wash the tomatoes very well and cut away any soft spots or bruises. Remove and discard the stems, coring the tomatoes with a shallow cut. Slice them in chunks directly into a heavy saucepan large enough to hold all the fruit. Coarsely chop the rest of the vegetables and add them to the pan with about a tablespoon of salt, if

desired, and a small quantity of pepper. Add the olive oil. Stir the contents of the pan with a long-handled spoon to mix everything together.

Set the pan over medium heat and, when the tomato juices start to boil, cover it and cook for about 15 minutes, stirring occasionally. Lower the heat to medium-low or low—the liquid should simmer rather than boil rapidly. Cover again and cook for 15 to 20 minutes. Give it a stir now and then. At the end of this time the tomatoes should be thoroughly soft and should have yielded up all the juices. Now raise the heat to medium-high and cook, uncovered, rapidly to evaporate the juice and reduce the contents to a thick paste. The total time will depend on the juiciness and meatiness of the tomatoes.

When the tomatoes are soft and thick, put the contents of the pan through the large disk of a food mill (which is better than either a blender or a food processor because it will hold back much of the seeds and skins that can give the sauce a bitter flavor). Taste the sauce and add more salt and a little sugar if desired. You can also add a handful of slivered basil leaves—Mita doesn't, preferring to add the herbs later, when she uses the sauce.

The pureed sauce can be frozen—1-cup containers are very handy. Or you can preserve it the old-fashioned way in scrupulously clean preserving jars. Stand the jars on layers of newspaper or kitchen towels and fill them with *boiling* water. Heat the sauce up to simmering. When you're ready to fill a jar with sauce, tip the water out and immediately fill it with *hot* tomato sauce. When all the jars are filled, screw the lids on tightly and set them in a preserving kettle. Fill the kettle with boiling water to come just to the tops of the jars, set the kettle over medium-high heat, bring to a boil, and boil for 10 to 15 minutes. Remove from the heat and let cool slightly. Use tongs to remove the jars and set them on a rack or on the layer of newspaper or kitchen towels. Pretty soon you'll start to hear them ping and snap as the lids seal. Any jars that don't seal can be refrigerated and used within a week. ***The yield depends on many variables—the quantity of tomatoes obviously, but also the quantity of juice they throw off. This amount of tomatoes should make between 3 and 4 pints of sauce.***

Nutritional Data, per cup

| | | |
|---|---|---|
| Calories 303 | Carbohydrate 32g | Saturated Fat 3g |
| Protein 5g | Sodium 64mg | Monounsaturated |
| Fat 20g | Cholesterol 0 | Fat 15g |

# MOROCCAN PRESERVED LEMONS

**S**alt-preserved or pickled lemons have a strange and delectable flavor that utterly mystifies those who taste them for the first time in a fish or meat stew. These are used for Moroccan Chicken with Preserved Lemons and Olives (page 320) and Tunisian Fish with Preserved Lemons and Olives (page 264), but once you've tried them in those dishes, you'll find other uses for them as well. I was introduced to these years ago through Paula Wolfert's masterpiece *Couscous and Other Good Food from Morocco*, and they've been an important part of my pantry ever since. I sometimes even add a little slice of preserved lemon to a Bloody Mary for Sunday lunch.

Use a 3½- to 4-pint glass canning jar or any similar lidded jar (it need not be self-sealing since it is the salt that preserves the lemons).

24 **fresh whole lemons, preferably organic**
2 **cups pickling, kosher, or sea salt**

If you can't find certified organic lemons—and it isn't easy—scrub the lemons very well with a brush under running water.

Fill a scrupulously clean preserving jar with boiling water, first standing it on a layer of newspapers or kitchen towels. Leave it for 10 minutes or so, then turn the water out. If for any reason you are interrupted in your work and can't immediately start to fill the jar with lemons, repeat this process. The jar should be sterilized with boiling water immediately before you fill it.

Hold a lemon upright and slice down carefully from the bud end to the stem end, stopping about ½ inch from the stem end. Give the lemon a quarter turn and slice again. The lemon will be quartered, but the quarters will be firmly attached at the stem end. Open the lemon slightly and pack the insides with salt, then press the lemon down in the bottom of the jar. Do this with all the lemons, pressing them very firmly so that they yield up a considerable quantity of juice. Fill the jar up to the top, with an inch to spare.

American lemons are considerably less juicy than their equivalents in Mediterranean countries. If insufficient juice has been released to completely cover all the lemons, squeeze enough fresh lemon juice to cover them right up to the top. Add another 2 tablespoons pickling salt to the top of the jar and screw the lid on tight.

Now set the jar of lemons aside to pickle for at least 3 weeks—although pre-

DRESSINGS, SAUCES, CONDIMENTS, AND PRESERVES

served lemons will last a good deal longer, several months at least. Every couple of days, invert the jar and leave it standing on its head for a couple of days, then right it again. This will redistribute the salty juice over all the lemons. ***Makes 24 salt-preserved lemons***

Nutritional Data, per lemon

| | | |
|---|---|---|
| Calories 22 | Carbohydrate 12g | Saturated Fat trace |
| Protein 1g | Sodium 5,889mg | Monounsaturated |
| Fat trace | Cholesterol 0 | Fat trace |

# LEBANESE PICKLED TURNIPS

**P**ink pickled turnips are great favorites in Lebanon and Syria, where they often play a significant role on the meze table, their delicate rosy color as significant a contrast to the pale cream of hummus and baba ghanouj as their sharp fermented flavor is to the sweet earthiness of eggplant and chick-peas. Use small white turnips, the ones that have a light violet blush around the tops—the big yellow-fleshed, purple-skinned ones just won't do the trick. You will also need a 3½- to 4-pint mason or other type of preserving jar or two smaller ones. The jars need not be self-sealing.

2 **pounds white turnips**
1 **medium beet, peeled and sliced**
3 **garlic cloves, peeled (optional)**
**pickling, kosher, or sea salt**
1¼ **cups white wine vinegar**
2½ **cups water**

Make sure the preserving jar is scrupulously clean. Immediately before using it, fill it with freshly boiling water and let the water sit for 10 minutes before turning it out.

Scrub the turnips under running water with a soft brush. Quarter or halve them if large and fill the preserving jar with turnips, layering slices of beet in among them from time to time. If you wish, add the garlic cloves as well. For quart jars, add 1 tablespoon salt; for half-gallon jars, add 2 tablespoons. Mix the vinegar and water and pour the liquid over the turnips in the jar so that they are completely covered. Close the jar tightly and set aside in a cool (but not refrigerated) place. Invert the jars every few days to redistribute the salt. The pickles will be ready to eat in a week to 10 days but can be kept, refrigerated, for up to one month. **Makes 12 servings**

### Nutritional Data, per portion

| | | |
|---|---|---|
| Calories 27 | Carbohydrate 6g | Saturated Fat 0 |
| Protein 1g | Sodium 607mg | Monounsaturated |
| Fat trace | Cholesterol 0 | Fat 0 |

## FASTING AND FEASTING IN THE MEDITERRANEAN

At the beginning of this century l'Isle-sur-la-Sorgue, a substantial country town in the Vaucluse region of Provence, had only two butcher shops. Not surprising perhaps in a rural area where many people probably got their meat from farmyard animals like chickens and rabbits. What is surprising, though, René Jouveau, chronicler of Provençal food lore, tells us, is that the two butcher shops were open *only* twice a year, at Christmas and Easter.

Like other people of the Mediterranean at that time, the people of l'Isle-sur-la-Sorgue, it seems, scarcely ate meat at all, especially beef. Lamb was for Easter, turkey for Christmas, and for the rest, on Sundays if they were fortunate they might have a roasted chicken, rabbit, pigeon, or duck. And if they were not fortunate, Sunday might see little more than an extra dollop of olive oil and an extra cut of cheese to go with the daily beans and bread.

This was the pattern in country districts throughout the Mediterranean until sometime well after World War II, long periods of meager diet punctuated by brief and welcome bouts of feasting. It was the pattern in Greece in the 1950s when butcher shops were closed during Lent and other fasts, and it was the pattern in Crete and southern Italy when the Seven Countries Study (see Introduction) was initiated in the early 1960s.

*continued*

The cycle of fasting and feasting was reinforced by religious proscriptions, especially among Christians. In the Orthodox tradition, observant laypeople fasted during the following periods: Wednesdays and Fridays throughout the year except during Easter and Pentecost weeks and for 10 days after Christmas; the 48 days leading up to Easter; the 40 days before Christmas; the 15 days culminating in the Feast of the Assumption on August 15; and, in honor of the Apostles, from the end of Pentecost Week to June 29, the Feast of Sts. Peter and Paul. Fasting, for Greeks, Syrians, Bulgarians, and other members of the Orthodox community, means no meat, eggs, or dairy products all the time and no oil, wine, or fish during particularly acute periods. (During Lent, for instance, oil and wine are permitted on Saturdays and Sundays, and fish is allowed on the two feast days that fall in Lent, Annunciation, on March 25, and Palm Sunday.) Fully a third of the year, then, is given over to a very meager diet during which meat and dairy are completely excluded—and that's not counting Wednesdays and Fridays—although how many people in the Orthodox church still observe these stringent rules is not clear.

The Catholic tradition is more lenient. Long ago, a papal dispensation released Spaniards from the weekly obligation to abstain from meat so as to conserve their strength to battle the Infidel. In other parts of the Catholic community today, Lent is observed only by the pious and penitent, Fridays have ceased to be meatless, and other fasting periods seem to have been largely forgotten.

This is a pity, not just for religious reasons (perhaps for that as well), but because the obligation to abstain from meat and dairy products for long periods throughout the year was clearly beneficial to physical well-being as much as to spiritual health. I mention this particularly because it seems like a good practice, especially for people who have no interest in becoming totally vegetarian, to observe days or periods of abstention from meat and dairy products.

The total fast of Yom Kippur is also now but one day a year, but among pious Jews traditionally there were weekly abstentions on Mondays and Thursdays, the days when the Torah was read. Moslems fast in a rather

*continued*

different manner. Throughout Ramadan, the month-long period that commemorates the revelation of the Koran, Moslems abstain from food and drink (and tobacco and sexual intercourse as well) from daybreak until sunset, when traditionally the fast is broken with a few dates or a small cake like knaife or katayef, honey-drenched sweets with fresh cheese or chopped nuts. Men go to the mosque to pray; women prepare or supervise the preparation of an evening meal that must be nourishing enough to provide for the next 24 hours.

Throughout the Mediterranean, every long period of fasting was broken by a feast, and none more glorious in the Christian world than Easter. To me this is the quintessential Mediterranean feast, summing up in its emotional surge and its iconography the fundamental Mediterranean belief in a god (or goddess) who dies and returns to life and in some mystical way redeems humanity from the terror and mystery of our own dying. It is a powerful myth, deeply embedded in the history of the region.

In the Orthodox church, the long fast of Lent culminates in an even more rigorous Passion Week fast, when every scrap of fat is banned from the diet. Greeks break the fast on Easter Eve, after midnight Mass. When the Orthodox priest delivers the poignant and stirring pronouncement "Christ is risen!" it is the signal for a round of feasting that begins almost immediately with *magheritsa*, a rich thick broth of organ meats, butter, oil, and eggs, an eruption of goodness and flavors that burst or explode in the mouth after the long, lean weeks of Lent. *Magheritsa* is traditionally made with all of the innards, including the lungs, tripe, and carefully rinsed intestines, of the lamb that was slaughtered for the Easter feast. And the feasting continues the next day, with the same lamb roasted or stewed and shared abundantly among family and friends, along with buttery sweet cakes, often made in Easter symbols like the lamb and the dove.

This profusion of meat, butter, sugar, and eggs is typical of Easter celebrations throughout the Mediterranean. It is a way of eating that is not, of course, to everyone's taste and certainly not particularly healthful if it were to become an everyday affair. But it's worth remembering that a rich and meat-laden diet is *not* the stuff of everyday consumption. It's a feast, and a feast by its very nature is a very special occasion.

DRESSINGS, SAUCES, CONDIMENTS, AND PRESERVES

# CHAPTER SEVEN

# POULTRY AND MEAT

"We almost never eat red meat anymore."

It's a statement I hear over and over again from friends and colleagues and especially from their offspring as they grow into adulthood and start families of their own. Statistics bear it out: per capita, Americans are eating a good deal less red meat than they were a decade or more ago.

In most cases the reasons for this change are practical rather than philosophical. Scientists, nutritionists, dietitians, even some government health specialists advise us that our lives would be healthier, happier, and more productive if we would just cut down on the amount of meat we eat. The customary restaurant serving of a pound-per-person slab of well-marbled beefsteak, its edges curling with crisply browned fat, its cholesterol-rich juices forming a savory puddle for a butter-drenched baked potato topped with a dollop of sour cream, is assuredly nutritional madness.

But you just can't get around the fact that most of us who are not vegetarians really *like* to eat meat. There are complex physiological, psychological, and cultural reasons behind this, not the least of them being that meat adds depth, richness, and complexity of flavor to dishes that vegetables, no matter how fresh and delicious, can't supply. Moreover, quantities of meat on the table have always served as a cultural marker for high status, which is one good reason why government agencies like the federal Department of Agriculture promote the image of an American table groaning under the weight of all that meat.

I am not a vegetarian. But years of living and working in Mediterranean countries have taught me that meat does not need to be, in fact in those places seldom is, at the center of the plate. The trick in Mediterranean kitchens is to use meat in small quantities, more as a flavoring ingredient than as the focus of a dish.

The best example of this is a pasta sauce in which ½ to ¾ pound of meat makes enough sauce, with tomatoes and other vegetables, for six to eight servings. The sauce is savory with herbs, spices, dried wild mushrooms, and other aromatics, but the richness comes from the meat flavor.

Sauces are not the only example of this principle. Many traditional meat dishes are made with almost more vegetables than meat and are intended to be served, like a sauce, with a complex carbohydrate, whether pasta, rice, potatoes, or polenta. Even in home kitchens, Mediterranean cooks precede a meat course with a vegetable-sauced pasta or light soup and follow it with fruit, plain or cooked, depending on the season. Although meat is at the center of the plate in such meals, it is only one plate in the succession of the menu, and the rest of the plates are all determinedly nonmeat.

Please note that in the following recipes I have counted on a serving size, in general, of 3 to 4 ounces of whatever meat is served—not counting bones. All recent health and nutrition research concurs that there is no need for healthy, normal humans, whether children or adults, to consume more than that amount daily, and a growing body of evidence suggests that excess consumption can cause cumulative health problems that go well beyond weight and cholesterol counts.

If this looks like a small amount of meat on your plate, you should be adding more grains, legumes or beans, and vegetables to extend it. Most of the following preparations, for instance, go well with rice, baked or steamed potatoes, steamed bulgur pilaf, cornmeal polenta, steamed barley, or some of the small pasta shapes (small shells, orzo, elbows, etc., but not spaghetti or linguine) that are intended for this purpose.

Precede the meat dish with a light vegetable or bean soup, a salad of raw or cooked vegetables, or a plate of a single vegetable that is the star of the current season. (In early summer, for instance, try a plate of plain little green string beans. Fresh from a market garden, lightly steamed and dressed with oil, lemon, and a little garlic, they are ever so much more desirable than asparagus imported out of season from Mexico.) Follow the meat with a green salad and a small piece of cheese, or fresh fruit, or a simple, easy-to-make sweet, and you have a very substantial meal.

As much as possible I use meat from animals that have been raised humanely, in unconfined spaces with plenty of room to range. I also look for meat from animals that have been fed nonmedicated feed and have been given drugs only when necessary to fight off disease. The two conditions go hand in hand, for animals raised in confinement, whether chickens in battery cages or pigs and veal

calves in cramped stalls, are exposed to innumerable sources of infection and need to be medicated to stay alive long enough to be slaughtered. When I take an antibiotic or, heaven forfend, a hormone, I want a dosage prescribed by my medical advisers for my specific condition and not an obscure quantity prescribed by some distant animal-feed manufacturer and dosed to the animal willy-nilly by the factory farm manager.

I also wish to give voice to a respect for life that has been the source of ethical questions since the beginning of human self-consciousness. Since we take life to sustain our own lives, it seems to me unquestionable that we owe an indulgence to the life we take, at least that that life be lived in dignity and lost with a sense of respect on the part of those who take it.

For me, the finest food begins with the finest ingredients. All else being equal, the meat of animals raised humanely, whether chickens, hogs, or so-called "wild" venison, is better in flavor and texture and contributes more to the dish than that from commercial factory farms.

---

## ABOUT CHICKEN

Like most Italian farm women, my Tuscan neighbor Mita Antolini raises her own chickens and rabbits. The chickens run free in the farmyard, their diet supplemented only by cracked corn raised on the farm; the rabbits are in hutches, fed from herbaceous grasses that Mita gathers in huge bunches from the fields each day. The meat of these animals is incomparable, full of savor and juice and texture.

Our modern, commercially raised chickens are the tomatoes of the animal world—overbred, overmedicated, mass produced, tasteless, and with a mushy texture that adds nothing to soups or stews.

I seek out sources of good, naturally raised, preferably free-range birds, which, fortunately, are becoming more available—and less expensive as they do so. If you can't find free-running birds, insist on birds that have been fed pure, nonmedicated feed. They don't need that garbage in their diet, and neither do you.

---

# POLLO AL CHILINDRON

### Spanish Chicken with Sweet Peppers

In this Spanish way of cooking chicken, tomatoes are sometimes added and cooked down with the peppers. I prefer the purity of the sweet pepper flavor. If you can't find any slightly hot peppers (such as Anaheim or New Mexico peppers), add a very little cayenne, hot pepper flakes, or pure ground red chili to the pepper mixture. (But don't use chili powder, which is a mixture of chili pepper, cumin, and other seasonings for making chili con carne.)

The chicken parts should be small—legs separated from thighs, breast halves cut in half again. This is also a good way to treat skinless, boneless chicken breasts, if that's a cut you prefer, because the sauce compensates for the dryness of the meat. If you use boneless chicken, the quantity needed for the recipe will be less—2 pounds should be plenty for 8 servings.

4 pounds chicken parts

salt and freshly ground black pepper to taste

6 tablespoons extra-virgin olive oil

8 flavorful red and green peppers, preferably both sweet and slightly hot

2 medium onions, halved and thinly sliced

2 garlic cloves, sliced

1 teaspoon chopped fresh thyme, or ½ teaspoon dried, crumbled

12 fat green Italian or Greek olives, pitted and coarsely chopped

½ cup amontillado sherry

½ cup water or chicken stock (page 81)

2 tablespoons fresh orange juice, *not* canned or frozen concentrate

Cut away any excess fat or skin from the chicken pieces. You can discard the skin entirely if you wish. Sprinkle the pieces with salt if you wish and liberally with pepper. In a large skillet over medium heat, fry the chicken pieces in 4 tablespoons of oil until they are golden brown on all sides, 5 to 7 minutes to a side.

Meanwhile, slice the peppers lengthwise about ½ inch thick.

When the chicken is done, remove it from the skillet and set aside to drain. Discard the cooking fat and wipe out the pan. Preheat the oven to 375 degrees.

Add the remaining 2 tablespoons of oil to the pan and gently sauté the onions

and garlic over medium-low heat, stirring frequently, until the vegetables are very soft but not beginning to brown—about 10 to 15 minutes. Add the thyme and the pepper strips and continue cooking and stirring until the peppers are soft and limp, about 15 minutes. Mix in the olives.

Put the chicken in an ovenproof casserole or dish. Pile the pepper and onion mixture over the chicken pieces to cover them thoroughly. Add the sherry, stock, and orange juice to the skillet, raise the heat to medium-high, and boil, scraping up any brown bits left in the bottom of the pan. Pour the liquid over the peppers.

Bake the chicken for about 30 minutes (20 minutes for skinless, boneless breasts) or until the chicken is thoroughly cooked and the sauce is sizzling. *Makes 8 servings*

Nutritional Data, per portion

| | | |
|---|---|---|
| Calories 368 | Carbohydrate 11g | Saturated Fat 5g |
| Protein 29g | Sodium 227mg | Monounsaturated |
| Fat 22g | Cholesterol 88mg | Fat 11g |

# NIÇOISE CHICKEN WITH TOMATOES
## AND BLACK OLIVES

**T**his is a classic dish from the Comté de Nice, that bit of the Riviera that seems so much like Italy. Like the preceding recipe, it can be made successfully with skinless, boneless chicken breasts if you prefer.

6   tablespoons extra-virgin olive oil

3   medium onions, coarsely chopped

2   garlic cloves, chopped

1   tablespoon minced fresh thyme or 1 teaspoon dried, crumbled

a small handful of finely chopped flat-leaf parsley

3 to 4 pounds chicken breasts and legs, cut into 6 or 8 pieces, or

      2 pounds skinless, boneless chicken breasts

salt and freshly ground black pepper to taste

6   very ripe tomatoes, peeled (page 454) and chopped, or 1 28-ounce can

      whole tomatoes, well drained and chopped

½   cup dry white wine or vermouth

½   cup small black Niçoise olives

juice of ½ lemon

In a large skillet, heat 3 tablespoons of the olive oil, add the onions and garlic, and sauté over medium-low heat until the onions are very soft and starting to brown, about 10 to 15 minutes. Add the thyme and parsley and cook a few minutes longer, stirring to mix well. Set aside.

Cut away any excess fat or skin from the chicken pieces. (You can discard the skin entirely if you wish.) Rub the chicken pieces all over with salt and pepper. In a separate pan, sauté the chicken pieces in the remaining oil until they are well browned on all sides—about 5 to 7 minutes to a side. Add the tomatoes and wine, stirring to scrape up the brown bits from the bottom of the pan. Turn the heat up to medium-high and cook, uncovered, stirring occasionally, until the liquid has reduced and the tomato sauce is thickened—about 20 to 25 minutes. Test the chicken for doneness—there should be no trace of pink.

Stir in the reserved onion-herb mixture, the olives, and the lemon juice. Return

to a boil and cook for 5 minutes, stirring frequently—or just long enough to reduce the juices once more. Serve with rice, polenta, or bulgur pilaf (pages 201, 220, 222).
***Makes 6 to 8 servings***

Nutritional Data, per portion

| | | |
|---|---|---|
| Calories 437 | Carbohydrate 11g | Saturated Fat 7g |
| Protein 27g | Sodium 180mg | Monounsaturated |
| Fat 32g | Cholesterol 101mg | Fat 17g |

# LEBANESE GARLICKY ROAST CHICKEN

***Caution: For true garlic lovers only!***

**O**ne of my favorite street foods in Beirut was a humble chicken sandwich, made with tender roasted chicken piled in a sandwich roll that had been slathered with the garlic sauce called *toum bi zeit* in Arabic. The sandwiches were topped with a slice of pickled cucumber and toasted briefly. After a morning of intensive Arabic lessons, these were a welcome respite. And the garlic sauce is just as good served in dollops on a plate of roasted chicken.

1    **4- to 5-pound roasting chicken, preferably free-range**
2    **garlic cloves, minced**
2    **tablespoons extra-virgin olive oil**
2    **tablespoons fresh lemon juice**
     **salt and freshly ground black pepper to taste**
½    **cup Lebanese Garlic Sauce (page 294)**

Pull the fat out of the chicken cavity and discard. Dry the chicken well with paper towels. Mix together the garlic, oil, and lemon juice and smear all over the bird, inside and out. Sprinkle liberally with salt and pepper, inside and out, and set aside to marinate for an hour or more.

When you're ready to cook, preheat the oven to 400 degrees. Place the chicken on a roasting rack, pouring over it any excess marinade. Roast for about 30 minutes, basting every 10 minutes or so with the pan juices. Make the garlic sauce while the chicken is roasting, following the directions on page 294. Reduce heat to 325 degrees and continue roasting for 30 minutes.

The chicken is done when a leg moves loosely on its joint or when the juices run clear yellow when pricked with a fork. Remove from the oven and set aside to rest for 10 minutes. Carve the chicken and pass the garlic sauce heaped in a small bowl.
*Makes 4 to 6 servings*

### Nutritional Data, per portion

| | | |
|---|---|---|
| Calories  501 | Carbohydrate  6g | Saturated Fat  8g |
| Protein  43g | Sodium  302mg | Monounsaturated |
| Fat  33g | Cholesterol  133mg | Fat  17g |

# SPANISH ROAST CHICKEN WITH A SHERRY-ORANGE GLAZE

**R**oast potatoes in the pan with the chicken or serve it with a rice or bulgur pilaf (pages 201, 222). In summer, the chicken is delightful at room temperature with an abundance of green salad.

1    4- to 5-pound roasting chicken, preferably free-range

1½ teaspoons ground cumin

salt and freshly ground black pepper to taste

2    garlic cloves, minced

2    tablespoons extra-virgin olive oil

½    cup amontillado or oloroso sherry

¾    cup orange marmalade

¾    cup fresh orange juice

¼    teaspoon Tabasco sauce (optional)

Pull the fat out of the chicken cavity and discard. Dry the chicken well with paper towels. Sprinkle the carcass inside and out with 1 teaspoon of the cumin and the salt and pepper. Mix together the garlic, oil, and 2 tablespoons of the sherry.

Beat with a fork to mix well, then rub over the chicken inside and out. Set aside for an hour or more to marinate.

When you're ready to cook, preheat the oven to 400 degrees. Place the chicken on a roasting rack, pouring over it any excess marinade. Roast for about 30 minutes, basting every 10 minutes or so with the pan juices.

While the chicken is roasting, make the glaze. In a small saucepan, combine the remaining sherry and remaining cumin with the orange marmalade and orange juice. Bring to a boil, reduce the heat to low, and simmer, stirring frequently, until the sauce has thickened and reduced to about 1 cup. Remove from the heat and add a little Tabasco if you wish.

Remove the chicken from the oven and brush it with the hot glaze. Reduce the oven temperature to 325 degrees, return the bird to the oven, and continue roasting for 20 to 30 minutes, brushing it with glaze every 10 minutes or so. The chicken is done when a leg moves loosely on its joint or when the juices run clear yellow when pricked with a fork. Remove from the oven and set aside to rest for 10 minutes before serving. *Makes 6 servings*

Nutritional Data, per portion

| Calories 557 | Carbohydrate 33g | Saturated Fat 7g |
|---|---|---|
| Protein 43g | Sodium 154mg | Monounsaturated |
| Fat 28g | Cholesterol 133mg | Fat 13g |

# MOROCCAN CHICKEN WITH PRESERVED LEMONS AND OLIVES

**S**akina el-Alaoui is a fine Moroccan home cook who takes great pride in the quality of food on her table. She prepares her chickens, which are very small (a half chicken makes one serving) in the traditional manner, rinsing them thoroughly, inside and out, in cold water, then rubbing them all over, inside and out, with salt and cut lemon quarters. She removes all visible traces of fat and any fibrous elements from the birds and rubs the salt and lemon juice between the skin and the flesh on the chicken breasts. Once the birds have been thoroughly cleaned, she freezes each one individually for use later on.

Moroccan cooks use *olives rouges*, lovely red and violet half-ripened olives (Sakina's are preserved at home in a paste of salt and the juice of bitter oranges), but any good-quality salt- or brine-cured olives can be substituted. Preserved lemons add an unusual and enticing flavor, but they must be made a good three weeks in advance. If you wish, use fresh lemons—the flavor will not be the same, but it's still a good dish.

> **about 5 to 6 pounds chicken, preferably small chickens weighing no more than 2 or 2½ pounds, including livers and giblets**
>
> 1   **lemon, cut into quarters**
>
> **a handful of fine sea salt**
>
> ½   **cup minced cilantro**
>
> ½   **cup minced flat-leaf parsley**
>
> 2   **tablespoons minced garlic**
>
> 1   **tablespoon ground ginger**
>
> **freshly ground black pepper to taste**
>
> ¼   **teaspoon saffron threads**
>
> 2   **whole preserved lemons (page 305)**
>
> ¼   **cup water**
>
> ½   **cup extra-virgin olive oil**
>
> 4   **medium onions, halved and very thinly sliced**
>
> 1   **tablespoon sweet paprika**
>
> 1   **tablespoon unsalted butter (optional)**
>
> 1   **cup best-quality black or violet olives**

Remove all traces of fat and any fibers from the chickens. Rinse thoroughly, inside and out, in cool running water. Rub them all over, inside and out, with lemon quarters, being sure to rub between the skin and the flesh of the breasts. Rub salt all over the chickens. Set aside in a cool place to drain for at least 30 minutes or refrigerate the chickens, covered, overnight. Trim any greenish spots off the livers and pull away and discard the giblet linings.

When you're ready to cook, rinse the chickens again in cool running water and pat them dry with paper towels. Set aside.

In a heavy pot or kettle large enough to hold all the chickens, mix the cilantro, parsley, garlic, ginger, and pepper. Crumble the saffron into the herbs. Cut one of the preserved lemons into small pieces and add to the mixture along with the water.

Mix the seasoning together well, then put the chickens in the pot and use your hands to rub them all over, inside and out, with the seasoning sauce. Add the giblets to the middle of the pot, pour the olive oil over, and set the kettle over very low heat. As the chicken begins to sizzle in the sauce, add the onions and shake the pan to distribute them evenly around the birds. Cover the pan and cook very slowly until the chickens are thoroughly cooked and the onions have almost disintegrated into the sauce. After 30 minutes of cooking, add the livers to the pot, together with the paprika, shaking the kettle to distribute the paprika in the sauce. Total cooking time will be 1½ to 2 hours.

When the chickens are thoroughly cooked, remove them from the sauce. Cut whole chickens into halves or quarters and arrange them on a warm platter. Take the gizzards and hearts out of the sauce, cut them into small bits, and stir them back in. Using a fork, coarsely crush the livers in the sauce. The sauce should be quite thick; if it seems too thin, let it boil down, stirring frequently, until it is the right consistency. Add the butter if desired and the olives. Swirl the pan to distribute the olives and emulsify the sauce. Pour the sauce over the chickens on the platter and garnish with strips of peel from the second preserved lemon. (If you're not using preserved lemons, garnish the chickens with a little grated fresh lemon zest.) *Makes 8 servings*

Nutritional Data, per portion

| | | |
|---|---|---|
| Calories 666 | Carbohydrate 15g | Saturated Fat 12g |
| Protein 44g | Sodium 1,970mg | Monounsaturated |
| Fat 49g | Cholesterol 200mg | Fat 26g |

# LEBANESE GARLIC-MARINATED CHICKEN ON THE GRILL

This is a fine recipe for skinless, boneless chicken breasts since the olive oil compensates for the dryness of the meat. For the finest flavor and texture, do try to find chicken breasts from naturally raised free-range birds. The garlic sauce (*toum bi zeit*) on page 294 is delicious with this. Precede it with a chilled gazpacho (page 102) or ajo blanco (page 104) and serve the chicken with fresh pita bread (page 133) or slices of a crusty country loaf and a massive green salad for a memorable summer Sunday lunch.

2   pounds skinless, boneless chicken breasts

4   garlic cloves, crushed with the flat blade of a knife

1   teaspoon salt

½   cup fresh lemon juice

¾   cup extra-virgin olive oil

1   teaspoon sweet paprika

freshly ground black pepper to taste

Chicken breasts are usually sold split in half. Cut each breast half in half again and put them in a bowl.

Chop the garlic coarsely and in a small bowl crush it with the salt, using the back of a spoon, until you have a smooth paste. Stir in the lemon juice, oil, paprika, and pepper. Beat well with a fork and pour the marinade over the chicken pieces. Mix well, using your hands, and turn the pieces to coat them liberally with the marinade. Cover and refrigerate for 4 or 5 hours or overnight.

When you're ready to cook, prepare the grill, leaving plenty of time for it to heat up if you're using charcoal or wood. When the fire is hot enough, place the chicken pieces on the grill and set the grill a good 8 inches from the source of the heat. Use the marinade remaining in the bowl to baste the chicken frequently as it cooks. Grill for 10 minutes or longer on each side, turning each piece once. Test for doneness and serve hot or at room temperature. ***Makes 6 to 8 servings***

Nutritional Data, per portion

| Calories   219 | Carbohydrate   1g | Saturated Fat   2g |
|---|---|---|
| Protein   26g | Sodium   211mg | Monounsaturated |
| Fat   12g | Cholesterol   66mg | Fat   9g |

THE MEDITERRANEAN DIET COOKBOOK

# POLLO AL MATTONE OR AL DIAVOLO

### *Tuscan Grilled Chicken*

**T**uscans call this celebrated method of grilling pigeons or very young chickens *pollo al mattone* because the bird is traditionally flattened with a brick or *pollo al diavolo* because the peppery seasoning is as hot as the dickens. Tuscan chickens don't weigh much more than a couple of pounds each, so half a chicken, flattened with a weight, is ideal for each serving. Our chickens tend to be much larger. If you use larger chickens cut into parts, don't bother flattening them. Simply marinate and grill them.

1½ cups extra-virgin olive oil

1 teaspoon salt

1 tablespoon freshly ground black pepper

1 tablespoon hot red pepper flakes or to taste

1 tablespoon chopped fresh rosemary leaves

1 tablespoon finely chopped flat-leaf parsley

1 tablespoon fresh thyme or 1 teaspoon dried, crumbled

about 6 or 7 pounds chicken—3 very small chickens split in half or
      larger chickens cut into 6 or 8 pieces

juice of 1 lemon

lemon wedges for garnish

Mix the olive oil with the salt, black pepper, red pepper, rosemary, parsley, and thyme and set aside, covered, for several hours or overnight.

Prepare the chicken by cutting away excess yellow fat from the insides of the birds. (To reduce fat, you can discard the skin if you wish.) Flatten small chicken halves by laying them skin side up on a board (a flattened chicken will cook more evenly on the grill—a nicety that I don't always observe). Cut away the wing tips and pound each chicken half smartly with the flat side of a meat cleaver or a Chinese cleaver—this should crack the breastbone.

Place the chickens in a dish or on a platter large enough to hold them all in one layer. Cover them with the flavored olive oil. Leave to marinate in the oil, turning occasionally, for at least one hour. Or refrigerate, covered, for several hours or overnight.

Prepare the grill, leaving plenty of time for it to heat up if you're using charcoal or wood. When the fire is hot enough, place the chickens skin side down on the grill and set the grill a good 8 inches from the source of the heat. Add the lemon juice to the oil remaining in the platter and use the lemon-oil mixture to baste the chickens frequently as they cook. Grill for 15 minutes on each side, turning each piece once. Test for doneness: The juices should run clear yellow when chicken is thoroughly cooked.

Serve the chicken piled on a platter and garnished with lemon wedges. Accompany with ratatouille or one of its variations (page 44) and with an abundance of fresh salad greens, dressed simply with oil and lemon juice, and slices of crusty country-style bread. ***Makes 6 to 8 servings***

Nutritional Data, per portion

| | | |
|---|---|---|
| Calories  574 | Carbohydrate  1g | Saturated Fat  9g |
| Protein  44g | Sodium  271mg | Monounsaturated |
| Fat  43g | Cholesterol  143mg | Fat  25g |

## ABOUT RABBIT

Growing up in Maine, I never ate rabbit, nor did I know anyone who did. The first rabbit I ever knowingly consumed was in the home of a French friend in Paris, a woman who took great pride and pleasure in the fine, traditional table she set for her family after she came home from the office every day. The meal she prepared was *lapin à la moutarde*, a very typical and familiar French presentation with a wonderfully savory mustard sauce.

Rabbit is a farmyard animal throughout the Mediterranean, as familiar on the table as chicken or duck. My Tuscan neighbors raise rabbits in hutches along with their chickens and geese, and they often serve rabbit, fragrant with olive oil and rosemary, that has been braised in the outdoor bread oven after the bread has come out, as part of a Sunday feast. I have grown to love this meat for its delicious flavor, its supple texture, and its adaptability to many styles and sauces. Moreover, it's very low in fat— lower even than skinless white-meat chicken. As for the Thumper factor, well—we eat lamb and veal without any problems, so what's the big deal about rabbit?

If you're unfamiliar with rabbit, try these recipes, braising it in white wine with onions and plump green olives or in vermouth and stock with dried wild mushrooms. Rabbit also lends itself well to many traditional chicken stews—coq au vin, for instance, can as easily be made with tender pieces of rabbit. Or try *pollo al chilindron* (page 314) or the Niçoise-style braised chicken (page 316).

It's hard to find good fresh rabbit in this country, although persistence may pay off in a farmer who is willing to provide you with what you're looking for. Otherwise, you will have to make do with frozen rabbit. Thaw frozen rabbit slowly in your refrigerator so as not to toughen the delicate meat. If you can't find rabbit at all, you can use chicken in these recipes instead.

# BRAISED RABBIT GARNISHED WITH GREEN OLIVES AND ONIONS

**W**ith its peppery sauce, this dish is delightful with a lentil puree. Prepare the lentils as in the recipe on page 234 and, when they're very soft, whirl them with their juices in a food processor or put them through the medium disk of a food mill. Mashed potatoes with olive oil (page 404) also make a nice accompaniment.

Instant flour may seem like an anomaly in a traditional Mediterranean dish, but it's a trick restaurant chefs use to achieve a smooth sauce, and it works.

2  2- to 2½-pound rabbits, cut into about 6 pieces each
1  cup dry white wine, or more if necessary
6  tablespoons extra-virgin olive oil
½  garlic clove, crushed lightly
2  tablespoons minced flat-leaf parsley
1  teaspoon dried thyme, crumbled
2  bay leaves
½  teaspoon salt, or to taste
24  small pearl or pickling onions, peeled
1  tablespoon instant flour
24  plump green olives, pitted
1  teaspoon freshly cracked black pepper

Rinse the rabbit pieces under cool running water and set them in a large mixing bowl. Pour the white wine, ¼ cup of the oil, garlic, parsley, thyme, bay leaves, and salt over them and stir to coat the pieces with the marinade. Cover and set aside for several hours or refrigerate overnight.

In a heavy casserole or saucepan large enough to hold all the rabbit, sauté the onions in the remaining 2 tablespoons of oil over medium heat, stirring frequently, until they are golden brown—about 10 to 15 minutes. Remove the onions with a slotted spoon and set aside.

Remove the rabbit pieces from the marinade, reserving the marinade. Pat the pieces dry with paper towels and brown them in the oil remaining in the pan, turning frequently—about 10 minutes. When all the rabbit pieces are well colored, sprinkle the flour over them. Cook for about 5 minutes, stirring constantly with a

wooden spoon, to distribute and brown the flour. Return the browned onions to the pan and pour in the marinade, adding a little wine or stock or water if necessary to bring the liquid just to the top of the meat and onions. Bring to a boil, scraping up any bits that adhere to the pan. When the liquid is boiling, turn the heat down to a simmer, cover the pan, and simmer gently for about 1 hour or until the meat is falling off the bone.

Remove the meat and onions from the pan and arrange them on a heated serving platter, the meat in the center, the onions around the edge. Strain the sauce through a sieve to remove all the aromatics and let the strained sauce sit for a few minutes so that the fat rises to the surface. Skim away the fat and return the sauce to a clean small saucepan. Simmer the sauce over medium-low heat for about 5 minutes to reduce it and thicken it slightly. Add the olives for the last few moments, just long enough to heat them, then remove them with a slotted spoon and distribute them over the onions. Taste the sauce for seasoning, adding a little more salt if necessary. Stir in the cracked black pepper and pour the sauce over the meat in the platter. Serve immediately. *Makes 8 servings*

Nutritional Data, per portion

| | | |
|---|---|---|
| Calories 387 | Carbohydrate 2g | Saturated Fat 5g |
| Protein 39g | Sodium 694mg | Monounsaturated |
| Fat 24g | Cholesterol 111mg | Fat 11g |

# ANGELO PELLEGRINI'S BRAISED RABBIT WITH WILD MUSHROOMS

**A**ngelo Pellegrini was an accomplished cook and gardener, a wine maker of distinction (partly helped by the fact that his wine grapes came from the vineyards of his good friend Robert Mondavi), and a fine writer. "I am convinced," he once wrote, "that no one, much less one in moderate circumstances, can satisfy a cultivated palate every day of the year without a garden and a cellar of his own." He made this rabbit dish for me in the kitchen of his Seattle home one sunny summer morning shortly before he died. I will never forget it.

¾   ounce dried porcini

1   small celery rib, leaves included

4   flat-leaf parsley sprigs

2 or 3 fresh tarragon sprigs

3 or 4 fresh thyme sprigs

4   fresh sage leaves

2   wild mint sprigs, if available

1   small dried red chili, seeds and membranes removed

2   2- to 2½-pound rabbits, cut into about 6 pieces each

½   cup unbleached all-purpose or instant flour

salt and freshly ground black pepper to taste

¼   cup extra-virgin olive oil

2   ounces Italian pancetta or blanched bacon, minced almost to a pulp

kidneys and livers from the rabbits or 2 chicken livers, chopped

1   tablespoon tomato puree

¼   cup dry vermouth

½   cup clear white chicken stock (page 81)

½   teaspoon arrowroot

Put the mushrooms in a bowl and cover them with very hot water. Set aside to soak. Chop together the celery, parsley, herbs, and chili and set aside.

Put the rabbit pieces in a paper bag with the flour, salt, and pepper. Shake the bag vigorously to coat the meat. Over medium-high heat in a heavy stewing pan

large enough to hold all the meat, sauté the rabbit pieces in the olive oil, turning frequently. As the pieces brown—in about 15 to 20 minutes—remove them and set aside.

When all of the rabbit pieces are browned, add the pancetta to the pan and stir over medium-high heat. When the pancetta starts to brown, add the rabbit livers and kidneys or the chicken livers. Stir well and lower the heat slightly. Add the herb mixture and continue cooking for about 5 minutes, stirring occasionally and taking care not to burn the vegetables. Return the rabbit pieces to the pan with their juices.

Remove the mushrooms from their soaking liquid. *Do not discard the liquid.* Rinse the mushrooms rapidly under running water, chop them coarsely, and add them to the pan with the rabbit. Strain the mushroom liquid directly into the pan through a sieve lined with a paper towel. Add the tomato puree, vermouth, and stock, stir, and bring to a slow simmer. When the liquid starts to bubble, sprinkle the arrowroot over and stir to mix well. Cover the pan and leave the rabbit to cook over low to medium-low heat for 1 hour.

Dr. Pellegrini liked to serve this rabbit with polenta (page 220). **Makes 6 to 8 servings**

Nutritional Data, per portion

| | | |
|---|---|---|
| Calories 425 | Carbohydrate 9g | Saturated Fat 6g |
| Protein 44g | Sodium 215mg | Monounsaturated |
| Fat 22g | Cholesterol 152mg | Fat 10g |

# PARTRIDGE WITH A CHOCOLATE SAUCE

**R**abbit, hare, partridge, and other animals, once largely harvested from the wild and now largely grown on farms, are traditionally cooked in strong sauces to complement their gamy flavors. The addition of chocolate, typical of very old-fashioned country cuisine in France, Spain, and Italy, is a little startling at first, but if you think historically, it makes some sense. Could this be a Mexican mole, translated through Spain centuries ago to other parts of the Mediterranean?

I buy partridges from a game farm near my house in Maine, but in Italy and Spain in the fall butcher shops are full of hanging birds, their brilliant plumage adding liveliness to an already lively scene. If you are a bird hunter or know someone who is, try this with a wild bird that has been hung for a few days.

2   partridges, each about 1 pound dressed, split in half

1   tablespoon instant flour

salt and freshly ground black pepper to taste

2   tablespoons extra-virgin olive oil

6   shallots, chopped

2   large carrots, peeled and cut into chunks

4   garlic cloves, chopped

1   bay leaf

1   tablespoon chopped fresh thyme or 1 teaspoon dried, crumbled

¼   cup minced flat-leaf parsley

1   cup dry red wine

1   tablespoon balsamic vinegar

1   cup clear white chicken stock (page 81)

1   teaspoon sugar or more to taste

1   ounce unsweetened cooking chocolate

Preheat the oven to 350 degrees. Sprinkle the flour, a little salt, and pepper over the partridges. In a heavy saucepan large enough to hold them, brown the birds in the oil over medium heat, turning frequently. (You may have to do this in two

batches.) When the birds are golden all over—in about 20 minutes—remove them and set them in a roasting pan with a lid. They should just fit the pan.

Lower the heat to medium-low, and in the oil remaining in the saucepan gently sauté the shallots until soft but not brown—about 5 minutes. Add the carrots and garlic, stir to mix with the fat in the pan, and continue cooking for 5 minutes. Be careful not to brown the vegetables. Add the herbs and stir to distribute. Add the wine and bring it to a boil, stirring to bring up any bits that adhere to the bottom of the pan. Let the wine boil for about 5 minutes to throw off the alcohol, then add the vinegar, stock, sugar, and chocolate. Continue cooking and stirring until the chocolate has melted and combined with the rest of the sauce, about 10 minutes.

Pour the sauce over the partridges, scraping the pan well. Cover the roasting pan and bake for about 1 hour or until the partridges are thoroughly cooked and the sauce is thick and velvety.

The dish can be served immediately, but it is even better the day after. If you wish to make it a day ahead, refrigerate it overnight and skim any hardened fat off the surface of the sauce before reheating. If the sauce is bitter, add a very little more sugar to it.

Traditionally this would be served with triangles of country bread fried in olive oil, but that's a little rich for modern tastes. Try it on its own, with slices of plain country bread for sopping up the sauce. ***Makes 4 servings***

Nutritional Data, per portion

| | | |
|---|---|---|
| Calories  596 | Carbohydrate  15g | Saturated Fat  16g |
| Protein  30g | Sodium  37mg | Monounsaturated |
| Fat  47g | Cholesterol  0 | Fat  21g |

# MOROCCAN TAGINE OF BEEF, LAMB, OR VEAL WITH QUINCES OR TURNIPS

**S**akina el-Alaoui made this deservedly famous Moroccan dish for me one bright September morning in her sunny kitchen in Marrakesh with quinces that came from trees in her back garden. Round hard fruits that look like golden-greenish apples, quinces are not always easy to find in this country, although I have seen them occasionally in supermarket produce sections in the late summer and fall. They were once a staple of our kitchens, and 19th-century cookery books always include several recipes for quince jelly—the fruit is naturally very high in pectin. If you find them, stock up—they keep very well in a refrigerator or a cool room.

Many Moroccan recipes call for adding the quinces and sugar directly to the meat stew. Preparing the quinces as detailed here adds a complication to the dish, but Sakina's method of cooking the quinces in their syrup apart from the meat makes a great deal of sense to me. If you can't find quinces, or don't want to be bothered with them, you can substitute dried apricots or dried prunes, treating them in the same manner as the quinces and adjusting the cooking time to their smaller size. Or make the tagine with white turnips, the small round ones with a purple blush at the stem end, adding them directly to the stew. The taste will be quite different but still delicious. This is a tagine for a large party. It will easily serve 10 people and needs nothing more than a green salad and a simple dessert or fruit to follow. In Morocco the tagine was served with semolina bread (page 137); if you wish, serve it with plain rice or couscous.

3    pounds boneless lean beef, lamb, or veal, cut into small stewing
     chunks
½    cup extra-virgin olive oil
1    teaspoon freshly ground black pepper
1    teaspoon ground ginger
1    teaspoon saffron threads, crumbled
salt to taste
4    large red onions, halved and thinly sliced
3    garlic cloves, thinly sliced
3    medium tomatoes, chopped, or 1 14- to 16-ounce can whole tomatoes,
     drained and chopped

8   quinces, about 3 or 4 inches in diameter, or 8 small white turnips,
    peeled and quartered
1   3-inch cinnamon stick
3   tablespoons sugar
8   medium zucchini
¼   cup minced flat-leaf parsley
⅓   cup minced cilantro

Brown the meat in the oil over high heat in a large heavy saucepan or casserole, stirring occasionally so that the meat browns on all sides—about 15 to 20 minutes. Add the aromatics and salt and stir to mix well. When the aroma of the spices begins to rise, stir in the onions, garlic, and tomatoes, lower the heat, and cook, stirring frequently, until the onions begin to soften—about 15 minutes. Add enough water to the saucepan just to cover the contents, cover the pan, and cook over medium-low heat until the meat is done—about 1½ hours. Check the water level from time to time, adding *boiling* water as necessary. The contents of the pan should always be just covered with water.

While the meat cooks, prepare the quinces if you're using them. Rub away any fuzz (like peach fuzz) with a kitchen towel. Cut the quinces in half and core them, but leave the halves intact. Drop the quinces into another saucepan and cover them with water—about 2 cups should be enough. Add the cinnamon stick, bring to a boil, and cook, covered, for about 15 minutes, just long enough to soften the quinces.

Remove the pan from the heat. Take the quince halves out of the water and set aside while you make the syrup. Add the sugar to the water and cinnamon remaining in the pan and cook over medium-high heat until the liquid has reduced and become very syrupy—about 5 minutes. Add about ½ cup of the sauce in which the meat is cooking to the syrup and cook briefly, just long enough to mix the sauce and syrup. Stir the reserved quince halves into the syrup and cook the quinces until they're golden and napped with the cinnamon-flavored syrup. Discard the cinnamon and set the quinces aside in their syrup.

If you're using turnips, cook them apart from the meat stew in a little salted water until just barely tender—about 15 to 20 minutes. Set aside.

Cut the zucchini in half lengthwise, then in half again horizontally to make 32 chunks of zucchini. Add to the stew along with the parsley and cilantro, and turnips if you are using them. Stir to mix very well and cook for about 10 minutes or until the zucchini is very soft.

POULTRY AND MEAT

Serve the tagine on a large deep platter. Using a slotted spoon, transfer the meat from the stew to the center of the platter. Set the quinces, skin side out, around the edge of the meat and the zucchini chunks around the outer edge of the platter. If you've used turnips instead of quinces, arrange them alternating with the zucchini.

If the meat sauce is thin, bring it to a rapid boil and cook over high heat to reduce it and thicken it. Pour the thickened sauce over the meat and serve immediately. Any syrup remaining from the quinces may also be poured over the dish before serving. *Makes 10 to 12 servings*

Nutritional Data, per portion

| | | |
|---|---|---|
| Calories 327 | Carbohydrate 25g | Saturated Fat 3g |
| Protein 29g | Sodium 77mg | Monounsaturated |
| Fat 13g | Cholesterol 65mg | Fat 9g |

# STIFADO OF VEAL OR LAMB

**S**tifado is a Greek way of braising or stewing in red wine and red wine vinegar. Lamb or veal stifado is a typical dish in tavernas all over Greece, and on the island of Cyprus we ate stifados of octopus and tiny onions flavored memorably with cinnamon, cloves, and allspice. Many cooks like to marinate the meat beforehand in the wine and vinegar—this would be sensational with a piece of wild venison. With veal, lamb, or beef the marinating is not necessary.

This dish is especially delicious with garlic mashed potatoes with olive oil (page 404), although rice or tiny orzo pasta, cooked separately in a little of the stifado liquid, is more traditional.

3   pounds small white onions, peeled

4   garlic cloves, crushed with the flat blade of a knife

¼   cup extra-virgin olive oil

2   pounds boneless lean veal, lamb, or beef cut into small stewing pieces

1   small 14- to 16-ounce can whole tomatoes, drained and coarsely crushed

2   tablespoons tomato puree diluted with ½ cup water

2   bay leaves

1   3-inch cinnamon stick

4   allspice berries

4   whole cloves

1½ teaspoons ground cumin

1   cup dry red wine

½   cup red wine vinegar

salt and freshly ground black pepper to taste

In a heavy casserole over medium-low heat, gently sauté the onions and garlic in the oil until the onions are just starting to turn brown—about 10 to 15 minutes. Push the onions and garlic out to the edges of the pan and add the meat to the center. (Or remove the onions and garlic and set aside, if it is more comfortable, returning them to the pan after the meat has browned.) Turn the heat up to medium and quickly brown the meat on all sides—about 15 to 20 minutes.

When the meat is thoroughly browned, stir in the tomatoes, tomato paste, bay leaves, cinnamon, allspice, cloves, and cumin. Add the red wine and vinegar and enough water to barely cover the meat and vegetables, along with a very little salt and pepper if desired. Cover the pan closely and simmer very slowly for at least 2 hours. It can cook for as long as 4 hours and, like most wine and onion preparations, is even better reheated the day after it's made. If you're going to serve it immediately after cooking, however, let it stand away from the heat for about 30 minutes before serving. *Makes 8 servings*

Nutritional Data, per portion

| | | |
|---|---|---|
| Calories  272 | Carbohydrate  18g | Saturated Fat  2g |
| Protein  26g | Sodium  224mg | Monounsaturated |
| Fat  11g | Cholesterol  91mg | Fat  7g |

# ANDALUSIAN BRAISED LAMB SHANKS WITH HONEY

In contrast to most of these recipes, this is a very meaty dish. Still, the 5 pounds for six people is not as much as you might think, because the shank is a very bony cut. Most of the fat rendered by the meat is removed in the cooking process.

The recipe comes from El Caballo Rojo, a restaurant in Córdoba whose proprietor, Pepe Marin, traces Andalusian cuisine back to the Moors who held southern Spain for 700 years. If this is indeed Moorish, and I'm not so sure it is, then New World bell peppers and paprika are modern additions.

Because most of the cooking is done a day in advance, this is a good dish for busy cooks to serve at a dinner party. For a healthier presentation, serve it accompanied by Tuscan Beans with Olive Oil and Aromatics (page 225) or Baked Chick-Peas in Tomato Sauce (page 233) and plain steamed rice.

¼   cup extra-virgin olive oil

5   pounds meaty lamb shanks, cut crosswise into 2½-inch pieces

2   medium onions, finely chopped

½   medium green bell pepper, finely chopped

1½ teaspoons saffron threads dissolved in 3 tablespoons water

1   tablespoon sweet paprika

1   cup dry white wine

¼   cup brandy, preferably Spanish

2   tablespoons mild honey

3   tablespoons sherry vinegar

salt and freshly ground black pepper to taste

In a large heavy Dutch oven or casserole, heat 2 tablespoons of the oil over medium-high heat. Add a single layer of lamb pieces and cook, turning occasionally, until the meat is browned on all sides—about 10 minutes. Transfer to a platter and repeat with the remaining lamb. Pour the fat out of the pan and wipe it clean.

Add the remaining 2 tablespoons of oil to the pan together with the onions and bell pepper. Cook, stirring occasionally, over medium-low heat until the onions

are softened but not browned—about 10 minutes. Stir in the saffron water, paprika, wine, and brandy. Bring to a boil and cook until the liquid is reduced by half—about 10 to 15 minutes.

Return the meat to the pan and add enough water to come halfway up the meat. Cover and cook over medium-low heat, stirring occasionally, until the meat is very tender and falling off the bone, about 2½ hours. Remove from the heat and, using tongs, transfer the lamb to a deep platter. Cover lightly with foil and set in a warm oven while you finish the sauce.

Carefully degrease the sauce in the casserole by tilting the casserole and spooning out the fat that rises. (Or refrigerate the meat and the sauce separately overnight. Remove congealed fat from the top of the sauce before reheating.) When the fat is removed, set the pan over medium-high heat and stir in the honey, vinegar, and salt to taste. Boil until the sauce is reduced to 2 cups, about 10 minutes. Taste and add more salt if desired and pepper. Pour the sauce over the lamb and serve immediately. *Makes 6 to 8 servings*

Nutritional Data, per portion

| | | |
|---|---|---|
| Calories  240 | Carbohydrate  9g | Saturated Fat  3g |
| Protein  24g | Sodium  74mg | Monounsaturated |
| Fat  12g | Cholesterol  73mg | Fat  7g |

# BRAISED VEAL SHANKS WITH ARTICHOKES

**P**ilar Plana, a gifted home cook who lives in the old cathedral city of Zaragoza in the northeast of Spain, makes rich bread dumplings called *huevos tontos* or "stupid eggs" to go with this stew. I prefer plain steamed potatoes, drizzled with fruity extra-virgin olive oil and sprinkled with sea salt and freshly ground black pepper.

¼   cup extra-virgin olive oil

6   pounds veal shanks, cut crosswise about 1½ to 2 inches thick (the cut
      is sometimes called *osso buco*), or 2 pounds boneless veal, cut into
      stewing chunks

6   garlic cloves, thinly sliced

2   teaspoons sweet paprika

¼   teaspoon ground cinnamon

salt and freshly ground black pepper to taste

6   artichokes

1   tablespoon fresh lemon juice

a little minced flat-leaf parsley for garnish

In a large heavy casserole or Dutch oven, heat 3 tablespoons of the oil over medium-high heat. Working in batches, add the veal to the pan and cook, turning occasionally, until well browned on all sides—about 20 minutes. As the veal pieces brown, transfer them to a platter.

Reduce the heat to low. Add the remaining oil to the pan with the garlic and cook, stirring, until very lightly browned—about 15 minutes. Off the heat, add the paprika, cinnamon, salt, and pepper to the pan. Return the veal, with any juices that have collected on the platter, to the pan and stir to coat the veal with the spices.

Set the pan on the stove, increase the heat to medium, and when the meat starts to sizzle, add water to come halfway up. Reduce the heat, cover, and simmer, turning the veal once or twice, until the meat is very tender and falling off the bone, about 2 hours. (The meat can be prepared ahead of time up to this point and refrigerated

for several hours or overnight. Skim off the congealed fat before continuing with the cooking.)

Trim the artichokes, following the directions on page 455. Quarter the artichokes, remove the inner choke, and add the quarters to the stew. Add a little boiling water if necessary to keep the meat at least half covered by liquid. Cover the pan and cook for another 15 to 20 minutes or until the artichokes are tender.

Add the lemon juice to the sauce, taste, and adjust the seasoning. Arrange the veal shanks on a deep heated platter with the artichokes around the edge. Pour the sauce over the shanks and sprinkle with parsley. *Makes 6 to 8 servings*

### Nutritional Data, per portion

| | | |
|---|---|---|
| Calories  238 | Carbohydrate  11g | Saturated Fat  2g |
| Protein  26g | Sodium  195mg | Monounsaturated |
| Fat  11g | Cholesterol  98mg | Fat  7g |

## SOUVLAKIA OR KEBAB

### *Skewered Lamb with Grilled Vegetables*

In the early 1970s, when the terrible ethnic war that would soon wrack the nation was still just a small cloud on a very distant horizon, Lebanon was perfect picnic country. There were cobble beaches on the one hand, forests and mountain meadows strewn with blossoms on the other, and a full panoply of ruined Roman temples and Crusader castles where you could set up camp with a ravishing view of snowy mountain peaks, the shimmering sea, olive groves and orchards, hilltop villages, and, off in the distance, another Roman or Crusader ruin.

Lamb on skewers was a favorite picnic food, easy to prepare, easy to transport, easy to set up and cook on the spot. In the photographs in food magazines, the ingredients are craftily arranged on skewers, a cube of lamb, a cherry tomato, a piece of green pepper, a chunk of onion, and so on. The arrangement looks pretty, but it makes better sense, since all these ingredients cook at different rates, to skewer the lamb and roast the vegetables apart.

For picnics, whether in Roman ruins or American backyards, I like to serve this with çaçik (page 37) and rounds of pita bread (page 133). Tuck the grilled meat and vegetables into the bread and drizzle a little garlicky çaçik over for a Middle

Eastern sandwich. The gazpacho on page 102, served in chilled mugs, goes well with this too.

The meat should be abundant for eight people. Select the quantity of vegetables according to taste and what looks good in the market. The vegetables listed here are the traditional ones. Eggplant and zucchini, cut into thick slices, painted with olive oil, and grilled on both sides, are not bad with this either, and in America grilled fresh sweetcorn, still wrapped in its outer husks, goes splendidly with the rest. For a Mediterranean touch, try good extra-virgin olive oil with salt and pepper on your corn instead of butter—the combination is alluring.

3    pounds boneless lean lamb, preferably leg, cut into 1½-inch cubes
¼    cup extra-virgin olive oil
2    tablespoons fresh lemon juice
¼    cup minced flat-leaf parsley
3    garlic cloves, finely minced
½    teaspoon hot red pepper flakes
freshly ground black pepper to taste
2    bay leaves, crumbled
red onions, unpeeled, cut into quarters
red and green bell peppers, cut in half lengthwise and cored
fresh hot red and green chilies, cut in half lengthwise and cored
small ripe but firm tomatoes, cut in half, or whole cherry tomatoes
salt to taste
lemon wedges to squeeze over the grilled meat and vegetables

Mix the lamb with the oil, lemon juice, parsley, garlic, red pepper flakes, black pepper, and bay leaves. Stir with your hands to distribute the aromatics thoroughly. Cover and place in the refrigerator for several hours or overnight. Stir the meat occasionally. (If this is for an away-from-home picnic, prepare the vegetables at the same time and store each type in its own plastic bag in the refrigerator. If you're cooking at home, there's no need to prepare the vegetables until just before you're ready to cook.)

Prepare the grill when you're ready to cook, leaving plenty of time for it to heat up if you're using charcoal or wood. Set the cooking grid about 5 to 6 inches from the fire. Thread the meat cubes on skewers and prepare the vegetables if you didn't

do it the day before. You will want to grill the meat in the center of the grill and the vegetables along the side, where the fire is a little less intense. But the vegetables take longer than the meat, so start with them. Just be sure to leave enough room in the middle for the meat.

Brush the onion quarters all over with the marinade remaining in the bowl. Set the onion quarters skin side down on the outer edge of the grill. Now do the same with the peppers and chilies and then the tomatoes. In each case the vegetable will cook only on its skin side, but the heat of the grill will penetrate, and the blistering skin of onions, peppers, and tomatoes gives a wonderfully seductive aroma to the whole. Cherry tomatoes especially will cook much more quickly than anything else. Watch them carefully—if they split open, they may drop through to the fire. As soon as all the vegetables are in place, put the meat skewers in the center. They should take about 7 or 8 minutes—3½ to 4 minutes on each side, brushing them frequently with the remaining marinade. They are done when they are crisp on the outside and still pink within. Leave them on a little longer if you don't like rare meat, but don't overcook them.

If you time this carefully, everything will come out right at the same time. But don't worry. Most people don't time it that carefully, and the point of a picnic is to have a good time.

Sprinkle salt to taste over the meat and vegetables and serve with lemons to squeeze over.

One last thought: wrap pita breads in foil packages—no more than 4 breads to a package—and set them at the edge of the grill while it's warming up. Remove them when you put the vegetables on, but don't open them. The foil will retain enough heat to keep them warm until you're ready to open them and slip the meat and vegetables inside. ***Makes 8 servings***

Nutritional Data, per portion

| | | |
|---|---|---|
| Calories   407 | Carbohydrate   28g | Saturated Fat   4g |
| Protein   41g | Sodium   129mg | Monounsaturated |
| Fat   15g | Cholesterol   115mg | Fat   8g |

# SGHEENA: A ONE-POT MEAL
# FOR THE SABBATH

**B**eef and beans, lamb and chick-peas, chicken and cracked bulgur wheat— *adafina, dfeena, sgheena,* or *hamin* in Italy and Greece—the dish takes many shapes around the Mediterranean, but it's always a hearty, filling balance of meat and legumes or grains made to be served on the Sabbath for the simple reason that Jewish law prohibits the lighting of a fire on that holy day. Like Maine baked beans, which it resembles in concept if not in flavor, *sgheena* (the word most often used by Moroccan Jews) is meant to go in the oven before the Sabbath begins on Friday at sundown and cook all night in the falling heat of the gradually cooling oven. As the *sgheena* bakes, hermetically sealed in its round pot, an extraordinary exchange of flavors takes place, so that when the lid is finally lifted off at the Saturday lunch table, the irresistible aromas proclaim the Sabbath as much as the lighting of candles or the blessing of bread.

Arlette Benitah, an elderly Jewish Moroccan lady who was born in Gibraltar and lives in Casablanca, made this *sgheena* for me one day when I had just returned from Essaouira, down the coast south of Casablanca. There I had fallen in with a Jewish pilgrimage to the mausoleum of a miracle-working rabbi, a strange and disconcerting experience that somehow seemed an appropriate preparation for this meal. In both the pilgrimage and the *sgheena,* one seemed to confront the vitality of an older, more rudimentary and direct expression of Judaism without the rationalizing filter of the European Jewish culture that we know in America.

Madame Benitah's *sgheena* was made traditionally, with an ox foot to add gelatinous body to the sauce. Alas, this also adds a considerable amount of saturated fat. I prefer to leave the ox foot out, but if you want to try it, have the butcher split the ox foot in two and rinse it carefully before using it. Place the two halves of the ox foot in the very bottom of the pan and pile on the other ingredients as directed.

For the meat, I use a 2-pound piece of beef brisket, the exterior fat carefully cut away, and a thick 1-pound slice of veal shank—the cut also known as *osso buco*—to give body to the sauce.

Some cooks add meatballs or a meat "sausage" to the *sgheena*. The sausage is simply a long, fat roll of minced meat and seasonings tied up in a double roll of cheesecloth. There are sweet sausages, made with raisins, sugar, and sweet potatoes, and meatless ones, made with cracked wheat or rice.

You will need a very large lidded pot for this so that the grains have plenty of room to expand.

1    pound wheat berries, soaked in cold water for at least 2 hours

3    pounds boneless beef or veal

¼    cup extra-virgin olive oil

2    large onions, chopped

1    tablespoon sweet or hot paprika

1    teaspoon ground cumin

2    tablespoons harissa (page 301), diluted with ⅓ cup warm water

¼    teaspoon ground allspice

6 to 8 large waxy potatoes, such as Red Bliss or Yellow Finn, peeled and
        cut in half

6 to 8 small sweet potatoes, peeled and cut in half

8 to 10 large eggs

1    cup dried chick-peas, soaked overnight, or use the quick-soak
        method (page 454)

2    whole heads of garlic

1    cup long-grain rice

salt to taste

½    teaspoon saffron threads, crumbled

½    teaspoon ground cinnamon

Preheat the oven to 350 degrees. Drain the wheat berries and put them in a heavy lidded casserole large enough to hold all the ingredients, keeping in mind that the wheat and rice will expand during cooking.

In a heavy skillet, brown the meat in 2 tablespoons of the oil over medium-high heat, turning so that all sides brown well—about 10 minutes. Remove the meat and set it on top of the wheat berries.

Lower the heat to medium-low and add the onions to the oil in the skillet. Cook the onions gently, stirring frequently, until they are very soft and starting to turn golden—about 15 to 20 minutes. Off the heat, add the paprika, cumin, harissa, and allspice and stir to mix well. Transfer the onion mixture to the casserole.

Add the potatoes and sweet potatoes to the casserole and nestle the eggs in

among the potato quarters, leaving a space in the middle for the rice. Drain the chick-peas and sprinkle them around the potatoes and eggs. Rub the garlic heads to get rid of any loose skin, but don't peel them. Press each head down in among the potatoes, at opposite sides of the pan. Add boiling water just to the height of the potatoes and eggs.

Cover the pan and bring the liquid to a simmer, then place it in the preheated oven. Turn the heat down to 300 degrees and cook for about 1 hour, then turn the heat down to 250 degrees and cook for another hour.

At the end of the second hour, mix the rice with the remaining oil in a small bowl. Stir in about a teaspoon of salt and the saffron and cinnamon. Stir to coat the rice well with oil and aromatics. Tie up the rice in a loose bag made of a double layer of cheesecloth and bury it in the middle of the stew. Don't worry if the oil oozes out of the sides of the bag—that's what it's meant to do. Cover the casserole again and continue cooking for at least another 2 hours. Though Orthodox Jews leave it in the oven overnight, the stew will be thoroughly cooked by the end of 4 hours. Longer cooking makes the vegetables *very* soft.

When you're ready to serve, remove the eggs and peel them. Arrange them on a platter with the potatoes and sweet potatoes. Spoon the chick-peas over them and add a little of the sauce from the casserole. Serve as a first course, with more of the sauce in a bowl so that each diner can spoon it over the vegetables and eggs.

As a second course, serve the meat, wheat, and rice, again with a bowl of sauce to be passed at the table. ***Makes 8 to 10 servings***

Nutritional Data, per portion

| Calories 875 | Carbohydrate 112g | Saturated Fat 6g |
| Protein 51g | Sodium 200mg | Monounsaturated |
| Fat 26g | Cholesterol 276mg | Fat 12g |

**VARIATION:** Instead of cooking the chick-peas in the *sgheena*, cook them separately with about 2 pounds spinach or chard, steamed, chopped, and mixed with a little slivered onion and garlic and about ¼ cup olive oil. (See recipe for *garbanzos kon spinaka*, page 405.) Serve with the second course.

# DAUBE DE VEAU AU PHARE

*Mrs. Ramsay's Provençal Stew*

. . . An exquisite scent of olives and oil and juice rose from the great brown dish . . . with its shiny walls and its confusion of savoury brown and yellow meats and its bay leaves and its wine. . . .

The daube that Mrs. Ramsay served at her candlelight dinner in *To the Lighthouse* was actually made with beef. I prefer veal—so long as it is veal from an animal that has been raised in an unconfined environment. The meat of veal calves raised in confinement is tender to the point of lacking all texture and so anemically white that it's no wonder it has no flavor.

By all accounts, Virginia Woolf had an appreciative palate. Mrs. Ramsay's recipe for daube, she said, had been handed down from her French grandmother. Perhaps it was something like this. To be authentic, use a good red wine from Provence, a Mas de Gougonnier or a Bandol. California wines are, for the most part, too intense and round for this dish.

2½ pounds boneless lean veal, cut into 10 chunks

FOR THE MARINADE:

½   cup extra-virgin olive oil

1   medium carrot, peeled and sliced

1   medium onion, sliced

1   celery rib, sliced

¾   cup robust, dry red wine

¼   cup red wine vinegar

¼   cup brandy

2   tablespoons coarsely chopped flat-leaf parsley

1   4-inch strip of orange zest

2   garlic cloves, coarsely chopped

¾   teaspoon fresh thyme leaves or ¼ teaspoon dried, crumbled

3   bay leaves, broken in two

freshly ground black pepper to taste

FOR THE STEW:

**a little instant flour for sprinkling on the meat**

2   **tablespoons extra-virgin olive oil**

8   **medium carrots, peeled and cut into chunks**

18  **fat shallots or 18 very small pearl onions, peeled**

24  **pitted olives, preferably a mixture of black and green**

1   **14- to 16-ounce can whole tomatoes, drained and chopped**

**salt and freshly ground black pepper (optional) to taste**

Put the meat in a deep china or glass bowl and pour all the marinade ingredients over it. Turn the meat with your hands to distribute the aromatics evenly throughout. Cover the bowl and refrigerate overnight or for 4 to 5 hours.

The next day, preheat the oven to 300 degrees. Remove the pieces of meat, reserving the marinade. Dry the meat well with paper towels and sprinkle a little flour over it to help the browning. In a large heavy casserole, brown the meat in 2 tablespoons of olive oil over medium-high heat. (You may have to do this in batches, removing pieces as they brown.)

When all the meat is brown, return it all to the pan and pour the marinade over it. There should be just enough liquid to come to the top of the meat. Add a little more wine if necessary. Set the pan over medium-low heat and, while it is warming up, prepare the carrots, shallots, and olives and add them to the pan with the tomatoes.

When the sauce is simmering, cover the pan tightly and bake for at least 3 hours. It is actually better prepared a day ahead of time, in which case you can refrigerate the daube once it is cooked, first letting it cool down to room temperature. Before you heat it up the next day, remove the fat, which will have congealed on the surface. Taste the daube and adjust the seasoning, adding salt and pepper if you wish.

These daubes are often served with wide pasta noodles, like tagliatelle, though Mrs. Ramsay probably served hers with potatoes. *Makes 8 servings*

Nutritional Data, per portion

| | | |
|---|---|---|
| Calories 411 | Carbohydrate 19g | Saturated Fat 4g |
| Protein 31g | Sodium 444mg | Monounsaturated |
| Fat 24g | Cholesterol 114mg | Fat 16g |

# VEAL STEW WITH WILD MUSHROOMS

**W**hen we lived in Spain, we would go out in early December looking for a Christmas tree in the forests of the Gredos Mountains north and west of Madrid, where Spanish friends had a *finca*, a large farm. After a long day tramping through the pine groves we were treated to a late *merienda* in the cottage of the bailiff who managed the place. In the fireplace embers, his wife cooked a plain tortilla of potatoes and onions (page 65) to go with the rough wine of the farm and followed it with chestnuts so fresh they could be eaten out of hand like apples. One year, when we were ready to leave, the bailiff's wife handed me a piece of newspaper wrapped around a cache of chanterelles she had gathered that morning. They were dewy fresh, apricot-colored, and their aroma had some of the sweet fruitiness of apricots, too. They were perfect in the veal stew I was planning for supper.

Chanterelles are one of two kinds of wild mushrooms I feel comfortable about gathering, the other being porcini or boletus. (I would feel comfortable about morels too, but I never seem to find them.) They are unmistakable—though if you're unfamiliar with them, check carefully with a mushroom guidebook or preferably an experienced mushroomer before you try. If you come across them, by all means, use them in this very simple dish. Morels and porcini are also excellent choices, but if you can't find fresh wild mushrooms, use a mixture of commercially available fresh shiitake and white button mushrooms. Add a handful of dried porcini, soaked in warm water as in the directions for Angelo Pellegrini's Braised Rabbit with Wild Mushrooms (page 328).

This is especially good with a well-seasoned, freshly steamed polenta; or make the polenta ahead, slice it thickly when it is cool and firm, and sauté the slices on each side in a few tablespoons of good extra-virgin oil.

For the wine, you might try a sauvignon blanc from California (Sanford Vineyards is a personal favorite) or, for a slightly different flavor, a vernaccia from San Gimignano in Tuscany.

2 pounds fresh wild mushrooms

2 medium onions, finely chopped

½ garlic clove, minced

¼ cup minced flat-leaf parsley

3 tablespoons extra-virgin olive oil

1½ pounds boneless veal shoulder, cut into small stewing pieces

1 cup dry but fragrant white wine

1 teaspoon minced fresh thyme or ½ teaspoon dried, crumbled

salt and freshly ground black pepper to taste

a few drops of fresh lemon juice, optional

Wild mushrooms must be cleaned carefully before they are cooked, but they should never be washed. Trim the tough stem ends and any soft spots. (In Tuscany they say that if you throw the trimmings out the kitchen door, you'll get mushrooms next year in the spot where they landed.) Brush away any leaves or twigs that cling to the mushrooms, working gently with a soft brush or a sponge dipped in water and squeezed very dry. Chanterelles should be kept whole; large porcini should be sliced thickly, smaller ones cut into halves or quarters; morels can be kept whole unless they're large, in which case cut them in half. Set the prepared mushrooms aside.

In a heavy skillet large enough to hold all the ingredients, sauté the onions, garlic, and parsley in the oil over gentle heat, stirring constantly, until the onions are just soft—about 10 to 15 minutes. Push the vegetables out to the sides of the skillet, raise the heat to medium, and brown the veal pieces in the oil. (The vegetables can be removed for this process and returned to the pan after the meat is browned if that's more convenient.)

When the meat is brown, stir in the mushrooms and cook rapidly, stirring frequently. The mushrooms will absorb oil at first, then give off a good deal of liquid. When the liquid is bubbling—after about 15 to 20 minutes—add the wine and a little water or stock if necessary to bring the liquid just to the top of the meat. Add the thyme and salt and pepper to taste. Cook, uncovered, at a steady simmer for about 20 minutes. Then raise the heat to high and cook for 5 minutes. The liquid should reduce to about ⅓ cup of syrupy glaze. If the liquid reduces too much, add a little more wine or water during the cooking process. Remove from the heat, taste, and adjust the seasonings, adding a few drops of fresh lemon juice if you wish. Serve immediately. *Makes 4 to 6 servings*

# ÀRISTA DI MAIALE

### *Florentine Roast Loin of Pork*

**T**here is a story that's always told about àrista. It sounds apocryphal, but no less an authority than Pellegrino Artusi, the great 19th-century cook, gastronome, and recipe compiler, says the dish was served at a church council meeting in Florence in 1430 to, in Artusi's words, "smooth out some differences between the Roman and Greek Churches." When the Greek bishops were served this famous Florentine roast, they were heard to murmur "Àrista! Àrista!" which in Greek means "This is really terrific!" And àrista it has been ever since.

*Àrista di maiale*, pork loin roasted in rosemary and garlic, is served all over Tuscany, in farmhouse kitchens, at bourgeois tables, in trattorie and tavole calde. The best is roasted on a rotating spit, a *girarrosto*, before the fire, but it is also put into the bread oven after the bread comes out. It is good hot straight from the oven and even better cold the day after. Sliced very thinly and put between two slices of country bread, it makes a terrific sandwich, and it often appears on an antipasto tray along with sliced sausages and prosciutto.

Ask the butcher to bone out a loin roast of pork but leave the undercut attached. This will give you two pieces of unequal size, attached at the bottom. When opened out flat, it will look like a book that is open about two-thirds of the way through. You will also need butcher's twine to tie the roast once you have stuffed it.

Hot from the oven, this is delicious with garlic mashed potatoes with olive oil (page 404) or garlic-roasted potatoes with black olives (page 403). Or, if you wish, add peeled potatoes, carrots, and onions to the roasting pan for the final hour of cooking, turning the vegetables in the pan juices and basting them from time to time. Cold the next day, àrista makes a fine accompaniment to Lentil and Green Olive Salad (page 236).

POULTRY AND MEAT

4   pounds boneless pork loin in one piece

7 or 8 fresh rosemary sprigs

4   garlic cloves, chopped

1½ teaspoons salt

freshly ground black pepper to taste

2   tablespoons extra-virgin olive oil

½   cup dry white wine

Preheat the oven to 375 degrees. Open the pork loin out on a work table or cutting board. Strip the needles from 4 rosemary sprigs and combine them with the garlic. Chop the two together to make a coarse mixture. In a small bowl, combine the garlic and rosemary with a teaspoon of salt and a good quantity of black pepper. Add a tablespoon of the olive oil and mix well. Rub the inside of the pork with this mixture. Roll the two sides of the pork together and tie them with butcher's twine every 2 inches or so along the whole length of the roast. As you tie, work the remaining rosemary sprigs in under the twine so that the rosemary is evenly dispersed on the outside of the pork.

When the pork is tied up, rub the outside with the remaining salt and olive oil. Set it on a rack in a roasting pan and roast for 1 hour, basting with the wine and the pan juices every 20 minutes or so. Then reduce the heat to 325 degrees and continue roasting and basting. A 4-pound boneless loin should be done in about 1½ hours. If you prefer your pork very well done, leave it in the oven for 2 hours in all. As soon as it is done, remove from the oven and set aside for 10 minutes before slicing. Degrease the pan juices and serve them with the pork. *Makes 10 to 12 servings*

Nutritional Data, per portion

| | | |
|---|---|---|
| Calories  307 | Carbohydrate  1g | Saturated Fat  6g |
| Protein  31g | Sodium  336mg | Monounsaturated |
| Fat  19g | Cholesterol  94mg | Fat  9g |

# AFELIA

*Cypriote Braised Pork with Wine, Cinnamon, and Coriander*

**N**ote that coriander seeds rather than the fresh herb (cilantro) are used in this dish. Crush the seeds with a mortar and pestle or grind them coarsely in an electric coffee grinder. Cypriote red wines are quite heavy, so a richly flavored California cabernet sauvignon would be fine for the sauce—and to drink with it. Oven-roasted potatoes in olive oil or rice makes a nice accompaniment.

2   **pounds boneless lean pork, cut into 1- to 2-inch pieces**

2   **cups dry red wine**

2   **tablespoons crushed coriander seeds**

1   **3-inch cinnamon stick, broken in two**

½   **cup extra-virgin olive oil**

24 **small white onions, peeled**

2   **bay leaves**

**salt and freshly ground black pepper to taste**

Place the pork pieces in a bowl with the wine, coriander, and cinnamon. Stir to mix well, cover, and refrigerate for 8 hours or overnight.

When you're ready to cook, remove the pork from the marinade, reserving the marinade. Dry the meat with paper towels and brown it in the oil over medium-high heat in a pot large enough to hold the pork and onions. Turn the pork to brown it well on all sides. This will take about 20 minutes. As the pork browns, transfer the pieces to a plate and reserve.

When all the pork is brown, add the onions and stir them in the oil just until they start to take on a little color—about 10 to 15 minutes. Return the pork pieces to the pan together with the reserved marinade. Add the bay leaves, a little salt if desired, and several grinds of pepper. Cover tightly, turn the heat to low, and cook slowly but steadily for at least 2 hours or until the pork pieces are fork-tender and the sauce is thick and almost syrupy. If the pork pieces are done but the sauce is still watery, remove the pork and the onions and boil the sauce down to the desired consistency. Serve the pork with its sauce. ***Makes 6 to 8 servings***

Nutritional Data, per portion

| | | |
|---|---|---|
| Calories 304 | Carbohydrate 5g | Saturated Fat 4g |
| Protein 25g | Sodium 66mg | Monounsaturated |
| Fat 21g | Cholesterol 67mg | Fat 14g |

# BRAISED PORK WITH SWEET AND HOT PEPPERS

1   medium onion, chopped

2   garlic cloves, chopped

2   tablespoons extra-virgin olive oil

¾   pound lean boneless pork loin or tenderloin, cut into ½-inch slices

½   teaspoon salt or more to taste

freshly ground black pepper to taste

1   fresh rosemary sprig

¼   cup dry red wine

¼   cup water

1   tablespoon balsamic vinegar

6   red and green peppers, both hot and sweet, sliced into long strips

In a large skillet over medium heat, gently sauté the onion and garlic in the oil until the vegetables are soft and beginning to brown—about 15 minutes. Push the vegetables to the sides of the pan and add the pork pieces. Sauté the pork, turning to brown it on both sides—about 10 to 15 minutes. Sprinkle salt and pepper over the pork and add the rosemary needles, stripped away from the sprig. Add the wine, water, and vinegar and stir to mix everything together. Arrange the pepper slices over the top. Cover the pan and steam together gently, over medium-low heat, until the peppers are softened, about 20 to 25 minutes. Serve with rice or bulgur pilaf (pages 201, 222). *Makes 4 to 6 servings*

Nutritional Data, per portion

| | | |
|---|---|---|
| Calories 160 | Carbohydrate 8g | Saturated Fat 2g |
| Protein 14g | Sodium 223mg | Monounsaturated |
| Fat 8g | Cholesterol 36mg | Fat 5g |

# GRATIN DE HARICOTS AU PORC

### *A Simple Cassoulet*

The classic version of cassoulet is a production that nowadays is largely left to restaurant kitchens. It involves copious quantities of meat, both fresh and preserved, garlic sausages, and goose preserved in its own fat. All that aromatic fat gives the dish extraordinary succulence and a voluptuous texture, but it is not something modern palates will want to contemplate more than once or twice a year—or a lifetime.

This is a much simpler version and yet very good, another example of how a small amount of meat can be used to complement and flavor other elements of the meal, in this case beans.

The recipe might look complicated at first, but it is really very straightforward. Partially cook the beans, then roast the pork, then combine them for a final exchange of flavors in the oven. For ease of preparation, you can cook the beans and pork a day ahead and refrigerate them until ready to finish, an hour or two before you want to serve the gratin.

1    pound flageolets, small white beans, or cannellini, soaked overnight,
         or use the quick-soak method (page 454)

2    medium onions, 1 cut in half, 1 halved and thinly sliced

¼    cup coarsely chopped flat-leaf parsley

2    garlic cloves, crushed with the flat blade of a knife

1    bay leaf

2    medium carrots, peeled and chopped

freshly ground black pepper to taste

3    tablespoons extra-virgin olive oil

1¼ pounds lean pork in one piece for roasting

2    garlic cloves, thinly sliced

salt to taste

1    teaspoon chopped fresh thyme or ½ teaspoon dried, crumbled

½    cup dry white wine

1    cup fine dry unseasoned bread crumbs

Drain the beans, discard the soaking water, and combine the beans in a saucepan with the halved onion, parsley, garlic, bay leaf, carrots, pepper, and 2 tablespoons of the olive oil. Add boiling water to come to about an inch above the beans and set on medium-low heat. As soon as the water simmers, cover the pan, lower the heat to maintain a simmer, and cook for about 1 hour or until the beans are just tender but not falling apart. Check the water level from time to time, adding a little *boiling* water when necessary to keep the beans covered.

Meanwhile, preheat the oven to 350 degrees. Use the point of a knife to make little ½-inch-deep incisions all over the pork and insert a garlic slice in each slit. Rub the pork with the remaining olive oil and about a teaspoon of salt. Grind some pepper over the pork and rub it in with your hands. Strew the onion slices and the thyme over the bottom of a small roasting pan and set the pork on top of the onions. Pour half the wine over it and roast the pork for about 40 minutes, basting every 10 minutes with the pan juices. Remove the pork from the oven and turn the heat down to about 275 degrees.

Drain the beans, reserving the cooking liquid. Discard the onion halves and bay leaf. Spread half the beans in the bottom of a wide bean pot or casserole. Cut the pork into small pieces (don't worry if it's pink in the middle) and distribute the pieces over the beans, along with the onion slices from the roasting pan. Add the rest of the beans on top of the pork.

Pour the wine into the roasting pan and set it over high heat until the wine bubbles. Stir to bring up all the brown bits adhering to the pan, and when the alcohol has cooked off, add the liquid to the beans. Pour in about a cup of the reserved cooking liquid or more if necessary to come just to the top of the beans. Sprinkle half the bread crumbs over the top and set the casserole in the oven. After 30 minutes, gently stir the bread crumbs into the top layer of beans and add half the remaining bread crumbs. Repeat this after another 30 minutes or so. This will help to form a crust or gratin on top of the beans. The total cooking time will probably be about 1½ hours. Check the liquid level from time to time and add more cooking liquid or boiling water if necessary. If a crust has not formed by the end of the cooking time, drizzle a tablespoon of olive oil over the top, raise the heat to 400 degrees, and cook for another 10 minutes, until the top is golden. ***Makes 8 servings***

Nutritional Data, per portion

| | | |
|---|---|---|
| Calories 408 | Carbohydrate 50g | Saturated Fat 2g |
| Protein 30g | Sodium 176mg | Monounsaturated |
| Fat 10g | Cholesterol 45mg | Fat 6g |

**VARIATION:** This dish also works very well with lamb, in which case you might wish to add a good deal more garlic.

---

## ALMOST VEGETARIAN

The next three recipes are good examples of almost-vegetarian cuisine, preparations in which a small amount of meat acts as a flavoring or base for a dish that is made up primarily of vegetables. If you're trying to cut down on the quantity of meat you eat but don't want to become a vegetarian, these are for you.

The recipes call for lamb because they come from the eastern Mediterranean, where lamb is the treasured meat. Veal or beef can be substituted, and you can increase the quantity of vegetables or change the vegetables depending on what is available seasonally. Dishes like these have the added advantage that they can be made well in advance and, in fact, seem to benefit from a day of rest between cooking and serving. Bring them slowly back to serving temperature. Accompany with a rice or bulgur pilaf (pages 201, 222) and a green salad.

# LAMB BAKED WITH POTATOES, EGGPLANT, TOMATOES, AND ZUCCHINI

1   pound boneless lean lamb shoulder, cut into pieces no more than
     ½ inch to a side

3 to 4 tablespoons extra-virgin olive oil as needed

1   large onion, coarsely chopped

2   garlic cloves, crushed with the flat blade of a knife

2   large potatoes, peeled and cut into cubes

4   large very ripe tomatoes, cut into chunks, or 1 28-ounce can whole
     tomatoes, with liquid, coarsely chopped

2   medium zucchini, cut into ½-inch-thick slices

1   large eggplant, cut into 1-inch cubes

½   teaspoon ground cinnamon

2   tablespoons minced flat-leaf parsley

2   bay leaves

1   tablespoon sweet paprika

1   teaspoon dried thyme or oregano, crumbled

salt and freshly ground black pepper to taste

½   cup dry red wine

Preheat the oven to 325 degrees. In a heavy saucepan or skillet, brown the meat in 2 tablespoons of the olive oil over high heat, turning frequently so that the meat browns uniformly. When all the meat is brown—after about 20 minutes—remove it from the pan with a slotted spoon and distribute it over the bottom of an ovenproof casserole or large soufflé dish.

Add the onion and garlic to the oil remaining in the pan, lower the heat to medium-low, and cook, stirring frequently, until the onion has softened—about 10 to 15 minutes. Remove the onion and garlic and distribute over the meat. Add another tablespoon of oil to the pan, raise the heat to medium, and sauté the potato cubes, stirring, until they start to brown along the edges—about 10 minutes. Remove the potatoes and distribute over the onions.

Add the tomatoes, zucchini, and eggplant to the pan and cook, stirring to bring

up any bits that have adhered to the pan. Stir in the spices and herbs, a little salt and pepper, and the wine. Cook over medium heat for about 10 minutes to reduce the tomatoes to a thick sauce. Pour the sauce over the vegetables in the oven dish. Cover the casserole with aluminum foil and set in the oven. Bake for 1 hour, uncovering for the last 15 minutes of baking. The vegetables and meat should be very tender. Serve immediately. **Makes 8 servings**

Nutritional Data, per portion

| | | |
|---|---|---|
| Calories 229 | Carbohydrate 22g | Saturated Fat 2g |
| Protein 15g | Sodium 56mg | Monounsaturated |
| Fat 11g | Cholesterol 37mg | Fat 6g |

# LAMB OR VEAL WITH ARTICHOKES

**B**alqiss was the seventh daughter of a seventh daughter, a magical woman in Arab folklore. She kept house for us in Beirut and tended the baby while I delved ever deeper into the tenebrous realm of the Egyptian Twelfth Dynasty in the basement library of the American University. Walking home from a six- or seven-hour library stretch, dazed, thoroughly grubby, and longing for food and a bath, preferably in that order, I would catch the deliciously compelling aromas of her cooking from far down Rue de Californie. This was one of her favorite recipes, one that often greeted me when I arrived home.

3   tablespoons extra-virgin olive oil

1   pound boneless lean lamb or veal, cut into small cubes

6   fat scallions, both white and green parts, coarsely chopped

2   medium yellow onions, coarsely chopped

2   large garlic cloves, chopped

10  artichokes, prepared as directed on page 455 and quartered

2   teaspoons unbleached all-purpose flour

⅓   cup fresh lemon juice

¼   cup minced flat-leaf parsley

¼   cup minced cilantro

salt and freshly ground black pepper to taste

POULTRY AND MEAT

Heat the oil in a saucepan large enough to hold all the ingredients. Over medium heat, cook the meat cubes, turning frequently, until the meat is thoroughly browned—about 20 minutes. Lower the heat to medium-low and add the scallions, onions, and garlic. Sauté until the onions are soft but not brown, about 10 to 15 minutes, then add just enough water to come to the top of the meat, cover the pan, and cook gently for about 20 minutes.

Drain the artichoke quarters and add to the pan with the meat, stirring to mix well. Blend the flour with a little water to get rid of any lumps, then add more water to make ½ cup and stir the mixture into the stew. Add the lemon juice and more boiling water to bring the level up to the top of the artichokes and meat. Cover the pan and cook for 20 minutes longer or until the artichoke quarters are tender. Remove the lid and simmer for another 10 or 15 minutes to reduce and thicken the sauce. Add the parsley and cilantro, taste, and adjust the seasoning, adding salt, pepper, and lemon juice as desired. Serve the artichoke stew over a mound of rice or bulgur pilaf (pages 201, 222). **Makes 8 servings**

### Nutritional Data, per portion

| | | |
|---|---|---|
| Calories 230 | Carbohydrate 23g | Saturated Fat 2g |
| Protein 17g | Sodium 195mg | Monounsaturated |
| Fat 9g | Cholesterol 37mg | Fat 6g |

# TURKISH WINTER VEGETABLE STEW

### *Lamb or Veal with Celery Root, Carrots, Potatoes, and Leeks*

Gnarled and dusty-cream-colored celery root, or celeriac, is often available in produce markets in the winter. It should feel firm when you press it and hefty in the hand—lightweight ones are probably dried out and spongy inside. The flavor is decidedly celery and pleasantly pungent when raw. Cooking it softens and sweetens the flavor.

If you can't find celery root, use thoroughly un-Mediterranean parsnips instead—the flavor will be different, but the texture will be similar.

| | |
|---|---|
| 1 | pound boneless lean lamb, veal, or beef, cut into small cubes |
| 2 | tablespoons extra-virgin olive oil |
| 2 | medium onions, coarsely chopped |
| salt to taste | |
| 1 | tablespoon unbleached all-purpose flour |
| ½ | cup rich meat stock (page 83) or water |
| 5 | medium waxy potatoes, peeled and cut into large cubes |
| 2 | medium celery roots, peeled and cut into large cubes |
| 4 | medium carrots, peeled and cut into 2-inch lengths |
| 3 | fat leeks, trimmed, rinsed, and cut into 2-inch lengths |
| 2 | garlic cloves, crushed with the flat blade of a knife |
| 1 | teaspoon dried thyme, crumbled |
| freshly ground black pepper to taste | |
| 1 | tablespoon fresh lemon juice |

In a heavy saucepan or casserole over medium-high heat, brown the meat in a tablespoon of the oil, turning frequently to brown evenly on all sides. When the meat is brown, in about 20 minutes, turn the heat to medium-low and add the onions with another tablespoon of oil. Cook the onions gently, stirring frequently, until they are soft but not brown—about 10 to 15 minutes. Add a little salt and the flour and stir until the flour has been completely blended into the meat and onions. Pour in the stock, bring to a simmer, cover the pan, and cook for 20 to 25 minutes, stirring occasionally.

POULTRY AND MEAT

Uncover the pan and add the vegetables, stirring to mix them well with the meat sauce. Add a little more water or stock just to come to the top of the vegetables. Add the garlic, thyme, and black pepper, cover the pan again, and cook the vegetables until they are tender but not falling apart—about 20 minutes. At the last moment, stir in the lemon juice. Taste and adjust the seasoning, adding more salt, pepper, or lemon juice if desired. Sprinkle with the parsley and serve. *Makes 8 servings*

### Nutritional Data, per portion

| | | |
|---|---|---|
| Calories 254 | Carbohydrate 32g | Saturated Fat 2g |
| Protein 15g | Sodium 79mg | Monounsaturated |
| Fat 8g | Cholesterol 37mg | Fat 4g |

## LIVING AND EATING IN THE MEDITERRANEAN

Like most people in the late Middle Ages, Francesco di Marco Datini, the Prato merchant whose life was so brilliantly detailed by Iris Origo, took only two meals a day. In Italy these were desinare, or dinner, at terce—that is, the middle of the morning—and cena, or supper, at sundown. In summer, when the sun set late, a merenda or snack might fill the gap between. But two meals were recommended—for the sake of body as well as soul. Origo quotes a certain Paolo da Certaldo: "Order your day so that you do not eat more than twice, dinner in the morn and supper at night, and do not drink save at meals, and you will be much more healthy. . . . Cook once a day in the morning and keep part for the night; and eat little at supper, and you will keep well."

Certaldo's advice is followed throughout much of the Mediterranean today. Most people eat a very light, almost insignificant breakfast, a copious lunch sometime well after midday, followed by a rest if not a siesta, and a light, late supper, often made up of leftovers from lunch with perhaps a little plate of soup or fresh salad to enliven the meal. In between these meals there are small snacks—merende, meriendas, or casse-croûtes—often in

*continued*

the form of a tiny triangle of a sandwich or a little square of pizza, but always freshly made, never packaged or mass produced. (A bar that doesn't provide freshly made snacks like this doesn't survive for long.)

Is this a healthier way to live than America's on-the-run eating style, which, more often than not, features a very light lunch and a heavier meal in the evening? On the evidence, it would seem so, though it's almost impossible to structure a scientific test. Dietitians tell us that calories consumed at midday are metabolized more quickly than those consumed in the evening. And experience confirms that late, heavy meals lead to restless nights and dyspepsia in the morning.

Certainly the Mediterranean way is more civilized, even though times are changing and offices and shops are increasingly pressured to stay open through the day. Still, even in busy Mediterranean capitals, all who are able to do so, no matter what their social class or professional status, stop what they're doing at one o'clock in the afternoon and go home or to a restaurant for lunch with family and friends. This is not a mere pause in the day's occupation, but a full-scale halt, a shifting of the gears, for what is a social highlight and one of the most enjoyable moments of the day.

Whole families take part in mealtimes. It's not that they're all out in the kitchen chopping onions (usually there's a grandmother or an aunt or a sister temporarily out of work who takes charge of the cooking), but rather that they all have something to contribute, from the youngest on up. Mediterranean people have a limitless interest in food. You sense this when you sit down at a family table—everyone comments, usually favorably (usually with good reason), talking about how the sauce is flavored or the sweetness of the cheese, about what it was like the last time they had it, or how it's different at Aunt Elena's house, or remembering the time they all went mushrooming in the hills above Nice.

The merchant from Prato, though something of a Puritan, was also enormously interested in the quality of his victuals. When Francesco was working in Florence, his wife, Margherita, kept him supplied with the products of their country estate in Prato, sending down to Florence eggs, cheese, fresh produce, and the chickens, capons, and partridges that he

*continued*

especially loved. Francesco and Margherita paid strict attention to what was on their table, an attitude that holds true for many Mediterranean people to this day, rich and poor alike.

Even deep in the heart of a modern city, a guest at a noble table (noble by money or noble by blood but *magari*, as Italians say, noble all the same) will not be surprised to find that the food—the roasted chickens, the grilled meats, the fresh salads, the oil in the cruet, and the wine in the crystal glasses—all comes from the family's own estates, much of it produced under the direct and astute surveillance of the head of the family. And in that it will be no different from, if more abundant than, the same food served in a farmhouse kitchen.

Mary McCarthy once pointed out that in England and America rich and poor eat very differently, while in Italy and France rich and poor eat alike except that the rich eat more. That may not be as true as it once was, but in Mediterranean countries food is still a major link that ties together all social and economic classes in a network of common interests and values and pleasures.

Foreigners often remark that Italians spend their time at table talking about what they're eating right now, what they had at the last meal, and what they're going to have at the next. There's a certain sweet truth in that, and not just for Italians. When the gods of good eating are listening in heaven, they hear at mealtime the same welcome chorus all over the Mediterranean. *"Sahteen!"* they hear. *"Buon appetito! Bon appétit!"*

And we lack even the words to make a translation.

# CHAPTER EIGHT

# VEGETABLE DISHES

"*E*at more vegetables," government diet specialists thunder, and the American Cancer Society chimes in: "Five a day! Five a day!"

Everywhere the message is unmistakable—we Americans have to get more fresh vegetables into our diets, and the way to do that is not by doubling an order of french fries to go with a lunchtime burger. Most people who give even a little thought to the relationship between food and health need no persuading that fresh fruits and vegetables, full of vitamins and fiber along with important trace elements, are the very foundation of a healthy diet. They know too that we should all be consuming more vegetables, including beans and grains, and a good deal less meat and meat products.

Yet, if the message is unmistakable, the method is less than clear. Five a day of *what* exactly? And how am I supposed to do it? Say I have cereal and yogurt at breakfast (because I need the fiber and the calcium) and a half sandwich and a cup of soup at lunch (because I work in a midtown office and that's the most acceptable lunch available). Then I come home tired but willing to put a little effort into the evening meal both because cooking is a good way to come down off a high-tension workday and because I care about the quality of what I put into my body and the bodies of those I nurture and cherish. What should I cook for dinner?

Adding vegetables to the diet doesn't necessarily mean staring at a plate of naked broccoli at suppertime. As Mediterranean cooks know well, vegetables can be slipped into an overall menu plan in dozens of different ways, ways moreover that don't just add bald quotients of nutrients to the diet but add appetizing flavor and color, verve and excitement to the plate. Think of a piece of grilled meat or fish on a plain white dinner plate. It was prepared in the proper manner, brushed with olive

oil, sprinkled with fresh herbs, cooked until just done, and there it sits—interesting, but . . . as Gertrude Stein said of the city of Oakland, "There's no there there."

But add to that grilled meat or fish what Italians call the *contorno* (the word comes from the decorative arts and means "cornice" or "border"). Make the *contorno* broccoli, just for the sake of the argument. Only make it steamed lightly until very tender, so that the deep green color shines, then chopped coarsely and turned in a little *salsina* of warm olive oil with some minced garlic and broken fragments of red chili pepper. A few drops of lemon juice, a few grains of salt, and the *contorno* becomes what it was intended to be—delicious on its own and even more delicious as a border around that plainly grilled piece of meat or fish. It decorates, enhances, and adds to the value, both visual and gustatory, of the plate.

Vegetables are the heart and soul of Mediterranean cooking; grains and beans may be the backbone of the diet, but vegetables are what bring delight to these frankly rather stodgy staples. And not just as an accompaniment to what sits in the center of the plate, for vegetables are often served in their own right. An artichoke, at the height of its late-winter season, is seen as a special thing, something deserving of treatment on its own. As such it may be served as a first course with nothing more to garnish it than a little vinaigrette or green sauce into which the tender ends of the leaves are dipped before scraping them, in that sexy, intimate way of artichokes, between the teeth. Fresh peas in June, the tiny tender *piselli romaneschi* that are raised in little market gardens around Rome, issue forth from the kitchen almost as a stew, mixed with bits of cured-pork *guanciale* and impregnated with olive oil, a first course so tender and juicy it must be eaten with a spoon. Or leeks in winter, fat and alabaster-white, plainly steamed and cooled to room temperature, are served, with stunning simplicity, all by themselves with a mustardy vinaigrette that points up the sweet earthiness, the ancient nature of this fundamental vegetable.

Whatever the vegetable (and I could go on and on listing vegetables that are served on their own in this manner), the treatment makes it a star, to be appreciated for precisely what it is and nothing more. But it does something more than that, something a little more spiritual and philosophical. For in the Mediterranean it is a clear if unstated principle that you don't eat artichokes in August or fresh peas in February or leeks in June or fava beans in October. Acknowledging there is a season for each of these things forces us to recognize and salute their rarity and worth. It ties us ever more deeply to the agriculture that sustains us all, that is the foundation of our life on the planet, and it gives us (or at least it gives me) a sense of humble gratitude for all that went into creating this perfection, the skill of the farmer and the cook, the richness of the earth, the rain and sun and wind that urged the plant to fruition.

In shifting from a meat-based diet to a largely plant-based diet, keep in mind that you will need to increase the quantity of vegetables in each individual serving. Because they lack fat, vegetables are less filling than meat; moreover, vegetables prepared in a Mediterranean style are so delicious that people just naturally seem to want more of them. I find, for instance, that it takes ½ pound of a vegetable like broccoli to make one serving as an accompaniment to a main-course meat or fish. If I am serving broccoli on its own or with other vegetables, I might increase that to ¾ pound, depending on whether it's for lunch or dinner and how many courses come before or after.

Plainly cooked vegetables are made more interesting by adding some sort of very simple sauce. See Chapter 6 for some appropriate sauce recipes. The following are suggestions for combinations.

### Vegetables to Serve with a Light, Mustardy Vinaigrette

Steamed or poached artichokes, asparagus, beets, broccoli, green beans, leeks, steamed greens (spinach, chicory, broccoli rabe).

Mix up the vinaigrette (page 286), adding finely chopped or minced green herbs if appropriate, and simply toss the finished vegetables in it while still warm. For best flavor, serve the vegetables hot or at room temperature but not chilled.

### Vegetables to Serve with Extra-Virgin Olive Oil and Freshly Grated Cheese

Steamed or poached asparagus, broccoli, cauliflower, cabbage, green beans, zucchini.

When the vegetables are tender, drain them and return to the pan. Add about a tablespoon of very fruity olive oil and a tablespoon of freshly grated Parmigiano, feta, manchego, or other cheese for each pound of vegetables. Toss the vegetables over low heat just long enough to warm the oil and soften the cheese. With the oil and cheese you can also add salt, freshly ground black pepper, and minced fresh herbs if you wish.

### Grilled Vegetables

Eggplant, tomatoes, zucchini, onions, peppers.

Slice them thickly (leave peppers whole or in halves), paint with olive oil, and grill over charcoal or wood embers until tender. Serve sprinkled with a few drops of lemon juice.

### Pureed Vegetables

Beets, carrots, celeriac, potatoes, turnips, cut into chunks.

Steam until very tender, then put through a vegetable mill (much better than a food processor) and beat in a little yogurt and/or fruity olive oil, salt, pepper, and herbs.

### Quick Grated Vegetable Sautés

Turnips, beets, cabbage, carrots, celery root.

Grate on the large holes of a grater and sauté in 1 or 2 tablespoons of extra-virgin olive oil, adding salt, pepper, perhaps a little pinch of sugar or a thread of tomato sauce, if desired.

### Vegetables à la Grecque

Artichokes (hearts only), mushrooms, fennel, small baby onions, carrots, very fresh zucchini.

Poach in 3 parts water to 1 part extra-virgin olive oil along with the juice of ½ lemon, 1 teaspoon whole peppercorns, 1 teaspoon whole coriander seeds, a little thyme and parsley, and a bay leaf. Cook, uncovered, until the water boils away and the vegetables are very tender; serve with their aromatic juices poured over them.

## ARTICHOKES

In the early 17th century, Giacomo Castelvetro fled to England from Venice and the hounds of the Inquisition. A man of great culture and humanity, he became concerned that the English diet was poor in fresh vegetables. So, as one of the earliest advocates of the virtues of the Mediterranean diet, he set himself the task of introducing a more healthful table to his English friends. The result was *A Brief Account of the Fruits, Herbs & Vegetables of Italy*, dedicated in 1614 to that great gardener and patron of the arts, Lucy, Countess of Bedford.

This is a remarkable book, a treasure chest of honest, sage, and lucid advice about cultivating and cooking a range of fruits and vegetables so amazing that our modern produce markets look humble by comparison. What makes the book exceptional is Castelvetro's sensibility in the kitchen as much as in the garden. The book rings as true today as it must have done nearly 400 years ago. The Italian original is now available, in a lovely translation by Gillian Riley and with an introduction by the late great British food writer Jane Grigson, called *The Fruit, Herbs & Vegetables of Italy* (Viking, 1989).

Of artichokes Castelvetro writes: "When they are about the size of a walnut they are good raw, with just salt, pepper and some mature cheese to bring out the flavor." The following recipe is based on his instructions for cooking artichokes.

# GIACOMO CASTELVETRO'S ARTICHOKES BRAISED IN BROTH

salt to taste

8   firm, plump artichokes, prepared as directed on page 455, the stalks
      cut back to the base of the fruit

4   cups rich meat stock (page 83) or rich clear white chicken stock
      (page 81)

8   ½-inch-thick slices of crusty country-style bread

4 to 6 tablespoons coarsely grated Parmigiano cheese

freshly ground black pepper to taste

Bring a large pan of lightly salted water to a rolling boil. Drop in the artichokes and cook, uncovered, for about 20 minutes or until the artichokes are just tender. (To test for tenderness, poke the base of an artichoke with a kitchen fork or skewer. It should be slightly resistant.)

Drain the artichokes. Add the stock to the pan in which they cooked, bring it to a boil, and add the artichokes to the stock to finish cooking—about 20 minutes longer.

Meanwhile, toast the bread under the broiler on both sides until golden.

To serve, set the toast in individual soup plates. When the artichokes are done, remove them from the pan, reserving the stock. Spoon about ½ cup stock over each toast slice. Sprinkle with a little of the grated cheese and salt and pepper. Set an artichoke upright on the toast slice and serve. Eat the artichokes, dipping them in the stock and accompanying them with morsels of soaked toast. *Makes 6 to 8 servings*

Nutritional Data, per portion

| | | |
|---|---|---|
| Calories  156 | Carbohydrate  28g | Saturated Fat  1g |
| Protein  9g | Sodium  348mg | Monounsaturated |
| Fat  2g | Cholesterol  3mg | Fat  1g |

VEGETABLE DISHES

# BRAISED ARTICHOKES AND POTATOES

**D**own by the Tiber in the old Roman ghetto, a few restaurants still specialize in Roman Jewish food. Probably the most famous dish is deep-fried *carciofi alla giudea*, whole artichokes plunged into a vat of olive oil and fried until they look like bronzed chrysanthemum souvenirs of a long-ago football game. Because they're made with chokeless Roman artichokes, you don't have to worry about any nasty spines when you eat them. The flesh of the artichoke is roasted and sweet. An unforgettable treat!

Well, you can't really do this without spineless artichokes, something we don't seem to have in this country (although an enterprising grower could develop a good market). This recipe is a takeoff on the idea, with potatoes added.

8   small, firm artichokes

8   small potatoes, peeled

1   medium onion, halved and finely sliced

2   garlic cloves, coarsely chopped

salt and freshly ground black pepper to taste

¼   teaspoon dried thyme, crumbled

2   small bay leaves

⅓   cup extra-virgin olive oil

juice of ½ lemon

lemon wedges for serving

Prepare the artichokes as described on page 455, quartering them and removing the chokes. Drain them and put them with the potatoes in a saucepan large enough to hold all the ingredients. Sprinkle the onion and garlic around the other vegetables; add a little salt and pepper and the thyme and bay leaves. Pour the olive oil over the vegetables and set the pan over medium heat.

When the oil starts to sizzle, add the lemon juice and enough boiling water to come about halfway up the artichokes. Cover the pan tightly and cook for 30 minutes. Then remove the lid, raise the heat, and cook until all the water has evaporated and the artichokes and potatoes are sizzling in the oil, about 10 to 15 minutes longer.

Remove from the heat and serve immediately, with lemon wedges for squeezing over the vegetables. *Makes 6 to 8 servings*

## ASPARAGUS

This is one of the many vegetables that has suffered from overexposure. We now have asparagus in markets year-round, much of it grown in Mexico and of indifferent quality. My asparagus memories go back to my Maine childhood, when it was the first green vegetable, if you don't count dandelions, of the spring. Like many Maine professional men, my father, although a lawyer with a busy practice, was a first-rate gardener. He was particularly proud of his asparagus patch and would go out to the garden in season to gather enough fresh asparagus for our favorite breakfast, poached asparagus on toast. That early Maine asparagus had a flavor (still has) that nothing from Mexico can beat. I still believe that asparagus should be eaten only when it's in season locally. If in Mexico that means year-round; in Maine, as in the Mediterranean, it still means springtime.

# CASTELVETRO'S GRILLED ASPARAGUS

This recipe is based on the 17th-century gentle gourmet's directions for grilling asparagus.

3    pounds plump seasonal asparagus
¼    cup extra-virgin olive oil
salt and freshly ground black pepper to taste
3    tablespoons fresh bitter (Seville) orange juice or 2 tablespoons sweet
         orange juice and 1 tablespoon lemon juice

Preheat the oven broiler or prepare a charcoal fire for grilling. Rinse the asparagus and trim it of any tough ends. The stalks should be roughly equal in length. Place the asparagus in a shallow bowl and add the olive oil. Roll the asparagus around to coat it well with the oil.

Sprinkle another plate with salt and lots of freshly ground black pepper, stirring

VEGETABLE DISHES

with a fork to mix the grains well. Roll each spear of asparagus in the salt and pepper mixture to coat it, not too thickly. Lay the spears on a grid and broil or grill carefully, about 6 to 8 inches from the heat. The asparagus should cook through and be lightly and pleasantly browned on the outside in about 10 minutes.

Heap the asparagus in a clean shallow bowl and pour the citrus juice over, stirring gently to mix well. Serve immediately or set aside at room temperature, stirring occasionally, to absorb the flavors. **Makes 6 to 8 servings**

Nutritional Data, per portion

| | | |
|---|---|---|
| Calories 82 | Carbohydrate 4g | Saturated Fat 1g |
| Protein 3g | Sodium 2mg | Monounsaturated |
| Fat 7g | Cholesterol 0 | Fat 6g |

# ANDALUSIAN ASPARAGUS

Clara Maria de Amezua is Spain's foremost cooking teacher and a tireless promoter of Spanish ways in the kitchen. This is her method for cooking asparagus in a manner that's typical of Spain's vast southern region of Andalusia.

2   **pounds young asparagus**
¼   **cup extra-virgin olive oil or more if needed**
4   **garlic cloves, peeled**
12  **blanched almonds**
1   **2-inch slice of crusty country-style bread, crusts removed, cut into**
        **cubes**
1   **tablespoon very-good-quality sherry vinegar**
**salt and freshly ground black pepper to taste**
1   **cup water**

Preheat the oven to 400 degrees. Trim the asparagus, rinse, and set aside.

Heat half the olive oil in a saucepan over medium heat. Add the garlic, almonds, and bread and sauté, stirring constantly, until all the ingredients are nicely browned—about 5 to 7 minutes. Do not let them burn. Transfer the almonds, garlic, and bread cubes with a slotted spoon to a food processor or

blender. Add the vinegar and about ½ teaspoon salt and process briefly until the mixture is a coarse meal.

In the oil remaining in the pan, sauté the asparagus over medium-low heat until the stalks change color and start to become tender—about 5 to 7 minutes. (You may need to add another tablespoon or two of oil.) Remove the asparagus and place in an ovenproof gratin dish. Bring the water to a boil and pour it over the asparagus. Then sprinkle the almond-bread mixture over the top. Bake for 15 minutes or until the asparagus is thoroughly cooked and most of the liquid has boiled away. Serve immediately. ***Makes 4 to 6 servings***

### Nutritional Data, per portion

| | | |
|---|---|---|
| Calories 162 | Carbohydrate 13g | Saturated Fat 2g |
| Protein 6g | Sodium 85mg | Monounsaturated |
| Fat 11g | Cholesterol 0 | Fat 8g |

## BEETS

If beets are young and tender, their tops can be cooked and served with them. Cook the tops and roots separately so that any sand clinging to the roots will not get mixed into the tops. Cut the tops to within an inch of the roots, rinse them carefully, chop into 1-inch pieces, and steam them in about 1 inch of boiling water. In a separate pan, boil the rinsed beets. Drain, slip the skins off, and cut them into slices or chunks, depending on their size. Mix them in with the beet tops and serve with a vinaigrette (page 286) or with olive oil and lemon juice.

In Greece, small young beets, boiled in abundant salted water until they are tender, are drained, the skins slipped off, and served with skordalia (page 291).

VEGETABLE DISHES

# THE ALL-IMPORTANT BRASSICAS

Broccoli and broccoli rabe, cauliflower, Brussels sprouts, cabbage and kale, turnip greens and mustard greens, and their many sisters and cousins are all members of a family botanists call the *brassicas*—*B. oleracea* for broccoli, *B. rapa* for turnips and mustard greens. (You will also sometimes see the family referred to as cruciferous vegetables because of the cross-marking at the tip of the emerging flower bud that is characteristic of all family members.)

Brassicas are worth mentioning because they are all, without exception, nutritional powerhouses, full of beta-carotene and vitamins C and K; of minerals like calcium, phosphorus, and potassium; and of riboflavin and folacin. While the balance of these elements may change from one variety to another, they are all important. Moreover, they're excellent sources of dietary fiber. So critical are these vegetables that at least one of them should appear on your table every day.

Fortunately this is not difficult. Throughout history people have recognized the importance of these vegetables, and one or more of them are characteristic of just about every food culture in the earth's temperate zones (they are difficult to grow in the tropics). This means that the family has become wide-ranging, with an enormous variety of textures, shapes, and flavors—though always with that underlying peppery sharpness, especially in their raw state, that marks all brassicas. Don't assume that only brassicas typical of Mediterranean kitchens and gardens are suitable to use in Mediterranean-style cooking. Asian cuisines also have an interesting range of brassicas (bok choy, gai choy or Chinese mustard, gai lon or Chinese broccoli, and many more). They are increasingly available in American produce markets, and I often use them in these Mediterranean recipes.

## BROCCOLI AND BROCCOLI RABE

Italian cooks are in a class by themselves when it comes to broccoli and its stronger-flavored relative broccoli rabe—or broccoletti di rape or rapini, two other names by which this amazing vegetable is also known in American markets. Broccoli rabe's Chinese cousin, called variously *choy sum* or *Chinese (white) flowering cabbage*, is equally good in these recipes.

George Bush to the contrary, broccoli and its relatives are delicious vegetables, full of the antioxidants beta-carotene and vitamin C and important trace elements. See also the recipe for *orecchiette alla Barese* (page 182), little ears of pasta with a sauce of broccoli rabe.

# STEAMED BROCCOLI WITH GARLIC AND HOT PEPPERS

3    pounds fresh broccoli or broccoli rabe
2    garlic cloves, thinly sliced
½    cup extra-virgin olive oil
1    small dried hot red chili pepper or more to taste
½    teaspoon salt or more to taste

A head of broccoli can be cooked as a single unit, but it's easier to trim away the thick lower stems and cut the head into individual florets with a couple of inches of stem attached. Rinse in a colander and set aside.

Broccoli rabe should be rinsed carefully and any yellow or slimy leaves and coarse stems discarded. For convenience in cooking, cut the flowering stems and leaves into 2-inch-long pieces.

In a saucepan large enough to hold all the broccoli, start to sauté the garlic gently in the oil over medium-low heat. Add the chili pepper, broken into smaller pieces or sliced. (If you want less heat, discard the seeds and membranes.) Cook the garlic and pepper together, stirring, until the garlic slices are soft but not brown, about 7 to 10 minutes.

Add the broccoli with the water clinging to it and more water to come about 1 inch up the sides of the pan. Cover the pan and give it a shake to distribute the oil and flavorings. Cook over medium-low heat for 12 to 15 minutes or until tender. Serve immediately, using the pan juices as a sauce. ***Makes 6 to 8 servings***

### Nutritional Data, per portion

| | | |
|---|---|---|
| Calories 151 | Carbohydrate 6g | Saturated Fat 2g |
| Protein 3g | Sodium 165mg | Monounsaturated |
| Fat 14g | Cholesterol 0 | Fat 11g |

## CABBAGE AND KALE

Cabbage is a vegetable that is so easily ruined by overcooking that it's a wonder anyone bothers to eat it anymore. And in fact, not many people do. It's one of those vegetables people seem to get more often in restaurants than anywhere else, and there too it's served with an indifference that borders on contempt. The obligatory creamy coleslaw in a sticky sweet and sour sauce is not cabbage at its finest. Nor is the smell of overcooked cabbage—the cabbage in a big pot of water that sat on the back of the stove and simmered all day, lending its unforgettable aroma to tenement staircases.

Poor cabbage! Fortunately, smart young chefs are beginning to take a look at the maligned vegetable and devise ways to make it more acceptable. It isn't hard, especially when you combine cabbage with olive oil, garlic, and aromatic herbs. Cabbage should be cooked either briefly in a large quantity of water or—if you must cook it a long time, as in recipes for braised cabbage—in a small quantity of oil and/or stock.

## SIZZLING CABBAGE WITH GARLIC

**U**se small, firm round cabbages or crinkly-leaved Savoy cabbages. Peel away the outer layer of leaves and rinse before using.

2   small cabbages
salt to taste
1   garlic clove, minced
½   cup extra-virgin olive oil
freshly ground black pepper to taste

Preheat the oven to 400 degrees. Cut the trimmed cabbages into quarters and remove part of the central stem, but leave enough to hold the leaves together.

Bring a large quantity of lightly salted water to a rolling boil. Plunge the cabbage quarters into the water and boil rapidly for 5 to 7 minutes or until the cabbage starts to soften but does not get limp.

Combine the garlic and oil in a shallow bowl like a soup plate. When the cabbages are done, drain them and immediately dip each quarter in the garlicky olive oil, turning it to coat each side of the cabbage. Then set it in an oval gratin dish and sprinkle with salt and pepper. When all the cabbage quarters have been done, pour any remaining oil over the cabbages in the dish, cover the dish with aluminum foil, and slide the dish into the oven for about 5 minutes or just long enough to set the oil really sizzling. Remove the foil and let the cabbages sizzle a little longer—no more than 5 minutes—then serve immediately in the sizzling pan with slices of crusty country-style bread for sopping up the juices. *Makes 8 servings, ¼ cabbage per serving*

Nutritional Data, per portion

| | | |
|---|---|---|
| Calories  161 | Carbohydrate  9g | Saturated Fat  2g |
| Protein  2g | Sodium  31mg | Monounsaturated |
| Fat  14g | Cholesterol  0 | Fat  11g |

# BRAISED CHESTNUTS WITH KALE

**P**eeling chestnuts is tedious but worth it for the fine rich flavor and the textural contrast they add to any cabbage dish. When we're in Italy for Thanksgiving, this robustly flavored dish is a favorite on our table, made with *cavolo nero*, a type of very dark green kale that stands in the garden all winter, getting sweeter with each frost. It's an important source of vitamins when there's nothing else fresh to eat. You can't find *cavolo nero* in this country unless you grow it yourself, but our kale is almost as good.

24  fresh chestnuts

1  medium onion, diced

2  tablespoons extra-virgin olive oil

2  ounces slab bacon, diced (optional)

1  cup rich meat stock (page 83)

2½ pounds kale

salt and freshly ground black pepper to taste

Preheat the oven to 350 degrees. Meanwhile, prepare the chestnuts. With a sharp paring knife, carefully cut a cross on the rounded side of the chestnut, cutting right through the tough peel and into the flesh. When all the chestnuts are done, spread them out on a cookie sheet and roast for about 15 minutes or until the chestnuts have burst open along the cuts. Remove from the oven and peel the chestnuts, pulling away both the outer shell and the furry inner skin that clings to the nut. Stubborn chestnuts should be returned to the oven for further toasting.

In a pan large enough to hold all the chestnuts, cook the onion in the olive oil until it is soft but not brown—about 10 minutes. Add the bacon if desired and continue cooking until the bacon starts to render its fat—about 5 minutes. Turn the peeled chestnuts into the pan, raise the heat to medium, and stir the chestnuts to coat them with fat. When the fat starts to sizzle, pour in the stock, cover the pan, lower the heat to medium-low, and cook for 20 to 35 minutes, until the chestnuts are tender but still firm.

Meanwhile, clean the kale and cut away the hard stems. Hold a bunch of kale leaves together in your hand and sliver the leaves every ½ inch or so. When all the kale is prepared, rinse it carefully in a colander under running water. Add the kale to a large saucepan and cook it in the water clinging to the leaves, watching carefully and adding a very little boiling water if necessary to keep it from sticking. Cook for about 20 to 35 minutes or until the kale is very tender.

When the kale and chestnuts are done, combine them with their juices. Set over medium-high heat and cook rapidly, stirring frequently, to reduce the juices and concentrate them. Taste and add salt and pepper if desired. A few drops of lemon juice can also be added. **Makes 6 to 8 servings**

Nutritional Data, per portion

| | | |
|---|---|---|
| Calories 165 | Carbohydrate 28g | Saturated Fat 1g |
| Protein 4g | Sodium 47mg | Monounsaturated |
| Fat 5g | Cholesterol 0 | Fat 3g |

## CARROTS

Finely chopped carrot and celery, along with onion and garlic and sometimes a little minced parsley, form the *battuto* or *soffrito*, which, like the French mirepoix, forms the basis of so many soups, stews, and sauces in the Mediterranean kitchen. I mention this because, in our urge to get more fresh vegetables into the diet, we might ignore this very good and efficient source. A medium carrot, minced and cooked in a sauce that will eventually serve six or eight people, may not seem like much in the way of a vegetable, but looked at as one part of a multifaceted and vitamin-rich combination, it takes on more importance.

See also the recipes for carrot salads, pages 58–60.

# CARROTS IN AGRODOLCE

### Italian Sweet and Sour Carrots

Cooking vegetables in a sweet and sour sauce is an old Italian technique that I learned years ago from Elizabeth David's *Italian Food*. Mrs. David suggested the method for zucchini, but I find it works very well with fresh sweet carrots.

3   pounds firm, tender carrots, peeled and sliced no more than ½ inch
       thick

salt to taste

1   tablespoon minced shallot or onion

¼   cup extra-virgin olive oil

freshly ground black pepper to taste

3   tablespoons red wine vinegar

1   tablespoon sugar

2   tablespoons minced flat-leaf parsley

Drop the carrots into a pan of rapidly boiling lightly salted water. Cook for about 5 minutes or long enough to tenderize the carrots slightly but not cook them through. Drain the carrots.

Cook the shallot or onion in the olive oil over medium-low heat until just softened—about 5 to 10 minutes. Add the drained carrots and stir to coat the slices well with the oil. Grind some black pepper over, add a few tablespoons of hot water, cover the pan, and cook gently for about 5 minutes. Uncover the pan and pour in the vinegar. When the vinegar is boiling, add the sugar and stir the carrots in the liquid while it cooks down to a small amount of syrup that coats the carrots nicely. When the carrots are cooked, turn them out in a warm serving bowl, sprinkle with the parsley, and serve immediately. *Makes 6 servings*

### Nutritional Data, per portion

| | | |
|---|---|---|
| Calories  178 | Carbohydrate  23g | Saturated Fat  1g |
| Protein  2g | Sodium  71mg | Monounsaturated |
| Fat  10g | Cholesterol  0 | Fat  7g |

# OVEN-BRAISED CARROTS

2    medium onions, halved and sliced
¼    cup extra-virgin olive oil
3    pounds young, tender carrots, peeled
1    cup rich meat stock (page 83) or rich clear white chicken stock
       (page 81)
**salt and freshly ground black pepper to taste**
⅓    cup freshly grated Parmigiano cheese

Preheat the oven to 375 degrees. In an ovenproof casserole, gently stew the onions in the olive oil over medium-low heat until they are soft but not browned—about 10 to 15 minutes.

Cut the carrots in half lengthwise, then into sections about 2 inches long. Add the carrots to the casserole and stir to mix well. Pour in the stock with salt to taste and a good quantity of black pepper. When the stock comes to a boil, cover the casserole with a lid or heavy aluminum foil and bake for about 40 minutes or until the carrots are very soft.

Remove the casserole from the oven, stir the carrots, and sprinkle the cheese over the top. Return to the oven, uncovered, and cook until the stock has reduced to a few tablespoons of bubbling syrup and the cheese is melted. Serve immediately.
*Makes 6 to 8 servings*

Nutritional Data, per portion

| Calories  162 | Carbohydrate  20g | Saturated Fat  2g |
| Protein  4g | Sodium  130mg | Monounsaturated |
| Fat  9g | Cholesterol  3mg | Fat  6g |

# CARROTS IN A CHERMOULA SAUCE

**A** Moroccan mixture of aromatics suspended in oil, chermoula is used as a sauce for vegetables or a marinade for fish. Feel free to change the quantities or to add and subtract—each cook in Morocco has his or her own balance, which, it is always claimed, is the only authentic and genuine chermoula. Only cumin and sweet paprika seem to be constants, although cilantro is almost always present. If you don't care for the flavor of cilantro, use parsley instead. This is the version Sakina el-Alaoui, a fine Marrakesh cook, uses for carrots and zucchini. I've also used it successfully with autumn squashes.

2   **pounds carrots, peeled and cut into 2-inch chunks**

FOR THE CHERMOULA:

1   **garlic clove, crushed with the flat blade of a knife**

2   **tablespoons minced cilantro**

2   **tablespoons minced flat-leaf parsley**

½   **teaspoon salt**

1   **teaspoon sweet paprika**

¼   **teaspoon ground cumin**

3   **tablespoons extra-virgin olive oil**

**juice of 1 lemon**

If the carrots are very thick, cut each chunk in half lengthwise. Put the carrots into a saucepan and just barely cover with boiling water. Cook, partially covered, until they are soft and tender—about 15 minutes.

Meanwhile, chop the garlic and mix with the cilantro, parsley, salt, paprika, and cumin. Beat in the oil and lemon juice. Taste and adjust the seasoning, adding more salt or lemon juice if you wish.

As soon as the carrots are done, drain them and while they are still hot pour the chermoula sauce over. Stir gently to cover the carrot pieces with the sauce. Set aside to marinate for at least 30 minutes before serving. Serve at room temperature. *Makes 6 to 8 servings*

| Calories   91 | Carbohydrate   11g | Saturated Fat   1g |
| Protein   1g | Sodium   173mg | Monounsaturated |
| Fat   5g | Cholesterol   0 | Fat   4g |

## CAULIFLOWER

# CAULIFLOWER WITH A VEIL OF GRATED CHEESE

1   tablespoon extra-virgin olive oil

about 3 pounds firm white cauliflower

2   cups light clear white chicken stock (page 81)

½   cup coarsely grated aged cheese, such as aged pecorino or manchego,
       Asiago, or Parmigiano

salt and freshly ground black pepper to taste

Preheat the oven to 250 degrees. Lightly oil a gratin dish large enough to hold all the cauliflower.

Break the cauliflower into small florets of uniform size. Bring the stock to a boil in a pan large enough to hold the cauliflower. (The stock should fill the pan to a depth of 1 inch; add water if needed.) When the liquid boils, add the cauliflower. Cover and steam for about 8 to 10 minutes or until the cauliflower is just tender. Using kitchen tongs, remove the cauliflower, reserving the cooking liquid, and place in the gratin dish. Drizzle the remaining olive oil over the cauliflower and place the dish in the oven while you finish the sauce.

Rapidly boil down the stock remaining in the pan until you have just a few tablespoonfuls of syrupy sauce. This should take about 7 to 10 minutes.

Remove the gratin dish and raise the oven temperature to 400 degrees. Spoon the sauce over the cauliflower, then distribute the cheese over the top. Add salt and pepper. Return the dish to the oven just long enough for the cheese to melt and brown very lightly. Remove from the oven and serve immediately. *Makes 6 to 8 servings*

**Nutritional Data, per portion**

| | | |
|---|---|---|
| Calories  66 | Carbohydrate  4g | Saturated Fat  2g |
| Protein  4g | Sodium  135mg | Monounsaturated |
| Fat  4g | Cholesterol  5mg | Fat  2g |

## EGGPLANT

One of the most endearing traits of the Turks is their candid pride in their own cuisine. Every Turkish cookbook begins with two pronouncements: (1) that Turkish is one of the world's three great cooking styles, the other two being French and Chinese; and (2) that there are at least 200 recipes for preparing eggplants in traditional Turkish cookery. One might dispute the primacy of the "great" cuisines, but one would not dispute the prominence of the eggplant in Turkey and in every country from the Balkans around through North Africa where the influence of Turkish culture and the Turkish kitchen has been felt. Eggplants have a uniquely voluptuous flavor and texture—which is probably why the Turks, a sensuous people, love them so much.

Eggplants, or aubergines to give them their English name (which is closer to the names used in the Mediterranean), actually came into the Mediterranean with the Arabs, but the vegetable achieved apotheosis with the introduction of New World tomatoes, so much so that there is scarcely a recipe for eggplant that doesn't include tomatoes in some form, even if it's just a tablespoon of tomato paste diluted with water and added to a sauce.

The greatest problem with eggplant is its ability to soak up oil or any other kind of cooking fat. For traditional cooks this was hardly a problem, particularly when the fat was something as delicious as fresh green olive oil or perhaps the salt-preserved tail fat from a fat-tailed sheep.

For contemporary cooks the problem of fat absorption is said to be solved by salting the cut eggplants, whether in slices or chunks, and setting them aside to let the bitter juices drain away. I don't find our eggplants to be particularly bitter, and I am not persuaded that salting them reduces their ability to absorb oil to any significant degree. Sometimes I salt them; sometimes I don't—it really depends on the amount of other work a dish entails.

When it's appropriate, you can control the amount of oil by slicing the eggplants rather thickly, painting the slices on both sides with a small amount of oil, and grilling or broiling them. This is one of the best vegetables for grilling over charcoal or wood embers. The creamy flesh absorbs a delightful smokiness from

the fire. Small eggplants can be cut in half, the cut sides scored and drizzled with olive oil, before grilling; larger eggplants should be sliced—lengthwise if you wish. For other eggplant recipes, see ratatouille (page 44), baba ghanouj (page 34), and eggplant dip with yogurt (page 35).

The number of eggplant types available in American produce markets seems to increase each season. Best for Mediterranean preparations are the familiar dark violet to black pear-shaped ones, sometimes called *Italian*. Look for eggplants that are not more than 6 to 8 inches long and have a good heft to them.

# KARNI YARIK

### *Turkish Eggplant Stuffed with Meat and Rice*

**O**f the whole repertoire of Turkish ways with eggplant, this is one of the most popular and a good illustration of how a small amount of meat can be used as a flavoring, rather than a primary ingredient, to add richness to main-course vegetable presentations. Serve *karnı yarık* as a main course with çaçik (page 37) on the side and a copious salad such as fattoush (page 73).

Dried mint, rather than fresh, is used here for its sweet intensity.

1¼ cups finely chopped yellow onion

about ¼ cup extra-virgin olive oil or more if needed

1    cup finely chopped sweet green pepper, preferably cubanelle or
       Italian long peppers

½    pound lean ground lamb

1¼ cups chopped fresh or well-drained canned Italian plum tomatoes

1    tablespoon dried mint

1    tablespoon ground cumin

½    teaspoon hot red pepper flakes

salt and freshly ground black pepper to taste

1    cup cooked long-grain rice (about ½ cup raw)

¼    cup minced flat-leaf parsley

8    Italian eggplants

1    very ripe tomato, thinly sliced

⅓    cup freshly grated Parmigiano cheese

VEGETABLE DISHES

Prepare the stuffing: In a skillet over medium-low heat, gently cook the onion in 2 tablespoons of the olive oil. After about 5 minutes, when the onion starts to soften, add the green peppers. Cook for 10 to 15 minutes or until the vegetables are soft but not browned. Remove the vegetables from the skillet, along with the cooking oil, and set aside.

Add the lamb to the skillet and sauté quickly, raising the heat and stirring constantly until the lamb is thoroughly browned—about 5 to 7 minutes. (If the lamb is especially lean, you might need to add a teaspoon or more of olive oil.) Scrape the lamb with its fat into a sieve to drain. Discard the fat and return the lamb to the skillet along with the onion-pepper mixture. Add the chopped tomatoes and seasonings and mix well. Cook, stirring occasionally, over medium-low heat until the tomatoes have released all their liquid and the sauce has thickened but not dried out—about 15 minutes. Taste and adjust the seasonings.

Remove the skillet from the heat and stir in the rice and parsley, mixing well. Set aside until you're ready to use it. (The stuffing can be prepared a day or more ahead of time and refrigerated, but bring it back to room temperature before proceeding with the recipe.)

Preheat the oven to 350 degrees. Rinse the eggplants. Leave them whole, but prick them with a fork in half a dozen places. (If you use larger eggplants, cut them in half lengthwise, score the cut surfaces in a crisscross pattern no more than ½ inch deep, and then paint them with a very little olive oil.) Place the eggplants on a lightly oiled baking sheet (cut side up if you're using halves) and bake for 30 to 40 minutes or until the flesh is soft. Set aside until cool enough to handle.

Using a table knife and spoon, gently cut a slit down one side of the whole eggplants so that you can open them up and push the flesh to either side—but don't cut them into two separate halves. Pile up several heaped tablespoonfuls of stuffing in the center of each eggplant. (If you're using halved eggplants, break up the cooked flesh with the tines of a table fork to make room for the stuffing.) Be careful not to cut through the eggplant skin.

Set the stuffed eggplants in a lightly oiled rectangular roasting pan. Raise the oven temperature to 450 degrees. Place 1 or 2 tomato slices on top of each eggplant and drizzle a teaspoon of olive oil over each. Sprinkle a little grated cheese on top of the tomato slices. Bring a teakettle of water to a boil and pour water into the roasting pan to a depth of about ½ inch. Bake for 15 to 20 minutes or until the tops are nicely browned.

Set the eggplants aside until you're ready to serve. They should be served warm or at room temperature but not cold. ***Makes 6 to 8 servings***

<u>Nutritional Data, per portion</u>

| | | |
|---|---|---|
| Calories  290 | Carbohydrate  36g | Saturated Fat  3g |
| Protein  13g | Sodium  112mg | Monounsaturated |
| Fat  12g | Cholesterol  23mg | Fat  8g |

# GRATIN OF EGGPLANT WITH AN ORANGE-TOMATO SAUCE

**T**his dish can easily be made vegetarian by simply eliminating the bacon, in which case you should increase the olive oil to 2 tablespoons.

Salt the eggplant slices if you wish, but a strong-flavored sauce like this one will conceal any lurking acerbity.

1   ounce slab bacon, diced, about ⅓ cup

⅓   cup extra-virgin olive oil

1 or 2 medium onions, chopped

½   garlic clove, crushed and minced

1   small carrot, chopped

1   celery rib, chopped

1½ pounds tomatoes, seeded and chopped, or 1 28-ounce can whole
      plum tomatoes, drained

zest of 1 medium orange, cut into julienne strips or chopped

salt and freshly ground black pepper to taste

¼   cup chopped or slivered fresh basil leaves

1½ pounds eggplant

2 or 3 tablespoons freshly grated Parmigiano cheese to taste

In a sauté pan over medium heat, gently cook the bacon in 1 tablespoon of the olive oil until the bacon fat starts to run and the edges of the bacon begin to

VEGETABLE DISHES

brown—about 5 to 7 minutes. Stir in the onions, garlic, carrot, and celery and continue cooking, stirring occasionally, until the vegetables are soft but not browned—about 10 minutes. Add the tomatoes and orange zest, turn the heat up to medium-high, and cook, stirring, until the tomato juice has nearly evaporated and the sauce is thick and jammy—about 15 minutes. Taste the sauce and adjust the seasoning, adding a little salt and a lot of freshly ground pepper. Off the heat, stir in the basil and set the sauce aside. The sauce can be prepared well ahead of time and refrigerated until you're ready to continue cooking. Add about ¼ cup water to the sauce to keep it from scorching and reheat before continuing with the recipe.

Preheat the oven to 400 degrees. Slice the eggplant no more than ½ inch thick. Use some of the remaining oil to oil a baking sheet lightly. Lay the eggplant slices on the sheet and, using a paintbrush or pastry brush, paint each slice with a thin coating of oil. Roast the eggplant slices for about 20 minutes or until they are brown on top and creamy inside. Remove the baking sheet from the oven.

Preheat the broiler. Top each eggplant slice with a heaped tablespoon of the orange-tomato sauce, then sprinkle with a little grated cheese. Return to the oven and broil for 5 to 7 minutes or just long enough to melt the cheese and bubble the sauce.

For a more handsome presentation, lightly oil an oval gratin dish and spread a very thin layer of orange-tomato sauce over the bottom. Set the eggplant slices on the sauce, top with more sauce and cheese, and broil. Serve directly from the gratin dish. *Makes 6 servings*

Nutritional Data, per portion

| | | |
|---|---|---|
| Calories 219 | Carbohydrate 18g | Saturated Fat 3g |
| Protein 4g | Sodium 104mg | Monounsaturated |
| Fat 16g | Cholesterol 5mg | Fat 11g |

# EGGPLANT STUFFED WITH RICOTTA AND HERBS

**T**his is a rare recipe for eggplant, one that doesn't include tomatoes. It goes back to pre-tomato Italy and was inspired by the great gourmet Castelvetro's instructions for preparing eggplant.

2  pounds small eggplant

salt to taste

1  medium onion, chopped

2  garlic cloves, minced

⅓  cup extra-virgin olive oil

⅓  cup long-grain rice, parboiled for about 8 minutes to soften the grains

¼  cup minced flat-leaf parsley

¼  cup minced green herbs such as borage, lovage, basil, summer savory,
       thyme, oregano, or a combination

¾  cup ricotta cheese

dash of Tabasco sauce or cayenne pepper (optional)

freshly ground black pepper to taste

½  cup toasted unseasoned bread crumbs

¼  cup freshly grated Parmigiano cheese

Cut each eggplant in half lengthwise and, using a small paring knife or a grapefruit spoon, carefully hollow out the halves, leaving a shell not more than ½ inch thick. Sprinkle a little salt over the eggplant shells and turn them upside down to drain in a colander or on a cake rack while you proceed with the recipe. Coarsely chop the eggplant flesh.

In a sauté pan over medium-low heat, gently sauté the chopped eggplant with the onion and garlic in 2 tablespoons of the olive oil until the vegetables are thoroughly softened but not brown—about 15 minutes. Remove the pan from the heat and stir in the rice, herbs, and ricotta. Add Tabasco if you wish. Mix well, taste, and add salt and pepper if desired.

Preheat the oven to 350 degrees. Rinse the eggplant shells to rid them of excess salt and pat the insides dry with paper towels. Lightly oil a baking dish. Mound the stuffing loosely in each shell and set the shells in the baking dish. Sprinkle the tops with the bread crumbs and cheese and drizzle the remaining oil over them.

Add about ½ inch of boiling water to the baking pan and bake for 30 to 40 minutes or until the tops are golden brown. Remove from the oven and let cool slightly before serving. *Makes 6 to 8 servings*

Nutritional Data, per portion

| | | |
|---|---|---|
| Calories  228 | Carbohydrate  21g | Saturated Fat  4g |
| Protein  7g | Sodium  209mg | Monounsaturated |
| Fat  14g | Cholesterol  14mg | Fat  9g |

## FAVAS OR BROAD BEANS

Broad beans, to give them their proper English name, are hardly known at all in this country. All the more curious since they were a familiar staple of colonial kitchen gardens. Nowadays, they're more likely to be known by their Italian name, *fave* or *favas*, and to be available only in Greek or Italian neighborhood produce shops. Why this should be so is a culinary mystery. The fact is that they are delicious, with a delicately earthy flavor that becomes exaggerated and even unpleasant as they mature.

Most American cookbooks, if they mention broad beans at all, suggest not only shelling them from the thick green pods (lined with a soft fuzz in which the beans lie like green babes in a nursery) but also peeling away the outer skin from each bean. To which I say, if you have to go through all that, favas ain't worth eating.

Broad beans should be eaten as they are in the Mediterranean, when they are young and tender and the pods are limber rather than stiff and tough. Shell them if you wish, although the most slender beans can be eaten pods and all, just topped and tailed and cut into lengths like string beans. Or you can mix the two together, shelled beans and beans in the pod, as Middle Eastern cooks do. It is hard to find fava beans of this quality here, but they are very easy to grow and don't take up a lot of space in the home garden, where they happily tolerate cold weather. (In Mediterranean gardens the seeds are planted at Christmas, about 3 inches underground, and the plants spring up in early March, so there are usually plenty of broad beans for a late Easter.)

The market gardens that surround Rome and supply much of the produce for the city are famous for the quality of their broad beans, as well as for the tiny, sweet *piselli romaneschi*, Roman peas, that arrive next after broad beans. Faith Willinger, a

food writer who has lived in Italy for many years, introduced me to the word *scorpacciata*, which my dictionary translates as "blowout." This is precisely the term for what Romans do during the brief season when these broad beans and later peas are around—eat their fill and then eat some more, because their time is so brief.

Don't even think of trying the next two recipes unless you raise your own vegetables or otherwise have access to the very finest quality of fresh, young produce.

## FAVA (BROAD) BEANS OR PEAS ROMAN STYLE

Like many Roman preparations, these are traditionally made with *strutto*, a very fine and tasty lard, and *guanciale*, the cured cheeks of pork, a mixture of fat and lean. That is still the best way (and remember that lard is lower in cholesterol than butter), but since good lard and cured pork cheeks are all but impossible to find in this country, I have adapted the recipe.

¼ cup finely diced onion

⅓ cup extra-virgin olive oil

2 or 3 slices of prosciutto, diced, or 2 ounces slab bacon, blanched in
     boiling water and diced

3 to 4 pounds tender young fava (broad) beans, shelled or, if the pods are
     tender, cut up like string beans

1 cup light clear white chicken stock (page 81) or water

salt and freshly ground black pepper to taste

1 tablespoon minced flat-leaf parsley

½ teaspoon minced fresh thyme or ¼ teaspoon dried, crumbled

In a saucepan large enough to hold all the beans, gently cook the onion in the olive oil until it is very soft but not brown—about 10 to 15 minutes. Add the prosciutto and stir until the fat starts to run, about 5 to 7 minutes. Add the beans and stir to coat them well. Pour in the stock and add the salt, pepper, parsley, and thyme.

Raise the heat to a fast boil. Cook quickly, without covering, so that the beans

VEGETABLE DISHES

retain their bright color and all their flavor. By the time the cooking is done and the beans are tender, there should be just a few spoonfuls of rather syrupy liquid in the bottom of the pan, good for sopping up with wedges of country bread. Remove from the heat and serve immediately. ***Makes 6 to 8 servings***

### Nutritional Data, per portion

| | | |
|---|---|---|
| Calories 244 | Carbohydrate 23g | Saturated Fat 2g |
| Protein 14g | Sodium 266mg | Monounsaturated |
| Fat 12g | Cholesterol 7mg | Fat 7g |

# KOUKIA ME ANGINARES

### *Broad Beans with Artichokes*

**T**his Greek dish, which is substantial enough to be a main course (perhaps with some bread and a good sheep's milk cheese to go along with it), requires not only top-quality broad beans but also fresh small young artichokes, preferably the lovely violet ones, two to a serving. These are almost impossible to find in this country, so use larger artichokes, counting on one to a person.

12  **small artichokes or 6 large ones**

1½ **pounds fresh young broad beans**

1   **medium onion, coarsely chopped**

2   **tablespoons minced fresh dill**

1   **teaspoon minced fresh mint leaves**

½   **cup extra-virgin olive oil**

**juice of 1 lemon**

**salt and freshly ground black pepper to taste**

Prepare the artichokes as described on page 455. Large artichokes should be quartered and the chokes removed.

Shell the broad beans. The youngest and slenderest can be kept in the pods but should be topped and tailed, like green beans, and cut into approximately 1½-inch lengths. Put the beans, onion, and herbs in a pan large enough to hold all the vegetables. Add the olive oil and set the pan over medium-low heat. Cook, stirring

frequently, for 10 to 15 minutes or until the onions have softened but not browned. Then push the drained artichokes into the bean mixture and add the lemon juice, a little salt and pepper, and water just to come to the tops of the vegetables. Cover tightly and cook, just simmering, for about 20 minutes or until the artichokes are tender enough to be pierced by the point of a knife. Remove from the heat and let stand for 20 to 30 minutes before serving. ***Makes 6 servings***

Nutritional Data, per portion

| Calories 342 | Carbohydrate 36g | Saturated Fat 3g |
|---|---|---|
| Protein 13g | Sodium 237mg | Monounsaturated |
| Fat 20g | Cholesterol 0 | Fat 15g |

## FENNEL

For inexplicable reasons, fennel (the blanched white bulb, that is, not the seeds) is often called *anise* in American produce markets. If you don't know what to look for, ask the produce manager for anise—that's fennel, and you won't find it called anything else in cookbooks.

Italians believe raw fennel cleanses the palate and often serve it as an end-of-the-meal salad, thickly sliced and dressed with a little olive oil and lemon juice or wine vinegar. It is also occasionally served braised with a sprinkling of grated Parmigiano or aged pecorino cheese; follow the directions for Cauliflower with a Veil of Grated Cheese (page 381).

## GREEN BEANS

What kind of green beans? Well there are the flat, broad ones called *romano beans* and little haricots verts, as narrow as shoelaces, and deep violet beans that turn green when cooked and sturdy crisp round pole beans, like Blue Lake and Kentucky Wonder, cherished by American gardeners. Fresh green beans, like sweetcorn and dead-ripe juicy tomatoes, are one of summer's great pleasures, not to be confused with the flaccid long-distance things that decorate supermarket produce sections out of season. Test the beans before you buy: if they break in two with a satisfying snap, they are ready to eat.

Green beans, steamed whole if they're small, broken into 2-inch pieces if they're larger, are an elegant hot first course, dressed with a light vinaigrette or just with plain olive oil, lemon juice, and salt and pepper. Cook a large quantity, at least

¾ pound per serving, and heap them in a big china bowl. They're so good they're addictive, like potato chips, and there are almost never enough.

Cooking times in the next two recipes may come as a surprise since we've heard for years about not *over*cooking vegetables. Yet Mediterranean cooks often stew green beans, and other vegetables too, for a long time, especially in combinations like these. The result is a remarkably good-tasting exchange of flavors.

# GREEN BEANS WITH OLIVE OIL AND TOMATOES

Green beans stewed until meltingly tender in a thick and aromatic sauce of fresh tomatoes are ubiquitous throughout the Mediterranean. When fresh green beans are at their peak in local markets, consider increasing the quantities and making this a main course, perhaps with salad, a wedge of cheese, and some good bread. It's a way of honoring the goodness of things as simple and ordinary as beans.

3 pounds green beans, topped and tailed, cut into 2-inch lengths if desired

1 cup finely chopped onion

1 garlic clove, finely chopped

¼ cup extra-virgin olive oil

2 cups chopped fresh tomatoes or chopped drained canned whole tomatoes

1 teaspoon sugar

1 teaspoon salt or more to taste

1 tablespoon fresh lemon juice

In a saucepan large enough to hold the beans, cook the onion and garlic in the oil over medium heat until the onion is thoroughly golden and starting to brown—about 10 to 15 minutes. Rinse the beans and, with the water that clings to them, turn them into the onions. Stir to mix everything together well, cover, and lower the heat to medium-low. Cook for about 5 minutes, just to meld the flavors.

Uncover the pan and add the tomatoes, sugar, and salt. Cover again and cook for about 40 minutes or until the beans are thoroughly softened and the tomatoes have dissolved into a sauce that naps the beans. Stir in the lemon juice. Taste and adjust the seasoning, adding more salt if necessary. ***Makes 6 to 8 servings***

Nutritional Data, per portion

| | | |
|---|---|---|
| Calories 127 | Carbohydrate 15g | Saturated Fat 1g |
| Protein 3g | Sodium 289mg | Monounsaturated |
| Fat 7g | Cholesterol 0 | Fat 6g |

# FASSOLAKIA YIAHNI

### *Ragout of Fresh Green Beans*

**D**iane Kochilas, a young Greek-American who has readopted her parents' homeland, was one of the first to introduce Americans to the great and delicious variety of regional Greek food. This recipe is adapted from her book, *The Food and Wine of Greece.* Diane tops the dish with crumbled feta cheese to make a main-course offering.

¼ cup extra-virgin olive oil

2 medium onions, halved and very thinly sliced

1 garlic clove, chopped

3 pounds fresh green beans, topped and tailed

4 medium potatoes, peeled and cut into chunks

4 or 5 tomatoes, peeled (page 454) and coarsely chopped, or 1 28-ounce
     can whole tomatoes, drained and coarsely chopped

1 small dried hot red chili (optional)

salt and freshly ground black pepper to taste

In a pan large enough to hold all the vegetables, warm the olive oil over medium-low heat. Add the onions and garlic and cook, stirring occasionally, until the onions are meltingly soft—about 10 to 15 minutes. Add the beans and potatoes and stir with a wooden spoon for a few minutes, until the vegetables are coated with oil and beginning to soften.

VEGETABLE DISHES

Add the tomatoes and chili and season with salt and pepper. Add a few tablespoons of water and cover the pot tightly. Simmer for about 1 hour, adding a little boiling water from time to time if necessary. The vegetables are done when they are very soft and the tomatoes are reduced to a thick sauce that naps the vegetables. The dish can be served hot but is more traditionally served at room temperature. *Makes 6 servings*

### Nutritional Data, per portion

| | | |
|---|---|---|
| Calories 251 | Carbohydrate 39g | Saturated Fat 1g |
| Protein 7g | Sodium 27mg | Monounsaturated |
| Fat 10g | Cholesterol 0 | Fat 7g |

## LEEKS

Leeks are an essential ingredient in most broths and stocks, but they are also quite wonderful on their own, milder than onions but with a similar rich flavor. Gardeners blanch leeks, usually by hoeing soil up around the growing stems to retain their creamy whiteness. This leaves sandy traces between the leaves, so they need careful cleaning. To clean leeks, insert a knife tip about 1½ inches from the base and slide it back toward the green tips to slice the leek in half, leaving it attached at the base. Cut away the tough green leaves, but leave a little green for a more attractive presentation. Rinse very well in running water to get rid of the sand.

# OVEN-BRAISED LEEKS

8    fat leeks, rinsed well

2    cups light clear white chicken stock (page 81)

⅓    cup extra-virgin olive oil

juice of 1 lemon

1    celery rib, cut into 1-inch pieces

¼    teaspoon dried oregano, crumbled

1    bay leaf

1    teaspoon black peppercorns

1½ teaspoons coriander seeds

salt and freshly ground black pepper to taste

Preheat the oven to 375 degrees. Arrange the leeks in a single layer in a shallow ovenproof pan or gratin dish.

In a medium saucepan, combine all the remaining ingredients except salt and pepper. Bring to a boil and simmer for about 10 minutes, then pour over the leeks. Add a little salt and ground pepper to taste.

Cover the pan tightly with aluminum foil and bake for 15 to 20 minutes or until the leeks are just soft. Remove the foil and continue cooking for 5 to 10 minutes or until the juice in the pan is reduced to a syrupy liquid and the leeks are starting to brown. Set aside and cool to room temperature before serving. Serve with crusty country-style bread for sopping up the juices. *Makes 6 to 8 servings*

### Nutritional Data, per portion

| | | |
|---|---|---|
| Calories  151 | Carbohydrate  16g | Saturated Fat  1g |
| Protein  2g | Sodium  36mg | Monounsaturated |
| Fat  10g | Cholesterol  0 | Fat  7g |

## MUSHROOMS

Mushrooms used in Mediterranean cooking are almost always wild, and the variety is staggering. Among the favorites most frequently seen in market stalls are fat porcini or cèpes (*Boletus edulis*), lovely apricot-colored chanterelles, and trompettes de la mort (a sort of black chanterelle that, despite the name—trumpets of death—is thoroughly safe to eat). There are also the dangerous but delicious ovoli or *Amanita caesarea*—dangerous because they are closely related to the deadly *Amanita phalloides*, or death cap, especially in the infant, egglike stage that gives them the name *ovoli*. Italians make a delicious salad from fresh ovoli, thinly shaved and combined with julienne strips of celery and shards of Parmigiano cheese, all dressed with good oil and lemon juice and sometimes with a few shavings of white truffle over the top.

Mushrooms like these grow in deciduous woods and fields throughout the United States, but I cannot in good conscience recommend that you gather your own unless you know what you are about. If you are ignorant but curious, get in touch with a local mycological society—your local extension agent or state university department of botany should be able to help you.

Porcini or cèpes are the easiest mushrooms to recognize and are abundant in many parts of this country. If you find a lot, you might want to dry them for a source of intense flavor to add to stews, soups, and sauces. Here's how you do it:

Collect firm, healthy specimens, without any trace of bugs or slugs. Brush away any earth or leaves clinging to them, but *do not wash them*. Slice them about ½ inch thick and arrange the slices on a screen. Place the screens in the sun on a dry day and just leave them. You'll have to turn them occasionally and bring them in at night when the dew starts to collect. If they don't dry sufficiently in one day, set them out again in the morning. Alternatively, you can set them in a very slow oven—best is an oven with only the pilot light lit, but those are rare. Or use a commercial dehydrator. When the slices are thoroughly dry and powdery, they can be stored in a tin canister, but don't put them in plastic bags, or they'll mildew and turn soft.

Fresh wild mushrooms are increasingly available in the produce sections of specialty food stores. Shiitake, portobello, and cremini mushrooms, although cultivated, often have good flavor. But if you can't find wild or flavorful cultivated mushrooms, cook dried porcini with fresh commercial button mushrooms, as in the following recipe, to give the supermarket variety a taste of the wild.

# GRATIN OF POTATOES AND MUSHROOMS

**D**ried mushrooms should be soaked before being used in very hot, but not boiling, water, then drained (don't discard the water!) and thoroughly rinsed to remove all traces of grit. The soaking liquid should be strained through a fine-mesh sieve and added to the cooking juices for flavor; or it can be frozen and added to soups and sauces. The flavor of dried wild mushrooms can vary enormously from one packet to the next. Keep that in mind in following this recipe and don't hesitate to alter the amount suggested if you find the flavor stronger or milder than you expected.

¾   **ounce dried porcini or more to taste**

½   **pound fresh button mushrooms**

¼   **cup extra-virgin olive oil**

1   **pound baking potatoes, peeled and thinly sliced**

**salt and freshly ground black pepper to taste**

2   **medium tomatoes, thinly sliced, or 4 canned whole tomatoes, drained**
      **and coarsely chopped**

¼   **cup grated sharp provolone or Parmigiano cheese**

¾   **cup grated fresh mozzarella cheese**

Soak the mushrooms, following the directions above. When they're softened, strain the liquid into a bowl through a sieve lined with a double layer of cheesecloth. Rinse the mushrooms carefully, squeeze dry, and chop coarsely.

Wipe the button mushrooms with a damp paper towel to remove any grit. Slice them about ¼ inch thick and sauté in 2 tablespoons of the olive oil in a heavy skillet over medium-high heat. Cook for about 5 minutes, stirring frequently. The mushrooms should be golden and just starting to soften.

Preheat the oven to 400 degrees. Brush an oval gratin dish with a tablespoon of the remaining olive oil. Arrange the potatoes in a layer in the dish and pour in the mushroom-soaking liquid with a little salt and pepper. Scatter the fresh mushrooms and the porcini over the potatoes. Arrange the tomatoes in a layer over the mushrooms. Sprinkle with a little more salt, if desired, and more pepper. Drizzle the remaining tablespoon of olive oil over the top. Bake until the potatoes are just tender, 20 to 25 minutes.

Remove the dish from the oven. Combine the provolone and mozzarella and sprinkle the cheese on top of the tomatoes. Return the dish to the oven and bake until the cheese is melted and forms a golden crust, about 10 minutes. Remove from the oven and let stand for about 15 minutes before serving. *Makes 6 to 8 servings*

Nutritional Data, per portion

| | | |
|---|---|---|
| Calories  157 | Carbohydrate  13g | Saturated Fat  2g |
| Protein  5g | Sodium  46mg | Monounsaturated |
| Fat  10g | Cholesterol  10mg |  Fat  6g |

## ONIONS

# SWEET AND SOUR BABY ONIONS

**T**hese are often served as an antipasto or on an hors d'oeuvre tray, but they are a delightful accompaniment to a plain roast pork or a grilled salmon fillet. The onions should be the small variety sometimes called *pickling* or *pearl onions*. The important thing is that they be of uniform size.

1½ **pounds small onions, peeled**

¼   **cup white wine vinegar or sherry vinegar**

1   **tablespoon sugar**

2   **tablespoons extra-virgin olive oil**

3   **tablespoons tomato puree**

2   **small bay leaves**

**salt and freshly ground black pepper to taste**

1   **cup water**

Combine all the ingredients in a saucepan; the onions should just be swimming in liquid. Bring to a boil and cook, uncovered, at a gentle simmer for about 20 minutes or until the onions are softened but not falling apart. The sauce should reduce and become quite syrupy. If the sauce is still too thin when the onions have finished cooking, remove the onions with a slotted spoon and rapidly boil the sauce down to a syrup. The onions can be served hot but are better at room temperature. *Makes 6 servings*

Nutritional Data, per portion

| | | |
|---|---|---|
| Calories 92 | Carbohydrate 12g | Saturated Fat 1g |
| Protein 1g | Sodium 34mg | Monounsaturated |
| Fat 5g | Cholesterol 0 | Fat 4g |

# ROASTED ONIONS

An old-fashioned but delicious way to treat very large onions. Once upon a time, these were roasted in the fireplace embers—imagine the fragrance that perfumed the room!

3   tablespoons extra-virgin olive oil

6   very large yellow (Spanish) onions, unpeeled

salt and freshly ground black pepper to taste

Preheat the oven to 375 degrees. Rub the unpeeled onions with 1 tablespoon of the oil. Place them on the oven rack and roast for 40 minutes or until the onions are tender all the way through.

Transfer the onions to a warm serving dish. Peel them as soon as you can handle them and cut them into quarters or smaller pieces if you wish. Drizzle the remaining oil over them, sprinkle with salt and pepper, and serve immediately.

For a more dramatic presentation, serve the roasted onions in their skins and let diners peel them at the table. Pass a cruet of extra-virgin olive oil to pour on them, along with salt and pepper. *Makes 6 servings*

Nutritional Data, per portion

| | | |
|---|---|---|
| Calories 178 | Carbohydrate 31g | Saturated Fat 1g |
| Protein 6g | Sodium 36mg | Monounsaturated |
| Fat 5g | Cholesterol 0 | Fat 4g |

## PEAS

"The noblest of vegetables," Castelvetro called them in the early 17th century, "especially those whose pods are good to eat as well"—proof that we clever moderns didn't invent edible-podded peas the day before yesterday.

VEGETABLE DISHES

# PISELLI ALLA ROMANA

### *Roman Sweet Young Peas*

**P**iselli alla romana are cooked exactly as in the fava (broad bean) recipe on page 389, adjusting the cooking time to the more tender peas. Do be sure to cook them very thoroughly, however—they should be very soft and almost soupy in this presentation.

## PEPPERS

# RED AND YELLOW PEPPERS WITH GARLIC AND BLACK OLIVES

**S**erve these peppers on their own as a first course or as a garnish for a simple risotto or pilaf.

| | |
|---|---|
| 2 | pounds bell peppers, preferably red and yellow |
| 6 | garlic cloves, chopped |
| ¼ | cup extra-virgin olive oil |
| ⅓ | cup pine nuts |
| ½ | cup pitted black olives, preferably Kalamata |
| 1 | 3-inch strip of orange zest, finely slivered |
| ⅓ | cup slivered fresh basil leaves |
| salt to taste | |

Roast and peel the peppers as directed on page 455. Slice them lengthwise about ½ inch thick and set aside.

In a skillet over medium heat, sauté the garlic in the oil, stirring constantly, until it is soft—about 7 minutes. Add the pine nuts and continue cooking until the nuts start to take on a little color, then stir in the black olives and orange zest. Cook, stirring, for 3 to 4 minutes to let the flavors develop. Stir in the peppers with their juice, the basil, and a little salt if desired. Cook for another few minutes to reduce the pepper liquid slightly. Serve hot or at room temperature. *Makes 4 to 6 servings*

**Nutritional Data, per portion**

| | | |
|---|---|---|
| Calories 174 | Carbohydrate 11g | Saturated Fat 2g |
| Protein 3g | Sodium 102mg | Monounsaturated |
| Fat 15g | Cholesterol 0 | Fat 10g |

## POTATOES

# PATATAS A LA RIOJANA

### *Potatoes Simmered in a Spicy Stew*

**A**na Espinosa comes from a little pueblo near the cathedral city of Burgos in Old Castile, the heartland of Spain. These potatoes are her grandmother's recipe, but a similar sort of potato stew is served almost daily throughout the region. Sometimes, she says, it's the main dish of a meal, especially if enriched with sausages or meaty pork spareribs cooked along with the potatoes. This version has just a small amount of sausage for flavoring. Vegetarians can omit the sausage.

The chilies used in Spain have just enough heat to make you sit up and take notice. The best ones to use here are dried New Mexico (Anaheim) chilies. Removing seeds and inner membranes before soaking will also cut down on the heat of the chilies.

½   **cup chopped onion**

¼   **cup extra-virgin olive oil**

3   **pounds potatoes, peeled and thickly sliced**

**about 6 ounces Spanish-style paprika-flavored chorizo or garlicky**

      **kielbasa, cut into ¼-inch-thick slices**

2   **cups water**

1   **green bell pepper, thickly sliced**

¼   **cup coarsely chopped flat-leaf parsley**

2   **tablespoons sweet paprika**

3   **dried red New Mexico (Anaheim) chilies, soaked in water**

¼   **teaspoon hot paprika**

**salt to taste**

VEGETABLE DISHES

In a deep kettle that will hold all the ingredients, sauté the onion in the oil over medium-high heat until it starts to soften but is not browned—about 10 minutes. Add the potatoes and continue cooking, stirring to mix well. Add the sausage, again stirring, and when the potatoes are just beginning to brown along their edges— about 10 minutes—add a cup of the water. Cook for about 5 minutes. The potatoes will absorb much of the water during this time.

Add the second cup of water when the first has been pretty well absorbed, together with the green pepper, parsley, and sweet paprika.

Remove the chilies from the soaking liquid and discard the seeds and membranes. With a spoon edge, scrape away the inner red pulp. Discard the skins and add the pulp to the potatoes, stirring to mix well. Cook for 8 to 10 minutes, until the potatoes are tender. Add the hot paprika and stir carefully to mix without breaking up the potatoes. Taste and add salt if desired. The potatoes should be fork-tender with just a little rich red sauce to spoon over their tops. Serve immediately. ***Makes 6 to 8 servings***

### Nutritional Data, per portion

| | | |
|---|---|---|
| Calories 256 | Carbohydrate 29g | Saturated Fat 3g |
| Protein 7g | Sodium 240mg | Monounsaturated |
| Fat 14g | Cholesterol 14mg | Fat 8g |

# GRATIN OR TIAN OF POTATOES

**T**his traditional Provençal preparation is an indication that a good gratin need not be swimming in butter, cream, and cheese like the delectable ones from the Dauphiné. Potatoes are much more frequently used in the Mediterranean than we might expect.

¾ **cup light clear white chicken broth (page 81)**

3 **pounds waxy potatoes, such as Red Bliss, peeled and thinly sliced**

2 **garlic cloves, minced**

⅓ **cup fruity extra-virgin olive oil**

**salt and freshly ground black pepper to taste**

2 **bay leaves**

Preheat the oven to 375 degrees. Bring the broth to a simmer in a small saucepan.

Toss the potatoes and garlic in a bowl with the olive oil until the potatoes are well coated. Arrange the slices in an oval gratin dish. Add salt and pepper to taste and tuck the bay leaves in with the potatoes. Pour the simmering stock over them. Cover the gratin dish with aluminum foil and bake for 40 minutes, by which time the potatoes should have absorbed most of the stock. Uncover the pan and continue baking for 10 minutes to brown the tops of the potatoes. Serve immediately. *Makes 6 to 8 servings*

Nutritional Data, per portion

| | | |
|---|---|---|
| Calories 208 | Carbohydrate 28g | Saturated Fat 1g |
| Protein 3g | Sodium 16mg | Monounsaturated |
| Fat 10g | Cholesterol 0 | Fat 7g |

## GARLIC-ROASTED POTATOES WITH BLACK OLIVES

2 pounds potatoes, unpeeled, cut into chunks, or whole small new
   potatoes

4 garlic cloves, chopped

3 fresh rosemary sprigs

1 small hot dried red chili, crumbled

salt and freshly ground black pepper to taste

¼ cup extra-virgin olive oil

24 large black olives, pitted and coarsely chopped

2 tablespoons minced flat-leaf parsley

Preheat the oven to 425 degrees. In a bowl, toss the potatoes with the garlic, rosemary, chili pepper, salt and pepper, and olive oil. Spread the potatoes about an inch or more thick in a small roasting pan or a gratin dish—thick enough so that you can't see the bottom of the pan through the potatoes. Roast, stirring occasionally with a wooden spoon, for about 25 minutes or until they are golden brown.

Remove from the oven and stir in the olives. Taste and add more pepper and salt if desired—the olives may be sufficiently salty. Sprinkle with parsley and serve. *Makes 6 servings*

VEGETABLE DISHES

# GARLIC MASHED POTATOES
# WITH OLIVE OIL

If you thought potatoes could be mashed only with masses of butter and cream, try this for a new vision of that essential accompaniment to the blue-plate special. Baking potatoes, because of their drier flesh, seem to take more kindly to mashing than waxy potatoes. Don't try to mash potatoes with a food processor—they just get gluey.

2½ **pounds baking potatoes**

**salt to taste**

6   **garlic cloves, peeled**

⅓   **cup extra-virgin olive oil or more to taste**

**freshly ground black pepper to taste**

Peel the potatoes if you wish. Or peel half and leave the other half with the skins on. Cut the potatoes in half and plunge them into a large pot of rapidly boiling water. Add the whole garlic cloves and cook, covered, until the potatoes are very tender—about 25 minutes.

Drain the potatoes and garlic well and turn them into a warm serving bowl. Using a potato masher, mash them coarsely, adding the olive oil a little at a time. When all the oil has been added, taste and add more salt if needed and an abundance of black pepper. Serve immediately. *Makes 6 servings*

THE MEDITERRANEAN DIET COOKBOOK

## SPINACH

Spinach is said to have originated in the East, possibly in Persia, and was brought into the Mediterranean by the Arabs when they swept across North Africa and into Spain, southern France, and Sicily. Certainly the many preparations of spinach with pine nuts and dark or golden raisins suggest an Arab origin.

# GARBANZOS KON SPINAKA

### *Sephardic Spinach with Chick-Peas from Greece*

This recipe is adapted from a favorite and most unusual book, *Cookbook of the Jews of Greece*, by Nicholas Stavroulakis, founder of the Jewish Museum of Athens and a profound scholar of Mediterranean culture. Greek Jews came from two directions, the Sephardic from Spain, from which country they were expelled in 1492, and the Romaniote Jews from Palestine, who emigrated much earlier. Stavroulakis points out that there were Jews in Thessalonica at the time St. Paul visited them in his evangelizing efforts, and they must have been there long before.

As with many Jewish recipes, nothing marks this as specifically Jewish—spinach is cooked with chick-peas all over the Mediterranean. But it was given to Stavroulakis by a Greek Jew from Larissa. And its name is Ladino, the language of Sephardic Jews, a dialect of old Spanish mixed with words of Turkish and Greek origin. It's tempting to see this as a recipe the Sephardim brought with them from Arab Spain to Greece.

This is delicious served over steamed rice and makes a first-rate vegetarian main course.

1   **large onion, thinly sliced**

2   **tablespoons extra-virgin olive oil**

1½ **cups chick-peas, soaked overnight, or use the quick-soak method**
      **(page 454)**

1   **pound fresh spinach**

½   **cup minced fresh dill**

**juice of 2 lemons**

**salt and freshly ground black pepper to taste**

Gently sauté the onion slices in the olive oil over medium-low heat until the onions are soft but not browned—about 10 to 15 minutes. Drain the chick-peas and add them to the onions, turning them to coat with the oil. Cover with water—about 1 cup will do—and simmer gently until the chick-peas are tender, about 40 minutes, adding a little *boiling* water from time to time if necessary.

Meanwhile, clean the spinach thoroughly, rinsing it in several changes of water and cutting away the thick stems. When the chick-peas are tender, add the spinach with the water clinging to its leaves and the dill and continue cooking very slowly until the spinach is tender—about 10 minutes. At the end of the cooking time, stir in the lemon juice and adjust the seasoning, adding salt if necessary and pepper.
**Makes 6 servings**

Nutritional Data, per portion

| | | |
|---|---|---|
| Calories 253 | Carbohydrate 37g | Saturated Fat 1g |
| Protein 12g | Sodium 58mg | Monounsaturated |
| Fat 8g | Cholesterol 0 | Fat 4g |

## LIGURIAN SPINACH WITH GOLDEN RAISINS AND PINE NUTS

2   pounds fresh spinach

¼   cup golden raisins

¼   cup pine nuts

3   tablespoons extra-virgin olive oil

½   medium onion, minced

½   garlic clove, minced with the onion

salt and freshly ground black pepper to taste

pinch of freshly grated nutmeg (optional)

Rinse the spinach carefully in 2 or 3 changes of water. Place the spinach in a large pot over medium heat, cover, and cook, stirring occasionally, in the water clinging to the leaves for about 10 minutes—don't overcook the spinach. Drain thoroughly and chop coarsely. You should have about 3 cups spinach. (The spinach can be cooked and chopped well ahead of time and then refrigerated until you're ready to use it.)

THE MEDITERRANEAN DIET COOKBOOK

Cover the raisins with very hot water and set aside to refresh and plump.

In a saucepan over medium-low heat, gently sauté the pine nuts in the olive oil until golden, about 7 to 10 minutes, being careful not to burn them. Remove them from the oil and set aside. Add the onion and garlic to the oil and cook, stirring frequently, until soft but not brown—about 10 minutes. Stir in the chopped spinach and mix to combine thoroughly. Just before serving, drain the raisins and stir them into the spinach along with the toasted pine nuts. Add salt, pepper, and a little nutmeg if desired. Serve immediately. *Makes 4 to 6 servings*

Nutritional Data, per portion

| Calories | 148 | Carbohydrate | 12g | Saturated Fat | 2g |
|---|---|---|---|---|---|
| Protein | 6g | Sodium | 121mg | Monounsaturated | |
| Fat | 11g | Cholesterol | 0 | Fat | 7g |

## SQUASH

Except for zucchini, we don't think of squash as a Mediterranean vegetable. Yet pumpkins and winter squash also have a role to play, most often in combination with other vegetables, as in couscous (page 195). One of the most stunning dishes I've ever been presented was a *risotto alla zucca*, made with golden pumpkins (page 204). Moroccan chermoula makes a fine sauce for barely steamed chunks of autumn squash.

# STEAMED SQUASH WITH A
# CHERMOULA SAUCE

about 1½ pounds autumn squash such as turban, acorn, butternut, or
    kabocha
ingredients for chermoula sauce (page 380)

Cut the squash in half and remove the seeds and fibers from the center. Peel the
squash and cut into 2-inch chunks. Place the squash in a steamer basket over
rapidly boiling water. Cover and cook for 10 to 15 minutes or until the squash is just
tender.

Meanwhile, mix together the chermoula sauce, following the directions on
page 380. As soon as the squash is done, remove it from the heat and while it is still
warm pour the chermoula over it, stirring gently to mix well without breaking up
the squash. Set aside to marinate for at least 30 minutes before serving. Serve at
room temperature. *Makes 6 to 8 servings*

### Nutritional Data, per portion

| | | |
|---|---|---|
| Calories 74 | Carbohydrate 7g | Saturated Fat 1g |
| Protein 1g | Sodium 139mg | Monounsaturated |
| Fat 5g | Cholesterol 0 | Fat 4g |

## TOMATOES

What would the Mediterranean table be without tomatoes? Well, it would be an
ancient Mediterranean table since this amazing New World fruit arrived in the
Mediterranean only after 1492 and did not become widely used until long after that.
Giacomo Castelvetro's great compendium, written in 1614, doesn't even mention
tomatoes, and although they appeared as botanical curiosities in early herbals, the
first European recipes that we know of are in Antonio Latini's cookbook published
in Naples in 1692. Still, tomatoes did not become widespread until the later 19th
century.

Today they flourish: in early summer there are pinkish-green salad tomatoes,
plump and tasty and intended to be eaten raw and somewhat underripe; later there
are dead-ripe tomatoes, packed with juice, and plum-shaped tomatoes full of flesh

to be turned into sauces; and later still, in the dead of winter, you can glimpse the welcome sight of little winter tomatoes, small globes as bright red as a Christmas ornament, the whole plant inverted and hanging by its roots from a market stall.

Recently I've been alarmed to see crates of flavorless Dutch hothouse tomatoes on sale in Mediterranean markets, obviously one of those achievements of which the European Community is so proud. But I refuse to believe that cooks and diners will readily give up their recently acquired heritage.

## PROVENÇAL STUFFED TOMATOES

6    large very ripe but firm tomatoes

½    teaspoon salt

1    large garlic clove, crushed with the flat blade of a knife

1    oil-packed anchovy fillet or 1 salted anchovy, prepared as directed on
      page 471

3    tablespoons finely chopped flat-leaf parsley

3 to 4 tablespoons toasted unseasoned bread crumbs to taste

3    tablespoons extra-virgin olive oil

1    tablespoon chopped fresh basil leaves

freshly ground black pepper to taste

Cut each tomato in half horizontally and gently squeeze out the seeds inside. Set the tomato halves, cut side up, on a lightly oiled baking sheet. Preheat the oven to 425 degrees.

Mix the salt and garlic in a mortar and pound with the pestle until you have a paste. Then pound in the anchovy and the parsley. When the parsley has been thoroughly incorporated, add a tablespoon of the toasted bread crumbs and mix well. Add a tablespoon of the olive oil and stir to make a thick paste.

Using a narrow spatula, smear some of the garlic paste on each tomato half. Mix the remaining bread crumbs with the basil leaves and sprinkle over each tomato half. Then drizzle the remaining oil over the halves.

Bake the tomatoes on the baking sheet for about 20 minutes or until they are thoroughly softened and starting to brown on top. Remove and serve hot, or set aside and serve at room temperature later. ***Makes 6 servings***

Nutritional Data, per portion

| | | |
|---|---|---|
| Calories 111 | Carbohydrate 10g | Saturated Fat 1g |
| Protein 2g | Sodium 255mg | Monounsaturated |
| Fat 8g | Cholesterol trace | Fat 6g |

## HOTHOUSE TOMATOES MADE TO TASTE LIKE SOMETHING ELSE

This is not so much a recipe as a trick, to be used when you can't get good fresh tomatoes and still feel they must be a part of your table. What the trick does is concentrate the small amount of flavor in these tomatoes and intensify it. It comes from my daughter Sara, who, after a childhood spent happily munching her way around the Mediterranean, grew up, to the surprise of no one but her parents, to become a restaurant chef.

Preheat the oven to 200 degrees. Rinse as many tomatoes as you need, cut out their cores (where the stems are), sprinkle in a few grains of salt and pepper and a few drops of extra-virgin olive oil, and set them in a well-oiled roasting pan. Place the pan in the oven and, after about an hour at this slow heat, sprinkle a little more salt and drizzle a little more oil over each tomato. The skins of the tomatoes will have cracked and the tomatoes themselves settled in the pan a little as their juice has evaporated. After another hour of roasting, sprinkle a little finely minced garlic over the cracked tomatoes, along with a few grains of sugar. Continue roasting for up to 3 hours, from time to time adding a little more oil, salt, and sugar—but the sugar in very small quantities because you don't want the tomatoes to dissolve into jam.

## TURNIPS

Another neglected vegetable, like cabbage, that is starting to find favor with bold restaurant chefs. Smaller turnips are usually sweeter than larger ones. For most uses I prefer the small white turnips with purple-blushing tops to the yellow rutabagas or swedes.

# GRATIN OF PURPLE-TOPPED TURNIPS

2   tablespoons extra-virgin olive oil, plus a little to oil the dish

2½ pounds purple-topped turnips, scrubbed and sliced not more than
      ¾ inch thick

salt to taste

¼   cup finely chopped shallot

½   garlic clove, finely chopped

1   cup rich meat stock (page 83) or clear white chicken stock (page 81)

¼   cup minced flat-leaf parsley

2   tablespoons finely grated Parmigiano cheese

freshly ground black pepper to taste

Preheat the oven to 400 degrees. Lightly oil an oval gratin dish. Prepare the turnips while you bring a large pan of lightly salted water to a rolling boil. Drop the turnip slices in and cook for about 5 to 7 minutes, until they're just tender. Drain and arrange the slices in the gratin dish.

Meanwhile, cook the shallot and garlic in the olive oil in a saucepan over medium-low heat, stirring occasionally, until the vegetables are tender but not brown—about 10 minutes. Add the stock and parsley and, when the stock is boiling, pour it over the turnip slices in the gratin dish. Sprinkle with the cheese and a little pepper. Cover with aluminum foil and bake for 20 to 30 minutes or until the turnip slices are very tender. Remove the foil, baste the slices with a little of the pan juices, and bake for 5 minutes more, just to glaze the top of the turnips. Serve immediately. ***Makes 6 servings***

**Nutritional Data, per portion**

| | | |
|---|---|---|
| Calories 109 | Carbohydrate 14g | Saturated Fat 1g |
| Protein 3g | Sodium 168mg | Monounsaturated |
| Fat 5g | Cholesterol 2mg | Fat 4g |

## ZUCCHINI AND ZUCCHINI BLOSSOMS

Young, firm zucchini, not more than 6 inches long, can be steamed whole in lightly salted water for just a few minutes until tender, then cut into chunks and turned while still hot in the chermoula described on page 380. Sliced zucchini are very good sautéed in olive oil, or use them in the recipe for *agrodolce* (page 378); zucchini need not be parboiled, as the carrots are, before being cooked in the sauce.

# CASTELVETRO'S ZUCCHINI WITH SWEET HERBS

Castelvetro, the great 17th-century gourmet, took pains to explain to his English readers what he meant by "sweet herbs": "It is the name our housewives give to a special mixture of parsley, spinach beets, mint, borage, marjoram, basil and thyme (but with more of the first two since the others are so strongly flavoured), which they wash and then chop very fine. We use this mixture to season many dishes."

3   pounds zucchini, about 6 to 8 inches long, sliced no thicker than
        ½ inch

salt to taste

2   bunches of scallions

⅓   cup extra-virgin olive oil

2   tablespoons minced flat-leaf parsley

1   teaspoon minced fresh mint leaves

1   teaspoon minced fresh borage, if available

½   teaspoon minced fresh thyme

freshly ground black pepper to taste

¼   cup water

In a pot large enough to hold the sliced zucchini, bring about 2 inches of lightly salted water to a rolling boil. Tip the zucchini in, cover, and cook for about 3 to 5 minutes or until the zucchini is just tender. Drain and set aside.

Slice the scallions on the diagonal, green tops included, into 1-inch-long pieces. In a skillet large enough to hold the zucchini comfortably, cook the scallions in the olive oil over medium-low heat until the scallions have started to soften, about 10 minutes. Stir in all the herbs and the salt and pepper. Add the zucchini and stir gently in the oil to mix everything together well. Raise the heat and, when the zucchini starts to sizzle, add the water. Continue cooking until the water has boiled away, the zucchini and scallions are tender, and the sauce is syrupy. Taste and adjust seasoning, adding salt, pepper, or, if desired, a few drops of fresh lemon juice. Serve immediately. *Makes 6 to 8 servings*

Nutritional Data, per portion

| | | |
|---|---|---|
| Calories 113 | Carbohydrate 7g | Saturated Fat 1g |
| Protein 3g | Sodium 10mg | Monounsaturated |
| Fat 10g | Cholesterol 0 | Fat 7g |

# KOLOKYTHIA YAKHNI

### *Greek Zucchini Stew*

This method can be adapted for many other vegetables, such as green beans, broad beans, or even little new potatoes. Or a combination of two or three vegetables might be used.

2   medium onions, sliced

⅓   cup extra-virgin olive oil

1   pound tomatoes, chopped, or 1 14- to 16-ounce can whole tomatoes,
      drained and chopped

1   teaspoon sugar

½   cup water

salt and freshly ground black pepper to taste

2   pounds small zucchini, cut in half lengthwise unless very small

1   teaspoon minced fresh mint leaves

1   teaspoon minced fresh dill

VEGETABLE DISHES

In a saucepan over medium-low heat, gently stew the onions in the olive oil until soft but not brown—about 10 minutes. Add the tomatoes and sugar and cook for another 10 minutes. Then pour in the water, add salt and pepper, and stir well. When the tomato sauce has come back to a boil, add the zucchini with the mint and dill. Cook gently until the zucchini is very tender, about 15 minutes. Let stand for 20 minutes before serving. *Makes 6 servings*

Nutritional Data, per portion

| | | |
|---|---|---|
| Calories  167 | Carbohydrate  13g | Saturated Fat  2g |
| Protein  3g | Sodium  13mg | Monounsaturated |
| Fat  13g | Cholesterol  0 | Fat  10g |

## FIORE DI ZUCCHINI FRITTI

### *Fried Zucchini Blossoms*

For those who have access to the flowers of zucchini, this is a wonderful way to use them. One is always told to use only the male flowers of the zucchini, but I must confess I can't tell the difference. Don't worry about using female flowers (the ones that produce the zucchini fruit)—I have never met a gardener who complained about an underabundance of zucchini.

These are as addictive as potato chips—and probably about as healthy too. Be prepared to spend your time at the stove frying up zucchini blossoms while your loved ones gather around and consume them as fast as they emerge.

Pure olive oil (see page 459) has a higher smoke point at 410 degrees than unrefined extra-virgin oil and is better for deep frying. Use it alone or in combination with flavorless vegetable oil.

24  **just-picked zucchini blossoms**
1  **quart pure olive oil or 2 cups olive oil and 2 cups flavorless vegetable
      oil**
1  **cup cool water**
1  **cup unbleached all-purpose flour**
**salt and freshly ground black pepper to taste**
**coarse salt for serving**

Rinse the blossoms lightly in running water and set aside in a colander to drain. Put the oils in a frying pan or deep fryer and heat up gradually over medium heat.

Put the water in a bowl and sift over it about ½ cup of the flour, beating with a fork as you sift it in. Continue adding flour, beating as you do so, until the batter is the consistency of light cream. Add salt and black pepper.

Test the oil temperature by dropping a little cube of plain bread in it. When it's hot enough, the bread cube will sizzle and quickly turn golden brown. Dip a zucchini blossom in the batter, coating it completely. Briefly hold it over the bowl to let excess batter drain off, then drop it in the hot fat. Let it sizzle on one side until golden brown, then turn with a long-handled kitchen fork and cook briefly on the other side. Remove with the fork or a slotted spoon and set on a rack over paper towels to drain.

You can do about 6 of these at a time without reducing the temperature of the oil too much. Don't try to crowd the pan. When all the zucchini blossoms have been fried, if they have not already been eaten, pile them up in a bowl, sprinkle with a little coarse salt, and serve. *Makes 6 servings, counting 4 blossoms for each person (You may need more—in fact, you may end up frying until all the zucchini plants in the garden have been stripped of their flowers.)*

Nutritional Data, per portion

| | | |
|---|---|---|
| Calories 138 | Carbohydrate 12g | Saturated Fat 1g |
| Protein 2g | Sodium 1mg | Monounsaturated |
| Fat 9g | Cholesterol 0 | Fat 7g |

# MISTA DI VERDURA COTTA

In Roman restaurants you will find *mista di verdura cotta*, cooked mixed greens, richly dressed with oil and vinegar or lemon juice, served at room temperature as a first course or starter. There will be small portions of three or four different kinds of greens, almost inevitably including spinach, as well as other seasonal greens and green vegetables—chicory, broccoli, broccoli rabe, the first little green beans of the season, perhaps asparagus, or "wild asparagus," which is actually hop shoots—Romans call them *lùpoli*. Every part of the selection will have come from the remarkable fields and gardens that surround Rome and provide so much of the city's foodstuffs. This dish is a great favorite with Roman weight watchers.

Quality (as usual) is what counts in this preparation: Seek out the freshest produce, rigorously excluding any suggestion of wilt and rejecting out-of-season vegetables such as those big tasteless asparagus. Try to balance the selection between bitter (broccoli rabe, turnip greens, etc.) and sweet (spinach, chard, etc.). Or prepare any one of these and serve it on its own or as a *contorno*, an accompaniment, for a main-course meat or fish.

> 1½ pounds each of at least 2 of the following greens: spinach, chard,
> broccoli rabe, turnip greens
>
> ¾ pound slender asparagus
>
> ¾ pound small green beans or haricots verts
>
> FOR EACH SEPARATE VEGETABLE:
>
> 2 garlic cloves, minced
>
> 2 tablespoons extra-virgin olive oil or more to taste
>
> 2 teaspoons fresh lemon juice or more to taste
>
> salt and freshly ground black pepper to taste
>
> lemon wedges and extra-virgin olive oil for serving

Pick over the greens, discarding any that are wilted or otherwise unsuitable. Wash them very well in several changes of water. If chard ribs are very thick, cut them away and use only the green leafy portion. Cook spinach leaves whole; chop

other greens coarsely. Steam each green separately in the water clinging to the leaves, adding a very little more water if necessary to keep it from catching on the bottom of the pan. Cooking times vary, depending on the vegetable. Count on about 10 minutes for spinach and perhaps 15 minutes for broccoli rabe or chard. Each vegetable should be tender but not soggy.

When each of the greens is very tender, drain separately, chop them separately, and set aside.

Trim the asparagus or top and tail the green beans. Steam in about 1 inch of rapidly boiling water until the vegetable is tender. Do not undercook. Count on 10 minutes for green beans, 12 to 15 for asparagus. Drain and set aside.

Gently cook the garlic in the oil in a sauté pan until the garlic is melted and soft but not brown—about 5 minutes. Turn one of the cooked vegetables in the garlicky oil to warm it slightly and coat it thoroughly. Add the lemon juice and, if you wish, salt and a very little pepper. (Greens absorb more oil than either green beans or asparagus. Add more if necessary.) Divide into 6 servings and arrange on plates, leaving room for the other vegetables to follow. Continue with the others, following the same procedure.

When all of the vegetables are done, garnish each plate with a lemon wedge and serve along with a glass cruet of olive oil for those who wish to add more. This is delicious on its own, accompanied simply by good bread. ***Makes 6 servings***

Nutritional Data, per portion

| | | |
|---|---|---|
| Calories  249 | Carbohydrate  18g | Saturated Fat  3g |
| Protein  8g | Sodium  140mg | Monounsaturated |
| Fat  20g | Cholesterol  0 | Fat  15g |

VEGETABLE DISHES

# TURKISH-STYLE OVEN-BRAISED
# WINTER VEGETABLES

**T**here is something comforting about the mixed vegetable dishes of the eastern Mediterranean. Greek and Turkish cooks are particularly gifted at roasting, braising, and stewing vegetables for hours in a little savory extra-virgin olive oil and whatever aromatics the cook has to hand. These are substantial dishes that can easily be the focus of a meal, especially with a good crusty country loaf and a chunk of feta or other firm cheese.

Don't be limited by the vegetable suggestions here—if others are available, use them. Fennel, artichoke or celery hearts, and beets are all good suggestions, though beets should be added with caution to avoid turning the whole thing pink.

1  cup dried small white beans, soaked overnight, or use the quick-soak
  method (page 454)

about ½ cup extra-virgin olive oil

1  medium celery root, peeled and cut into 1-inch cubes

½  pound Jerusalem artichokes, peeled and cut into 1-inch cubes

3  large carrots, peeled and cut into 1-inch cubes

3  small white turnips, peeled and cut into 1-inch cubes

2  medium potatoes, peeled if desired and cut into 1-inch cubes

15  scallions, green tops sliced diagonally and white parts left whole

4  large garlic cloves, crushed with the flat blade of a knife

juice of ½ lemon or more to taste

salt and freshly ground black pepper to taste

lemon wedges for serving

Preheat the oven to 450 degrees. Drain the soaked beans and place in a saucepan with water to cover to a depth of 1 inch and 2 tablespoons of the olive oil. Cook gently until the beans are tender—time depends on the age and size of the beans. When done, set aside in their cooking liquid.

Place all the vegetables except the scallion greens in a large roasting pan with the remaining olive oil, the lemon juice, and salt and pepper. Fill the pan halfway with boiling water and place, uncovered, in the preheated oven for 30 minutes or

until the vegetables are thoroughly cooked and starting to brown on top. Remove and sprinkle the chopped scallion greens over the vegetables. Cover the roasting pan lightly with foil and set aside until the beans are ready.

When the beans are tender, add them with their cooking liquid to the roasted vegetables, distributing them evenly. The dish can be reheated, covered with foil, in the oven before serving, but it is usually served at room temperature. Serve with lemon wedges. **Makes 8 servings**

Nutritional Data, per portion

| | | |
|---|---|---|
| Calories   305 | Carbohydrate   39g | Saturated Fat   2g |
| Protein   9g | Sodium   73mg | Monounsaturated |
| Fat   15g | Cholesterol   0 | Fat   11g |

# MEDITERRANEAN SUMMER STEW OF VEGETABLES

This is a dish for people like me, who are weary of the so-called crisp-tender vegetables served in fashionable restaurants. Don't be limited by the vegetable suggestions in the recipe. Your local farmer's market may provide a different and equally enticing selection—perhaps fresh young fava beans, so tender you can eat them pod and all, or later in the season shell beans, okra, and any of the variety of summer squashes. When young spring onions are available, the kind with the outer skin still fresh enough to eat, I like to use them, with their green tops, instead of yellow or white onions.

A heavy terra-cotta braising dish, wider than it is tall, is traditional for these vegetable preparations, though it should be used with a gas burner and a Flame-Tamer. Send the vegetables to the table in the handsome dish in which they are cooked.

VEGETABLE DISHES

¼ cup extra-virgin olive oil

2 medium fresh spring onions or yellow or white onions (not scallions), thinly sliced

3 garlic cloves, crushed with the flat blade of a knife

2 medium potatoes, peeled and cut into chunks, or 12 small new potatoes

1 pound or more green beans, topped and tailed and broken in half if very long

3 small bell peppers, both green and red, cut into strips

3 or 4 fresh thyme or oregano sprigs to taste

3 long narrow zucchini, cut into 1-inch chunks

3 large firm but ripe tomatoes, cut into chunks

salt and freshly ground black pepper to taste

1 tablespoon minced flat-leaf parsley

Warm the olive oil over medium-low heat in a pan large enough to hold all the vegetables. Add the onions and garlic and stew very gently, stirring occasionally, until the onions are meltingly soft—about 10 to 15 minutes.

When the onions are soft, arrange the potatoes over them, then add the beans and peppers. Distribute the thyme over the beans. Add the zucchini chunks and then the tomatoes. Sprinkle a little salt, if desired, and pepper on top, cover tightly (use a double layer of heavy-duty aluminum foil to cover a terra-cotta pot), and stew over low heat for about 45 minutes or until the vegetables are thoroughly cooked. Check the liquid occasionally—there should be plenty, but if necessary add up to ¼ cup boiling water.

When the vegetables are soft and meltingly tender, remove the dish from the heat and set aside, still covered, until ready to serve. If necessary, they can be warmed up a little just before serving, but they are best a bit warmer than room temperature. Sprinkle with the parsley just before serving. *Makes 6 to 8 servings*

Nutritional Data, per portion

| | | |
|---|---|---|
| Calories 141 | Carbohydrate 18g | Saturated Fat 1g |
| Protein 3g | Sodium 14mg | Monounsaturated |
| Fat 7g | Cholesterol 0 | Fat 6g |

# A GRAND ARRAY OF STUFFED VEGETABLES

**A**ll over the eastern Mediterranean and in southern Italy you find stuffed vegetables as part of the meze or antipasto table. A big platter of stuffed tomatoes, peppers, zucchini, and onions makes a handsome presentation for a summer buffet. I give two stuffings—one with meat, one a meatless Lenten stuffing for vegetarians. The procedure is the same for both. The stuffings can be made ahead and refrigerated, but bring them back to room temperature before stuffing the vegetables.

| | |
|---|---|
| 4 | medium firm but ripe tomatoes |
| 2 | large bell peppers, preferably red and yellow |
| 4 | large zucchini |
| 4 | medium yellow onions |
| | stuffing (recipes follow) |
| ¼ | cup extra-virgin olive oil |
| ⅓ | cup unseasoned bread crumbs |
| ⅓ | cup freshly grated Parmigiano cheese |

Preheat the oven to 350 degrees. Cut the tops off the tomatoes about a quarter of the way down and use a serrated grapefruit spoon to scoop out the insides, leaving the outer shells intact. Chop the insides, drain in a colander, then place in a small bowl.

Cut the peppers in half lengthwise and remove the seeds and inner membranes.

Cut the zucchini in half lengthwise and, using the serrated spoon, gently scoop out the insides, leaving about ¼ inch of shell all around. Chop the zucchini flesh and add to the drained tomatoes. You should have about 1½ to 2 cups of zucchini and tomatoes.

Slice off the root ends of the onions with a shallow cut, just enough to make them stand upright. Cut the stem ends about a quarter of the way down. Peel the onions and gently scoop out the insides, leaving a ¼-inch-thick shell all around. Chop the onion flesh and set aside in another bowl. You should have about 1½ to 2 cups of onion.

Using a paper towel, smear a little of the oil over the bottom of a roasting pan large enough to hold all the vegetables without crowding. Arrange the vegetables in the pan. Stuff each vegetable loosely with one of the stuffings, allowing room for the

stuffing to expand. (Each stuffing recipe makes enough for this quantity of vegetables.) When all the vegetables are stuffed, sprinkle with the bread crumbs and cheese and drizzle a little of the oil over the tops. Pour the remaining oil into the pan along with about ½ inch of boiling water. Slide the pan into the oven and bake for 1 hour. If the vegetables are not brown on top, increase the heat to about 425 degrees and drizzle a little more olive oil over the tops. Return to the oven for 10 minutes or so until the vegetables brown. Let the vegetables cool to lukewarm or room temperature before serving. *Makes 8 servings*

# MEATLESS STUFFING

½ cup extra-virgin olive oil

the chopped onion removed from the vegetables

the tomato and zucchini flesh removed from the vegetables

2 green bell peppers, finely chopped

1 28-ounce can whole tomatoes, drained

1 teaspoon hot red pepper flakes

½ cup long-grain rice

½ cup coarse (number 3) bulgur

½ cup minced flat-leaf parsley

1 tablespoon dried thyme, crumbled

2 tablespoons chopped fresh mint leaves

¼ teaspoon ground cinnamon

salt and freshly ground black pepper to taste

Warm the olive oil in a large skillet over medium heat and gently sauté the onion for about 5 minutes or until it starts to soften. Add the tomato-zucchini mixture and the peppers and stew gently for about 15 minutes or until the vegetables are soft but not brown. Add the canned tomatoes and red pepper flakes. Break up the tomatoes with a wooden spoon while they come to a simmer. Then add the rice and stir to mix well. Simmer for 10 minutes or until the tomatoes have reduced to a thick sauce and the rice is starting to soften. Off the heat, stir in the bulgur, parsley, thyme, mint, and cinnamon. Taste and adjust the seasoning, adding salt and freshly ground black pepper.

# PORK OR VEAL STUFFING WITH RICE

the chopped onion removed from the vegetables

the tomato and zucchini flesh removed from the vegetables

2   garlic cloves, minced

½   cup minced flat-leaf parsley

¼   cup extra-virgin olive oil

½   pound boneless very lean pork or veal, ground

1   small dried hot red chili, chopped or broken into bits

½   cup long-grain rice

½   cup boiling water

⅓   cup unseasoned bread crumbs

1   tablespoon dried oregano, crumbled

¼   cup freshly grated Parmigiano cheese

salt and freshly ground black pepper to taste

Combine the onion with the tomato-zucchini mixture, garlic, and parsley. In a skillet over medium heat, gently sauté the combined vegetables in the olive oil until they are soft but not brown, about 15 minutes. Push the vegetables to the edge of the pan and add the meat to the center. Raise the heat slightly and sauté the meat until it has lost its pink color, about 5 minutes, stirring with a wooden spoon to break the meat up. Add the dried chili and stir to mix well.

Add the rice and boiling water and mix well. Cook for about 5 minutes, just to soften the rice a little.

Off the heat, stir in the bread crumbs, oregano, and cheese, mixing everything together very well. Taste and add salt and pepper as desired.

Nutritional Data, per portion, meatless stuffing

| | | |
|---|---|---|
| Calories  384 | Carbohydrate  40g | Saturated Fat  4g |
| Protein  8g | Sodium  291mg | Monounsaturated |
| Fat  23g | Cholesterol  3mg |   Fat  17g |

Nutritional Data, per portion, pork or veal stuffing

| | | |
|---|---|---|
| Calories  373 | Carbohydrate  25g | Saturated Fat  5g |
| Protein  12g | Sodium  238mg | Monounsaturated |
| Fat  26g | Cholesterol  25mg |   Fat  18g |

# CHAPTER NINE

# A FEW SWEETS

It is six o'clock in the afternoon, late spring in Tuscany, and warm enough to go about without a jacket even in the narrow, deeply shaded streets of Cortona. Along the stone-paved via Nazionale, which ambles through the heart of the old Etruscan hill town, corrugated steel shutters bang up, one after the other, as shops reopen after the long siesta. It is the hour of the *passeggiata*, not just in Cortona but all over the Mediterranean, in bustling cities and quiet towns, even in country villages. The streets fill gradually, but by seven o'clock they are thronged with strollers of all ages, young, old, babies in prams, elderly ladies arm in arm, students clutching book bags, little children darting between the legs of their parents, people coming and going, stopping to chat, moving in and out of cafés and bars, sharing coffee, a glass of wine or something stronger, and above all sweets.

This is the time of day when all over the Mediterranean people pause in whatever they're doing for a little social intercourse over something sweet. It might be as simple as an ice cream or sherbet, as elaborate as the syrup-and-nut confections of Greece and Lebanon, a little wedge of fruit-and-rum-laced cake in southern Italy, butter-filled cookies in Barcelona, a dollop of rice pudding in Turkey, or a crust of sweet pastry with jam on top in Tuscany.

At holiday time the sweets grow more elaborate—special sweet breads and cakes associated with Christmas and Easter, marzipan candies for All Souls' Day, fried delights for Hanukkah, Carnival, or the end of Ramadan, rich tortes for the Feast of the Epiphany when the Three Kings arrive at the manger bearing gifts. One characteristic that all these confections share, along with those consumed during the late-afternoon *passeggiata* or *paseo*, is that they are almost never made at home. Elaborate sweets are made in the pastry shop, the pasticceria, zacharoplasteion, or pâtisserie, which is often a very different place from the bakery, just as daily bread is a very

different thing from such sweet delights. Only rarely, in farmhouses in the country-side, are sweets made at home, and then they are usually of the very simplest sort.

The kind of sweet desserts we Americans consume at the end of a meal—cakes, cookies, fudgy chocolate confections—are regarded with bewilderment in Medi-terranean countries, where more often than not a meal ends with fruit, plain and simple, raw or cooked, or on special occasions perhaps a glass of sweet wine and a hard biscuit to dip in it. It is a much saner way to conclude a repast. If the meal has been abundant—and the abundance may mean nothing more than good bread and cheese and a hearty vegetable soup—nothing more is required.

I've selected the sweet cakes and puddings in this chapter with that in mind. The fruit desserts and suggestions are self-explanatory. The rest, although made in home kitchens, are either special holiday sweets or intended to be served, for instance, to guests who drop in on Sunday afternoon.

If you feel you must serve a sweet at the end of the meal, keep the quantities very small—Paula Wolfert pointed out to me that the sweets served in Turkish homes with little cups of strong black Turkish coffee are no bigger than the coffee cups themselves.

---

### SERVING FRESH FRUIT

As with other produce, I like as much as possible to put only organically produced, pesticide-free fruits on my table. That's not always easy to do, however, and during apple season in New England, for instance, I'd rather have apples from regional farms, raised under principles of integrated pest management (using pesticides selectively and only when necessary, rather than systematically throughout the growing season) than organically raised strawberries from Chile.

Still, you can't buy everything locally. There's no way we'll ever get local citrus fruits in New England or even very good figs. Buying locally is a good principle, but it's not the whole story.

A dramatic and appetizing presentation might focus on just one variety of fruit, piling it up in extravagant abundance in a handsome bowl—translucent yellow Bartlett pears, for instance, or Macoun apples, dark, velvety plums too juicy to eat except over a plate, New Jersey peaches when they're so tender a thumb can dent the flesh, Door County cherries,

*continued*

red and glowing like currants, or the first tangerines and mandarin oranges of the season, enhanced with some of their dark green leaves. In decorator's terms, an opulence of fruit piled up in a bowl like this "makes a statement." But it's also an invitation to a certain delicious kind of greed—and we all need more fresh fruit in our lives, so a little greed is in order.

Another fine way to serve fruit is in a fresh fruit salad, perhaps calling it *macédoine* or *macedonia* to give it new dimension. Cut a selection of fruit into uniform pieces, peeling those varieties that seem to warrant it, mix them together in a glass bowl, and add a very little sugar and a few tablespoons of liqueur or wine or citrus juice.

Don't overdo the varieties, however—three or four different fruits, carefully selected to balance each other's flavors, present a better display than eight or nine. Too many fruits in the macédoine leads inevitably to the supposition that the cook simply cleaned out the refrigerator fruit drawer before dinner.

Don't overdo the addition of other flavorings either—it's a mistake to think that, if 2 tablespoons of Grand Marnier are good, 4 tablespoons will be that much better. Restraint is the key. The point is simply to enhance the flavors, which is why fortified sweet wines and herbal liqueurs are used. Lemon juice, orange juice, or the juice of bitter or Seville oranges can be just as sharp and interesting with fresh fruit.

Other suggestions for serving fresh fruit:

- peaches, peeled and sliced and dressed with a very little aromatic red wine (not more than a tablespoonful per serving) and a sprinkling of sugar
- fresh little seasonal strawberries, rinsed briefly and served with a little balsamic vinegar (artisanally made if you can find it) and a saucer of powdered sugar to dip them in
- berries of any sort—raspberries, blackberries, blueberries, huckleberries, cloudberries—with the juice of blood oranges or Meyer lemons
- oranges, the skin and white pith peeled away, thinly sliced and dressed with a little sweet white moscato wine (try this with a few grains of freshly cracked black pepper for a startling contrast)
- melons with wedges of lemon or lime to squeeze over them (more traditional at the start of the meal but also good for dessert)
- figs: if you can find them, fresh figs, so ripe they fall apart in your hands, are too extravagantly delicious to need garnishing with any other flavor; eat them out of hand, preferably sitting in the sun under the fig tree

A FEW SWEETS

# NICHOLAS'S FAVORITE
# BRAISED PEARS IN BAROLO

**M**y son Nicholas was six years old when he discovered these pears in a restaurant on the via Crispi in Rome. He was just coming off a two-year diet of peanut butter and jelly sandwiches (on whole-wheat bread, of course), and I thought he would slide off his chair with pleasure at the soft buttery winy taste of them. Nearly 20 years later, he still asks for via Crispi pears when he comes home.

The pears should be firm. Overripe pears will cook too quickly and disintegrate. They can be cooked on top of the stove but are best baked in the oven at a low temperature. I use a copper pan that is small enough that all the pears can stand upright and tall enough so that their stems aren't crushed when the pan is covered.

6   very firm yellow or green pears with their stems attached

½   lemon

1   3- to 4-inch cinnamon stick, broken in two

2   cups strong red wine—a Barolo, if you can afford it, or a California
       cabernet sauvignon

½   cup water

½   cup sugar

Preheat the oven to 275 degrees. Peel the pears with a vegetable parer, leaving the stems intact. Place them upright in a deep ovenproof dish. Pare the zest away from the lemon half and add it to the pears. Cut away and discard the white pith and thinly slice the lemon half. Add the slices along with the cinnamon to the pears.

Bring the wine, water, and ¼ cup of the sugar to a boil. Pour the boiling wine over the pears, cover them with a lid or a piece of heavy-duty aluminum foil, and bake for 1½ hours or until the pears are very soft.

Remove the pan from the oven. If the liquid is not syrupy, remove the pears from the pan and set them aside, standing upright on a small platter, to cool to room temperature. (Do not refrigerate; they'll get too cold.) Boil the liquid down, adding more of the sugar if necessary, until it is a thick syrup. Discard the cinnamon, lemon slices, and zest. Spoon the syrup over the pears, a little at a time. Serve at room temperature. ***Makes 6 servings***

# A COMPOTE OF TURKISH DRIED FRUITS AND NUTS

**O**ne of Turkey's leading exports is high-quality dried fruits, especially apricots and figs, and the country is also the world's leading producer of hazelnuts, so this winter dessert is particularly apt. You can use all figs or all apricots, but the two together, alternating in the dish, are particularly attractive.

These are traditionally served with a clotted cream called *kaymak*, but they are also good with drained yogurt (page 299) that has been sweetened to taste with sugar or honey and flavored with ¼ teaspoon vanilla extract if desired.

To toast the nuts, spread them on a baking sheet in a 350-degree oven for about 15 minutes or until they are a light golden brown. Be careful not to overroast them.

**about 1½ pounds mixed dried figs and apricots**

½ **cup finely chopped toasted hazelnuts**

½ **cup finely chopped toasted walnuts or almonds**

½ **cup sugar**

1 **cup water**

Put the dried fruits in a large mixing bowl and pour boiling water over them to cover. Set aside to soften for about 15 minutes. Butter the bottom of a shallow round straight-sided ovenproof dish just large enough to hold all the fruit. Preheat the oven to 350 degrees.

Combine the nuts in a food processor with ¼ cup of the sugar. Process very briefly in spurts to grind the nuts coarsely—they should not become a paste.

When the dried fruits are softened, drain them and alternate them in the prepared dish.

Mix the remaining sugar with the water, bring to a boil, and cook for 5 minutes. Pour the syrup over the fruits in the dish, cover with foil, and bake for about 20 minutes. Remove the foil, sprinkle the sugar and nut mixture over the fruits, and return the dish to the oven for 15 minutes. ***Makes 8 servings***

Nutritional Data, per portion

| | | |
|---|---|---|
| Calories 356 | Carbohydrate 69g | Saturated Fat 1g |
| Protein 5g | Sodium 15mg | Monounsaturated |
| Fat 10g | Cholesterol 1mg | Fat 5g |

# TURKISH APRICOTS STUFFED WITH SWEET, THICK YOGURT

In Turkey these luscious apricots are stuffed with *kaymak*, a sweet, rich but rather bland cream made traditionally, like Italian mozzarella, from the milk of water buffalos. There's nothing remotely like that here, but yogurt, drained over-night to make labneh and mixed with sugar, can be used instead. The taste is quite different but still delicious. Use nonfat yogurt if you wish. Turkish cooks would not add the wine, but I think it lends a little complexity to the flavors.

¾ **pound dried apricots, preferably imported from Turkey**

¼ **cup granulated sugar plus more to taste for the labneh**

½ **cup labneh made from 1 pint yogurt (page 299)**

2 **tablespoons sweet dessert wine such as moscato or sauternes**

2 **tablespoons finely chopped pistachio nuts or more if desired**

Put the apricots in a pan with water to cover to a depth of 1 inch. Bring to a boil and simmer, uncovered, until the apricots are plump—10 to 15 minutes.

Drain the apricots, reserving the cooking water. Measure out ¾ cup of the cooking water and return it to the pan with the ¼ cup sugar. (Discard the rest of the cooking water.) Cook, stirring, until the sugar has dissolved, then add the wine. Return the apricots to the pan and continue cooking for about 20 minutes or until they are very soft. Remove the apricots and set aside to cool. Do not discard the cooking syrup.

While the apricots are cooking, blend the labneh with sugar to taste until it is smooth. Start with 2 tablespoons of sugar and add more if desired.

When the apricots are cool enough to handle, open each one and spoon in a rounded tablespoon or more of the yogurt, pressing the apricot halves around it to hold it in place. (The apricots should not be closed up over the yogurt, however. They should look like an old-fashioned whoopie pie, with the yogurt oozing out.)

Arrange the apricots on a serving dish and spoon some of the reserved syrup over each one. Garnish with pistachios. *Makes 6 servings*

### Nutritional Data, per portion

| | | |
|---|---|---|
| Calories 217 | Carbohydrate 47g | Saturated Fat trace |
| Protein 6g | Sodium 33mg | Monounsaturated |
| Fat 2g | Cholesterol 0 | Fat 1g |

# ZALETI

### *Venetian Cornmeal Cookies*

**Y**ou can find *zaleti* year-round in the territory around Venice, but they are traditional for Carnival and the pre-Lenten frenzy. Like many sweets and savories from that time of the year, they hark back to ancient magic related to worship of the sun, and they remind us of that in their shape and color—round and bright yellow with cornmeal and egg yolks. Some cooks add grated lemon zest instead of vanilla, and some add chopped candied fruit instead of the currants and pine nuts. (The currants here are dried black Zante grapes, not red currants. If you can't find them, use raisins instead.) In fact there may be as many different recipes as there are cooks, and each has its own claim to authenticity.

½   **cup dried currants or raisins, either black or golden**

¼   **cup grappa, vodka, or rum**

¾   **cup yellow cornmeal**

¾   **cup unbleached all-purpose flour**

**pinch of salt**

1   **teaspoon baking powder**

½   **cup (1 stick) unsalted butter plus butter to grease the cookie sheet**

3   **large egg yolks**

½   **cup sugar**

⅓   **cup pine nuts**

A FEW SWEETS

Preheat the oven to 375 degrees. Put the currants in a little bowl with the liquor and set aside to macerate for 20 to 30 minutes.

Combine the cornmeal, flour, salt, and baking powder and sift to mix well. Set aside.

Use a little butter to grease a cookie sheet. Heat the stick of butter in a small pan over low heat until it is just barely melted but not separated and foaming.

Beat the egg yolks until thick and lemon colored. Slowly beat in the sugar and then the melted butter. When all the butter has been incorporated, add the sifted dry ingredients and mix well with a wooden spoon.

Drain the currants and add to the batter together with the pine nuts. Stir to distribute throughout the batter. Set aside to rest for about 15 minutes, then drop by spoonfuls on the greased cookie sheet. Bake for 10 minutes, until the cookies are browning around the edge. Remove to a wire rack to cool. ***Makes about 32 cookies***

Nutritional Data, per cookie

| | | |
|---|---|---|
| Calories  83 | Carbohydrate  10g | Saturated Fat  2g |
| Protein  1g | Sodium  21mg | Monounsaturated |
| Fat  4g | Cholesterol  28mg | Fat  1g |

# BISCOTTI DI PRATO

*Hard Almond Biscuits*

These hard biscuits, sometimes called *cantucci*, come originally from Prato, just north of Florence. They are meant to be dipped and softened in a glass of sweet wine or Tuscan vin santo after a meal. Originally *biscotto* meant "twice cooked" or "cooked again," and these are among the few baked goods called *biscuits* that still reflect that meaning.

It's a little unnerving to see what is happening to biscotti in this country. Having thoroughly ruined scones and croissants by adding all kinds of garbage to them, we now seem well on our way to doing the same thing with biscotti, increasing the size, softening the texture, and adding chocolate flavoring and chocolate coating. In the end it is the simplicity of the thing that appeals, as the original recipe shows.

To toast the almonds and hazelnuts, put them on a baking sheet in a 350-degree oven for about 15 minutes or until they are a light golden brown. Be careful not to overroast them.

    **a little olive oil for the cookie sheet**
4    **cups unbleached all-purpose flour plus a little more for the cookie
        sheet and work surface**
2    **cups sugar**
1    **teaspoon baking soda**
½    **teaspoon salt**
4    **large eggs**
1    **teaspoon vanilla extract**
1    **cup very coarsely chopped toasted almonds**
¾    **cup very coarsely chopped toasted hazelnuts**
1    **large egg white**
1    **teaspoon water**

Preheat the oven to 375 degrees. Grease a cookie sheet with a paper towel dipped in a little oil and flour it lightly.

Mix the flour, sugar, baking soda, and salt in a bowl and toss with a fork to combine well. Set aside.

In a separate bowl, beat the whole eggs briefly, just to combine the yolks and whites. Add the vanilla and stir—don't beat—the eggs into the flour mixture, kneading with your hands in the bowl until you have a homogeneous mixture. Turn the dough out onto a very lightly floured wooden board. Sprinkle the nuts over it and continue kneading for a few minutes until the nuts are distributed throughout the dough.

Leave the dough to rest for 10 minutes or so, then divide it into 6 pieces. Using your hands, shape each piece into a long thin log no more than 2 inches in diameter. Set each log as it is finished on the cookie sheet—the logs should be far apart because they expand when they bake. Press the top of each log to flatten it slightly; the log should be oval in section rather than round.

Using a fork, beat the egg white with the water in a small bowl. Paint each log with egg white, using a pastry brush. Bake for 20 to 30 minutes or until the logs are dry and lightly colored. Remove from the oven and set aside until they are cool enough to handle. Reset the oven to 300 degrees.

When the logs are cool enough to handle, slice them on the diagonal no more than ½ inch thick, using a long sharp knife. Lay the biscotti, flat side down, on the cookie sheet and return to the oven for 15 to 20 minutes.

Transfer the biscotti to a rack to dry, cool, and harden for several hours. They can be kept in a cookie tin for 6 weeks or more. ***Makes about 36 biscotti***

### Nutritional Data, per biscotti

| | | |
|---|---|---|
| Calories 141 | Carbohydrate 23g | Saturated Fat trace |
| Protein 3g | Sodium 75mg | Monounsaturated |
| Fat 4g | Cholesterol 24mg | Fat 3g |

# KOURABIEDES

### *Greek Butter-Almond Cookies*

I first met these in their Greek incarnation, although they are deservedly popular throughout the eastern Mediterranean. Rich with butter and sugar, they are especially treasured at Christmastime, when Greek cooks stick a whole clove into each cookie, a symbol of the gifts of the magi. I don't do that—I don't like biting down on a whole clove, and these are so good you can quickly forget, in your enthusiasm, to remove the clove beforehand.

To toast the almonds, spread them on a baking sheet in a 350-degree oven for about 15 minutes or until they are a light golden brown. Be careful not to overroast them.

2   cups blanched almonds, toasted

2   tablespoons granulated sugar

2   cups (4 sticks) unsalted butter

1   large egg yolk, lightly beaten

¼   cup good cognac

1   teaspoon vanilla extract

2½ cups cake flour

½   teaspoon baking powder

pinch of salt

1   cup confectioners' sugar

Preheat the oven to 350 degrees. Divide the almonds into 2 batches. Process one batch in the food processor with the granulated sugar until it is finely ground but not a paste, being careful not to overprocess. Finely chop the second batch of almonds on a cutting board with a sharp knife. They should be smaller than rice grains but not as fine as coarse cornmeal.

In a large mixing bowl, beat the butter until it is very light, pale colored, and fluffy. Using a spatula, stir in the egg yolk, cognac, and vanilla and beat briefly just to combine with the butter.

Combine the flour, baking powder, salt, and ½ cup of the confectioners' sugar. Sift this over the butter, about a quarter of it at a time, folding in after each addition. Add all the almonds and stir or knead with your hands to mix together very

A FEW SWEETS

well. The dough should be soft but not sticky, and you should be able to roll a small ball of it easily between your palms. If it's too sticky, refrigerate for 20 minutes to chill.

Shape and bake the cookies in batches. Roll a rounded tablespoon of the dough, gently and quickly, between your palms to make a ball and set the balls on an ungreased cookie sheet, leaving about ½ inch between them. Bake for about 10 to 12 minutes or until the cookies are pale golden. They should not be brown.

Transfer the cookies to a wire rack set over a sheet of aluminum foil. Let them cool for 10 to 15 minutes, then sift the remaining confectioners' sugar over them. (The sugar that falls between the cookies onto the aluminum foil can be reused in the next sifting.) The cookies keep very well in a tin for several weeks. *Makes 3 to 4 dozen cookies*

Nutritional Data, per cookie

| | | |
|---|---|---|
| Calories 160 | Carbohydrate 10g | Saturated Fat 6g |
| Protein 2g | Sodium 11mg | Monounsaturated |
| Fat 13g | Cholesterol 29mg | Fat 5g |

# YOGURT-LEMON TORTE

**B**ecause the lemons we get in this country have none of the exquisite flavor of those from the Mediterranean, I use lemon-flavored yogurt to boost the flavor of the torte. Use the best-quality yogurt you can find; it should have no added gelatin or other ingredients to stabilize and thicken it. This is a rich, if simple, cake, but that's no reason to avoid it—just don't eat it every day. If you're following a Mediterranean pattern, your everyday diet will be so full of good things that an occasional high-fat sweet should do no harm.

**Butter and flour for a round 9-inch cake pan**

½ **cup (1 stick) unsalted butter, cut into chunks**

1¼ **cups sugar**

2 **whole eggs plus 4 egg whites**

1 **cup nonfat lemon yogurt**

**grated zest and juice of 1 lemon**

1   tablespoon pure vanilla extract

2¼ cups cake flour

1   teaspoon baking powder

½   teaspoon baking soda

¼   teaspoon cream of tartar

pinch of salt

about ¼ cup confectioners' sugar in a sifter or shaker

Butter the insides of the cake pan very lightly. Shake a little flour into it and shake the pan to distribute the flour in an even layer all over the inside. Preheat the oven to 325 degrees.

In a medium mixing bowl, beat the butter to a cream and add the sugar, a little at a time, beating constantly. Add the eggs and egg whites, one at a time, beating after each addition. Add the yogurt and beat it in; then beat in the lemon zest and juice and the vanilla.

Combine the flour with the baking powder, baking soda, cream of tartar, and salt. Sift over the butter and egg batter. Using a spatula, gently fold the flour into the batter. Pour the batter into the prepared cake pan. Set in the lower part of the preheated oven and bake for one hour. (The cake is done when it is golden and springs back nicely, or when a toothpick inserted in the middle comes out clean.) Turn out to cool on a cake rack and dust with a little confectioners' sugar. *Makes one 9-inch cake; about 8 to 10 servings*

Nutritional Data, per portion

| Calories 330 | Carbohydrate 53g | Saturated Fat 6g |
|---|---|---|
| Protein 6g | Sodium 176mg | Monounsaturated |
| Fat 11g | Cholesterol 68mg | Fat 3g |

**VARIATION:** Substitute ¼ cup very strong coffee (use instant espresso) and 2 or 3 tablespoons Italian grappa or brandy for the grated lemon zest and juice.

# TORTA DI POLENTA GIALLA

*Cornmeal Cake*

**T**his is a lovely, light citrusy cake, based on one that's made throughout Italy's Po Valley region. It will keep for a week or more, but it's so delicious it will doubtless disappear long before then. Serve it, if you wish, with a little sherbet on the side or with lightly sweetened berries.

butter and flour for the cake pan

1   vanilla bean

1   cup sugar

¾   cup (1½ sticks) unsalted butter

3   large eggs, separated

½   cup very finely ground blanched almonds

3   tablespoons fresh orange juice

½   cup yellow cornmeal

½   cup unbleached all-purpose flour

1   teaspoon baking powder

pinch of salt

2   tablespoons potato starch or arrowroot

¼   cup confectioners' sugar (optional)

Preheat the oven to 325 degrees. Lightly butter and flour a 9-inch round cake pan.

Chop the vanilla bean as finely as you can and put it in a blender with the sugar. Blend until the vanilla is thoroughly pulverized. (If you don't have a vanilla bean, you can simply stir in ½ teaspoon pure vanilla extract with the orange juice later.) In a medium mixing bowl, cream the butter until light and fluffy. Using a sifter to hold back any pieces of vanilla that didn't disintegrate, slowly sift the vanilla sugar into the butter, a little at a time, beating continuously. Add the egg yolks, one at a time, beating after each addition. Stir in the almonds and orange juice. Add the cornmeal and stir to mix very well. Set aside.

Mix together the flour, baking powder, salt, and potato starch. Place in a sifter and set aside.

In a separate bowl using clean beaters, beat the egg whites to stiff peaks. Stir about a quarter of the egg whites into the batter, then sift about a third of the flour mixture over it. Fold the flour into the batter with a spatula. Continue adding egg whites and flour two more times, folding after each addition, ending with the remaining egg whites.

Pour the batter into the prepared pan and bake for 20 to 30 minutes or until the cake is golden brown and springs back to the touch.

Set aside on a rack to cool. Remove from the pan and sift a little confectioners' sugar over the top before serving if you wish. *Makes one 9-inch cake; about 8 to 10 servings*

Nutritional Data, per portion

| | | |
|---|---|---|
| Calories   313 | Carbohydrate   34g | Saturated Fat   10g |
| Protein   4g | Sodium   84mg | Monounsaturated |
| Fat   18g | Cholesterol   102mg | Fat   6g |

# BEAUMES-DE-VENISE CAKE WITH OLIVE OIL

This luscious cake is based on a recipe developed by Alice Waters, chef and owner of Chez Panisse in Berkeley, California. If you can't find Muscat de Beaumes-de-Venise, a French sweet wine, use a good-quality sauternes or a moscato from Italy.

**butter and flour for the cake pan**

5   **large eggs**

2   **large egg whites**

¾   **cup sugar**

1   **tablespoon grated lemon zest**

1   **cup sifted unbleached all-purpose flour**

½   **teaspoon salt**

½   **cup Muscat de Beaumes-de-Venise**

⅓   **cup plus 2 tablespoons extra-virgin olive oil**

A FEW SWEETS

Preheat the oven to 375 degrees. Liberally butter an 8-inch springform pan and shake a little flour around the inside. Cut out two 8-inch circles of parchment paper or wax paper. Set one in the bottom of the pan. Butter the other circle on one side and set aside.

Separate the eggs, putting all the whites in one bowl. Beat the yolks with the sugar in a separate bowl until they are light and lemon colored. Add the lemon zest and mix well.

Combine the flour and salt, tossing to mix well. A little at a time, add the flour to the batter, beating continually. Add the wine and oil, a little at a time, beating continually, until everything is thoroughly incorporated.

In a separate bowl and with clean beaters, beat the egg whites until they stand in stiff peaks. Stir about a quarter of the egg whites into the batter. Add about half the remaining egg whites and fold in. Then add the last half and fold in.

Pour the batter into the prepared springform pan and bake for 20 minutes, rotating the cake if necessary to ensure even cooking. Lower the oven temperature to 325 degrees and bake for another 20 minutes. Turn off the oven, cover the cake with the circle of buttered parchment, buttered side down, and close the oven door. Leave the cake for 10 minutes more. It will deflate, like a soufflé.

Remove the cake from the oven, invert it onto a serving plate, remove the springform, and allow the cake to cool completely. It can be stored in a tightly covered container for several days or weeks. ***Makes one 8-inch cake; about 8 servings***

Nutritional Data, per portion

| | | |
|---|---|---|
| Calories 305 | Carbohydrate 33g | Saturated Fat 3g |
| Protein 6g | Sodium 192mg | Monounsaturated |
| Fat 17g | Cholesterol 135mg | Fat 12g |

# GREEK OLIVE OIL AND CITRUS CAKE

**U**se black currants (dried tiny Zante grapes) if you can find them; otherwise substitute black or golden raisins.

**butter and flour for the cake pan**

- 1   orange
- 1   lemon
- 3   cups cake flour
- 1   teaspoon baking soda
- 1   tablespoon ground cinnamon
- 2⅓ cups dried currants
- 1   cup light-flavored extra-virgin olive oil
- 1½ cups sugar
- 1   tablespoon brandy

Butter and flour a 9-inch round cake pan and set aside. Grate the zest of the orange and lemon and mix together. Squeeze the orange and lemon juice and mix with the zest.

Sift the flour with the baking soda and cinnamon. Add the currants, stirring to distribute them evenly throughout the flour.

In a medium bowl, beat the oil, adding the sugar a little at a time. When all the sugar has been added, fold in about a third of the flour mixture. Add about a quarter of the juice and zest and fold in. Continue alternating flour and juice, folding after each addition, until it has all been mixed. Finally, add the brandy and mix well. Pour the batter into the prepared pan and bake for 1 hour. Remove from the oven and cool on a rack before removing from the pan. ***Makes one 9-inch cake; about 8 to 10 servings***

Nutritional Data, per portion

| | | |
|---|---|---|
| Calories   530 | Carbohydrate   82g | Saturated Fat   3g |
| Protein   4g | Sodium   130mg | Monounsaturated |
| Fat   23g | Cholesterol   1mg | Fat   18g |

# PASTIERA DI GRANO

*A Neapolitan Easter Pie*

**W**hat I love about holiday sweets, especially Easter sweets, from the Mediterranean is the ease with which they can be decoded. Below the surface sweetness and richness, they remind us that the drama of the Easter Passion goes back to a time long before Christianity and that the Resurrection is a fulfillment of a very old and powerful—some might say archetypal—longing for new life and the profound belief that life will return. Easter in its origin is an agricultural festival, and that's why grains of wheat play a role in this extravagant pie.

The wheat berries or grains should be of a variety of hulled soft wheat, the kind of wheat that's used in this country almost solely for cake flour. You can find various hulled soft wheats at health food stores. If it's not marked *soft wheat*, look for kamut or spelt, both of which are soft-wheat grains. Or use farro, a soft, old-fashioned Italian wheat available in specialty stores and by mail (see Resources at the back of the book). Orange-flower water is available in Middle Eastern groceries; if you can't find it, substitute pure vanilla extract.

*Pasta frolla* is a basic Italian pastry dough for sweet tarts, very soft and not like the usual piecrust. The pie is not as complicated as it looks if you take it one step at a time, and it is well worth the effort. Carlo Middione, a great Italian chef in San Francisco, helped me understand how to construct this.

**FOR THE WHEAT BERRIES:**

1 cup whole soft-wheat berries or grains, soaked in water for at least 24 hours to soften

1 cup whole milk

1 tablespoon unsalted butter

1 cup sugar

**FOR THE PASTA FROLLA:**

2 cups unbleached all-purpose flour

½ cup cake flour

½ cup sugar

pinch of salt

¾ cup (1½ sticks) unsalted butter at room temperature

2   large eggs

grated zest of 1 lemon

FOR THE PIE FILLING:

¾   pound ricotta cheese

grated zest of 2 lemons

grated zest of 1 orange

1   tablespoon orange-flower water or vanilla extract

1   teaspoon pure vanilla extract (omit if you substitute vanilla for the
    orange-flower water)

3   large eggs, separated

2   large egg yolks

⅓   cup finely slivered candied orange peel

¼   cup pine nuts

butter and flour for the pan

1   teaspoon cold water

sugar for sprinkling on top


Drain the wheat berries and place them in the top of a double boiler with the milk and butter. Bring the water in the bottom of the double boiler to a boil. Cover and cook the wheat over the boiling water for about 2½ hours, adding more boiling water to the bottom as needed. The wheat should be soft but in separate grains, like properly cooked long-grain rice. If it seems dry, add about ⅓ cup more hot milk and stir well. At the end of 2 hours, add the sugar and cook for 30 minutes longer. Set aside to cool.

While the wheat is cooking, make the *pasta frolla*. Mix together the flours, sugar, and salt, tossing with a fork. Add the butter, cut into pieces, and, working rapidly, rub it into the flour mixture. Make a well in the center. Separate one of the eggs, adding the white to the pastry along with the second egg. (Reserve the yolk for painting the crust.) Add the lemon zest and use a fork to stir the eggs into the dough. When the eggs are thoroughly incorporated, form the dough into a soft ball, wrap it in plastic or foil, and refrigerate for at least 1 hour. When rolling it out, work quickly—the dough becomes crumbly with frequent handling.

When the wheat is cool, make the filling. In a large bowl, beat the ricotta with the citrus zests, orange-flower water, and vanilla until it is light and fluffy. Add the 5

A FEW SWEETS

egg yolks, one at a time, beating after each addition. Stir in the candied peel and pine nuts, then add the wheat and stir to mix well. Set aside.

Preheat the oven to 375 degrees. Lightly butter and flour a 10-inch springform pan and set it in the middle of a baking sheet. Using about two-thirds of the *pasta frolla*, roll it out into a 12-inch circle, about ⅛ inch thick, and line the pan. (It is easier to roll this soft dough between 2 sheets of wax paper.)

Beat the 3 egg whites until stiff. Stir about a quarter of the whites into the ricotta mixture, then fold in the remaining whites. Spoon the filling into the pasta frolla shell and smooth over the top.

Roll out the remaining pastry and cut it into strips about ¾ inch wide. Arrange the strips in a lattice pattern over the filling. Beat the reserved egg yolk with the teaspoon of cold water and paint the top of the pie all over, both strips and filling, with the egg wash. Sprinkle sugar over the top. Bake the pie for 45 minutes to 1 hour, until the filling is set and the crust golden brown. Cool on a rack to room temperature, but do not chill, before serving. ***Makes 10 to 12 servings***

Nutritional Data, per portion

| | | |
|---|---|---|
| Calories 490 | Carbohydrate 61g | Saturated Fat 12g |
| Protein 12g | Sodium 76g | Monounsaturated |
| Fat 22g | Cholesterol 176mg | Fat 7g |

# KARYDOPITA NISTISIMI

### *Lenten Walnut Cake*

**A**t a remarkable conference on the foods and wines of Greece that was held in Thessaloníki and organized by Oldways Preservation & Exchange Trust the highlight was a banquet, if that's not an oxymoron, of Greek Lenten foods called "The Joys of Fasting." The traditional Orthodox Lenten fast is rigorous—not only no meat, but no animal products of any kind, including eggs and butter. Yet the foods offered at this festive fast table were rich with the flavors of fresh vegetables and perfumed with herbs and good olive oil. *Karydopita*, topped with poached apricots in a sauce flavored with orange-flower water, was the fitting conclusion.

The recipe was devised by Aglaia Kremesi and Vali Manouilidi for the conference. This version is adapted somewhat from their recipe.

**a little olive oil for greasing the pan**

FOR THE SYRUP:

½  cup sugar

½  cup honey

1  cup water

1  tablespoon orange-flower water or fresh lemon juice

FOR THE CAKE:

1  teaspoon baking soda

¼  cup brandy

½  cup sifted unbleached all-purpose flour

½  cup sugar

1  teaspoon baking powder

½  teaspoon ground cinnamon

¼  teaspoon ground cloves

½  cup extra-virgin olive oil

½  cup fresh orange juice

2  cups walnut halves, finely chopped, about 1½ cups

¾  cup dry unseasoned bread crumbs

1  tablespoon grated orange zest

FOR THE TOPPING:

½  cup apricot jam

2  tablespoons water

Preheat the oven to 375 degrees. Using a paper towel dipped in olive oil, grease a 9-inch round springform pan.

Make the syrup: Boil the sugar and honey with the water for 15 to 20 minutes, until it is reduced to about ¾ cup. Off the heat, mix in the orange-flower water or lemon juice. Set aside to cool, then refrigerate.

Add the baking soda to the brandy. In a large mixing bowl, combine the flour with the sugar, baking powder, cinnamon, and cloves, tossing to mix well. Make a well in the center. Pour in the oil, orange juice, and brandy and gradually mix together, stirring with a wooden spoon. Mix in the nuts, bread crumbs, and orange zest and pour the batter into the prepared pan. Bake for 40 to

60 minutes or until the cake is firm in the center and pulling away from the sides of the pan.

When the cake is done and while it is still hot, pour the cold syrup over it and set aside in the cake pan to cool. Over very low heat, melt the jam with 2 tablespoons of water, stirring constantly. When the cake is cool, remove the springform and brush the apricot topping over the cake. *Makes 8 servings*

Nutritional Data, per portion

| | | |
|---|---|---|
| Calories  554 | Carbohydrate  74g | Saturated Fat  3g |
| Protein  6g | Sodium  318mg | Monounsaturated |
| Fat  29g | Cholesterol  0 | Fat  15g |

# CROSTATA DI MARMELLATA

### *Italian Jam Tart*

This Italian farmhouse tart is made very simply with *pasta frolla* and either very-good-quality jam or fresh fruit cooked with sugar to make a jam. Cherries, peaches, apricots, apples, plums in their seasons can go into the *crostata*.

This recipe uses nothing but very-good-quality jam. If you wish, make your own, using about a pound of soft fruits such as cherries, raspberries, or blackberries and cooking them down with about ½ cup of sugar to make about 1½ cups of jam.

**butter for the pan**

½  **recipe *pasta frolla* (page 442)**

1½ **cups good-quality jam, preferably homemade**

1   **large egg for the glaze**

1   **teaspoon water**

Preheat the oven to 350 degrees. Butter a 9-inch straight-sided tart pan, preferably one with a removable bottom.

Roll out approximately two-thirds of the *pasta frolla* very quickly into a 10-inch circle. This is easiest to do between sheets of wax paper. Line the tart pan. Or, if it is easier, press the pastry dough into the tart pan and up the sides. The dough should be about ⅛ inch thick. Spread the jam over the tart.

Between sheets of wax paper, roll out the remaining pastry dough, cut it into strips, and make a lattice on top of the tart.

Beat the egg with the water and brush a little of the wash over the lattice. Slide the tart into the oven and bake for about 20 minutes or until the crust is golden. Cool and serve at room temperature. ***Makes 8 to 10 servings***

Nutritional Data, per portion

| | | |
|---|---|---|
| Calories  268 | Carbohydrate  48g | Saturated Fat  5g |
| Protein  3g | Sodium  39mg | Monounsaturated |
| Fat  8g | Cholesterol  52mg | Fat  2g |

# TORRIJAS

### *Spanish Sweet French Toast with Citrus Syrup*

**A** universal Spanish favorite, *torrijas* are similar to *pain perdu* or sweetened French toast. In Jerez, Rosario Vazquez sprinkles a little cinnamon sugar over her *torrijas*, while in Madrid, Ana Espinosa serves this simple dessert with an appealing orange sauce. Other cooks might dip *torrijas* in warm honey or sugar syrup. The garnish changes from region to region, but the *torrijas* are the same.

1¼ cups fresh orange juice, from 4 oranges

1   tablespoon fresh lemon juice

⅓   cup plus 1 tablespoon Spanish brandy

⅓   cup plus 1 tablespoon orange liqueur such as Grand Marnier

⅓   cup plus 1 tablespoon port

zest of ½ orange, cut into julienne strips

5   tablespoons sugar

1   quart whole milk

zest of ½ lemon

1   3½-inch cinnamon stick

6 or 8 ¾-inch-thick slices of crusty plain white bread

¼   cup extra-virgin olive oil

3   large eggs, well beaten

A FEW SWEETS

Mix the juices, liquors, orange zest, and sugar together in a small saucepan and bring to a boil over medium-low heat. Simmer for about 25 minutes or until the liquid is reduced to about 1¾ cups of syrup. Set aside, but keep warm. (Or prepare the syrup ahead and heat it up when you're ready to make the *torrijas*.)

In another saucepan, combine the milk with the lemon zest and cinnamon and bring just to a simmer over low heat. Steep over very low heat (not even simmering) for about 20 minutes.

Place the bread slices in a rectangular dish in which all the slices will fit without overlapping. (If you don't have a large enough dish, prepare the *torrijas* in 2 or 3 batches.) Remove and discard the lemon zest and cinnamon stick. Pour the milk over the bread and leave for a few minutes.

When you're ready to cook, heat the skillet over medium heat. Add 2 table-spoons of the olive oil. Carefully dip a slice of soaked bread in the beaten egg, turning it to coat both sides. Cook, turning once, until nicely browned and firm, exactly as you would for French toast. Repeat with the remaining oil and bread.

Arrange the *torrijas* on a platter, drizzle a little of the orange syrup over each slice, and pass the remaining syrup in a pitcher. ***Makes 6 servings***

Nutritional Data, per portion

| | | |
|---|---|---|
| Calories  447 | Carbohydrate  53g | Saturated Fat  6g |
| Protein  13g | Sodium  380mg | Monounsaturated |
| Fat  19g | Cholesterol  129mg | Fat  10g |

# SÜTLAÇ

### *Turkish Rice Pudding*

**S**oft, sweet, and delicately perfumed, this is one of the most soothing desserts imaginable. In Istanbul you buy your sütlaç ready-made at the pudding shop, but it's very easy to prepare at home.

1  **quart whole milk**

**zest of 1 lemon**

1  **3-inch cinnamon stick**

½  **cup short-grain rice (rice for risotto is fine)**

**pinch of salt**

2  **cups water**

1  **tablespoon rice flour**

1  **tablespoon cornstarch**

¾  **cup sugar**

GARNISH (OPTIONAL):

**ground cinnamon, rose water, and/or finely chopped pistachios**

In a saucepan, heat the milk almost to boiling, add the lemon zest and cinnamon, and steep the milk for about 30 minutes. Keep it just below boiling temperature.

In a covered pan over medium-low heat, simmer the rice with a pinch of salt in 1½ cups of the water until it is very soft and all the water has been absorbed—about 30 minutes. If the water is absorbed before the rice is soft, add a little more *boiling* water to the pan. When the rice is soft, remove the lemon zest and cinnamon stick from the milk and pour the milk into the pan with the rice. Bring to a simmer and cook for 30 minutes.

Put the rice flour and cornstarch in a small bowl and slowly mix in about ½ cup water to make a smooth paste. Add this slowly to the simmering milk and rice, stirring constantly. Cook for 10 minutes, stirring constantly. Finally, add the sugar and continue cooking for 10 to 15 minutes or until the mixture is thickened.

The hot pudding may be served in a bowl or in 8 individual pudding dishes. If you wish, add 2 tablespoons of rose water to the pudding while it is still hot and

A FEW SWEETS

before you spoon it into the bowls. Or, once it is in the serving dishes, sprinkle a little cinnamon on top. Add a little spoonful of chopped pistachios and serve lukewarm or at room temperature. *Makes 5 cups; about 8 servings*

Nutritional Data, per portion

| | | |
|---|---|---|
| Calories   201 | Carbohydrate   36g | Saturated Fat   3g |
| Protein   5g | Sodium   77mg | Monounsaturated |
| Fat   4g | Cholesterol   17mg |   Fat   1g |

# BAKLAVA

**T**his is probably the most famous sweet dish of the entire eastern Mediterranean. The recipe comes from Malvina Azzi, the mother of an old friend from Beirut.

2    **cups sugar**

¾    **cup water**

¼    **cup rose water**

2    **cups (4 sticks) unsalted butter**

1½  **cups finely chopped walnuts**

1    **16-ounce package frozen filo pastry, thawed**

Make the sugar syrup: In a saucepan, boil 1½ cups of the sugar with the water for about 2 minutes over high heat, taking care not to let it burn or boil over. Just before removing it from the heat, stir in 2 tablespoons of the rose water. Let cool slightly, then refrigerate until you're ready to use it.

Clarify the butter by melting it in a pan over gentle heat and spooning off the milky froth that rises to the top. Pour off the butter, leaving behind the solid residue that settles to the bottom. You should have about 1½ cups clarified butter. Set it in a bowl over hot water to keep it liquid while you work.

Put the walnuts and remaining rose water in a food processor and process in spurts until the walnuts are finely minced. (The rose water helps keep the walnuts from getting oily.) Add the remaining ½ cup sugar and process briefly to mix well. Preheat the oven to 350 degrees.

Spread a sheet of plastic wrap or aluminum foil on a work surface. Open the filo pastry and spread it on the surface. Cover it with a barely dampened cloth. (Filo dries out quickly when exposed to air and should be kept covered whenever you're not working with it.)

Using the clarified butter and a pastry brush or clean paintbrush, butter a 10-by 14-inch baking pan liberally, bottom and sides. Place a sheet of pastry in the bottom of the pan (only half the sheet will fit). Butter the surface of the pastry, then fold the other half over and butter it. Proceed with the remaining sheets, buttering each one, until you have used about half the sheets in the box. The filo sheets should be somewhat crowded in the pan, folded up a little along the sides and at the ends.

Distribute the walnut mixture over the pastry in an even layer.

Place the remaining filo sheets over the walnut mixture, again buttering liberally between layers. When all the sheets have been used, cut the pastry with a sharp knife lengthwise into strips about 1 inch wide, then on the diagonal to make diamonds. Be sure to cut right down through to the bottom of the pan. Pour any remaining clarified butter over the top of the pastry.

Bake for 30 minutes, then raise the heat to 425 degrees and bake for 10 minutes more or until the pastry is puffed and golden brown on top. Remove from the oven and immediately pour the cold syrup over the hot pastry. Set aside to cool to room temperature before serving. ***Makes 25 to 30 pieces***

Nutritional Data, per piece

| Calories 226 | Carbohydrate 22g | Saturated Fat 7g |
|---|---|---|
| Protein 2g | Sodium 74mg | Monounsaturated |
| Fat 15g | Cholesterol 27mg | Fat 4g |

# MEDITERRANEAN METHODS, MATERIALS, AND INGREDIENTS

$D$on't be obsessive about methods and materials: that is the motto of the Mediterranean kitchen.

If you can't quite master a new technique, don't tell anyone. I can almost guarantee you they won't know the difference.

Flavor counts far more than elaborate techniques and presentations, and flavor begins with the best ingredients. Each separate ingredient should be the finest you can afford, but if you can't afford it or you've run out of it, don't worry. Mediterranean cooks are notable for making do with what's at hand. That's an attitude I try to cultivate in my own kitchen.

With the exception of pastries, which often require a fairly precise balance of ingredients, nothing in this book is written in stone. If you don't happen to have an ingredient, or if you don't have enough to satisfy the recipe requirements, don't let that stop you from preparing it. If you get halfway through a recipe only to discover that the tomatoes you thought were fine have gone soft, or someone in a midnight feeding frenzy ate up all the pine nuts, just leave out the pine nuts. Or change fish in a tomato-parsley sauce to fish in a parsley sauce and add lemon juice or wine or just plain water to make up for the missing liquid from the tomatoes.

On the other hand, a well-stocked pantry is a great comfort in life. If you have the space, there's nothing like a wall of shelves filled with the sort of things that keep well: olive oil, vinegars, dried mushrooms, beans, and grains.

## METHODS

### The Soffrito or Battuto

You will find, as you flip through the recipes in this book, that many begin with sautéing a mixture of finely chopped vegetables in olive oil or sometimes pork fat such as pancetta. This step is called the *battuto* or *soffrito* in Italy and the *sofrito* in Spain. I mention it because it's a useful technique for all sorts of soups, sauces, and sauced preparations, whether vegetables, meat, chicken, or fish. In Italy, the ingredients for the battuto—called *odori*, aromatics—might consist of a carrot, a rib of celery, and a little bunch of parsley or a sprig of rosemary. The stall holders in street markets give them away to favorite customers. "*Odori, signora?*" says the market lady from whom you've just bought artichokes, and she tucks a little bundle in the bag almost as an afterthought. When you get home, you chop your aromatics with maybe ½ onion and ½ clove of garlic, add a little finely chopped pancetta, and sauté it all in a spoonful of olive oil. It's the foundation of an aromatic pasta sauce or soup for lunch. It's also a way of adding vegetables to your daily diet without even being aware of it.

### Soaking Beans

Most beans and legumes should be soaked before cooking—lentils are a notable exception. To soak them, simply place them in a bowl with twice their quantity of fresh cool water. Set aside overnight. In the morning, discard the soaking water and start the cooking process with fresh water.

If you forget to soak the beans the night before (how many times I have forgotten!), you can use the quick-soak method: Set the beans in a saucepan with twice their quantity of fresh cool water. Bring the water to a boil over high heat and boil rapidly, covered, for 1 to 2 minutes. Then remove from the heat and set aside, still covered, for an hour or more. Drain the beans and use fresh water for cooking.

### Peeling and Seeding Tomatoes

To peel tomatoes, bring a large pot of water to a rolling boil, drop in one or two tomatoes (more will lower the heat of the water too much), and leave them for a slow count to 15. Then extract them with a slotted spoon and proceed until all the tomatoes are done. The skins should lift off easily, without using a knife.

Sometimes a recipe requires seeding tomatoes to make a very dry preparation.

Simply cut the skinned tomatoes in half and press each half gently so that the seeds ooze out. (You don't need to get every last seed.) I do this over a sheet of newspaper, then simply fold the paper up to discard it.

## Roasting Peppers

The method is the same, whether the peppers are sweet or hot, red, green, or yellow. Charcoal or wood embers are best for roasting peppers because of the smoky flavor they impart. If you have a grill, set the peppers on a grid about 4 inches above the hot and glowing coals. Turn the peppers frequently so that the skins become thoroughly blackened and blistered. If you don't have live coals, the peppers can be toasted over a gas flame on top of the stove. Use a long-handled fork and turn them constantly to toast as much of the skin as possible. Or if necessary, they can be toasted under an electric broiler. The point is to soften the peppers and turn the skins very black and loose, making them easy to peel.

No matter which procedure you follow, when the peppers are done, take them off the grill and set them aside under a kitchen towel until they're cool enough to handle. Then slit them and drain the juices into a bowl. (The flavorful pepper juices can be added to the preparation.) Peel the peppers by pulling and rubbing the blackened skin away with your fingers. Use a sharp knife if necessary to scrape away remaining bits of skin. Peeling the skins under running water washes too much of the flavor away, but a bowl of water is handy for rinsing off difficult bits.

The seeds and interior white membranes of sweet peppers are usually discarded for appearance's sake. With hot peppers, you may wish to retain some seeds and membrane, because this is where a large part of the pepper's heat is located. Taste a little bit of pepper, and if it seems not quite hot enough, add some of the seeds and membrane to the preparation.

This procedure can be done well in advance and the peppers refrigerated, if necessary, until you're ready to cook.

## Trimming Artichokes

Even artichokes that are to be served whole must be prepared before cooking. You'll need a bowl large enough to hold all the artichokes, filled with cool water to which the juice of a lemon has been added to keep the artichokes from darkening. To prepare the artichokes, cut the stems back to about an inch from where they join the fruit; or, if the artichokes are to be served whole, standing up on the plate, trim the artichoke stem off flush with the fruit. Break off the very tough outer leaves. For a fancier presentation, trim the tough points of the remaining leaves with kitchen

METHODS, MATERIALS, AND INGREDIENTS

shears to present a uniform appearance. As you work, rub the cut surfaces of the artichoke with a lemon half to keep the exposed flesh from darkening. Toss each finished artichoke into the bowl of lemon water. When all the artichokes are trimmed, drain and proceed with the recipe.

To prepare artichoke hearts, trim off most of the leaves until you have only a few layers left around the heart. Using a sharp knife, cut off the tops of the artichokes down to where the heart begins. Using a serrated grapefruit spoon, pull out the spiny choke that lies on top of the heart. Again, rub the cut surfaces with lemon and toss the finished artichokes into lemon water.

Some recipes call for quartered artichokes. For this, you need not go all the way down to the heart, but when you reach the tender leaves, cut the tops off, cut the artichokes into quarters, and use a serrated grapefruit spoon to scrape away the choke. Again, place in lemon water.

## MATERIALS

### Kitchen Paraphernalia

The part in Mediterranean cookbooks that I love best is the introductory chapter on *batterie de cuisine*, with its evocation of a lost old world of craftsmanship and caring—artisanally sculpted earthenware pots, each form carefully molded to a specific purpose; hammered copper skillets and soup kettles so heavy they must be lifted with both hands; and an intricate variety of tools, implements, and other handy gear like a French *chinois*, a conical sieve for straining sauces, or an Italian *mezzaluna*, a half-moon-shaped knife that makes chopping parsley a breeze, or a Spanish *plancha*, a flat iron griddle for *gambas a la plancha* (shrimp on the grill) and other similar treats.

These are all eminently useful objects and often very beautiful ones too. Collecting such paraphernalia and learning how to use them is a source of great pleasure—especially when they are sought out on their home ground. Real food lovers traveling in the Mediterranean always find a trip to the local market far more enlightening than a visit to any three-star restaurant. Not only will you find food products that are perfectly legal to bring back,* but markets are always surrounded, naturally enough, by little shops selling whatever else is needed in the kitchen.

---

* As a general rule of thumb for Customs, no meat products and no fresh fruits and vegetables may be brought back by travelers. But you can bring back dried beans, dried mushrooms, dried fruits, nuts, dried herbs and spices, rice and other grains, pasta, olive oil, and most cheeses.

The reality in most Mediterranean kitchens, however, is rather different. Even in the hands of truly gifted cooks, the batterie de cuisine often consists of cheap, dented aluminum pots with lids that don't quite fit, dull stainless-steel knives that are impossible to sharpen, and various catchall, makeshift, often comical, and sometimes out-and-out dangerous arrangements for preparing and serving food. Most Mediterranean cooks make do with what's on hand. And an ordinarily well-equipped American kitchen would almost always put what's on hand to shame.

Although you don't need any specialized equipment to adopt a Mediterranean way of cooking, there are a few tools, most of them inexpensive, that I consider essential. Here's my short list of essentials (see Resources):

*Good carbon-steel knives*, kept sharp with a stone. You'll know a good knife when you heft it—it feels well balanced and comfortable in the hand. A repertoire of knives might include an 8-inch chef's knife, indispensable for chopping and slicing, a couple of 5-inch paring knives, a serrated bread knife, and a smaller stainless-steel serrated knife for slicing tomatoes, lemons, and other fruit. Carbon-steel knives are very expensive and should be treated like jewels—washed after use, dried to prevent rust, sharpened before being put away in a special knife drawer or stand where each blade lies separate from the others, and sharpened again just before being used.

*A large, heavy cutting board* or a wooden countertop. Try to have at least two boards—one for chopping garlic and onions, cutting up meat and fish, and so forth; one for making breads and pastry—so the *pasta frolla* won't taste of onions. Keep your boards or countertops scrupulously clean and scrubbed, especially after cutting up chicken. One way salmonella spreads is through raw salad greens that have been contaminated by being cut up on a board used to cut chicken. Thorough cooking kills off the salmonella in chicken, but the uncooked salad becomes a fertile breeding ground for the invisible bugs. (A plastic cutting board, contrary to what we were told recently, is actually more likely than wood to engender this type of accidental contamination.)

*A mortar and pestle* is not just a nostalgic symbol of Old World craftsmanship, but a useful and necessary tool. More easily than with a food processor or blender, you can see when the food you're working with reaches precisely the right texture and consistency. Garlic, especially, should almost always be pounded in the mortar rather than tossed into the food processor—I'm persuaded that mechanical processing and blending give garlic a bitter aftertaste. And for small batches of food—½ cup or so of nuts, for instance—it's actually easier to use a mortar and a whole lot quicker to clean up.

I keep two mortars—one for pounding garlic and other strong-flavored foods, one for sweet spices and nuts; this way you'll keep the cookies from tasting of garlic and anchovies.

*Spice mills*: Because the flavor impact of freshly ground spices like allspice, cinnamon, and clove is so important in eastern Mediterranean dishes, I buy whole spices instead of previously ground ones. I keep a separate, small pepper mill with allspice berries in it and a separate small electric coffee grinder that I use when necessary for cinnamon, cloves, and other hard spices. These appliances, if they deserve such a fancy name, are cheap, and the convenience and flavor they afford is worth every penny.

*A hand-turned food mill*, with three different disks, along with the mortar and pestle, is indispensable for pureeing—especially for tomatoes since, unlike the processor or blender, it holds back seeds and bits of skin that can embitter a tomato sauce. And now and then, when you want an elegantly strained, velvety pureed soup or sauce, you will find it can really be done only with a food mill. Mechanically processed or blended purees must be further strained through a fine sieve to achieve this consistency.

*Tongs* are not something you see in domestic kitchens in the Mediterranean, but all professional chefs, there as well as here, find them so indispensable that, slid into the apron strings in back, they become part of the professional costume. I was introduced to tongs only a few years ago, but I can't cook without them today. Both my kitchens have three or four sets of the spring-loaded variety. For turning fried or grilled foods, for moving hot pots about on top of the stove, they are without peer.

*A baking stone* and a wooden peel are not quite mandatory but are certainly very useful if you intend to bake bread or pizza. For my money, the heavy, rectangular stones are superior to so-called pizza disks. The stone mimics, to some degree, the action of a traditional baking oven lined with fireproof brick. You can devise your own system, using unglazed ceramic tiles, available at building supply houses.

Whichever you use, the stone or tiles *must* heat up for at least 30 minutes before you put in the bread or pizza. (Be sure to put the cold stone into the cold oven to prevent cracking.) Even when the oven light goes off, indicating that the proper ambient temperature has been reached inside, the temperature of the stone may be lower.

Note too that the bread or pizza is placed *directly* on the stone, not in a pan or on a baking sheet. This is known as *casting* and imitates the action in a traditional oven where the bread or pizza is cast directly onto the floor or hearth of the oven.

(Traditional American baking powder biscuits, by the way, are terrific baked on a baking stone.)

*A long-handled wooden peel* is also useful in baking, especially for pizza. The best peels have a beveled edge so that pizza or bread loaves slide off the peel and onto the stone with a quick jerk of the hand, an action that seems to give most people who practice it an enormous amount of pleasure and satisfaction.

## INGREDIENTS

### Olives and Olive Oils

The subject of olive oil raises questions in the minds of American consumers, probably because for many of us it's a new product, a new taste, one we're not accustomed to using. Why is olive oil so expensive? Are we really getting what we pay for? If we buy cheap oils, are they bound to taste like rancid crankcase grease? What is extra-virgin oil, and why should I buy it?

The International Olive Oil Council, a United Nations–backed organization of oil-producing countries, sets world standards for different grades of olive oil. Only two concern us as consumers. The finest is extra-virgin oil, an unrefined product that is produced simply by extracting the oil from the olives through mechanical or physical (but not chemical) processes, whether an old-fashioned crush-and-press operation or a new-fangled centrifugal extractor. No matter how it's produced, extra-virgin oil must have a free acid content of less than 1 percent and "perfect" aroma, color, and flavor.

The second quality of oil is called *pure olive oil* or just plain *olive oil*—somewhat confusingly, since both extra-virgin and pure oils are pure in the sense that they are clean and contain nothing but the oil of olives. Pure oil is extracted from lesser-grade olives, those that, for a number of reasons, have undesirable characteristics of acidity, odor, and taste. This oil is refined to make a colorless, odorless, flavorless oil; then extra-virgin or virgin oil (an intermediate category that is not generally for sale) is added in small quantities to give the oil some character.

Extra-virgin olive oil is a great food product, lending taste and structure to dishes in which it is used. Each extra-virgin oil has its own particular color, flavor, and aroma—what professional tasters call *organoleptic characteristics*. I compare it to wine: in oil, as in wine, the complex of flavors and aromas in the finished product depends on a number of critical variables—the variety of the plant, whether vine or tree, the structure of the soil, the microclimate of the immediate

environment, the quantities of fertilizer and irrigation used during the growing season, the time and method of harvest, and finally the care with which the raw fruit is turned into the finished product, bottled, and stored. Like wines, the finest extra-virgin oils vary from one region to another and from one season to another. But they are almost invariably made from low-acid immature olives that are hand-picked and pressed quickly in cool temperatures before the oil starts to oxidize and ferment.

One caveat in comparing olive oil to wine: unlike wine, extra-virgin olive oil doesn't necessarily improve with age. Anyone who's had the privilege of tasting olive oil in the first few weeks after pressing knows that the fresher it is, the better it tastes. While a freshly pressed and unfiltered oil is not especially good for high-temperature cooking, since the unprecipitated vegetable matter may burn in the process, it is superb for consuming raw. A sauce in and of itself, it needs no embellishment beyond perhaps a few grains of salt.

Carefully stored in a sealed metal or glass container, preferably in a cool (but not refrigerated), dark cupboard, olive oil is good for up to two years, but after that the oil will have passed its prime and should be used as quickly as possible. Olive oil that is exposed to heat and light for a period of time, on the other hand, can turn rancid. Keep a small quantity in a metal oil can by the work counter and store the rest in the cupboard.

Which olive oil is best? It's hard to say, truthfully. I always have a good half dozen varieties of extra-virgin oils in the cupboard at any one time, primarily because the subject is an endlessly varying source of curiosity and interest. I taste and compare and sometimes use Lebanese oil in dishes of Middle Eastern origin or Spanish oils in Catalan dishes and sometimes vice versa.

I often hear it said that extra-virgin oil is not good for cooking and should be reserved for raw use in salads and as a garnish. I take my cue from chefs in the best restaurants in Tuscany and Umbria, where they've been producing and using olive oil for a lot longer than most of us. I use extra-virgin oil except for deep-fat frying; then I use refined olive oil since its smoking point is higher than that for unrefined extra-virgin oil.

Good commercial extra-virgin olive oils are widely available in this country, especially Italian oils from houses like Bertolli, Berio, and Colavita. These are fine for all-purpose cooking. But the relationship between commercial oils and specialty extra-virgin olive oils, often estate-produced and -bottled and usually from smaller producers or cooperatives, is like the relationship between good, commercial vin ordinaire or table wine and more unique and flavorful estate-

blended and -bottled wines. Like fine wines, these specialty oils have richness and complexity that change from one region to another and from one harvest to the next.

Here is a list of specialty oils I've tried and liked. There are many other oils that I haven't had the opportunity to taste. These oils are *generally* available in this country, though not from all suppliers and not all the time (see Resources, page 473).

**From Spain:**  Spain is the world's largest producer of olive oil, and much Spanish oil is shipped to Italy for bottling as Italian oil, a practice that is completely legal if somewhat questionable in the eyes of connoisseurs. Spain has also led the way in establishing controlled denominations that guarantee the origin of oil (like a wine appellation contrôlée), although Italy is following suit. The oils listed here are all from controlled denominations:

- L'Estornell (Catalonia, certified organic from Arbequina olives)
- Lerida (Catalonia, produced by the same family that makes L'Estornell)
- Montserrati (Catalan Pyrenees, certified organic from Arbequina olives)
- Siurana (Catalonia)
- Nuñez de Prado (Andalusia; unfiltered extra-virgin oil, and *flor del aceite* or "flower of the oil," produced by partial extraction before pressing the olives)

**From France:**  Provence and Corsica are the only regions in France that produce olive oil, and production is very limited. Provençal extra-virgin olive oils are consequently hard to find but worth seeking out. They are very light in flavor compared to Spanish and Italian oils. My favorites are organically produced Domaine de Gautière and Vallée des Baux.

**From Italy:**  Italy produces almost too many specialty extra-virgin oils to enumerate. Among my favorites are the following:

From Liguria: Ligurian oils are very light and clear, traditionally used to garnish fish preparations.

- Raineri "Mosto" (unfiltered)
- Roi Certificato Bio (certified organic)
- Ardoino

From Umbria and Tuscany: These two neighboring regions produce dark green oils, very fragrant and fruity with a typical *pizzica*, or peppery aftertaste, that's felt in the back of the throat. Tuscans are credited with putting extra-virgin olive oil on the American culinary map through skillful marketing techniques, but the oil itself stands on its own, marketing or not. Umbrian oils are less well known here but equally high in quality and deserving of attention.

- Trevi Umbro (Umbria)
- Lungarotti (Umbria)
- Mancianti (Umbria; extra-virgin olive oil and *affiorato*, produced by partial extraction)
- Badia a Coltibuono (Tuscany)
- Castello Banfi (Tuscany)
- Fonterutoli (Tuscany, unfiltered)
- Impruneta (Tuscany, unfiltered)
- Laudemio (Laudemio oils are produced under stringent guidelines by a consortium of 55 Tuscan producers known as the Olivanti. Each Laudemio oil is produced by an individual estate—Frescobaldi is the only one available in this country at this writing.)
- Tenuta del Numerouno (unfiltered)

From Calabria and Apulia: Southern Italy produces more oil than any other region, but it is less well known here than the central Italian oils. Southern oils are clear yellow in color, robust, and full-flavored, with a pronounced olive taste. The best of these oils are for true connoisseurs who love rich texture and flavor.

- La Giara (Calabria)
- Prodital Regale and Prodital Amphora (Calabria)
- Dentamaro (Apulia, from the Balduccis' hometown, Corato)

**From Greece:**

- Kydonia (Crete, made from Koroneiki olives)
- Greek Gourmet (Messina, made from organically grown Koroneiki olives)

**From California:** California is just beginning to produce classy extra-virgin olive oils, and the production is very limited. Among those available are E.V.O. (for extra-virgin olive oil) and Olio Santo.

You may also come across extra-virgin oils from other parts of the Mediterranean, especially Lebanon, Turkey, Tunisia, and Morocco. These oils vary in quality

METHODS, MATERIALS, AND INGREDIENTS

but can be very good. I'm especially drawn to Lebanese oil with its rich green flavor, at least in part because it's the first olive oil I learned to cook with when I went to live in Beirut in the early 1970s. If you prefer lighter oils, you'll want to try North African and Turkish oils when you find them. They are on the whole sweeter and with a bland, but not unattractive, flavor.

## Grains and Flours

*Wheat* is the very foundation of the Mediterranean diet, whether in the form of bread, pasta or couscous, or bulgur. The many types of wheat range from very soft farro or emmer (*Triticum dicoccum*), an old strain newly popular in Italy, to very hard durum (*T. durum*), the high-protein wheat preferred by commercial pasta and bread makers, grown primarily on the western prairies of the United States and Canada. *Soft* and *hard* refer not just to the texture of the wheat but also to the protein content—most hard wheats are higher in protein and higher in the gluten necessary for bread making than are soft wheats. In Italy, soft wheat is used in commercial pizzerias and for homemade *pasta al uovo*, with eggs added. Semolina is extracted from durum wheat for commercial pasta making; it is also used to make couscous and, in Morocco, for homemade bread. It is grainier than ordinary bread flour and produces bread with a lovely yellow crumb (see recipe, page 137).

All-purpose flour is a blend of hard and soft wheats. The best all-purpose flour is unbleached and unbromated. I use King Arthur unbleached all-purpose flour for most baking, adding a little soft-wheat pastry flour for pizza and pastries. King Arthur flour is widely available in the Northeast but not in the rest of the country. Southerners swear by White Lily soft-wheat flour for cakes, and it seems like a good pizza flour—but, again, it is not available outside the Southeast. Both companies will ship by mail (see Resources, page 474).

*Farro* is an ancient Mediterranean strain of soft wheat, said to be the wheat that supplied the Roman armies. In Tuscany and Umbria, farro is most often served as a whole grain, cooked in soups and stews. Dean & Deluca can supply farro by mail order.

*Bulgur* (in Turkish, the word most commonly used in this country) or *burghul* (in Arabic) is made of whole wheat berries that are steamed, then dried and cracked. It needs no further cooking for salad preparations but should be soaked in warm water to soften it before using. (Cover it with warm water—2 cups of water to 1 cup of bulgur—and set it aside for 20 to 30 minutes. Then drain and squeeze

dry in a kitchen towel.) Bulgur also makes an elegant pilaf (see recipe, page 222); for cooking, it does not need to be soaked beforehand.

Bulgur is commonly available at health food stores and specialty shops, as well as in Arab and Armenian neighborhood stores. (For mail-order shipments, try Dean & Deluca or Sultan's Delight.) It comes in three grades, depending on the size of the cracked grain. Number three (coarse) is best for pilaf. Number two (medium) is best for tabbouleh and other salads. Number one (fine) is for making kibbe.

*Couscous* is not a distinct grain but rather a type of pasta, made, like commercial pasta, from hard semolina (durum) wheat and water—nothing more. Once upon a time couscous was made at home, but nowadays, even in North Africa, most cooks use commercially prepared couscous (but not instant couscous—that's like using instant rice in a pilaf).

*Pasta* comes in hundreds of shapes and sizes, mostly classifiable as either long and skinny noodles or short, stubby forms that capture dense sauces. Whatever shape it takes, however, pasta is made from wheat flour and water, with eggs added in the north of Italy but not generally elsewhere.

Among the commercial pastas that are widely available, my favorites are De Cecco and Delverde, both imported from Italy and sold in American supermarkets. I haven't found an American-made fresh or dried pasta that is acceptable.

*Rice* is almost as complex a subject as wheat, but fortunately, in the Mediterranean it is simplified into two types—short-grain, used in risotto and paella, and long-grain, used in pilaf. (And, yes, there is a medium grain, grown in Spain and also used in paella.) Arborio is the most widely available short-grain rice, traditionally used for risotto but also an acceptable rice for paella. If you can find them, Carnaroli and Vialone Nano are superior for risotto—Balducci's (see Resources) has these two by mail order. The best rice for paella is *arroz bomba* or *calasparra* from Spain's eastern rice-growing regions, but you'll have to bring it back from Spain because it doesn't seem to be available in this country. Alcazaba rice is available, however, and it's also very good.

For pilaf, any long-grain rice is good. The best is basmati, a very fragrant rice originally from India but now grown in California and Texas. Other long-grain specialty rices grown in this country, like popcorn rice and pecan rice, are also good in pilaf.

*Polenta* is just cornmeal, either white or yellow, though yellow is more typical. In polenta recipes you can use any American cornmeal (except self-rising cornmeal, which contains chemical leavening), and it is often a better choice than run-

of-the-mill imported polenta, which may be less than fresh. The best Italian polenta, like the best American cornmeal, is stone ground using the whole grain, including the germ. For polenta, a rather coarse-textured meal is preferred. An interesting variation, available from Balducci's, Dean & Deluca, and Vivande, among other suppliers (see Resources), is *polenta taragna*, a mixture of cornmeal and ground buckwheat. It can be substituted for plain polenta in any recipe.

Two of the best stone-ground American cornmeals come from Rhode Island—Gray's Grist Mill in Adamsville and Kenyon Cornmeal Company in Usquepaugh. But there are small mills all over the country that are good sources for this native American product.

## Dairy Products

*Yogurt:* Fernand Braudel quotes Busbecq the Fleming, writing in 1555: "The Turks are so frugal and think so little of the pleasures of eating that if they have bread, salt, and some garlic or an onion and a kind of sour milk which they call yoghoort, they ask nothing more. They dilute this milk with very cold water and crumble bread into it and take it when they are hot and thirsty . . . it is not only palatable and digestible, but also possesses an extraordinary power of quenching the thirst."

The Turks probably introduced yogurt into the Mediterranean, and it is still more often used in the old Ottoman Empire countries of the eastern Mediterranean than it is in the West. Yogurt, sweetened with a little honey, is sometimes served for dessert in France, but it is not otherwise used in cooking. In the East, travelers will find rich and tangy yogurts made from sheep's or goat's milk, and these are becoming more available in this country from small dairies like Hollow Road Farms in the Hudson Valley. Look for these products in specialty and health food stores.

Another useful yogurt product is labneh or yogurt "cheese" (it's not really a cheese at all), made by straining the whey from ordinary yogurt (page 299).

Look for pure yogurt with live acidophilus cultures and no added gelatin or other stabilizers.

*Cheeses: Parmigiano* is, to my mind, the finest cheese in the world. Only the genuine product, Parmigiano-Reggiano, should be used. It comes in giant wheels of cheese stamped proudly all over their waxy outsides with the words *Parmigiano-Reggiano*. Avoid Argentine Parmesan or the previously grated stuff that comes in a

shiny green tube (*any* freshly grated cheese is better than that). Real Parmigiano has a remarkable nutty, sweet, slightly caramel flavor and a texture that is smooth and hard with pleasing bits of crunch from the embedded crystals that form as the cheese ages. It is expensive, but a little goes a long way. If you can't afford Parmigiano-Reggiano for cooking, use a well-made local hard cheese, even a local cheddar. The flavor will be totally different, but the integrity of the dish will remain.

Parmigiano should not be cut with a knife but rather broken away from the mother wheel using a wedge-shaped cutter so that the grain and texture of the cheese are exposed. Grate it freshly to use in cooking or serve it in chunks with the salad or fruit or to finish off a bottle of fine red wine. Parmigiano can be kept in the refrigerator, wrapped in paper and then loosely in plastic wrap, for months. It may get too hard for eating but will still be an excellent grating cheese.

*Mozzarella* is traditionally made from the milk of water buffalo cows that graze in pastures in the territory around Naples. Imported mozzarella di bufala is increasingly available in this country, but, alas, it is made by machine rather than the old-fashioned way by hand. Mozzarella from cow's milk is properly called *fior di latte* but may be marketed just as mozzarella or muzzarel'. You can often find handmade fior di latte in cheese shops in Italian neighborhoods. It can also be ordered from Paula Lambert's Mozzarella Company (see Resources). What is not to be used is the skim-milk cheese called mozzarella available in supermarket dairy cases. It bears no relationship whatsoever to the real thing, and how it came to be called mozzarella is a mystery.

Mozzarella is not meant for long keeping and should be used within a few days of purchase.

*Pecorino*, a sheep's milk cheese, is increasingly available in fine cheese shops in this country. The best is 100 percent sheep's milk; it is aged for varying periods of time. At three months it has a lovely nutty flavor and a creamy paste, a fine eating cheese. Aged longer, it becomes hard and dense and is best for grating. Pecorino romano is a very hard cheese with a distinctive sour flavor that is very good in some strong-flavored dishes but not universally appropriate. Manchego, a Spanish sheep's milk cheese that is found with increasing frequency, is very similar to pecorino and every bit as good.

*Feta* is the most characteristic Greek cheese. In Greece it is made only from sheep's or goat's milk, while in this country it is most often made from cow's milk. For this reason only imported Bulgarian or Greek feta is recommended in the recipes in this book, but if you can find feta from a local sheep or goat dairy, by all means use it. Feta is cured in a salt brine, and it varies in quality and in saltiness—

ask to taste a bit before you buy. If you don't use it right away, store feta in the brine that comes with it in the refrigerator.

*Manouri or manourgi* is a soft, fresh Greek cheese, made from whey with cream added, which makes it high in fat. *Mizithra* is similarly soft and fresh, made from the whey rendered in feta production, but without the added fat of manouri. Like most soft cheeses, they are not meant for long keeping.

### Cured Meats

*Pancetta* and *prosciutto* are Italian cured pork products. Pancetta is best described as unsmoked, salt-cured bacon, and it is widely available, especially in shops in Italian neighborhoods. Like bacon, pancetta, well-wrapped in foil, may be stored in the freezer for months, but freezing will destroy the fine texture of prosciutto. Wrap prosciutto in plastic wrap and store it in the refrigerator for no more than a week or 10 days.

Prosciutto is a fine dry-cured ham. The best, according to many, comes from Parma and is now imported to this country, but if you're traveling in Italy you'll want to try local prosciutto, such as San Daniele from Friuli or local hams, called *prosciutto nostrano*, in country districts. In Spain, travelers can sample *jamon serrano* and *jamon de jabugo*, two exceptional artisanal products that are not imported, because, unlike prosciutto di Parma, the pigs are not slaughtered under U.S. Department of Agriculture inspection. (There's absolutely nothing wrong with them—it's just that, to be imported, USDA inspection on site in the slaughterhouse is required of all pork products.)

Prosciutto and pancetta are used in very small quantities (a tablespoon or so of very finely chopped meat) in the *battuto* that forms the basis of many Italian sauces. If you can't find prosciutto (and it is very expensive), use pancetta instead. And if you must substitute bacon, blanch it in water for 5 minutes or so to rid it of smoky flavors.

### Tomatoes

The best tomatoes are of course the ones you grow in your own garden and harvest at the peak of ripeness about 30 seconds before you slice and eat them. Failing that, a farmer's market is a close second.

Like most Mediterranean cooks, I use canned tomatoes when fresh ones are not suitable. For those who live in New England and are fortunate enough to have gardens, the season usually lasts about two and a half days before the first frost, so when I'm in Maine I use a lot of canned tomatoes. The best canned tomatoes used

METHODS, MATERIALS, AND INGREDIENTS

to be imported, usually from Spain or Italy, but American brands are vastly improved. I like Hunt's whole canned tomatoes for their firm texture, their thick juice, and their flavor, which is thoroughly tomato, with nothing added. Canned organic tomatoes are particularly good. Whatever brand you use, make sure it contains nothing but whole tomatoes—often processors add other ingredients to boost the flavor.

*Estratto di pomodoro* is a pure tomato extract, about the same texture as tomato paste (the stuff that comes in a tube or a squat little can) but worlds apart in flavor. Unfortunately it's not exported, but if you're ever in Sicily, look for the *estratto* made by Anna Tasca Lanza, with a sweet, intense flavor. In this country I use either Hunt's tomato puree, adding a very little sugar to overcome residual bitterness, or imported Pomi strained tomatoes. Tomato paste or concentrate affects my palate with an unpleasant "cooked" flavor—like the sauce in bad Italian-American restaurants.

## Herbs, Spices, and Condiments

I mention here only those herbs and spices that seem to need comment.

Use *flat-leaf parsley* if at all possible, and if your supermarket can't or won't stock it, grow your own—it's very easy, in a pot on the window ledge if nowhere else, although you'll probably need several pots to supply a Mediterranean kitchen. (Cilantro will also grow well in a pot.)

*Thyme* is used both fresh and dried, both garden cultivated and wild, throughout the Mediterranean. It's a typical plant of the macchia or maquis, the low scrub forest that covers barren lands of the region. The flavor varies in intensity, depending on where the plant grows, but wild thyme generally contains more of a powerfully fragrant essential oil called *thymol*, a disinfectant, which is probably why I was given an infusion of wild thyme in Morocco to cure an unhappy stomach. Wild thyme, called *za'atar* in Arabic, is an ingredient in a fragrant mixture of thyme, sesame seeds, and sumac that is mixed with olive oil and sprinkled over freshly baked bread in the morning. (Confusingly, the mixture itself is also called *za'atar*. You can find both the mixture and the thyme in shops in Middle Eastern neighborhoods, so be sure you know what you're getting.)

*Oregano* is, like thyme (basil too, for that matter), a pungent member of the mint family (*Labiatae*) that is used in both cultivated and wild versions. It is a quintessential ingredient in true Neapolitan pizza. Oregano, called *rígani*, is also important in the Greek kitchen, and the wild version is used in Greece to make tea. Dried wild oregano, which has a delightfully astringent aroma, can be found in

shops in Greek neighborhoods, often tied up in pretty bundles. (Mexican oregano is a different plant, botanically, but with a similar pungency. Marjoram is a variety of oregano, with a sweeter and more delicate flavor.)

*Bay leaves*, or laurel, are not hard to find, but do use Turkish bay leaves if possible rather than the stronger, more medicinal-tasting bay leaves from California. McCormick's packages the Turkish ones, as do other commercial spice companies, and they are worth seeking out for the subtler flavor.

*Sumac*, the pleasantly astringent red berries of a Mediterranean shrub related to the sumac that grows in this country, is used in the eastern Mediterranean to impart an agreeably acid flavor to everything from salads to meat and chicken stews. It is part of the breakfast spread called za<sup>c</sup>atar in Lebanon and always used in the Lebanese salad fattoush (page 73). In Turkey, sumac is sprinkled on kebabs and other grilled meats. You'll find both whole berries and ground powdered sumac in shops in Middle Eastern neighborhoods.

*Saffron* came with the Arabs to Spain—the word for saffron in Arabic is *zafaran*, meaning "yellow." It's said to be the most expensive aromatic in the world since it takes the hand-collected stigmata of about 75,000 wild autumn-flowering crocuses to make a pound of saffron. Don't buy powdered saffron, which is often just cheap coloring with none of the musky, earthy flavor of true saffron. Saffron threads can be crumbled directly into a dish or steeped in water or broth first, then the saffron with its steeping liquid tipped into the sauce. Be discreet with saffron— too much can be overpowering.

*Mahleb* is made from the seeds of a certain wild black cherry (*Prunus mahaleb*, according to Turkish food authority Ayla Algar). It gives a soft, almondy sweetness and unique flavor to Greek, Turkish, and Lebanese sweets and sweet breads like *tsoureki* (page 141). Mahleb is available in Greek and Middle Eastern neighborhood stores. It's best to buy the whole seeds and grind them right before you need to use them. Good mail-order sources for mahleb are Massi's in Watertown, Massachusetts, and Sultan's Delight in Brooklyn, New York (see Resources).

The best *salt* I have ever tasted comes from the island of Gozo in the Maltese archipelago. It has a crisp, penetrating, but never acrid flavor that is more appreciated as a garnish added at table than as an ingredient in a stew or sauce. It may seem strange to attach so much importance to salt, but if you don't believe it's important, try a taste test: Buy several different varieties of salt, including sea salt, kosher salt, and ordinary shaker salt. Taste them on their own, completely nude. I think you'll be amazed at the difference.

In the Mediterranean, a squeeze of lemon juice or a splash of vinegar, what the

METHODS, MATERIALS, AND INGREDIENTS

French call *un filet de vinaigre*, often serves the same function as salt in bringing out the flavors of a dish. In places like Turkey and Tuscany, where meat is important in the cuisine, grilled meat always comes with a garnish of lemon wedges so that each diner can add a refreshing fillip of lemon juice to his or her plate. For people who must watch the amount of sodium in their diets this is an especially good practice.

*Vinegar* is almost as important for discriminating cooks as olive oil. Use red wine or white wine vinegar, depending on the color of the sauce. Many wine vinegars strike my palate as too acerbic and acid; I prefer imported aged sherry vinegar for its mellow yet robust flavor.

Balsamic vinegar (aceto balsamico) became hugely popular a few years back, and for a while chefs were throwing it indiscriminately on all kinds of preparations. It's a unique product, and the best artisanally made balsamic vinegar, called *aceto balsamico tradizionale di Modena*, is produced under stringent regulations in and around Modena and aged in fragrant wooden casks for 10 years or more. It's a rare treat, with a price to match, and should be reserved for very special occasions.

Once at Badia a Coltibuono, a fine Tuscan wine estate (also makers of excellent olive oil), I sampled 100-year-old aceto balsamico, served around the table, from small silver spoons, like some strange gourmet rite of communion. It was dark colored, almost black, with flashes of red lights, rather syrupy, and with an extraordinary flavor, penetrating and lush, mellow and palate-filling, all at the same time. Another time, in Florence, a particularly fine Parmigiano from Lodi, north of Parma, was served with drops of aceto balsamico poured lovingly on each shard of cheese. This is the best way to serve aceto balsamico tradizionale—with love, awe, and respect.

A more commonly available, but still rather expensive, balsamic vinegar is produced commercially of wine vinegar to which caramel and herbal essences have been added, producing a rather similar, but by no means comparable, product. Even this should not be used with a lavish hand, however. A few drops in a salad dressing are all that is necessary. Among balsamic vinegars generally available in this country, the best is produced by Fini and aged six years.

*Tahini* is a paste, the consistency of peanut butter, made from ground sesame seeds. I have tried health-food-store tahinis and mostly find them wanting, insipid in flavor and sticky in texture. The best I've found is Joyva, made in Brooklyn but widely available. Tahini may separate in the can—just stir it back together with a fork. Once you've opened a can of tahini, store it in the refrigerator.

*Peppers* used in Mediterranean recipes are usually sweet (not hot) peppers, either round bell peppers or long skinny ones such as are marketed in this country

as Italian or cubanelle long peppers. Fiery peppers, like the chilies we're used to from Mexican cuisine, are appreciated only in parts of North Africa. The small hot red pepper used in Italy is called *peperoncino rosso*, but it is used in *very* small quantities. For the rest, though Spaniards and Turks may *tell* you their dishes are hot, you probably won't find them so. A single hot dried chili or a teaspoon of hot red pepper flakes will flavor a sauce to serve six people.

*Anchovies* are at their best when packed in salt. In Greek, Middle Eastern, and Italian neighborhood shops you will find them in big round cans to be purchased by the piece or by the pound. Buy them in quantity if you find them: wrap carefully in foil and place in a sealable plastic bag to avoid contaminating other food with their strong aroma. They will keep for several months in the refrigerator. Before using, rinse each anchovy well under a running tap to rid it of salt. Then pull the two fillets away from the spine and discard the backbone and tail. Don't worry about the tiny side bones—they will be unnoticeable in a sauce or pizza topping.

The flavor of anchovies is unique and not to everyone's taste, but you might be surprised, if you say you detest anchovies, at the number of times you have eaten them thoroughly disguised in a sauce. The best chefs know that anchovies give a deep and complex flavor to dishes in which they're used.

In the absence of salt-packed anchovies, canned oil-packed anchovy fillets can be used instead. Because the fillets are so small, I substitute on a roughly two-to-one ratio—two oil-packed fillets to one salt-packed fillet.

Like anchovies, salt-packed *capers* are best. What are capers exactly? The unopened bud of a flowering plant that grows in crannied walls all over the Mediterranean. They are gathered in the late spring and preserved by packing in salt or pickling in brine. Brine-cured capers are widely available, but if you can find salt-cured ones in Greek or Italian neighborhood stores, they are superior. Rinse them under running water to rid them of salt before using.

# RESOURCES

**Yogurt cheese funnels**
The Baker's Catalogue (King Arthur Flour), P.O. Box 876, Norwich, VT 05055; 800-827-6836
Harvest Direct, Inc., P.O. Box 4514, Decatur, IL 62525-4514; 800-835-2867
Sur La Table, 84 Pine St., Pike Place Farmers' Market, Seattle, WA 98101; 800-240-0853

**Baking stones and wooden peels for bread and pizza**
The Baker's Catalogue (King Arthur Flour)
Sur La Table
Williams-Sonoma, P.O. Box 7456, San Francisco, CA 94120-7456; 800-541-2233; also available in stores nationwide

**Paella pans**
Sur La Table
Often available in Williams-Sonoma stores

**Couscousières**
Sur La Table

**Olive oil**
Balducci's, 42-26 12th St., Long Island City, NY 11101; 718-786-9690 or 800-225-3833; shop located at 424 Avenue of the Americas (Greenwich Village), New York, NY 10011
Dean & Deluca, 560 Broadway, New York, NY 10012; 800-221-7714, ext. 270
MAD.61, 10 E. 61st St., New York, NY 10021; 212-833-2222 for orders
Todaro Brothers, 557 Second Ave., New York, NY 10016; 212-679-7766

Vivande, 2125 Fillmore St., San Francisco, CA 94115; 415-346-4430
Zingerman's Delicatessen, 422 Detroit St., Ann Arbor, MI 48104-3400; 313-663-3400

## Wheat Flour and Cornmeal
Balducci's, Dean & Deluca, Vivande, Zingerman's
Gray's Grist Mill, P.O. Box 422, Adamsville, RI 02801; 508-636-6075
Kenyon Cornmeal Company (white and yellow cornmeal), Usquepaugh, West
    Kingston, RI 02892; 401-783-4054
The Baker's Catalogue (King Arthur Flour)

## Imported Cornmeal Polenta and Polenta Taragna
Balducci's, Dean & Deluca, Todaro's, Vivande, Zingerman's

## Rice for paella and risotto
Balducci's, Dean & Deluca, MAD.61, Todaro's, Vivande, Zingerman's

## Dried herbs and spices
The Spice House, 1048 N. Old World Third St., Milwaukee, WI 53203; 414-272-0977

## Sherry vinegar
Dean & Deluca, MAD.61, Vivande, Zingerman's

## Aceto balsamico tradizionale di Modena
Balducci's, Dean & Deluca, MAD.61, Todaro's, Vivande

## Parmigiano-Reggiano cheese
Balducci's, Dean & Deluca, MAD.61, Todaro's, Vivande, Zingerman's

## Mozzarella
Mozzarella Company (handmade fior di latte mozzarella), 2944 Elm St., Dallas,
    TX 75226; 800-798-2954; also, Balducci's, Dean & Deluca, and MAD.61 carry
    both handmade fior de latte and imported mozzarella di bufala; Vivande and
    Zingerman's both have imported mozzarella di bufala

## Salt-packed Anchovies
Vivande

## Dried wild mushrooms (funghi porcini)
Balducci's, Dean & Deluca, Todaro's, Vivande, Zingerman's

RESOURCES

**For Greek, Turkish, and Middle Eastern ingredients**

Massi's Bakery, 569 Mt. Auburn St., Watertown, MA 02172; 617-924-0537

Sultan's Delight (strictly mail order, no retail operation) (a division of Nuts About Nuts, Inc.), P.O. Box 090302, Brooklyn, NY; 718-745-6844 or 800-852-5046

Titan Foods, 25–50 31st St., Astoria, NY 11102; 718-626-7771

# THE TRADITIONAL HEALTHY MEDITERRANEAN DIET PYRAMID

"*T*raditional Diets of the Mediterranean" was the title of an extraordinary conference held in Cambridge, Massachusetts, in January 1993. Jointly organized by Oldways Preservation & Exchange Trust, a Boston-based educational organization, and the Harvard School of Public Health (a World Health Organization/Food and Agriculture Organization Collaborating Center), the conference brought together a distinguished group of scientists, public health officials, scholars, and experts on diet and health from around the globe to consider the traditional Mediterranean diet and the health benefits that might derive from it.

There was a considerable and cohesive body of research to examine. During the year following the conference, more than two dozen scientists from Europe and the United States reviewed and revised this material. The following document is the result of the conference and subsequent review. The World Health Organization, acting through its Regional Office for Europe, has joined Harvard and Oldways in endorsing the Mediterranean pyramid and its accompanying notes. The document, printed here for the first time, includes a dietary pyramid similar to the U.S. Department of Agriculture pyramid but differing radically in certain key respects; an outline of the characteristics of the diet; and a series of discussion notes defining current research and proposing directions for future investigation.

For those of us who are not scientists, yet who are concerned about the relationship between diet and disease, the important consideration is: how does the Mediterranean diet pyramid differ from the USDA pyramid?

Although the base of each pyramid is the same—a solid foundation of complex

carbohydrates in the form of bread, rice, pasta, and other grain products—thereafter they differ considerably. The most striking contrast is in the relative importance the USDA pyramid gives to meat, along with poultry, fish, and eggs—two to three servings a day are recommended from this group, which also includes dry beans and nuts. The inclusion of dry beans with red meat, as if the two had equal value, startled many nutritionists and food journalists; the importance given meat was widely seen as evidence of the Department of Agriculture's historically cozy relationship with the meat industry.

A close reading of the USDA pyramid materials is even more revealing: since portion sizes for this part of the pyramid are set at 2 to 3 ounces, and nothing suggests that choices within the meat group must be rotated, the clear impression remains that up to 9 ounces of red meat (3 servings, 3 ounces each) per day is fully within the range of healthy eating!

In the traditional Mediterranean diet, on the other hand, red meat comes at the very top of the pyramid, above even eggs and sweets, with the recommendation that it be consumed *only a few times a month* or somewhat more often in very small amounts—a little meat used to season a pasta sauce, for instance, or, mixed with vegetables in a soffrito, as the base for a soup. Beans, legumes, and nuts, on the other hand, are given a prominent place along with fruits and vegetables and are recommended for daily consumption.

Another crucial difference is the conspicuous role played by olive oil in the Mediterranean diet pyramid—unmentioned in the USDA pyramid, it is presumably included in the undifferentiated fats and oils that are to be "used sparingly." In the Mediterranean diet, olive oil is used liberally, as the primary cooking medium, and while expert opinions vary on the quantity of fat that should be included in the diet (see pages 484–486), there is *no* question that the fat should be olive oil.

Finally, note the figures to either side of the Mediterranean pyramid, one denoting regular physical activity, the other denoting wine in moderation. To me these signify an overriding consideration—that a diet pyramid, whatever its other merits, does not stand on its own. Food is part of the whole human picture that includes how we lead our lives away from the table (the activity figures) and how we conduct ourselves around it (the wineglass), sharing in a sustaining experience that is fundamental to our culture.

*Nancy Harmon Jenkins*

THE MEDITERRANEAN DIET PYRAMID

**HARVARD**
SCHOOL OF
PUBLIC HEALTH

**LDWAYS**
OLDWAYS PRESERVATION
& EXCHANGE TRUST

**WORLD HEALTH
ORGANIZATION**
REGIONAL OFFICE FOR EUROPE

# INTRODUCTION

*T*his preliminary concept of a pyramid to represent a traditional healthy Mediterranean diet is based on the dietary traditions of Crete, much of the rest of Greece, and southern Italy circa 1960, *structured in light of current nutrition research.* The selection of these regions and this time period as a basis for the design follows from three considerations:

1. Recognition that the rates of chronic diseases were among the lowest in the world and adult life expectancy was among the highest for these populations at that time, even though medical services were limited;
2. Availability of data describing the character of food consumption patterns of the areas at that time; and
3. The convergence of the dietary patterns revealed by these data and our current understanding of optimal nutrition based on epidemiological studies and clinical trials worldwide.

Variations of this diet have traditionally existed in other parts of Italy, parts of Spain and Portugal, southern France, parts of North Africa (especially Morocco and Tunisia), parts of Turkey, other parts of the Balkan region, as well as parts of the Middle East (especially Lebanon and Syria). The diet is closely tied to traditional areas of olive oil cultivation in the Mediterranean region.

Given these carefully defined parameters of geography and time, the phrase *traditional Mediterranean diet* is used here as shorthand for the healthy traditional diets of these regions at that time.

The design of the pyramid is not based solely on either the weight or the percentage of energy (calories) that foods account for in the diet, but on a blend of these that is meant to give relative proportions and a general sense of frequency

THE MEDITERRANEAN DIET PYRAMID

of servings—as well as an indication of which foods to favor in a healthy Mediterranean-style diet. The pyramid describes a diet for most healthy adults. Whether changes need to be made for children, women in the reproductive years, and other special population groups is an issue that needs further consideration.

A principal objective of this graphic illustration is to foster a dialogue within the international scientific, public health, food and agricultural, governmental, and other communities as to what specific elements and configurations of the traditional diets of the Mediterranean should be regarded as healthful.

For Americans, northern and eastern Europeans, and others who want to improve their diets, this model provides a highly palatable, healthful framework for change. Equally positive results can be obtained either by entirely adopting a Mediterranean-style diet or by alternating meals based on this Mediterranean model with meals inspired by healthful dietary traditions of other cultures in other parts of the world. For those living in the Mediterranean region, this pyramid provides a basis for preserving and revitalizing within a modern lifestyle centuries-old traditions that contribute to excellent health and a sense of pleasure and well-being and that are a vital part of our collective cultural heritage.

The pyramid is the first in a series that will be developed over the next few years to illustrate graphically the healthy traditional food and dietary patterns of various cultures and regions of the world. This initiative is an outgrowth of a multi-year conference series, "Public Health Implications of Traditional Diets," jointly organized by Harvard School of Public Health, a United Nations World Health Organization/Food and Agriculture Organization (WHO/FAO) Collaborating Center, and Oldways Preservation & Exchange Trust. These pyramids, taken as a collection, offer substantive refinements of the United States Department of Agriculture's Food Guide Pyramid, refinements that reflect the current state of clinical and epidemiological research worldwide and our understanding of what constitutes optimal human nutrition status.

*This pyramid together with its accompanying notes should be viewed as preliminary and subject to modification.*

## CHARACTERISTICS OF TRADITIONAL HEALTHY MEDITERRANEAN DIETS

Dietary data from those parts of the Mediterranean region that in the recent past enjoyed the lowest recorded rates of chronic diseases and the highest adult life expectancy show a pattern like the one illustrated on page 481. The healthfulness

THE MEDITERRANEAN DIET PYRAMID

# THE TRADITIONAL HEALTHY
# MEDITERRANEAN DIET PYRAMID

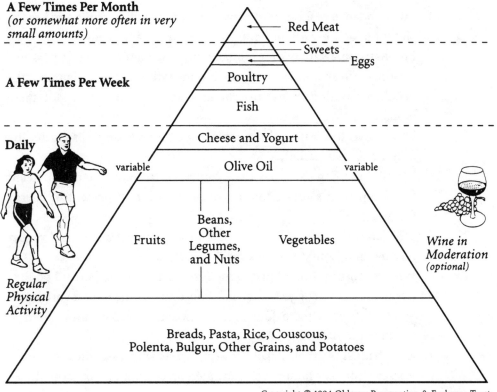

**A Few Times Per Month**
*(or somewhat more often in very small amounts)*

**A Few Times Per Week**

**Daily**

*Regular Physical Activity*

Red Meat

Sweets

Eggs

Poultry

Fish

Cheese and Yogurt

variable    Olive Oil    variable

Fruits    Beans, Other Legumes, and Nuts    Vegetables

*Wine in Moderation (optional)*

Breads, Pasta, Rice, Couscous,
Polenta, Bulgur, Other Grains, and Potatoes

of this pattern is corroborated by epidemiological and experimental nutrition research. The average amounts given are in most cases intentionally nonspecific, since variation is known to have been considerable within this pattern. The historical pattern includes the following (with several parenthetical notes adding contemporary public health perspectives):

1. An abundance of food from plant sources, including fruits and vegetables, potatoes, breads and grains, beans, nuts, and seeds;

2. Emphasis on a variety of minimally processed and, wherever possible, seasonally fresh and locally grown foods (which often maximizes the health-promoting micronutrient and antioxidant content of these foods);

3. Olive oil as the principal fat, replacing other fats and oils (including butter and margarine);

4. Total fat ranging from less than 25 percent to more than 35 percent of energy, with saturated fat no more than 7 to 8 percent of energy (calories);

5. Daily consumption of low to moderate amounts of cheese and yogurt (low-fat and nonfat versions may be preferable);

6. Weekly consumption of low to moderate amounts of fish and poultry (recent research suggests that fish should be somewhat favored over poultry); from zero to four eggs per week (including those used in cooking and baking);

7. Fresh fruit as the typical daily dessert; sweets with a significant amount of sugar (often as honey) and saturated fat consumed not more than a few times per week;

8. Red meat a few times per month (recent research suggests that if red meat is eaten, its consumption should be limited to a maximum of 12 to 16 ounces per month (340 to 450 grams); where the flavor is acceptable, lean versions may be preferable);

9. Regular physical activity at a level that promotes a healthy weight, fitness, and well-being; and

10. Moderate consumption of wine, normally with meals; about one to two glasses per day for men and one glass per day for women (wine should be considered optional and *avoided when consumption would put the individual or others at risk*).

THE MEDITERRANEAN DIET PYRAMID

# CONTEMPORARY PERSPECTIVES ON THE TRADITIONAL DIETS OF THE MEDITERRANEAN REGION: SOME NOTES FOR FURTHER RESEARCH AND CONSIDERATION

## Note 1: Foods from Plant Sources at the Center of the Plate

The traditional diets of the Mediterranean region circa 1960 were based mainly on foods from a rich diversity of plant sources and included fruits and vegetables, breads and grains, beans, nuts, and seeds.

These foods from plant sources made up the core of the diet, while foods from animal sources were more peripheral. In North Africa, couscous together with vegetables and legumes formed the center of the diet; in southern Europe, it was pasta, rice, polenta, and potatoes together with vegetables and legumes. In the eastern Mediterranean, bulgur and rice together with vegetables and legumes such as chick-peas and beans constituted the core of many meals. Throughout the Mediterranean, bread was and remains fundamental to the diet. It is eaten and enjoyed without butter or margarine. An abundance of fruit together with nuts, seeds, and olives rounds out the healthful use of foods from plant sources in the region's traditional diets. A diet based on these traditional patterns is likely to be sufficient in all essential nutrients that we are aware of today and might even today be expected to reduce rates of chronic diseases to a greater degree than the food patterns recommended in many current official dietary guidelines.

We are only beginning to understand the potential health effects of numerous micronutrients and nonnutritive substances in foods from plant sources, let alone the complexities of their interactions. It is premature to predict confidently which plant foods, in what amounts, and in what interactive blends, are important for health, so prudent dietary recommendations emphasize a high and varied intake of these foods.

A diet comprised *entirely* of foods from plant sources needs some care in selecting foods of sufficient variety and quality to ensure a balance of nutrients, and some groups such as women in the reproductive years require significantly more care to address their special needs. Therefore, the ratio of plant foods to animal foods found in the traditional Mediterranean diets—and the traditional diets of other regions such as parts of Asia—may provide the best, safest strategy for good nutrition for most people. Introducing a modest amount of foods from animal sources will also enhance the palatability of the diet for many.

THE MEDITERRANEAN DIET PYRAMID

The consumption of large amounts of vegetables and legumes (pulses) in much of the Mediterranean region, but most notably in Greece, is made easier by the concomitant use of liberal amounts of olive oil which enhances the taste and increases the energy density of these foods.

In the traditional Mediterranean diets, fruits and vegetables were, for the most part, locally grown or gathered, seasonally fresh, and often consumed raw or minimally processed. This may be crucial to a proper appreciation of the health-promoting mechanisms of these diets, given our emerging understanding of the potential protective character of dietary fiber, antioxidants, and other micronutrients and nonnutritive substances found in plant foods.

Consumption of sugar, which may displace foods containing important quantities of micronutrients, was very low in the traditional diets of the Mediterranean.

Some specific Mediterranean foods—such as garlic and various herbs and greens—may have health promoting properties that warrant further investigation.

### Note 2: Olive Oil and Total Fat

Olive oil, high in monounsaturated fat and a good source of antioxidants, is the Mediterranean region's principal source of fat. It appears that various levels of total fat (where the fat was mostly olive oil) can be associated with the excellent health seen in the region at that time, given the overall low levels of chronic diseases and high adult life expectancy throughout much of the Mediterranean in the 1960s.

Evidence suggests that the traditional diets of southern Italy and many other parts of the Mediterranean region in the 1960s had 30 percent or less of total energy from fat. Data from Greece in the 1960s, however, indicate that, with the lifestyles prevailing in those years (see page 489), an intake of more than 35 percent of total daily energy from fat was also compatible with good health. Saturated fat was very low and most of the balance of fat in the diet came from monounsaturated fat in olive oil. The Seven Countries Study reported that men in rural Crete in 1960 were apparently safely consuming 40 percent of their energy (calories) in the form of fat, following this pattern: 29 percent monounsaturated fat, 8 percent saturated fat, and 3 percent polyunsaturated fat. Regardless of varying fat levels, this proportional mix of types of fat in the diet—or fat profile—was typical of the Mediterranean region prior to significant shifts in eating habits over the last 30 years toward increased amounts of meat and dairy products.

In the early 1960s, heart disease rates in Greek populations were found to be nearly 90 percent lower than those measured among U.S. cohorts (Greece had 48 deaths per 100,000 population from ischemic heart disease in men aged 50 to 54,

THE MEDITERRANEAN DIET PYRAMID

while the United States had 466). At the same time, rates of other chronic diseases were similarly low throughout Greece (breast cancer rates, for example, were one-fourth to one-third of those in the United States and almost as low as those of Japan), and Greek adult male life expectancy was the highest in the world. Furthermore, rates of most chronic diseases that are now thought to be diet-related were lower in Greece than they were in other Mediterranean countries. Apparently, for an active person with no weight problem a traditional Mediterranean diet as represented by Crete is compatible with excellent health.

For more than 30 years, researchers have known that the high intake of fat in the form of olive oil in the traditional Greek diet did not have any apparent negative health consequences. In the 1960s, researchers believed that olive oil with its high level of monounsaturated fat was *neutral* with respect to effects on serum cholesterol, and consequently they did not further explore its possible health-promoting potential. Current research into the relation between diet and blood levels of HDL-cholesterol (which is protective against coronary heart disease) sheds new light on the role of olive oil in the traditional Mediterranean diet. In many studies, replacing carbohydrates with olive oil increases HDL-cholesterol levels, but has little effect on the serum level of LDL, or "bad," cholesterol. It might be speculated that the higher fat level and fat profile of some traditional Mediterranean diets *may* have been protective, not just neutral. On the other hand, in a context such as that which exists in parts of Asia—where for whole populations diets high in complex carbohydrates but very low in total fat are associated with very low total cholesterol levels and coronary heart disease rates—this HDL phenomenon appears not to have adverse consequences on public health.

Future research may determine whether two of the basic varieties of the Mediterranean diet have equally good effects on health. The two are:

- High intakes of complex carbohydrates (cereals), with moderate intakes of olive oil, fruits, and vegetables
- High intakes of olive oil, fruits, and vegetables, with more moderate intakes of complex carbohydrates (cereals)

Olive oil should always *replace—and not be added to*—other sources of fat, especially butter and margarine. Butter rarely featured in the traditional diets of Crete, southern Italy, and much of the rest of the Mediterranean region in 1960. Margarine was completely unknown in the area until recently.

The value of using olive oil in preference to other plant oils, particularly those high in polyunsaturated fats, is based on the following considerations:

THE MEDITERRANEAN DIET PYRAMID

- High intakes of linoleic acid, the main polyunsaturated fat in many vegetable oils, may compete with Omega-3 fatty acids in biochemical processes and enhance the tendency of blood to clot.
- Some research has indicated that diets high in monounsaturated fat are less likely to lead to LDL oxidation, and this may reduce atherosclerosis or the formation of atheroma.
- In many animal studies, diets high in polyunsaturated fats have promoted the development of tumors, although this has not been documented in humans.
- Mediterranean people have been using olive oil as their major dietary fat for thousands of years. Polyunsaturated fats have been used at higher levels on a wide scale for only a short time. Without evidence that lifetime exposure to high levels of polyunsaturated fats is safe, it is premature to recommend that diets high in these fats are as healthful— or as safe—as, for example, a Mediterranean diet.
- Olive oil contains several substances other than monounsaturated fatty acids and vitamin E, some of which may also contribute to its apparent healthfulness.

Other populations with traditional low to very low levels of other plant oils in the diet—most notably those of parts of Asia—also have reduced risk of certain chronic diseases. This suggests that there is probably more than one cultural model for healthy eating and that these models may diverge substantially in levels of total fat intake, as suggested above, and type of plant oils used.

## Note 3: Low to Moderate Consumption of Dairy Products

Dairy products from a variety of animals, goat, sheep, water buffalo, cow, and camel, principally in the form of cheese and yogurt, were traditionally consumed in low to moderate amounts in most parts of the Mediterranean region. The use of small amounts of high-fat, full-flavored cheese grated over pasta is an example of the healthful Mediterranean approach to incorporating these items into a diet that minimizes chronic disease risk. In the early 1960s, per-capita consumption of cheese in Crete was 91 grams (3 ounces) a week, with about an additional cup (2.5 deciliters) of milk consumed per day, usually in the form of yogurt. In southern Italy in the 1960s, per-capita consumption of milk was 609 grams per week or the equivalent of about 61 grams (2 ounces) of cheese per week.

In the entire region, very little fresh milk was consumed, and meals were

normally accompanied by wine or water. The recent availability of good-tasting low-fat and nonfat dairy products makes the inclusion of somewhat higher levels of dairy products in the diet possible with little likelihood of adverse consequences. Some full-fat dairy products that may suffer in taste from having their fat removed, such as some cheeses, can be enjoyed on a daily basis in low amounts.

There is insufficient evidence to judge whether the live bacterial cultures of yogurt may have contributed to the traditional good health of the region, but this deserves further research.

Following Mediterranean tradition, butter and cream should be used only in very small amounts or on special occasions. Olive oil is the preferred fat (see Note 2).

## Note 4: Sparing Use of Fish, Poultry, Eggs, and Red Meat

All foods from animal sources, and especially red meat (e.g., sheep, lamb, goat, beef, veal, and pork), were used sparingly in the traditional Mediterranean diets, as illustrated in the pyramid. The total red meat, poultry, and fish consumed on a per-person basis in southern Italy was 434 grams (15.5 ounces) per week in 1960, and in Crete it was about 371 grams (13 ounces) per week.

In rural Crete and much of the rest of Greece in 1960, red meat, mostly in the form of sheep or goat meat, was consumed only a few times per month. According to this pattern, if red meat is eaten at all in a Mediterranean-style diet, its consumption should not exceed 12 to 16 ounces per month. Where the flavor is acceptable, lean versions may be preferred. It should be noted that, in general, meat in the traditional Mediterranean diet was leaner (except for pork) than much of the meat now familiar to consumers in industrialized countries because livestock in the region was not grain fed in feedlots.

Although the available data cannot be considered definitive, a substantial body of evidence now suggests that a high intake of red meat is commonly associated with increased risks of coronary heart disease, colon and prostate cancers, and possibly other cancers. At present, we cannot assume that the relationships are due only to the fat content of red meats. Other factors may contribute to increased risk, such as carcinogens formed in the cooking of red meat, protein, the cholesterol (largely contained in the lean component), or the highly available iron. Further, meat contains no fiber and no antioxidants, and fatty meat eaten in large quantities may displace plant-based foods that do contain these important elements. The essential nutrients contained in red meat may also be obtained from other sources, so meat is not an essential food. It seems likely that the low levels of red meat consumed in traditional Mediterranean diets are healthier for adults than past or

present high consumption levels in the United States and many northern and especially eastern European countries. Consumed only a few times per month, however, meat seems to pose little risk to health. Whether similarly low intakes of red meat are appropriate for children needs further consideration.

Fish consumption in the Mediterranean in 1960 varied from 126 grams (4.5 ounces) per person per week in Crete to 420 grams (15 ounces) per person per week in Corfu in individual dietary surveys, while FAO Food Balance Sheet data indicate that in the same year weekly per-capita supply of fish in Spain was 519 grams (18.5 ounces) and in Portugal was 1,057 grams (38 ounces). Both countries follow a traditional Mediterranean food and health pattern. In Japan, which now enjoys the highest life expectancy in the world, per-capita consumption of fish has ranged from 532 to 672 grams (19 to 24 ounces) per week over the last 25 years (this according to individual dietary surveys; FAO Food Balance Sheet data show even higher levels in recent years). These latter figures suggest a rationale for a more liberal use of fish in the diet, as is suggested by its position in the pyramid. This is corroborated by research indicating increased health benefits from moderate fish consumption.

The consumption of zero to four whole eggs per week, including those used in baking and in prepared foods, was also part of the traditional Mediterranean diet.

## Note 5: Wine in Moderation and with Meals

In the Mediterranean tradition (primarily the tradition of non-Moslem areas), wine was enjoyed in moderation and normally with meals and typically within a family context. Wine was sometimes mixed with water, and women often did not drink alcohol at all.

From a contemporary public health perspective, wine should be considered optional in a Mediterranean-style diet and *avoided whenever consumption would put the individual or others at risk*, including during pregnancy and before driving.

For men, moderation is defined as one or two glasses of wine per day. Moderate alcohol consumption for men appears not only to lower the risk of heart disease but also to reduce overall mortality.

For women, moderation is generally defined as one glass of wine per day. Moderate alcohol consumption decreases the risk of heart disease for women as well as for men. Recent research has suggested that even a modest amount of alcohol may be associated with a small increase in the risk of breast cancer.

People may find these and other considerations of value as they make their personal decisions about the use of alcohol.

THE MEDITERRANEAN DIET PYRAMID

## Note 6: Physical Activity and Other Lifestyle Factors

Regular physical activity was a typical feature of the rural Mediterranean lifestyle in the 1960s and is considered vital to maintaining good health and optimal weight.

Current scientific data does not tell us if a diet with over 35 percent fat coming mainly from olive oil, and much of the rest of the diet being fruit, vegetables, and bread, promotes obesity in a sedentary population any more than a diet with an equivalent level of energy (calories) but with less fat.

Other diet-related lifestyle factors may also have contributed to the low rates of chronic diseases and high adult life expectancy found in the Mediterranean region in the 1960s. Those deserving serious attention for research include the long-term benefits of exclusive breast feeding; sharing food with family and friends, an expression of the strong social support system and general sense of community that is typical of the region; the extensive amount of time spent relaxing over meals, offering a relief from daily stress; an insistence on well-flavored, carefully prepared foods that stimulate the enjoyment of healthy diets; and the postlunch tradition of siesta (a good, long afternoon nap) that also provides relief from stress.

## FOR MORE INFORMATION

For more information and to receive a set of citations for the data on which the pyramid and its written explanations are based, please contact Oldways Preservation & Exchange Trust at 45 Milk Street, Boston, MA 02109. Telephone: (617) 695-0600. Fax: (617) 426-7696.

(February, 1994)

# BIBLIOGRAPHY

## Scientific and Technical Publications Relating to Health Aspects of the Mediterranean Diet

Ferro-Luzzi, A., and S. Sette. "The Mediterranean Diet: An Attempt to Define its Present and Past Composition." *European Journal of Clinical Nutrition* 43, (Suppl. 2) (1989): 13–29.

Fidanza, Flaminio. "Changing Patterns of Food Consumption in Italy." *Journal of the American Dietetic Association* 77 (August 1980): 133–37.

Fidanza, Flaminio. "The Mediterranean Italian Diet: Keys to Contemporary Thinking." *Proceedings of the Nutrition Society* 50 (1991): 519–26.

Greco, Luigi. "Mediterranean Diet in Italy: Historical and Socioeconomic Perspective." *Nutrition, Metabolism and Cardiovascular Diseases* 1 (1991): 144–47.

Kafatos, Anthony, et al. "Coronary-Heart-Disease Risk-Factor Status of the Cretan Urban Population in the 1980s." *American Journal of Clinical Nutrition* 54 (1991): 591–98.

Keys, Ancel, et al. "The Diet and 15-Year Death Rate in the Seven Countries Study." *American Journal of Epidemiology* 124, no. 6 (1986): 903–15.

Kromhout, Daan, et al. "Food Consumption Patterns in the 1960s in Seven Countries." *American Journal of Clinical Nutrition* 49 (1989): 889–94.

Renaud, S., and M. de Lorgeril. "Wine, Alcohol, Platelets, and the French Paradox for Coronary Heart Disease." *The Lancet* 339 (June 20, 1992): 1523–26.

Serra-Majem, Lluís, and Elisabet Helsing, editors. "Changing Patterns of Fat Intake in Mediterranean Countries." *European Journal of Clinical Nutrition*, vol. 47, supplement 1 (September 1993). (The entire issue of the journal consists of papers, by the editors and other research scientists, delivered at a seminar on the subject held in Barcelona in 1992.)

Willett, Walter C., M.D., et al. "Relation of Meat, Fat, and Fiber Intake to the Risk of Colon Cancer in a Prospective Study Among Women." *New England Journal of Medicine* (Dec. 13, 1990): 1664–72.

Willett, Walter C., M.D., and Frank M. Sacks, M.D., "More on Chewing the Fat: The Good Fat and the Good Cholesterol." Editorial, *New England Journal of Medicine* (Dec. 12, 1991): 1740–42.

*World Health Statistics Annual/Annuaire de statistiques sanitaires mondiales,* 1991. Geneva: World Health Organization, 1992.

## Cookbooks and Books About Food

Algar, Ayla. *Classical Turkish Cooking.* New York: HarperCollins, 1991.

Amezua, Clara María, and F.J.M. Mataix Verdú. *La Cocina mediterránea y el aceite de oliva.* Madrid: Grafur, n.d.

Andrews, Colman. *Catalan Cuisine.* New York: Atheneum, 1988.

Artusi, Pellegrino. *La Scienza in cucina e l'Arte di mangiar bene.* Firenze: Giunti Marzocco, 1984.

Boni, Ada. *La Cucina romana.* Rome: Newton-Compton, 1983.

Camporesi, Piero. *Bread of Dreams: Food and Fantasy in Early Modern Europe.* Chicago: University of Chicago Press, 1989.

Castelvetro, Giacomo. *The Fruit, Herbs & Vegetables of Italy.* Gillian Riley, trans. New York: Viking, 1989.

Chatto, James, and W. L. Martin. *A Kitchen in Corfu.* London: Weidenfeld & Nicolson, 1987.

David, Elizabeth. *French Provincial Cooking.* New York: Harper & Row, 1962.

David, Elizabeth. *Italian Food.* Harmondsworth: Penguin, 1969.

Davidson, Alan. *Mediterranean Seafood,* rev. ed. Baton Rouge: Louisiana State University Press, 1981.

El Glaoui, Mina. *Ma Cuisine marocaine.* Paris: Jean-Pierre Taillendier/Sochepress, 1987.

Field, Carol. *The Italian Baker.* New York: Harper & Row, 1985.

Francesconi, Jeanne Caròli. *La Cucina napoletana.* Roma: Newton Compton Editore, 1965.

Giacosa, Ilaria Gozzini, *A Cena da Lucullo.* Casale Monferrato: Edizione Piemme, 1986.

Gianni, Guido, *La Cucina Aretina.* Padova: Franco Muzzio Editore, 1990.

Gray, Patience. *Honey from a Weed.* New York: Harper & Row, 1986.

Halici, Nevin. *Nevin Halici's Turkish Cookbook.* London: Dorling Kindersley, 1989.

Hamady, Mary Laird. *Lebanese Mountain Cookery.* Boston: Godine, 1987.

Hazan, Marcella. *The Classic Italian Cook Book.* New York: Knopf, 1976; revised and reprinted in *Essentials of Classic Italian Cooking.* New York: Knopf, 1992.

Jacobs, Susie. *Recipes from a Greek Island.* New York: Simon & Schuster, 1991.

Jouveau, René. *Cuisine provençale de tradition populaire.* Berne: Éditions du Message, n.d.

Keys, Ancel and Margaret. *Eat Well & Stay Well*. Garden City, New York: Doubleday, 1959.

Khayat, Marie Karam, and Margaret Clark Keatinge. *Food from the Arab World*. Beirut: Eastern Art, 1978.

Koronyo, Viki, and Sima Ovadya. *Sefarad Yemekleri: Sephardic Cooking Book*. Istanbul: 1990.

Kouki, Mohamed. *Cuisine et patisserie tunisiennes*. Tunis-Carthage: Las Charguia, 1991.

Kremezi, Aglaia. *The Foods of Greece*. New York: Stewart, Tabori & Chang, 1993.

Kochilas, Diane. *The Food and Wine of Greece*. New York: St. Martin's Press, 1990.

McConnell, Carol and Malcolm. *The Mediterranean Diet: Wine, Pasta, Olive Oil, and a Long Healthy Life*. New York: Norton, 1987.

Machlin, Edda Servi. *The Classic Cuisine of the Italian Jews*. New York: Dodd, Mead, 1981.

Man, Rosamond. *The Complete Meze Table*. London: Ebury Press, 1986.

March, Lourdes. *El Libro de la paella y de los arroces*. Madrid: Alianza, 1985.

Médecin, Jacques. *Cuisine Niçoise*. London: Penguin, 1983.

Middione, Carlo. *The Food of Southern Italy*. New York: Morrow, 1987.

Olney, Richard. *Simple French Food*. New York: Atheneum, 1983.

Roden, Claudia. *A Book of Middle Eastern Food*. New York: Vintage, 1974.

Romer, Elizabeth. *A Tuscan Year*. New York: Atheneum, 1985.

Romer, Elizabeth. *Italian Pizza and Hearth Breads*. New York: Potter, 1987.

Sada, Luigi. *La Cucina della terra di Bari*. Padova: Franco Muzzio, 1991.

Sevilla, María José. *Spain on a Plate*. London: BBC Books, 1992.

Simeti, Mary Taylor. *Pomp and Sustenance: Twenty-Five Centuries of Sicilian Food*. New York: Holt, 1991.

Stavroulakis, Nicholas. *Cookbook of the Jews of Greece*. Athens: Lycabettus Press, 1986.

Tamzali, Haydee. *La Cuisine en Afrique du Nord*. Hamamet, Michael Tomkinson, 1990.

Wolfert, Paula. *Couscous and Other Good Food from Morocco*. New York: Harper & Row, 1974.

Wright, Clifford A. *Cucina Paradiso: The Heavenly Food of Sicily*. New York: Simon & Schuster, 1992.

## Books About the Mediterranean

Attenborough, David. *The First Eden: The Mediterranean World and Man*. Boston: Little, Brown, 1987.

Bradford, Ernle. *Mediterranean: Portrait of a Sea*. Hodder & Stoughton, 1971.

Braudel, Fernand. *The Mediterranean and the Mediterranean World in the Age of Philip II*. New York: Harper & Row, 1972.

Braudel, Fernand. *The Structures of Everyday Life* (Vol. I of *Civilization & Capitalism*). New York: Harper & Row, 1981.

Fitzgerald, Robert, trans. *The Odyssey of Homer.* Vintage Classics, 1990.

Fox, Robert. *The Inner Sea: The Mediterranean and Its People.* New York: Knopf, 1993.

Norwich, John Julius. *The Kingdom in the Sun.* London: Longman, 1970.

Origo, Iris. *The Merchant from Prato.* New York: Knopf, 1951; reprinted, Boston: David Godine, 1986.

Simeti, Mary Taylor. *On Persephone's Island: A Sicilian Journal.* New York: Knopf, 1986.

Verdier, Minelle. *La Civilisation de l'olivier.* Paris: Albin Michel, 1990.

# INDEX

INDEX

INDEX

INDEX

INDEX

INDEX

INDEX

INDEX

INDEX

# METRIC CONVERSION CHART

## Liquid Measures

| U.S. Measures | Fluid Ounces | | Imperial Measures | Milliliters |
|---|---|---|---|---|
| 1 teaspoon | ⅙ | | 1 teaspoon | 5 |
| 2 teaspoons | ¼ | | 1 dessertspoon | 10 |
| 1 tablespoon | ½ | | 1 tablespoon | 15 |
| 2 tablespoons | 1 | | 2 tablespoons | 30 |
| ¼ cup | 2 | | 4 tablespoons | 56 |
| ⅓ cup | 2⅔ | | | 80 |
| ½ cup | 4 | | | 110 |
| ⅔ cup | 5 | | ¼ pint/1 gill | 140 |
| ¾ cup | 6 | | | 170 |
| 1 cup/½ pint | 8 | | | 225 |
| 1¼ cups | 10 | | ½ pint | 280 |
| 1½ cups | 12 | | | 420 |
| 2 cups/1 pint | 16 | | generous ¾ pint | 450 |
| 2½ cups | 20 | | 1 pint | 560 |
| 3 cups/1½ pints | 24 | | | 675 |
| 3½ cups | 27 | | | 750 |
| 3¾ cups | 30 | | 1½ pints | 840 |
| 4 cups/2 pints | 32 | | | 900 |
| 4½ cups | 36 | | | 1000/1 liter |
| 5 cups | 40 | | 2 pints/1 quart | 1120 |
| 6 cups/3 pints | 48 | | scant 2½ pints | 1350 |
| 7 cups | 56 | | 2¾ pints | 1600 |
| 8 cups | 64 | | 3¼ pints | 1800 |
| 9 cups | 72 | | 3½ pints | 2000/2 liters |
| 10 cups/5 pints | 80 | | 4 pints | 2250 |

## Solid Measures

| U.S. and Imperial | Metric Equivalent | | U.S. and Imperial | Metric Equivalent | | U.S. and Imperial | Metric Equivalent |
|---|---|---|---|---|---|---|---|
| 1 oz. | 25 g. | | 7 oz. | 200 g. | | 1¾ lb. | 800 g. |
| 1½ oz. | 40 g. | | 8 oz./½ lb. | 225 g. | | 2 lb. | 900 g. |
| 2 oz. | 50 g. | | 9 oz. | 250 g. | | 2¼ lb. | 1000/1 kg. |
| 3 oz. | 60 g. | | 10 oz. | 275 g. | | 3 lb. | 1 kg. 350 g. |
| 3½ oz. | 100 g. | | 12 oz./¾ lb. | 350 g. | | 4 lb. | 1 kg. 800 g. |
| 4 oz./¼ lb. | 110 g. | | 16 oz./1 lb. | 450 g. | | 4½ lb. | 2 kg. |
| 5 oz. | 150 g. | | 1¼ lb. | 575 g. | | 5 lb. | 2 kg. 250 g. |
| 6 oz. | 175 g. | | 1½ lb. | 675 g. | | 6 lb. | 2 kg. 750 g. |

## Oven Temperature Equivalents

| Fahrenheit | Celsius | Gas Mark | Heat of Oven |
|---|---|---|---|
| 225° | 110° | ¼ | Very cool |
| 250° | 120° | ½ | Very cool |
| 275° | 140° | 1 | Cool |
| 300° | 150° | 2 | Cool |
| 325° | 160° | 3 | Moderate |
| 350° | 180° | 4 | Moderate |
| 375° | 190° | 5 | Moderately hot |
| 400° | 200° | 6 | Moderately hot |
| 424° | 220° | 7 | Hot |
| 450° | 230° | 8 | Hot |
| 475° | 240° | 9 | Very hot |

# INGREDIENTS AND COOKING TERMS

| U.S. | British |
|------|---------|
| All-purpose flour | Plain flour |
| Baking pan | Baking tin |
| Baking soda | Bicarbonate of soda |
| Beets | Beetroot |
| Belgian endive | Chicory |
| Bibb lettuce | Webb lettuce |
| Broil, broiled | Grill |
| Celery root | Celeriac |
| Cheesecloth | Muslin |
| Cilantro | Fresh coriander |
| Cookies | Biscuits |
| Corn | Sweet corn |
| Eggplant | Aubergine |
| Fava or lima beans | Broad beans |
| Flame Tamer | Heat diffuser |
| Hard-cooked eggs | Hard-boiled eggs |
| Heavy cream | Double cream |
| Light cream | Single cream |
| Navy beans | Haricot beans |
| Peanut oil | Groundnut oil |
| Pie plate | Flan dish |
| Plastic wrap | Cling film |
| Powdered sugar | Icing sugar |
| Romaine | Cos lettuce |
| Rutabaga | Swede |
| Scallions | Spring onions |
| Skillet | Frying pan |
| Snow peas | Mange-touts |
| Sour cream | Soured cream |
| Tart dough | Shortcrust pastry |
| Tart pan | Flan tin |
| Tart shell | Pastry case |
| Vanilla bean | Vanilla pod |
| Walnut meats | Walnut kernels |
| Zucchini | Courgettes |

MP67